# Billy Bos

## Rugby League Foot

# Robert Gate

## London League Publications Ltd

**Billy Boston**
**Rugby League Footballer**
© Robert Gate. Foreword © Neil Fox MBE. Introduction © Phil Melling.

The moral right of Robert Gate to be identified as the author has been asserted.

Cover design © Stephen McCarthy. Photographs and illustrations © the photographer or contributor of the photograph. No copyright has been intentionally breached.

Front cover: Billy scoring against Widnes. Back cover photos: top – Billy when he was in the Army; bottom – Billy shrugging off a tackler and heading for the line.

Title page: One of Billy's four tries against Barrow on 10 October 1964, when he reached his milestone of 500 tries.

All photographs in this book are from the private collections of Robert Gate and Billy Boston unless otherwise credited. No copyright has been intentionally breached, please contact London League Publications Ltd if you believe there has been a breach of copyright.

A CIP catalogue record for this book is available from the British Library.

This paperback edition published in Great Britain in March 2010 by:
London League Publications Ltd, P.O. Box 10441, London E14 8WR

ISBN:               978-1903659-50-2

Cover design by:    Stephen McCarthy Graphic Design
                    46, Clarence Road, London N15 5BB

Layout:             Peter Lush

Printed and bound by:  MPG Books Group,
                    Bodmin and King's Lynn

This paperback edition has minor changes to the text from the original hardback edition.

# Foreword

Billy Boston and Mick Sullivan were the best two wingers I ever played with or against. They were both brilliant at crash tackling the opposing centre, taking man and ball. The difference was that Mick would take him whether he had the ball or not. Billy was fairer.

Billy was a gentleman on the field and he is a gentleman off it. Even today at rugby league functions, such as Lions dinners, big matches or gatherings at the George Hotel in Huddersfield, Billy is the number one attraction. Everyone wants to talk to him, to have a photograph taken with him, to shake his hand or to get his autograph. Everyone looks up to Billy. He is always the one who gets the biggest ovation – and not just in England. I have been on several supporters tours to Australia, organised by Peter Banner, with Billy and, I can safely say, he is admired everywhere he goes.

I first played against Billy and Eric Ashton in 1957, when I was a kid of 18. Billy was five years older than me and I regarded him as a big star even then. In fact he was the number one personality in the game by then. I soon learnt why. He was an awesome man to tackle. There was no point going high on Billy. He had such powerful shoulders and such a good hand-off that players would just bounce off him. But he was not just powerful, he was nimble on his feet too. I always felt sorry for any man left to tackle him alone because Billy could beat them with movement or pace. Failing that, he could blast them out of his way. Basically you didn't have a chance of stopping him unless you could get up on him before he got into his stride.

I suppose I first got to know Billy socially on the 1962 Lions tour, when I used to spend a lot of time with him, Eric Ashton, Gerry Round and Alex Murphy. Billy was always good company with a nice sense of humour, a very pleasant bloke and a fantastic asset to the tour party. I'll never forget the two tries he scored in Brisbane which helped to win the second test 17–10, when we took the Ashes. I also remember the fantastic tackle on him by the Australian full-back Keith Barnes, who just about got his bootlaces to stop him getting his hat-trick. I think I only actually partnered Billy once on that tour, when he swapped to my wing part way through the game against North Queensland. Billy scored four tries and at the final whistle sidled up to Eric Ashton, our other centre, and joked, "See, I told you I'd get more tries playing with a good centre!" Of course, they didn't come any better than Eric. Billy and Eric were just wonderful as a partnership.

Billy has always been generous with his time. I will always be grateful to him for appearing in my testimonial match at Belle Vue in 1979, when he had been retired for about 10 years. I think a lot of people came just to see Billy again. When he got the ball for the first time and started running down the touch-line the crowd really roared. It was just like the old days. The crowds loved him. He was still the number one attraction and I will always regard him as a true friend.

## Neil Fox MBE

Neil Fox MBE was one of the best British players of the post-war era, winning every honour in the game. He is the world record points scorer with 6,220, which is unlikely ever to be beaten.

# Introduction

It is fitting that Robert Gate should write a new biography of Billy Boston. For a quarter of a century Robert has been one of our foremost rugby league historians, blazing a trail that others have followed and creating new standards of research and understanding for our game. In his writings on rugby league, Robert has brought to life our hidden character, always accepting the risks that come with publication, especially in the early days when commercial publishers turned their nose up at rugby league as a serious subject of literary and historical study. Robert took no notice of entrenched prejudice and in the spirit of a radical non-conformist he wrote about the game not on the basis of what he was supposed to think, or had been told to think by the establishment, but simply on the basis of what he had seen from an early age.

The importance of doing what you know to be true and testifying to what you have seen and witnessed reminds us of the approach adopted by the young Ernest Hemingway in his bull-fighting opus *Death in the Afternoon*. In the opening section Hemingway tells the reader why he feels compelled to write about the corrida in the aftermath of World War I: "I was trying to write then and I found the greatest difficulty, aside from knowing truly what you really felt, rather than what you were supposed to feel, and had been taught to feel, was to put down what really happened in action; what the actual things were which produced the emotion that you experienced. In writing for a newspaper you told what happened and, with one trick and another, you communicated the emotion aided by the element of timeliness which gives a certain emotion to any account of something that has happened on that day; but the real thing, the sequence of motion and fact which made the emotion and which would be as valid in a year or in ten years or, with luck and if you stated it purely enough, always, was beyond me and I was working very hard to try to get it. The only place where you could see life and death, i.e. violent death now that the wars were over, was in the bull ring and I wanted very much to go to Spain where I could study it. I was trying to learn to write, commencing with the simplest things, and one of the simplest things of all and the most fundamental is violent death."

Robert Gate took the same journey as Ernest Hemingway and during a time of transition for the game he tried to write about 'the simplest things', the 'fundamental' components that had given rugby league since the break with rugby union at the end of the 19th century its distinctive character. He reminded us of the great players, the epic moments, the forgotten skills, the ferocity and violence that has always been a part of our game and the styles of art and sublime avoidance that characterise our finest players. Robert chose his subjects carefully. When he started writing in the 1970s and 1980s he understood instinctively where to go in order to uncover those diverse traditions and the histories of which they had been a part. For example, Robert chose to focus on the century-long migration of rugby players from the towns and valleys of South Wales to the North of England. In *Gone North*, a two volume study of Welsh players, Robert brought to our attention many of those – from Danny Hurcombe to Alan Edwards, from Billo Rees to Ronnie James – whose contributions and achievements had not been recorded and whose histories and identities had gone missing from the annals of our game.

With the exception of Harry Edgar and Trevor Delaney, Robert was out there on his own; very few people were doing what he was doing with such big subjects and presenting them to us with such clarity and panache. For Robert the Welsh heritage of rugby league was stylish, charismatic and high-definition. It was an historical phenomenon of fundamental importance that had shaped our game in a unique way. Welsh players had been coming into rugby league for over 100 years and their presence had transformed the way we thought about the game, the way we played it and, in the person of a genius like Jim Sullivan, the way we coached it.

Robert knew that of all those players who left Wales to play rugby league no one, after Jim Sullivan, had made a more significant impact on rugby league than W.J. Boston, a 19 year old winger from Tiger Bay, Cardiff, who signed for Wigan on 13 March 1953. Absolutely no one who grew up in Wigan in the 1950s could escape the influence that Billy Boston had on their daily lives.

Billy's effect on the town's imagination bore testimony to its love affair with Wales, a relationship which stretched back to the time of Johnny Thomas, Tommy Howley, Sid Jerram and 'Dodger' Owens and which, in the case of my father, achieved its first romantic expression with the arrival of Danny Hurcombe from Mountain Ash. Players like these had enjoyed distinguished careers in rugby league, not just at Wigan, but throughout the game. Alec Givvons played with distinction for Oldham and Roy Francis had been an international wing at Barrow and Hull. But no one, not even the great Jim Sullivan who had gone north from Cardiff as an 18 year old in 1921, was able to prepare the rugby league public for the explosive genius of Billy Boston and the uninhibited way in which he played our game.

In the 1950s Boston was the Oscar Peterson of rugby league. From Wigan to Sydney he was the supreme entertainer. At Central Park he could play 'The Maidens of Cadiz' in a drizzle and reduce his opponents to enthralled spectators. All that mattered was the virtuoso style. Colour was irrelevant. Just occasionally he was called The Brown Bomber, but more often than not he was simply Billy B or Bouncing Bill. Ces Mountford, the great New Zealand half-back, once summed it up when he described Billy as the 'blank cheque' player. Jack Winstanley, who wrote an early biography of Billy, agrees unreservedly. "If he came on the market today", says Winstanley, "you'd have to pay well in excess of a million – probably two million – pounds." "Wigan", he says, "made the most effort of any signing they ever made to get Boston's signature." According to Martin Ryan, the Wigan full-back, the club would have paid whatever it took. Ryan also noted that Wigan were ready to pay half a million to bring Wendell Sailor over from Brisbane. "And all he does is run into people", he said, smiling. "Billy ran around them. He had the feet."

Be it Adrian van Heerden in the 1920s, Green Vigo in the 1970s or Billy Boston in the 1950s, Wiganers have had a long affair with overseas wingers: Springbok, Aboriginal, African, Welsh. But Wiganers were not unique in their affections. A scan of the team lists of the 1950s and 1960s reveals that almost every continent, bar Asia, was represented in rugby league. This seemed to suit Billy's personality and it probably made him feel more at home. It might also have reminded him of the world he had left, the ethnic communities he had grown up with in Tiger Bay, the interracial way of life that drew him as a youth to seek fame if not fortune with the Cardiff International Athletic Club.

In the 1950s the CIACS rugby club was a cosmopolitan side formed in the heart of Cardiff's dockland with a huge range of players from many backgrounds: Greeks, Italians, Maltese, Arabs. According to Billy, they were a motley crew all dressed in coloured shirts, but they helped break down ethnic barriers and gave him some of his happiest moments on a rugby field. Many of the CIACS black players, like Johnny Freeman and Colin Dixon, went north with Billy and had glittering careers at Halifax and Salford.

Towns like Wigan, Halifax and Hull – where Clive Sullivan enjoyed a fabulous career – replicated the close-knit community of Tiger Bay and the raucous warmth of its streets. In Ince, Wallgate, Whelley and Scholes, an emigrant from Wales like Billy Boston could enter a tight, labyrinthine world of back-to-backs, Irish communities and working class clubs. Martin Ryan, second only to Sullivan as Wigan's greatest full-back, was convinced that the protective, communal environment of a place like Wigan, with its extended family structure, was an ideal breeding ground for the hard school of rugby. "It bred loyalty," said Ryan, "and whatever the draw-backs and the deprivation, it gave you the character to play a physical contact sport." "The team I played in after the war was just like a family", he added. "We relied on each other; shared our grief as well as our grub." Ted Ward, who played with Ryan, also made the same point when I met him in Garnant in the late 1970s. "Our trainer was a farmer, Frank Barton. After the war rationing was still on and Frank used to give us a side of pig to share out after training." Ted Ward and Billy Boston felt at home in Wigan. The CIACS motto: UNIS ET IDEM, one and the same, had magically reappeared.

In Wigan Billy was a man who lived the way he played. And Wiganers loved him for that. Billy was a showman without showing off. "He scored his tries and there was no bloody fuss", says Jack Winstanley. He was a naturally diffident man who achieved what he did on a rugby field without undergoing a change of personality. That's the way Billy had been brought up by his parents and the way he'd been taught to behave by Bernard Sullivan at the South Church Street School and Bill Barrett at the Cardiff Boys Club. Billy played his rugby the way he lived his life. At Central Park, the game recreated the non-egotistical, community spirit he felt comfortable with. In typical fashion, he puts it thus: "During my period Wigan had an absolutely wonderful set of players and I think that this should be made clear. No one man can make a team and I was no exception. You only have to think back and remember some of the names. Brian McTigue, Dave Bolton, Mick Sullivan, Terry O'Grady, Ernie Ashcroft, Jack Cunliffe, Norman Cherrington, Eric Ashton: the list is endless. I consider myself very lucky to have played at this time. I am convinced that these were truly great players."

Billy Boston brings to mind Garrison Keillor's Lake Wobegon's code from his novel *Wobegon Boy*: "Do your job, don't tell lies, don't imagine you're exceptional even if you are, be glad for what you have done, don't feel sorry for yourself." And Billy never did. That's why Wiganers took to him. As Jack Winstanley put it: "Billy had a nice smile. He liked kids. He had a great degree of humility about him. That's why he was asked to open church bazaars and crown rose queens."

In 1996 a joy-rider hit Billy Boston outside his home in Poolstock. Billy suffered serious leg injuries. Sentencing the young offender the magistrate placed him under a curfew order. "I'm doing this for your own good", he said. "There are people out there who are very unhappy with what you've done. If there's one person you don't knock down in Wigan, it's Mr Boston." Billy, who was inundated with flowers and get-well cards, was in hospital for a few weeks. The car apparently was a write-off.

## Phil Melling

Phil Melling was born and raised in Wigan, but has lived in Wales for over 30 years. He played a major role in developing student and amateur rugby league in west Wales. He has written widely about rugby league, including *Man of Amman*, a biography of Dai Davies and edited, with Tony Collins, *The Glory of Their Times*, a collection of articles on the historical contribution of players of colour in rugby league. His play, *The Day of the African*, was one of the inaugural productions at the George Orwell Heritage in Wigan in the 1980s. He was also a regular contributor to *Our Game*, and has written for many other rugby league publications.

He is Emeritus Professor of American Literature at the University of Wales, Swansea, and chairman and founder of Study Guatemala, a charity that provides free education to disadvantaged children in Central America.

# Preface

They have just named a stand after Billy Boston at Wigan's DW Stadium and he never even played there. Almost simultaneously Billy topped the poll conducted by a local newspaper to determine the greatest player to have graced a rugby pitch in Wigan or Leigh, that is, in Wigan Borough. As the winner Billy will be immortalised as part of a new exhibition in the Wigan History Shop. The History Shop is a combination of the town's reference library, archive and heritage centre and is currently undergoing a £1.6 million refurbishment.

Very few people would have been surprised that Billy came out on top, despite the high quality of the opposition, which included Jim Sullivan, Eric Ashton, Brian McTigue, Joe Egan, Johnny Ring, Ellery Hanley, Martin Offiah, Jimmy Ledgard, John Woods and Alex Murphy, to name just the tip of the iceberg.

Why?

Probably because Billy is a memorable figure in every respect. Billy Boston – once seen, never forgotten. How many players can be truly be described as unforgettable? On your deathbed how many players will still be indelibly imprinted on your fading memory bank? It's a fair bet that for rugby league fans of a certain vintage, Billy will. Yet it is 41 years since he last played for Wigan and an awful lot of water has flown down the River Douglas past Central Park and Tesco in the meantime.

Billy has just turned 75 and has been a Wiganer for 56 years, having been lured to Lancashire from his native Cardiff for £3,000 in 1953. He might not have believed it at the time, but it was the best move he ever made. Even if he didn't believe it countless thousands of Wigan supporters did and still do. They are grateful to have been allowed to follow the career of a genuine rugby league legend. According to modern hyperbole almost anyone seems to be able to attain the status of "legend". We all know that to be nonsense and that very few can be described as such in reality. Billy Boston is unquestionably one of the few.

I actually do not remember where I was when John Kennedy was assassinated, nor do I recall what I was doing when the Americans landed on the moon. When Kennedy died I was a schoolboy and when the moon was first walked upon I had progressed to college, but that is as much as I can say about those momentous events. But I do remember the first time I clapped eyes on Billy Boston. It was in 1956, on 29 September, to be precise. It was a lovely Saturday afternoon at Thrum Hall and Halifax were playing Wigan. I had been a Halifax rugby league supporter for all of seven weeks, but I already recognised a big match when I saw one and there were almost 15,000 fans in the ground who were expecting fireworks. My attention was focused on the Halifax number five, Johnny Freeman, Halifax's own Billy Boston, except that to the eyes of a junior school kid from Halifax Johnny was better than Billy. I realise now that I was probably wrong! I knew enough to spot that Johnny and Billy – both Tiger Bay boys - were heroes and that the crowd was on tenterhooks whenever they got the ball or even had a whiff of it.

I expected Halifax to win, as I would for years and years to come. During those childhood years I had not yet recognised that other teams might be better than Halifax. If we lost it must obviously have been for some other reason than being poorer than the opposition … perish the thought. However, I did twig that Billy Boston, in his striking cherry and white hooped jersey, was special, even if 'Fax's blue and white hoops appeared even more attractive. The Halifax crowd's "oohs" and "aahs" and blind sense of panic whenever the ball reached him left no room for doubt – this was one dangerous character. Halifax did win, 9–3. Joe Mageen scored Halifax's try and Brian McTigue scored Wigan's. Full-back Peter Briers, who always seemed to miss more goals than he landed, kicked two for us and Johnny finished the scoring with a miraculous penalty goal in the last minute. Bloody Billy Boston did not trouble the scorers. I remember watching the game from the bottom side of Thrum Hall, looking across to the main stand. At one point Billy suddenly and unexpectedly got away on the outside of Johnny and dashed along touch towards the Scratching Shed. Somehow he was driven infield and Johnny had enough speed to catch hold of him by the shorts, which disintegrated in his hand. That's the sort of thing you don't easily forget when you are a sprog, or even when you get to my age.

When I started to research my biography of Billy at the History Shop last year, I read every account of Billy's matches for Wigan between 1953 and 1968. I was pleased to read in the *Wigan Examiner* that my memory was not faulty. It noted that Freeman did indeed hang on to Billy's pants. It added that Billy went on a few yards minus his shorts and then passed the ball. I had no recollection of what had happened once his shorts came off! It also reported that the scrums were shared 15–15 but I never noticed the hookers!

Since that first sight of Billy it was impossible not to take any and every chance to watch him in action. He never disappointed, even if by his own standards he had a poor game. Billy could have had the dodgiest game known to man and he would still have generated more excitement than anyone had any right to expect from one player. Anyone who ever saw his blockbusting runs, with bodies strewn behind him wondering where the train had gone, will never forget them. As a child I found them terrifying and worried for my own safety... and I was generally standing behind a concrete wall. They were also strangely compelling. You could not take your eyes off Billy, you had to count the bodies, to cringe as the next would-be hero dashed himself against this rapidly accelerating piece of granite and then perhaps Billy would take pity and daintily sidestep the poor blighter. That was the thing about Billy – he could beat men in any manner he chose. He had the power and the pace but he also had the poise. And what about his defence – has anyone ever generated such a bone-crushing concoction of power and velocity as Billy in those ball-and-all crash tackles on opposing centres? If anyone has, I for one have never seen the bloke.

I first met Billy in 1988, when I visited him at his pub, The Griffin, in order to collect one of his caps for display in the newly established Rugby League Hall of Fame. Billy was one of the original nine inductees into the Hall of Fame and it is pretty certain that no one in their right mind would have omitted him, even if the quota had been smaller. Everybody had told me that Billy was a lovely man and I was not disappointed. Everyone likes Billy. He is affability personified and probably generous to a fault.

That was certainly how it seemed to me when he told me he had no Wembley jersey to loan to the Hall of Fame. He should have had six but he had given them all away, generally to charitable causes. He came unstuck once through doing so. He told me: "I gave one of my Wembley jerseys to a bloke who came into the pub asking for something to auction for a children's charity. Years later he came into The Griffin and told me, 'I've got a shirt of yours'. 'Oh, yes,' I said. 'Which one?' He said, 'It was one of your Wembley shirts. You gave it to me to auction for charity but I kept it!' I don't know whether he paid for it in the auction himself or just decided to keep it!" Another Wembley jersey, the 1965 version, turned up a few years ago and the Welsh Sports Hall of Fame acquired it. They presented it to Billy at a function but then Billy let them have it back to put in one of their exhibitions.

My second encounter with Billy was at the opening of the Hall of Fame, when I gave him a copy of Jack Winstanley's superb 1963 biography *The Billy Boston Story*, because Billy had, characteristically, given away all his own copies.

That's Billy – affable, generous, friendly, modest and maybe the most admired man in Wigan. His fame follows or precedes him everywhere he goes. Joan, his wife – "the best thing that ever happened to me", according to Billy, says: "He is too famous, I sometimes think. I am quite a quiet person really and I used to get a bit jealous when women used to come up and kiss him. It happened a lot. We couldn't go anywhere without someone knowing him. Once in Singapore we were minding our own business walking down a street famous for its restaurants. Suddenly a bloke on the other side of the street bawled out, 'Hiya, Billy. How you doing?' I couldn't believe it!"

It is not only Wiganers who cherish Billy. I was at the Wigan-Saints Wembley Challenge Cup Final in 1991, standing with some friends at the foot of the steps leading up to the Twin Towers before the game. There was a group of St Helens lads nearby and they were in a boisterous mood, giving everyone who went by a load of verbal welly. Much of it was crude. Some of it must have been rehearsed, because they appeared to have tirades of abuse suitable for any recognisable replica jerseys that hove into view. It was all good-natured though, in the usual spirit of rugby league buffoons on such occasions. All of a sudden, Billy Boston came into view and had to cross the line of ridicule. No problem. The singing Sintelliners immediately broke into "There's only one Billy Boston, one Billy Boston", cheered their heads off and clapped him until he disappeared at the top of the steps. They meant it too. That incident probably sums up the esteem in which Billy is universally held.

By the time I began to research this biography in the Wigan History Shop in 2008, Billy had been retired from playing for Wigan for 40 years. Surely his popularity would have nose-dived by now, I mused. Not a bit. Even in the quietness of the reference library his name resonated, especially when one bloke told the rest of the family history researchers that "this bloke from Halifax is writing a book on Billy Boston" and implied that Halifax must not have a library. Another chap had come to look up his wedding, but ended up reading about Billy's deeds in 1966. Another regaled me with comparisons of Billy and Ellery Hanley – the two best players who had played for Wigan in his time – but it was obvious that Billy was his favourite. Yet another bloke told me Billy was the finest player in history, Wigan's or anyone else's, and added: "I know a woman who has the house where Billy used to live in Swan Meadow Lane. She's as proud as Punch".

Wiganers have certainly taken Billy to their hearts, as has the wider rugby league community. His heart and soul might still be Welsh but a big part of him must now have Wigan imprinted on it. Perhaps a fellow Welshman, Aneirin Rhys Thomas, best encapsulates Billy's relationship with his adopted home. In his *Cewri Campau Cymru* (*Welsh Sporting Giants*) Thomas wrote: "All agreed on his proverbial abilities, and all describe him as the complete player. Boston lit up the town of Wigan with his brilliant skills. Wigan was a bleak industrial town in the 1950s. A town of coal mines and austere factories, a town that bore the scars of the Second World War all too clearly. Escaping the yellow fog on a cold winter Saturday to watch the sparkling genius of Billy Boston at Central Park lit up the soul and warmed the body. Here he was king... an amiable king, a king of the people. Maybe Wigan's back-to-back terraced houses, Wigan's smoke chimneys, the pub-and-club Wigan, the rugby-talking Wigan was akin to Tiger Bay when Boston was back in Wales."

Billy had the common touch, time for all and sundry. In quiet spells on the pitch he would exchange pleasantries with the spectators. After games he would sign endless autographs for the kids. He would open fetes, judge competitions, play in charity matches, talk to fans on the streets – and there was no charge. Nowadays he would have agents coming out of his ears and millions in the bank. But he certainly would not have stayed in Wigan for over half a century and people like Chris Hesketh, captain of Great Britain's 1974 touring team, would not be writing such eulogies as: "Billy Boston was 'Mister Wigan' really and a wonderful, shy man. I know Billy had his fall-outs with Wigan but he is the most charming of men. Talk about humility. It's humility gone mad with Billy. If you were lucky you'd see Billy walking through the town to the match from Poolstock, where he lived, wearing his club blazer. I don't like saying things like 'The greatest ever' but I never saw a better winger than Billy Boston and I certainly never met a nicer fellah – he is a class man." (Taken from *Captain Courageous: The Chris Hesketh Story*, by Chris Hesketh and Graham Morris, 2006)

It has been a privilege to write Billy's biography.

**Robert Gate**
September 2009

Robert Gate has been writing on rugby league history for over 30 years. Recent books include his biography of Neil Fox, a book on the Great Britain test matches, and one on the players in the Rugby League Hall of Fame.

## Acknowledgements

### Thanks to:
Billy and Joan, for their hospitality, openness and patience.
Neil Fox and Phil Melling, for their contributions.
Stuart Smith, for permission to reproduce his painting of Billy.
Tony Capstick, Jim Carter, Harry Edgar (*Rugby League Journal*), the late Harold Farrimond, Raymond Fletcher, Tony Lewis, Jo Moran, Eric Purdham, Alex Service and Andy Wheelwright, for help with information, illustrations or advice.
John Benn, Tom Groves, Cliff Webb and Jack Winstanley, whose reports in the *Wigan Examiner* and the *Wigan Observer* provided so much information and entertainment.
Simon Martin, librarian at the Wigan History Shop, who taught me several tricks with microfilms, thereby making my research easier and quicker.
Peter Lush and Dave Farrar at London League Publications Ltd, for bringing this book to fruition; Steve McCarthy for designing the cover and the staff at MPG Biddles for printing it.

## Select bibliography
Bevan Alun Wyn, *St Helen's Stories* (Gomer 2007)
Duarte Arthur, *The Boys from the Bay: A brief history of the Cardiff International Athletic Club* (2006)
Gate Robert, *Gone North* (Vol 1) (R.E. Gate 1986)
Gate Robert, *Rugby League Hall of Fame* (Tempus 2003)
Peacock V, *Living Legends of Rugby League: Billy Boston* (The Who's Who Series of Publications 1984)
Winstanley Jack, *The Billy Boston Story* (*Wigan Observer* 1963)

Also Phil Melling's essays in:
Phil Melling and Tony Collins (eds), *The Glory of their Times* (Vertical Editions 2004)
Huw Richards, Peter Stead and Gareth Williams (eds), *Heart and Soul: The Character of Welsh Rugby* (University of Wales Press 1998)

Statistics: dnp: Did not play, Cup: Challenge Cup, CH: Championship, FT: BBC2 Floodlit Trophy LC: Lancashire Cup, WD: Western Division.

Publishers' note: Some of the reports in this book use language to describe black players that would not be acceptable today. No offence is intended, and we have left the reports as originally written for historical accuracy.

# Contents

The Billy Boston stand at Central Park.
Now a stand at the DW Stadium has been named after Billy. (Photo: Peter Lush)

Stuart Smith's painting of Billy.
(Courtesy Stuart Smith)

# 1.    Reflections on Billy Boston

It is inordinately difficult to convey just how extraordinary a rugby league player Billy Boston was. Unless one played with or against him or witnessed his deeds from the safety of the stands or the terracing, it is virtually impossible to describe the frisson he engendered when he was in action. As charismatic figures go in rugby league, there was none to surpass the man variously known as Bouncing Billy, Billy B, Billy-oh, the Sepia Streak, the Brown Bomber, the Wigan Walloper or most simply, popularly and affectionately – Billy, plain Billy.

A few anecdotal, even apocryphal, tales can perhaps give some flavour of how Billy was regarded. The first, told to the author by Maurice Bamford, among others, goes something like this: "A young winger was in the dressing-room before a game against Wigan. He had not played in the first team before and naturally he was worried. It was nerve-wracking enough to be making his first team debut but the lad was also down to mark Billy Boston. He listened intently to the coach's pre-match instructions and tactical advice. The coach had himself been an international winger so when he had finished his team talk, the young winger was surprised that he had not said anything to him regarding how to deal with Billy. He finally plucked up the courage to ask the coach if he could give him some advice about how to stop Billy. The coach frowned, sighed and said matter of factly, "There's only one way to stop Boston, lad". "So, how's that?" asked the youngster, who was becoming more and more anxious. The coach replied, "You'll have to throw s..t at him". Looking decidedly alarmed, the winger asked, "Where am I going to get any s..t from?" "Don't worry about that lad", said the coach. "When Billy starts running towards you, you'll soon find some!"

Definitely apocryphal is the following from *Gone North* (Volume 1): "Rugby followers the world over are familiar with players who would undoubtedly run at the proverbial brick wall, should their team's cause demand it. One day, or so the story goes, Billy Boston's team-mates set him up to run at said wall. Billy charged but just before impact the wall stepped out of the way!" That wall may have been thick but it was not stupid.

Because of their innate capacity to exaggerate physical features and mannerisms, cartoonists and caricaturists are often better able to capture the essence of individuals more concisely than writers. Billy was a godsend to them for the mayhem they could portray in their works. A good example was Roy Ullyett's *Daily Express* cartoon of the 1965 Challenge Cup Final, when Wigan defeated Hunslet in one of the all-time classic Wembley finals. In it a super-sized Billy is roaring along, having left one dazed man flat on his back in the distance and broken another man in two. In that period of secret agent 007 mania, Ullyett comments, "Compared with Billy, James Bond firing gas bombs and cannon from that car of his is about as frightening as a kiddie on a tricycle armed with a fruit lolly".

Moving from the ridiculous to the sublime, Billy's great rival Tom van Vollenhoven, alias 'The Flying Springbok', recalled in a *Wigan Observer* interview of 4 October 1990, conducted by Neil Barker: "Strength was Billy's forte. He was immensely powerful and it normally took about six players to down him. He was phenomenally built and he was one of those players who entertained the fans - a truly great player. We were rivals on the field but always the best of friends off it." In the same interview Billy remembered: "Tom's going to pull me up about the time I knocked his teeth out! It only seems like yesterday – we were playing Saints at Knowsley Road and I saw Tom flying down the wing in typical fashion. He was a natural try-scorer, but there was no way through on this occasion. I guess I must have caught him with a really good belt but it was a case of giving as good as you got in those days." Tom replied: "I wondered what hit me and then I remember Billy coming into our dressing room at the end of the game and being ever so apologetic. I had to laugh at his manner, but it's like Billy says – you gave as good as you got. I cracked him but it just so happened he was a bit more effective on this occasion."

Alex Murphy, one of the few men who can rival Billy in rugby league sainthood, said of Billy when he finished at Wigan in 1968: "Billy has been the lot in my opinion. I would name him as one of the two best wingers who ever played rugby, the other one being Tommy van Vollenhoven. Boston could really run in defence and attack. What's more he always had the respect of the opposition, both forwards and backs, and you can't say that about many other players." In 1993 Murphy wrote: "No one could score tries like Billy. But he also had the ability to stop tries as well as score them. His tackling was so effective he often did more damage without the ball than with it."

Billy's team-mates at Wigan were not slow to praise him when he announced his retirement in 1968. Brian McTigue, whom Billy rates as the greatest of all forwards, asked, "What can you say about Billy that hasn't been said over and over again? Billy Boston was in a class of his own. The complete natural footballer. The greatest." The man most closely associated with Billy, his centre partner and Wigan captain, Eric Ashton stated: "It is very difficult to put into words the praise Billy deserves. It has always made my job far easier playing with a bloke as great as he was. Throughout his career, he has unquestionably put countless thousands on gates, not only at Central Park and in this country, but in Australia, New Zealand and France. More's the pity that there will probably never be another player like him. Unquestionably Billy was the greatest in my time."

Joe Egan, one of Billy's coaches at Wigan in his glory days, said: "Billy Boston was the most perfect rugby league player I have ever seen. If Wigan had paid £30,000 for him, they would still have had their money's worth. It was always a terrific psychological advantage to have Boston in the team. If Billy had set his mind to it, he could have broken Brian Nordgren's club record of 64 tries in a season without a great deal of trouble. But personal records never seemed to bother him particularly."

Vince Karalius, the renowned St Helens and Great Britain loose-forward and a hard man among hard men, wrote in his 1964 autobiography *Lucky 13:* "He has probably been the most magnetic crowd-puller in the history of post-war British rugby league … I personally rate him one of the three finest wingers I have ever played with or against … A great player is Boston, the human block-buster, with the baffling side-step and try-scoring technique."

Another fabulous loose-forward, the Australian Johnny Raper had immense admiration for Billy. Discussing great wingers in his 1997 autobiography *The Man in the Bowler Hat*, Raper wrote: "Three wingmen stood out in my time in football – Great Britain's Billy Boston, Ken Irvine and Eddie Lumsden. Right behind them were a number of top quality players such as Johnny King, Eric Grothe and Britain's Mick Sullivan. Billy Boston has to claim one of my [Dream Team] spots. He was so big and strong, so involved in any match he played. Off the paddock he was one of the finest people I have met – a magnificent ambassador for the game and for himself. Reg Gasnier used to grumble about Boston's speciality of flying in off the wing to crunch some poor centre – and hear the breath explode out of his body. A number of English wingers perfected the art of swooping infield like that. And even if a bloke like Billy stayed out, he would create uncertainty; you could bet on centres glancing out of the corner of their eyes just in case he was on the way. Boston's timing was always impeccable. Inevitably he would cut off the ball before the opposition centre could get the ball to the winger. Blokes like Ike Southward and Mick Sullivan were pretty good at it too. Boston played much of his football outside one of the great centres of the game, Eric

2

Ashton, and had the certain ability to capitalise on the opportunities created for him. Close to the line, he was unstoppable – a lethal opponent and great finisher."

Maurice Bamford, another former forward and in later life a Great Britain coach, has fond memories of Billy. Like Johnny Raper, Bamford selected Billy in his Dream Team in 2005 in his book *Play to win: Rugby League Heroes*: "Billy took the XIII-a-side code by the scruff of the neck and was an instant success. Big for a wingman then, his pace and power were awesome and his footwork for such a big man was unbelievable. My mind's eye can see him now, hugging the touchline challenging the unlucky tackler to knock him into touch. 'Come on, all you have to do is push me into touch', he seemed to say, and if the tackler took the bait you could guarantee it would be he who hit the dust... My only meeting with Billy on the field was around 1960 when I played for Dewsbury at Central Park and our coach, Bert Cook ... had a simple ploy to stop Billy scoring. The game plan was easy: just get as many players as possible to confront Billy when he had the ball, especially near our line. I remember breaking from a scrum, 10 yards from our try-line and seeing two tacklers hanging from Billy like Christmas decorations, and him still moving menacingly towards our line. Gritting my teeth, I flung myself round Billy's standing leg at the same time as our loose-forward hit the top of the pile of bodies, but that dreadful feeling of inadequacy came flooding over us as Billy literally carried four of us over the line for a try in the corner. Always the same when you meet him, Billy Boston has that remarkable gift of being able to walk with commoners and kings and treat them both the same."

Another famous forward, Ray French also recalled having problems when playing for St Helens against Billy. In his 1979 autobiography *My Kind of Rugby*, French wrote: "Teams would plan their strategies round stopping the likes of 'Billy B' and 'The Voll', and we at St Helens were no exception, but often with disastrous results in the case of Boston. I can well remember the planning which went into the attempted stopping of Wigan's famous right-wing pair Eric Ashton and Billy Boston on one cold Boxing Day clash. Along with Billy Major, then our loose-forward, I had arranged to break quickly from the scrum and go up into the Wigan line and take Boston while Major fell back deep to the touch-line and took Eric Ashton whenever the pair tried their dummy scissors move.

'Billy's calling for the ball, Ray. Break quickly and get up on him when he comes inside,' Billy Major whispered as he packed down behind me in the scrum. 'Let him have it if you catch him.' 'Fair enough,' I replied. 'I'll follow Ashton,' insisted Major.

Wigan duly won the ball from the scrum and up I went to try to stop Boston about to steam inside from Eric Ashton's reverse pass. Disaster struck, for Billy Major somehow got caught up with Eric Ashton as he sped for the touch-line in front of Boston, while I, seeing Boston in my sights, let go with my right arm in the direction of his head. Boston ducked and grinned. Up popped Billy Major to receive the blow intended for Boston. Boston crashed through; Major was led from the field, blood streaming from a cut eye, with the retort: 'Forget the move, Ray, concentrate on the scrum-half'."

In full flight Billy Boston was a fearsome prospect for any defender. Standing around 5 feet 10½ inches tall and latterly weighing around the 15 stones mark, Billy was not unusually big for a rugby league player. There were plenty who were just as big but they were usually prop forwards. No prop forward in history could move like Billy, perish the thought. When he began playing rugby league he was an athletic 12½ stones, often described as panther-like. His speed, swerve and side-step, allied to natural strength and innate footballing skills, were breathtaking and scoring tries seemed to be second nature to him. As he matured his weight increased but so did his skills. Crucially he hardly seemed to lose pace or the ability to move off either foot, which made him truly formidable and a nightmare for opposing backs to tackle. Many match reports talk of opposing wingers, full-backs or half-backs as being brave, courageous, valiant or even suicidal, when making successful tackles on Billy. Such terms simply did not apply to other wingers, apart maybe from Lionel Cooper or Jack McLean, two big wingers whose careers only just overlapped with Billy's. Critics really did not expect solitary opponents, especially backs, to ground him. Stopping Billy usually had to be done mob-handed.

Even great wingers like Swinton's John Stopford would worry about having to face Billy. He told Phil Melling in *Heart and Soul* in 1998: "The first time I played against Boston was an away game. I walked to Central Park on my own and went straight into a pub near the Drill Hall and ordered two rum and blacks. I shouldn't have done it, and I never did it again, but I was scared stiff that day. It was what he was going to do to me; how much he was going to hurt me. It got no better when I got stripped off: the trainer had forgotten my ankle strap. I went looking for Maurice Hughes, the Wigan physio, to see if I could borrow one. The door of the Wigan dressing-room was open, and Billy had his feet on a bench reading a comic. It was *Superman*. He just nodded and smiled. How I got through that match I'll never know. Billy scored a try on me but he didn't show me up. He congratulated me afterwards and we had a drink."

I once asked another test class winger, Huddersfield's Ken Senior, what it was like to face Brian Bevan and Billy Boston, the two most prolific try-baggers in history. He replied: "Bloody difficult. After the kick-off I would not get anywhere near Bevan and with Billy I just tried to keep out of his way!" One winger who usually made a good fist of containing Billy was Oldham's John Etty, a notably competent defender. In his 1996 autobiography, *A Rugby League Winner*, John recalled the 1957 Lancashire Cup Final: "Wigan selected Billy Boston at stand-off. Frank Daley, however, showed tremendous courage in tackling him. I recall making the last tackle of the closely-contested game on Billy Boston, when the referee, Matt Coates, blew the whistle for full time. Billy got up, shook hands with me, and gave a big grin, although Wigan had lost! A true sportsman."

Dai Bevan, another top defensive wingman with Belle Vue Rangers, Wigan and Halifax, had some success in preventing Billy from scoring tries. Dai had in fact partnered Billy on his debut for Wigan 'A' in 1953. Years later, in an interview with Phil Lyon for the *Halifax Evening Courier*, he recalled that before the game, "Wigan bosses asked him which wing he preferred and Billy said, 'I'm Welsh, I'll play with Dai'. Billy and I still argue about who played where. I'm convinced I played centre to his wing. He swears it was the other way round." Billy was right. Dai's tactic of playing almost on top of Billy was infuriatingly simple but Billy did not think much of such play. When Billy finally broke his duck playing against Bevan in the infamous Challenge Cup semi-final of 1956 at Odsal, Dai recalled, "I was shattered by it because I had Billy just where I wanted him – not head-on, but from the side and slightly behind. I just mis-timed the tackle". At least Bevan had sussed the one thing players must never do when faced with Billy on the burst – try to take him head-on. That really was suicidal.

Mick Sullivan, Britain's most capped test winger and at various times Billy's fiercest rival and team-mate, was a man who took no prisoners, to put it politely. Mick is on record as describing Billy as the hardest opponent he ever had to deal with and rated Billy and Lionel Cooper, who he partnered at Huddersfield, as the best wingers he encountered.

Perhaps the most eloquent testimony to Billy's prowess came from Ces Mountford, one of the all-time great stand-offs, who wrote: "Van Vollenhoven is obviously a great winger, the best over a distance with a chance. But Billy at short range is the better man for upsetting the tight-set defence. Boston has swerve and, for his bulk, a remarkably tight

4

side-step. He takes the good or the awkward ball, the long or the short flip of a pass, far better than any other winger. He can play an excellent game on either wing, at centre or stand-off. On attack, Boston can use all his weight, or waft through with the grace of a ballet dancer. He can, too, hurl that huge bulk on the shortest way to the line and score through sheer, shattering strength. Obviously he has courage. He never shirks 'having a go', however forlorn the hope. And his excellent games at centre and stand-off have not been in the easy obscurity of a league game but in the intense glamour games of Wembley, Championship and all that. On defence, Boston can have the shattering effect of a flying bomb. It needs a lot of courage when Billy is 'unleashed' – that's the word – to take man and ball fairly, but with such a bone-shaking tackle. I think Boston has taken the 'ginger' out of star back opposition more often than any other man in the game. He comes in for a lot of growls for his energy-sapping tackles ... but they are fair. And, to be honest, he has to take an awful lot of unceremonious treatment when three or four men at a time have got him down. Boston is the complete player. He has speed, he has weight. He is a match-winner from forlorn hopes. He is a man of many parts in defence and attack, and a man of many positions. Barring Alex Murphy, I know of no player able to fill one position as the very best and two other positions as well as the best. Defensively, I think Boston counts for more as the dread and fear of oppositions. With all these attributes I would have Billy Boston first for my cash".

Billy's versatility served Wigan well and underlined his outstanding ability as an all-round rugby player. In 486 starts for Wigan he filled the following positions: right wing 404, full-back 7, right centre 28, left centre 32, left wing 5, stand-off 8 and second-row 2. In his first-class career he made 562 starts: right wing 469, full-back 8, right centre 32, left centre 33, left wing 7, stand-off 8 and second-row 3. It should not be forgotten either that in many games Billy began in one position and moved to other positions during the 80 minutes.

However, it is primarily as a right winger that Billy is so fondly remembered. Although Billy asked me not to say that he "crashed over" for most of his tries, many people's memories are of him crashing over or crashing through serried ranks of dazed defenders.

There are tries of all descriptions in this book, but perhaps a distillation of Billy's prowess can be gleaned from Jack Bentley's description in the *Daily Dispatch* of his five-try performance against a nonplussed Whitehaven on 29 October 1955: "For sheer power football, Boston's running would be difficult to match. Indeed, two of his tries bordered on the miraculous. The first was when he streaked away from a Bolton pass and when faced with Jackson, McAvoy, McCourt and Dawson simply ran 'through' the Whitehaven defenders. The second was from an 'impossible' position close to the touchline. He pushed off one tackler, brushed aside two others, spurted past another two and then more or less ignored full-back Jackson's challenge as he went over. On another occasion Jackson hit the winger with everything he had, but a swing of Boston's hips and Jackson picked himself up from outside the touchline. Boston trotted over the line for his fifth try!"

The fact that Billy scored a record 478 tries for Wigan indicates what a magnificent player he was, but does not show that his efforts produced, possibly, hundreds of tries for others. The effort required to deal with Billy often so debilitated defences that chances were created elsewhere. Eric Thompson gave such an example in the *Lancashire Evening Post & Chronicle*, when reporting Wigan's Challenge Cup semi-final encounter against Swinton in 1965. Of Wigan's opening try, he wrote: "[Ray Ashby's link-up] resulted in sending the hard-to-hold Boston close at the right corner. As has happened so many times in his 12 years in a cherry and white jersey, Wigan lost no time in cashing in on the havoc which a Boston burst nearly always creates in getting the opposition defence lop-sided through the manpower needed to check him. A quick fanning of the ball across the Swinton line, through half a dozen pairs of hands, saw Holden finish things off on the left flank."

Although he was demonstrably one of the greatest individual players to have graced the sport, Billy was always a fine example of a team player. His willingness to play anywhere is well known, as is his apparent disdain for chasing records. He often played with injuries, which would have kept lesser mortals off the pitch. It is an issue about which he feels strongly: "I was often asked to play when I wasn't really fit. It used to annoy me but I just tried to do my best. A player's career could be ended if he was unlucky. Clubs didn't seem to be too concerned sometimes as long as they could get men on to the pitch. Considering I am supposed to have damaged a lot of people, it's amazing how much damage other players did to me! I have two plastic knees now. There's some metal in them though, because every time I go through Customs they set off the alarms. If I can, I point to my knees before the alarms go off so they can run their sensors over them. I have been taken to the search rooms several times now in airports like Singapore." Billy has indeed got the scars of battle as testimony to the damage inflicted on him. Anyone seeing the immense surgical scars on his arms and shoulders would soon realise the perils of playing such a hard game as rugby league.

Frank Collier recalled the injury that Billy covered up in the 1961 Wembley final: "I remember the build-up. Dave Bolton was always leaking, always one for the toilet. Eric Ashton would tape himself up repeatedly, as would Billy Boston. In 1961 they stuck a needle in Boston's shoulder. I'm not kidding. I wouldn't have done to a horse what they did to Billy for killing the pain of that injury he had. Billy always used to have a shoulder strap. Where the buckle was, they used to put padding soaked in ether, so he could breathe a bit easier. He had had a bad injury at Leeds when his breastbone got caved in."

Billy also suffered from bouts of bronchitis in the worst parts of the winter. Joe Egan revealed in Jack Winstanley's *The Billy Boston Story*: "Boston has played many, many matches with a mustard poultice on his chest so strong that other players near him in the dressing-room have been on the verge of 'crying'. Putting on one of those poultices was just like peeling onions – it made tears stream down your cheeks."

Billy remains humorous despite his injuries. One of his best friends for the past half-century, Brian Cole, once asked him about the scars on his shoulder. Billy says: "Brian knew that I had been a line tester for the Post Office. I didn't go up poles if I could help it though. When Brian asked me how I came by the scars, I told him I was up a pole on Pork Chop Hill in Korea and was shot by a sniper. He also knew that I was in the Army during the Korean War so he swallowed the tale. Years later Brian went to Korea on business and decided to go to a library or a museum to see if he could find out anything more about my tale. He spent about 10 hours researching but came up with nothing. In desperation he phoned me up saying he couldn't find any reference to Pork Chop Hill and could I tell him where it was? I had to confess that I had taken it from a Gregory Peck film and had never been anywhere near Korea! He wasn't pleased and his language proved it!"

One attribute Billy rarely displayed was his goalkicking. Although he had been accustomed to kicking goals in rugby union, he only landed seven for Wigan. However, Alan Prescott, his skipper in the 1956 Ashes series, told this tale in the *Liverpool Echo* of a pre-test training session at Castleford: "Let me take you behind the scenes at Castleford and impart a big secret. It is not often that players without goal-kicking ambitions practice such kicks. Generally they have enough to worry about minding their own business. It happened that while Phil Jackson was busily engaged with certain moves with the inside backs, Billy Boston found himself with nothing to do and a ball lying handy. Not for Billy those simple shots in front of the sticks, the sort which anyone can kick in practice, but are not so easy when points depend on it. Out he went to the touchline, just beyond the '25' line and as he placed the ball for his shot somebody called out, 'Bet you a tanner you don't kick it, Billy'. 'You're on,' said Billy, and immediately four of us who were also watching events, asked to be included. 'I'll take you all on,' said Billy, full of confidence, and so it was that when he took his run at the ball half a crown [12½p] was at stake. We all thought we were on easy money, but from the moment he kicked we knew that the laugh was on the other side of our faces. Straight over the bar the ball sailed, and Billy's grin lit up the ground.

'Take it out of that and let's see the colour of your money,' he added. 'It was a fluke,' we chorused. 'Do it again and we'll believe it was no accident'. Again it was sixpences all round as Boston took his second shot. We could scarcely believe our eyes as the Wigan winger again sent the ball straight and true for the posts and we were all one shilling down. The novelty had now completely departed. Instead, it was a challenge. Again Boston was invited to kick, and again, and again. It was almost like clockwork. I found myself thinking of George Langfield and some of the goals he kicked for St Helens at a time when the Saints used to need the points very badly. He certainly could not have improved on Boston. Nor could anybody else. It was precision kicking with a bang. After five shots it was the rest of us who called 'enough'. I think Billy would have gone on kicking goals all afternoon. He had earned 12s 6d [62½p] for himself with five kicks. Who could have been anything other than impressed with this one return? The beauty of it is that Boston does not claim to be a goal-kicker. He only kicks them when he has to do so."

If Alan Prescott's revelations about Billy's goalkicking prowess surprised readers, Billy's own view that Johnny Freeman was the best goalkicker he ever saw is just as surprising. Freeman kicked just 15 goals for Halifax. Of course, both Billy and Johnny had tries on their minds rather than goals.

Billy was a superstar, although he readily acknowledges that other players made life easier for him. He says: "That great Wigan side of the late 1950s and early 1960s was full of good players. I was also helped a lot when I first came into rugby league by men like Ernie Ashcroft, Jack Cunliffe, Brian Nordgren, Jackie Fleming and Ken Gee. Jackie Broome was the main man in helping me in the early days. He was my centre, more or less nursed me in my first year and kept me out of trouble. The main men later on were undoubtedly Eric Ashton and Brian McTigue. Eric was a terrific captain. He was very quiet off the field but he would give us a bollocking on the field if he needed to. He gave me some stick on occasions, I can tell you. He didn't care what he said to me! We had a fantastic understanding of each other's play and hardly had to talk to each other. Somehow we just clicked and I don't know how or why. It was almost telepathic between us. Early on in his career he was played on the left wing all the time and desperately wanted to play centre. He told me was on the point of finishing playing if Wigan didn't move him to centre. Fortunately, they did move him but I always thought it was funny that Eric moved from wing to centre and I moved the other way – from centre to wing. It all worked out all right, I suppose. Some people thought Eric was a bit soft but he wasn't. Mind you, I upset him once by getting him sent off. We played a cup tie at Leeds and drew and I had a tiff or two with their forward Jack Fairbank. In the replay at Wigan I was determined to get some of my own back on Jack. I waited and waited for ages before I saw a chance. So I came in off the wing, whacked him hard and he went down. I don't think Jack knew who had hit him so I stood over him at the play-the-ball so he would know who had done him. Eric rushed up and pushed me out of the way, telling me to get back onto the wing. I kept trying to tell him I would stay at the play-the-ball, but Eric wouldn't have it. Anyway, by the time we had finished arguing, Jack had come to his senses and rolled over to see Eric towering over him. Thinking it had been Eric who had flattened him, he came up fighting and they slugged it out and got sent off. Eric only ever got sent off that once and it hadn't even been his fault. We laughed about it in later years but he didn't think it was funny then. It was the first time TV footage was used by the RFL disciplinary committee to decide players' punishments.

Brian McTigue was definitely the best forward I ever saw, bar none. He was a funny fella and a hard man. He was very quiet and I don't think his family ever forgave him for not carrying on as a boxer. He could get through anywhere, even the slightest gaps, and slip the ball to supporting runners like Norman Cherrington. He would be the first forward I would put on any teamsheet. He was a clean player but could do things on the sly to anyone who upset him and no one could get away with hitting him. He had a beautiful short jab! I don't care what they say about the so-called star backs; Brian McTigue was of more use to Wigan than I was. He led a great pack that hardly changed for years. I liked Norm Cherrington. Could that man run! He was like Dick Huddart, always in support if anyone made a break. I remember when Jim Sullivan was coach: He would have us racing. He would give Norman a 10-yard start on me and say, 'Catch this man!' I would go after him and Norm would finish 10 yards ahead of me. Jim would keep doing it and I would tell him, "You want me to catch him, sir? He's as fast as me. Do you want me to catch the wind? You can keep sending me after him but he'll always finish 10 yards ahead of me!" Later on Geoff Lyon came into the second-row and he might have been a bit faster than Norm, but Geoff was built more like a sprinter than Norm. Frank Collier was a really solid player, a 'biff-bang' sort. John Barton was a good prop, quiet and solid but got the job done. He would take the ball on after McTigue made the inroads. John had been a good soccer player and had been an early "Busby babe" at Manchester United – a bloody big babe! Roy Evans was only a youngster when he became our loose-forward but turned out to be a real good player and was quick as well. And what a good hooker we had in Bill Sayer. He was so steady and did the job, nearly always got the ball. Later on Colin Clarke did well at hooker. He was more flamboyant than Bill and very fast for a hooker.

Dave Bolton was a star stand-off for Wigan. Now he was quick – quick enough to run round defenders, because he wasn't a side-stepper. He was a great support player, always backing up any half-breaks. Running and backing-up was his game. He wasn't a ball-player, like some of the other half-backs of that period. Then there was Mick Sullivan. I would have Mick in my team every time. It was a pleasure to play with him, although less of a pleasure to play against him! You had to watch him like a hawk because he could be a sly devil. He wasn't afraid of anyone and certainly not of me. People complain about his rough antics but Mick could take it as well as dish it out. I like that about a player.

Good though the Wigan side was, the best team I ever played with was the 1962 Lions. Even the Australians agreed that we were something special and that says it all. The backs were definitely the best I ever played with. Gerry Round was a good enough full-back but the others were world class – Eric Ashton, Neil Fox, Mick Sullivan, Dave Bolton and Alex Murphy. What a pleasure it was to play in that line-up. Fantastic."

Billy also awards a "fantastic" to Brian Bevan. Billy rates Bevan as the best winger ever: "I scored 571 tries but Bevan got over 200 more than me. No one is ever going to get near that number. He was the sort of player who would be touching down under the posts when you got up after missing him in a tackle. I played against him quite a lot for Wigan but, because we were both right wingers, we were usually on opposite sides of the field. One thing we all know is that there'll never be another Brian Bevan."

It is equally certain that there will never be another Billy Boston.

# 2.  The road to Wigan Pier

William John Boston entered the world on 6 August, 1934. He was the sixth child of John and Nellie Boston, a brother for Doris, Joe, Johnny, Delia and Helena. He was also a brother for five more children who were to follow him – Herbie, Patti, Jimmy, Joannie and Raymond. Counting his parents, the Boston family was large enough to form a rugby league team, although such a thought would never have occurred to any of its members.

The family lived in Angelina Street in the Butetown district of Cardiff – the city's dockland. More specifically they lived in the romantic sounding Tiger Bay area of Butetown. Tiger Bay was not a big place, maybe a mile and a quarter across, but it accommodated as diverse a population as can be imagined. The late nineteenth century witnessed huge immigration into Cardiff. One authority suggests that as many as 57 different nationalities could be found in Butetown. Many came from West Africa, the Caribbean, Egypt, Ethiopia and Somalia, while others originated in the Iberian Peninsula and Eastern Europe. This immigration was almost entirely of single men and the common factor was sea-work. They were often sailors, who served in the Merchant Navy, or were engine-room workers and stokers. They married local Cardiff girls and a population, which was estimated from 5,000 to 10,000, began to form a distinctive, colourful and close-knit community despite its very diversity.

It was not, however, immune to conflict. In 1919 in the aftermath of The First World War there was rioting in Butetown. Disgruntled white men argued that black men were taking both their jobs and their women and there were attacks by whites on blacks and their families. Thankfully, such ugly problems were few and far between. Even so, the area did acquire a reputation for toughness despite its overwhelmingly harmonious community relations, and it was indeed one of Cardiff's least prosperous districts.

John Boston, Billy's father, was a seaman from Freetown, Sierra Leone, who settled in Cardiff. He abandoned his seafaring when a heart condition forced him to take a job on shore. His wife Nellie came from Irish stock and was described in Jack Winstanley's *The Billy Boston Story* as "perky, ginger-haired and warm-hearted". The two certainly had their hands full with their 11 offspring and although it must have been difficult to make ends meet, their children were always fed and loved.

Billy only attended one school. South Church Street took children through school from the age of five to 14. Billy recalls: "I was not much of a scholar but I excelled at all sports and there was plenty at South Church Street. I don't know where I got my sporting ability from. It certainly wasn't from my dad. He was only about 5 feet 4 inches tall and not at all sporty. It was as much as he could do to play cards down at the pub. I could also never work out where I got my size from. I weighed 15 pounds when I was born, I was a whopper. I always had pace and that was a blessing. Still, I reckon I was only the third fastest in our family, behind my sisters Doris and Delia. Doris was really quick and ran against Maureen Gardner, who represented Great Britain in the Olympics. I loved sports. The only physical thing I was no good at was dancing. Our school didn't have its own playing field so we had to use Llandaff Fields and Sophia Gardens for games lessons. One year at the school sports I won 10 out of 12 events and tied for the other two. When I wasn't playing games at school I would be playing with the other lads at Loudoun Square, where the local park was. There would be games going off all over the place, all mixed up. There could be cricket, football and rugby matches all taking place at the same time. There would be balls all over the place and kids falling over bricks. It probably looked like absolute chaos but we loved it."

At school Billy was not initially enamoured of rugby, preferring cricket and association football. In fact he did not really like the idea of getting involved in rugby at all. He thought it was a bit rough and did not fancy all that rucking and mauling. His attitude changed when he came under the influence of Bernard Sullivan, a teacher with a passion for rugby union. Mr Sullivan got Billy playing, at first in the forwards and then with ever increasing success at centre and full-back. School rugby fixtures were played on Saturday mornings and in the afternoons Billy and his mates would end up watching Cardiff at the Arms Park. Pretty soon Billy had ambitions to play for Wales, but also to represent Glamorgan at cricket. He says: "I really enjoyed playing cricket and I think a lot more people thought I had a better chance of succeeding as a cricketer than a rugby player. I did have trials for Glamorgan Seconds and after finishing at school I played cricket for Cardiff International Athletic Club, as well as rugby union. I also played cricket in the Army with the Royal Signals. One of our side was Doug Padgett, who was a good batsman for Yorkshire and England. I've still got a picture of that team somewhere. When I ended up in Wigan I played for Highfield Cricket Club. Bowling - fast-medium - was what I was best at."

There was plenty of talent in Billy's school and neighbourhood. Among his rugby team-mates was Joe Erskine, who became the British and Empire heavyweight boxing champion. Joe was stand-off, while his cousin, Johnny Freeman, played full-back and centre. Freeman was to follow in Billy's footsteps in later life, becoming a record-breaking left wingman for Halifax Rugby League club. Church Street School later nurtured two more magnificent future rugby league players in Colin Dixon and Clive Sullivan, both of whom were in Great Britain's World Cup-winning squad of 1972. In the 1920s Gus Risman, one of the Rugby League Hall of Fame's inaugural inductees along with Billy, had been a pupil at the school.

Billy made rapid progress as a rugby player and represented Cardiff Boys, a side which took boys up to 15½ years of age. In 1948–49 Cardiff Boys were the outstanding School XV of the season and won the coveted Dewar Challenge Shield for the third successive season. That season Cardiff Boys won 15 of their 16 fixtures, with Billy playing magnificently in the centre. He and Joe Erskine were members of the XV which defeated Mynydd Mawr 8–3 in the Challenge Shield final at The Gnoll, Neath in "a game which inspired attractive football from two keen sides", according to *The Playfair Welsh Rugby Annual 1949-50*.

On leaving school Billy worked for a while for a coal merchant, lugging sacks and general labouring before moving to Elliot's Equipment, who manufactured dinghies and parachutes, among other items. Next door was a bigger concern, George Elliot's Wire Ropes, for whose Irish branch the future Wales and Lions stand-off Cliff Morgan would work. Like Billy, Morgan would soon become a massive magnet for the heathen northerners.

There was no natural bridge for Billy from schools rugby to club rugby so for a while he had to be content with playing football on an informal basis. However, after discovering the charms of the Cardiff Central Boys Club, where he could indulge his myriad sporting interests, his briefly interrupted rugby career was resurrected. He was invited to trial for the international XV of the Welsh Association of Boys Clubs. He and Joe Erskine played in three trials and were selected to play against The English Boys Clubs XV. Billy played full-back and kicked two goals in an 8–6 victory. He represented the Welsh Boys Clubs on two more occasions at Bristol and at Neath. Two of his opponents were to become especially familiar – Mick Sullivan, who twice scored tries in the corner at Bristol beating Billy in the process both times, and John Barton. Both later became his team-mates at Wigan. Billy captained

South Church Street team around 1949. Billy is sitting in the front row on the right. Joe Erskine and Johnny Freeman are in the team. Bernard Sullivan is in the back row on the left.

Captain of the Welsh Boys Club team 1951–52.

Wales in the international match at Neath and, playing centre, scored 17 points in a convincing 32–0 win. Billy recalls: "I remember those games for the Boys Clubs, especially because Mick Sullivan played for England. We were great rivals even at that age. Mick became a really great winger in rugby league. Later, when he put on the Great Britain shirt he became an even greater player. Just putting on that red, white and blue jersey seemed to inspire him. In one of those Boys Clubs games there were about seven Shaw Cross Boys Club players. Mick was one of them, but the star was supposed to be a lad called David Smith. Unfortunately for him he had a shocker and our players were queuing up to score against him. That's how it goes sometimes."

Before he was 17, Billy was playing in the first team for the Cardiff International Athletic Club (CIAC). The CIACs had been formed in 1946 by young men of the Tiger Bay area, many of whom had served in the forces. They were the sons and grandsons of those immigrants who had gravitated to Butetown over the last half century or so. Consequently, CIAC XVs were always a cosmopolitan lot. The club was granted membership of the Cardiff and District Rugby Union and soon became renowned for playing an attractive and open style of rugby. Billy was soon recognised as very hot property. He played for Neath at 17 and there was talk of him being invited to play for Combined Aberavon and Neath against the Springboks on 17 November 1951, but the game clashed with a Welsh Youth international and it was thought wiser to play him in the latter fixture. He represented Wales Youth on three occasions. Earlier in the season, on 5 September, Billy had the thrill of playing for the Cardiff District XV against Cardiff at the Arms Park, although a 33–0 drubbing had been the result.

Billy's reputation was burgeoning and good judges were singing his praises and predicting a bright future for him. At the close of the 1951–52 season, in *The Cardiff Times*, the renowned Welsh rugby union journalist John Billot named Billy in his Five Players of the Year in the Cardiff & District Rugby Union, which was a big accolade for a boy who had still not reached his 18th birthday. His fellow Players of the Year were Paddy Dee (Old Illtydians), Bruce Sanders (Old Howardians), Tim 'Boots' Harrington (GKB) and fellow CIAC, Danny James, a winger of great promise who had topped the 30-try mark. Billot wrote, "This has undoubtedly been Billy Boston's best season. Every year he shows advancement and 1951–52 has been a winter of great accomplishment. From the Cardiff & District XV and Glamorgan and Wales Boys Clubs teams he rose to the ranks of the Welsh Youth XV and gave a splendid performance in France. Young Billy the boisterous is the outstanding back player of the year; his rugby future is assured and the path of fame open to him should he tread it wisely."

Billy's admirers at Neath were anxious that the club did not let him slip through their fingers but were ultimately disappointed. Billy recalls playing several games for Neath: "I used to get the bus from Cardiff to Neath and the fare was three and nine pence (about 18p). That was my only expense really. After the games money was given out as expenses in the clubhouse at a table under the stairs. I was amazed when I got a white five-pound note. That was a lot of money and I don't think I had ever handled one before. It showed how hypocritical things could be in rugby union. I was only a lad of 17, so how much were they giving to the others? Some were internationals and maybe even Lions. We obviously couldn't spend white fivers in Neath, apart from perhaps at the café one of the players owned. I was disappointed that Cardiff never showed any interest in me and I think that was because of my colour. They certainly wouldn't let me into their clubhouse after I turned professional. I don't think I would ever have been picked for Wales at union."

Bearing in mind Billy's proven qualities, it is hard to believe that he would never have won a Welsh cap, or indeed a shed full of them. That may, however, be just wishful thinking. The unpalatable fact remains that Wales, unlike England, did not cap any black players until the 1980s. After Billy other black players who forewent the opportunity of trying to win Welsh caps included Johnny Freeman, Colin Dixon, Frank Wilson, Mike Elliott and Clive Sullivan. It is surely stretching credulity to its limits to suggest that none of those were good enough to warrant capping.

Although Billy never got to play for Cardiff he did captain the Cardiff & District Rugby Union XV against them on 3 September 1952. He was then barely a month past his 18th birthday and became probably the youngest player ever to have had that honour. The result, a 22–0 defeat, was a bit better than on his only other appearance in this fixture the previous September.

Just as night follows day, rugby league scouts began to follow Billy Boston. Gus Risman, with his local knowledge and widespread Welsh contacts, had been interested in signing Billy for Workington Town since he was 15 and most rugby league clubs had agents looking out for likely converts in the valleys. There was no way Billy could have got under their radar, much though he would have preferred it. Before Risman could make a move Hunslet got in first. Their secretary George Richardson made persistent attempts to lure Billy to Parkside, several times accompanying club directors to watch Billy playing for the CIACs and also visiting his home, where his parents insisted that Billy was too young to consider such a step. Gus Risman upped the ante by arranging for Billy to accompany him on a trip to see what Workington had to offer him. Gus drove Billy all the way from Tiger Bay to Cumberland and back, but Billy and his parents were still adamant that he was too young to leave home and anyway he would soon enough be called up for military service. It would be better to leave such decisions until his National Service was over.

Billy was not at all ready to leave home and came to dread the ever increasing approaches which rugby league club officials and agents were making. He says: "I used to come back to Angelina Street, stop at the bottom and look along the street to see if there were any cars outside our house. It was always the rugby league people because no one had cars round us in those days. If I saw a car I would wait until it had gone before returning to the house."

Billy had no choice about leaving home in 1952, however. He was called up and despatched to Catterick in the North Riding of Yorkshire. If he thought that joining the Army would help him to avoid the attentions of the rugby league clubs, he could not have been more mistaken. He had been headhunted by 1 Training Regiment, Royal Signals. The Signals were the top rugby union playing unit in the services. Between 1948 and 1954 they won the Army Rugby Union Challenge Cup five times and even won the Yorkshire Cup in 1952, when they beat Halifax 11–10 at Otley, a few months before Billy arrived, and in 1954, when they despatched Roundhay 17–3.

The Signals were so successful that in June 1954 at the Annual General Meeting of the Army Rugby Union there were protests that the Signals had an unfair advantage over other units. In *The History of Army Rugby*, published in 1986, Lt Col John McLaren wrote: "[The Army Rugby Union committee] were satisfied that the present predominance of the Regiment arose from no improper means but from a powerful combination of favourable factors, namely:

a. The location in a rugby playing county and the strong connections which had been built up with local clubs and schools.

b. The nature of the training in the Regiment which was for high category trades demanding the type of young man produced by these clubs and schools.

c. The abnormally long training period for these trades (6 months).

d. The football reputation which had been built up attracted further keen footballers.

e. A very capable organiser.

The upshot was that the Royal Signals decided to temporarily withdraw from the Army Challenge Cup, which must have been a big blow, albeit a back-handed compliment, to that "very capable organiser". That very capable organiser was undoubtedly Major Gordon (GM) Fraser, a bespectacled, elderly officer with an unalloyed passion for rugby union, who was also well acquainted with some officials in the dark world of rugby league. Major Fraser was the honorary secretary of the Royal Signals rugby section, as well as its honorary fixture secretary and its honorary treasurer. He was also a member of the sub-committee for the North Riding Clubs in the Yorkshire Rugby football Union. In other words, he knew everyone and everything in Army and Yorkshire rugby union and he wanted Billy Boston in his team.

Billy remembers Major Fraser with some fondness: "He was rugby mad. For most of the week he seemed grumpy and went around with a frown on his face but on match days his face would light up and he became a changed man. He seemed to live for rugby. How he got all the rugby players into his unit always amazed me. We never knew how he managed it but he did."

Major Fraser had an abundance of talent at his disposal. Among Billy's team-mates over the two years of his service were young men who went on to stardom in both codes of rugby. One of the key men in the Signals XV was centre Phil Jackson, who had played for Barrow at Wembley in 1951 and was already regarded as one of league's finest three-quarters. He and Billy were to prove a lethal partnership in the centres. The man who provided the ammunition for Billy and Phil was fly-half Brian Gabbitas, a flaxen-haired will o' the wisp, who had already made an impact with Hunslet and would go on to represent Yorkshire and Great Britain. More rugby league influence came from goalkicking full-back Jimmy Dunn, a Leeds player, and Norman Mackie, a hooker, who signed for Bradford Northern. Flanker Reg Higgins came from a famous Widnes rugby league dynasty, although he made his name in union, winning 13 England caps and touring South Africa with the 1955 Lions. Phil Horrocks-Taylor had to be content with a place on the Signals' wing, although he would later represent Yorkshire and England at fly-half and captain the national XV. Billy's compatriot Russell Robins from Pontypridd was another distinguished back-row forward, who won 13 caps for Wales and accompanied Higgins on the 1955 Lions tour. He later turned professional with Leeds.

Although Billy was destined for Major Fraser's rugby-playing brotherhood, he got quite a shock on the day he was assigned to it: "We were square bashing during basic training when we were instructed to line up and be detailed for particular units. These units were specialised by sport – boxing, football, rugby, etc. I was instructed to join the boxing unit. I didn't fancy that at all. I didn't want to be a boxer. Then another bloke told me to join the rugby section, which was more like it. The first bloke noticed, came back to me and barked, 'I thought I told you to go to the boxing unit'. 'You did', I said, 'but that other chap told me to join this one'. Anyway, thank God, I ended up safely in Major Fraser's mob."

Billy rose from Signalman to Lance Corporal and became a Physical Training Instructor (PTI) after being sent on a course at Aldershot. It suited him down to the ground. When he was not actually playing, travelling and training for rugby, he was putting other soldiers through their physical training and becoming ever fitter himself. He even swam for the

Signals. Among the men he put through their PT were budding football stars Albert Quixall and Mel Charles, who would become English and Welsh internationals respectively.

From his arrival at Catterick Billy was a sensation. Within days he had announced his brilliance by scoring 37 points in his first game for his unit and by the end of his first season he was reported to have scored 126 tries in 30 matches, although no one has ever published a list of those scores. Many would have come in inter-unit matches but the Signals also played many first-class teams in Yorkshire. Huddersfield, Middlesbrough, Otley, Halifax and Harrogate, for example, appeared on their fixture list, along with more northerly clubs such as Percy Park, West Hartlepool and Durham City. They enjoyed trips to Lancashire to play top clubs Waterloo and Liverpool and there were annual fixtures at the universities of Oxford and Cambridge, as well as games against other regiments and military academies. The Army also provided plenty of representative rugby for its finest exponents and Billy was quickly drafted into Northern Command sides. Ultimately he won his Army cap at Twickenham, an especially coveted honour in the era of National Service when the competition was fierce.

Phil Jackson recalled in Keith Nutter's biography of him, *A Prince Among Centres:* "Billy is remembered as the very big block-busting winger who went through would be tacklers rather than around them. But in those days ... he was very big in the shoulders but slim in the hips and legs. He was very fast and elusive and when he got the ball with room to move it was 'shut the gate' time. He was a natural athlete. Obviously a magnificent rugby player but he was also a fine soccer player, was very good in the ring with the gloves on and was good at snooker, darts, anything. A lot like Willie Horne in that regard.

Sometimes we came up against teams who had heard what we were like and they would position one of the wing forwards out alongside their stand-off in order to shut our backs down. It must have been allowed then. In training we would practise some of the moves that we used at Barrow, send their defence in the wrong direction and give Billy some room and it was all over. I found that my three years at Craven Park was invaluable in these situations. I had clearly learned a great deal without ever realising it. It wasn't just about Billy and me though. We had a great rugby team and I can't remember us being beaten, though I am sure we must have been sometimes. Most of us were between 18 and 23, very fit... In fact the whole side was comprised of very, very good rugby players, a good mix too of Union lads and us boys from League. On our day we were untouchable. I remember the Waterloo Rugby Union Club was very highly rated... and we went to their ground and put about 40 points into them. I seem to remember Billy scored three tries. Their side included several International players but we threw the ball about in Rugby League fashion and they didn't know what had hit them. They were absolutely stunned... Myself and Billy and a couple of others from our team who were selected for the Army team would travel to London on the Wednesday for training, live at the Waldorf Hotel, play maybe at Twickenham on Saturday and travel back to Catterick on Sunday before taking off on Wednesday again for another game on the following Saturday.

The food at the Waldorf was fantastic. We would sit down for about two hours and wade through the many courses. However, Billy wouldn't eat what he called 'that rubbish' and when we went out for the evening he would buy himself a couple of pies from the pie cart! No wonder he signed for Wigan." Contrary to what Phil Jackson says about the pies, Billy insists he never bought any pies and in fact has never liked pies. That is a pity for Joan, he says, because she does like pies but hardly ever gets to eat any.

Far from hiding Billy from the persistence of the rugby league scouts Army life put him in the public limelight. Big services matches were heavily covered in the quality press, while any games played by the Signals in Yorkshire would be reported in the local press and it was hard for anyone to hide their light under a bushel when they were scoring tries in the quantities that Billy did. Hunslet were still the most persistent of his pursuers and their secretary, George Richardson, was one of the league men who were on familiar terms with Major Fraser. They kept coming to watch his progress and test his resolve.

Increasingly voices in the Welsh and wider union press were singing his praises and warning that it would be a huge blow to Welsh rugby if Billy were to succumb to the lure of northern gold. The former Wales and Lions full-back Vivian Jenkins wrote an article in the *News of the World* in 1952 warning that losing Billy Boston to rugby league would be akin to losing Jim Sullivan. In short, his loss would be a disaster for Welsh rugby union. A couple of years later, when it was already too late, Pat Marshall, who had long been singing his praises in services match reports in the *Daily Express,* wrote: "If he had not signed professional forms he must have been in the current Welsh Rugby Union side. Quite simply, he is one of the greatest running backs I have ever seen." Billy was 19 when Marshall wrote that. Unsurprisingly, the rugby league press was soon speculating as to which club would be signing him and how much his signature would cost. If any clubs had been unaware of Billy's prodigious talents before his call-up, they were certainly aware of them once he wound up in the Army. Apart from all the publicity about his exploits with the Signals, Billy was practically on the doorstep for scouts to watch his every move as so many of his games were played in Yorkshire.

It was in January 1953 that Wigan decided to enter the hunt for Billy. If he was as good as Sullivan, it was Wigan who could not afford to lose him, never mind Welsh rugby union. Bad weather, bad luck and bad intelligence prevented the Wigan board from actually seeing Billy in action until 21 February, when five directors came away suitably impressed after watching the Signals beat Old Roundhegians 24–8 in the sixth round of the Yorkshire Cup. However, board members Billy Gore and Joe Taylor had already made contact with Billy's parents and visited their home a couple of times while on scouting trips in Wales. The ground had, as it were, been prepared. Billy was due to play for the Signals in the Army Cup Final against the 1st Battalion Welsh Guards at Aldershot on 11 March and Wigan deputed chairman Joe Taylor, Tom Brown (vice-chairman), Frank Fairhurst and Billy Wood to attend and sign him, if possible and practicable.

The Signals had romped through to the final, scoring 281 points against 12 in the six preceding rounds. However, the Welsh Guards were the Cup holders and a hard struggle was anticipated. Billy disabused everyone of that idea by running over for two tries early in the proceedings, one of which Jimmy Dunn converted. In the second half Billy ran riot to add four more tries to his tally, including a 75-yard interception. Dunn added another three conversions, kicked a penalty goal and the Signals ran out winners by 35–0. If any of the Wigan directors had any lingering doubts about signing Billy they had been completely obliterated as they witnessed those six tries. At the final whistle Billy was swamped by soldiers from his regiment, who had been bussed down for the game, and carried in triumph to the presentation ceremony.

If the Wigan men thought they would have a chance to talk to Billy they were mistaken. So too was Oldham's representative, who had been an interested spectator. The celebration dinner was held at the Queen's Hotel in Farnborough that evening and Major Fraser made sure the Wigan and Oldham men were kept out. George Richardson was admitted, however, and the Major told Oldham's man: "Nobody touches Boston except Hunslet".

Wigan's board decided to take swift action. Joe Taylor hatched a plan to visit Billy's parents with Billy Gore on Friday, 13 March, persuade them to travel to Catterick with them and put them up at a hotel. Then they would get Billy and his parents together and talk business. They were authorised to pay whatever it took to acquire Billy's services and they were accompanied to the bank by secretary Jack Wood to withdraw £3,000 to take with them to Cardiff. In hindsight it was a pretty haphazard plan. Anything could have gone wrong and the Army certainly would not have let Billy off duties just because his parents and some men from Wigan had suddenly turned up in North Yorkshire.

However, Taylor and Gore got lucky. When they arrived at 7, Angelina Street, his parents told them Billy was there on leave and due to play for Neath the following afternoon. Billy did not arrive until 10.30 pm. The Wiganers began by offering £1,000 which Billy's parents suggested was nowhere near enough. Billy recalls: "I really didn't want to go north. The directors then put down £1,500 in real fivers and basically I just wanted to get rid of them. I left the room and my mother realised that I was unwilling to sign and thought she could get rid of them by asking them to raise the offer to £3,000. She thought that they would never pay that much and give up. When they agreed she was astonished but had to keep her word. I didn't see much of the money!"

Wigan had agreed to pay £1,500 there and then and the final £1,500 when Billy was demobbed. Billy later told Jack Winstanley: "I can say now that it was the best mistake I ever made. But I'm not ashamed to tell you that when the two Wigan directors left our house that night I burst into tears wondering what lay ahead of me as a professional rugby league player. I didn't sleep at all that night. Suddenly I realised that now I would never wear the red jersey of Wales in a rugby union international and I can't say I was happy about it. I honestly thought that when my mother told Wigan I wanted £3,000 to turn professional, she hoped it would frighten them off... I suppose I could have got more than £3,000 even in those days. Soon after I signed for Wigan, another club offered me an open cheque. But I don't regret having come to Wigan."

There were complications. Billy's parents insisted that the signing be kept secret. He was under enough pressure without the newspapers crawling all over him. Major Fraser would probably not have given him an easy time and he still had more than a year to serve at Catterick. Billy's signing could not, however, be kept from the RFL, who were required to register him as a Wigan player. Bill Fallowfield was sworn to secrecy too and bearing in mind rugby league's inability to keep secrets for any length of time, it was remarkable that news of his capture was not revealed for more than five months. The Wigan club too was very tolerant in this matter because they must have been itching to see their investment actually playing in a cherry and white jersey rather than the Royal Signal's dark blue.

Billy was in a state of turmoil after signing his amateur status away and told Jack Winstanley: "I must say I felt guilty on the Saturday morning when I jumped aboard the coach to play rugby union for Neath at Cheltenham. I was scared stiff in case the news had leaked out." His fears were probably nothing compared to Joe Taylor's and Billy Gore's, when they saw their new signing knocked out and concussed by the Cheltenham full-back.

The silence about Billy's signing meant, of course, that other clubs still thought they had a chance of capturing him. Hunslet became suspicious and their chairman Hector Rawson went to Catterick, accompanied by George Richardson and Eddie Waring of the *Sunday Pictorial*, to test the water again. They put the wind up Billy by asking him directly if he had signed for Wigan. Billy dissembled and told them he had not.

Billy admits that he told Mr Richardson that he would only sign for Hunslet, but only to get him off his back. He says: "I actually signed a letter to that effect, when he and Eddie Waring came up to Catterick to watch a game. It said, I would not sign for any other club. I wasn't lying because I had already signed for one – Wigan! Harry Jepson, who was

Hunslet's assistant secretary at the time, still has the letter and every time I see him at rugby league functions he brings it up and tells me Hunslet should have sued me!"

After the excitement of signing for Wigan, things settled down again. Billy carried on playing rugby and getting other soldiers fit for service. He was in demand for all sorts of fixtures. One involved him playing for Huddersfield at their Waterloo ground against Nim Hall's International XV on 29 April. His fellow Signalman Russell Robins had been invited to play in the International XV. Hall was a Huddersfield native who had risen to the captaincy of England and it would no doubt have given many of the participants heart attacks if they had known they were playing with a closet professional. Some of them were Army officers. The programme pen picture of Billy, perhaps his first, read: "From the Royal Signals and Neath. A player tipped for a great future, he has figured prominently for Welsh touring sides in Ireland and France this season. Native of Cardiff."

Four days earlier at the same venue, Billy had played for the Royal Signals in the Huddersfield sevens tournament. He impressed everyone, particularly the players of the Heriot's Former Pupils VII. The Edinburgh team were expert sevens players and were appearing for the first time at this event. K.T. Shaw, in his *Huddersfield RUFC: The First 75 Years (1909-1985)*, recalled: "Signals had a fine team and included a young winger from South Wales who was destined to become a household name in international rugby league circles, one Billy Boston. He had been the undoubted match winner for the Signals and hopes were high he would do the trick in the final [after the Signals had beaten Huddersfield 13-3 in the semis]. They had not reckoned on the sheer professionalism of Heriot's Sevens rugby. Boston failed to get a pass during the whole of the final, the Heriot's pack wheeling away from him at every scrum with their backs changing the direction of their attack similarly. His only chance came from a cross kick and sure enough he touched down but the Scots controlled possession and won 12–6."

When the summer of 1953 arrived Billy's defection was still unknown to the wider world and his thoughts turned to cricket. He still harboured hopes of playing for Glamorgan and was invited to play for their second team while on leave in Cardiff. Unfortunately, his leave was not long enough, lasting only until Friday. So he went to a local doctor and wangled a sickness certificate, believing it would cover his absence from Catterick. He was contentedly sitting in the darkness of a Cardiff cinema, when he felt the heavy hand of a police constable on his shoulder. He was, according to the Army, absent without leave (AWOL). He had not thought to send the certificate to Catterick. He knew what to say when the policeman asked him: "Do you want to go back under escort or make your own way?" He made his own way.

There was, however, no escape from the rugby league newshounds, especially Eddie Waring. Wigan had kept their word in keeping Billy's signing secret, although by August 1953 there was little chance that they could keep it quiet much longer. It was agreed that the official announcement would be made while Billy was at home on leave between 21 and 23 August. However, it became apparent that Waring would be spilling the beans in his *Sunday Pictorial* column and the Wigan board brought the announcement forward to Tuesday, 18 August. To their credit, they despatched Joe Taylor and Billy Gore to Catterick to warn Billy about it. To their dismay, Billy was not there and the pair had to hotfoot it to Darlington, where he was swimming in an Army championship competition. They were anxious to show that they had not broken their promise but had had their hands forced. Billy was given £50 as a token of their good faith. At least it was all out in the open now. No more need for subterfuge.

The Army rugby union team who beat the RAF 16–3 at Twickenham on 27 March 1954. Back: Morgans (referee), McCrae (RS), Watchorne, Hancock, Marques, Turner, Jackson (RS), Swan, McLeod, Clarke (touch judge); seated: Bazley, Boston (RS), Beringer, Edwards, Higgins (RS); front: Gabbitas (RS), Evans (RS). RS: Royal Signals. Brian Gabbitas and Phil Jackson were already rugby league players, John Hancock subsequently joined Salford.

Army rugby union: Scoring a try for the Royal Signals against the Scots Guards at Aldershot.

At Aldershot training to be a Physical Training Instructor. Yorkshire and England cricketer Doug Padgett is on the extreme left of the middle row.

Billy scoring his first try for Wigan, in the 'A' team match against Barrow 'A' in October 1953. Dai Bevan is supporting Billy on the touch-line. (Photo: Jo Moran)

# 3. 1953–54 Central Park at last

Billy finally made his debut in rugby league on the Saturday afternoon of 31 October 1953, when his appearance attracted a remarkable attendance of 8,525 to Central Park to watch Wigan 'A' take on Barrow 'A', the £335 gate money going some way to paying back Wigan's outlay on him. Wigan's reserves won 21–12, Billy scored two tries and the fans went home happy. The *Wigan Observer* reported proceedings on the following Tuesday. Under the headline "Boston tries thrill crowd – Welsh centre's promising debut", Billy was showered with praise: "Billy Boston made a splendid debut... He started hesitantly but once he settled down most of his actions, especially on attack, bore the stamp of class. He showed a keen positional sense after only 10 minutes when he took the ball with one hand (the pass from Wood was low and behind him) to score a try. He scored another in the second half and was twice unlucky. His weakness lies in cover defence, a fault which will be remedied with coaching. Boston's main asset is his penetrating attack which he varies constantly. In Saturday's game alone, he beat his man in three different ways – body swerve, side-step and hand-off. He is never still and literally 'always on his toes'. He uses his weight and has a deceptively long stride."

Of that first try Billy recalls: "I was lucky. I scored it off my first touch of the ball. Ab Wood, a lad from Leigh, gave me the pass. Nobody touched me and I didn't have to beat anyone for it. Having that bit of good luck gives you confidence". Billy's second try was harder earned, however, when he brushed off Newby and raced past the Barrow full-back to score a spectacular touchdown.

Billy's performance had certainly whetted the Wigan fans' appetite. They needed a new hero. The first team had lost 22–7 at Barrow and were not looking like an honours-chasing side. A couple of weeks later the almost unthinkable happened and ignominious defeat at Bramley was only averted by a last minute penalty goal landed by player-coach Ted Ward to earn a 19–19 draw. Wigan were then 14th in the league table, way behind leaders Halifax, Huddersfield and St Helens. So there was unbridled anticipation when it was announced that Billy would be arriving by car on weekend leave from his unit at Catterick Camp on Friday 20 November to make his first team debut the following day – coincidentally, again against Barrow at Central Park. Barrow had a fine side, stood sixth in the table and fielded Billy's Royal Signals colleague Phil Jackson at right centre, partnering the formidable winger Jim Lewthwaite. Billy was to play in direct opposition to Lewthwaite.

A crowd of 18,247 turned up and were not disappointed. The *Wigan Observer* declared the match the best seen at Central Park for years: "Above all it was full-blooded rugby, clean but robust and virile rugby as it is intended to be played". Wigan overturned a 10–7 half-time deficit to win 27–15. Ernie Ashcroft, playing out of position at stand-off, completely outshone Barrow icon Willie Horne and Norman Cherrington continually blasted through the Barrow forward screen. However, Billy was undoubtedly the centre of attraction and again snared the headlines, the *Wigan Observer* leading with "Boston thrills Wigan crowd – scoring dash against Barrow".

The *Wigan Observer* reported: "He was most impressive. It seems that Boston cannot fail to make the grade for on this showing he is one of Wigan's best ever prospects. Probably because his defence is suspect at the moment, Boston was played on the left wing but he may be even better as a centre. He is a well-equipped natural footballer, with a real swerve and side-step and an ability to change his pace at will. He has great powers of acceleration and eats up the ground with a most devastating stride. The try he scored showed his fine finishing powers and at the same time set the hallmark on his courage. Wigan spectators will look forward to seeing him again".

For the record, the teams on Billy's first class debut in rugby league were:
*Wigan:* Cunliffe, Ratcliffe, Broome, Roughley, Boston, Ashcroft, Alty, Gee, Mather, Collier, Silcock, Cherrington, Street.
Scorers: Tries: Broome, Boston, Ashcroft, Silcock, Cherrington; Goals: Cunliffe 6.
*Barrow:* Gibson, Lewthwaite, Jackson, Goodwin, Castle, Horne, Toohey, Pearson, McKeating, Barton, Grundy, Parker, McGregor.
Scorers: Tries: Castle 2, Gibson; Goals: Gibson 3.

Billy's next appearance, against minnows Liverpool City a fortnight later, saw a 55–10 victory. He played for the first time on the right wing, the position with which he became synonymous. Backing up a break by Nat Silcock, he scored from 40 yards out for the first try after only 50 seconds and added a second later in the game. Wiganers were in no doubt that Billy Boston was going to be a big star.

Other black players were also making headlines at the same time as Billy. Rugby league had, of course, a long tradition of lionising players from different backgrounds and races. When Billy entered the game Roy Francis, player-coach at Hull, and Cec Thompson at Workington, were the most prominent black players in the sport, both having won test caps, while Bramley enjoyed the services of a small coterie of Maori. Francis had trodden the same path from South Wales to Wigan as Billy, just before the war as a teenage winger. His impact had also been spectacular, although the arrival of Queenslander Harry Sunderland as Wigan manager precipitated his sudden and inexplicable transfer to Barrow. Francis and his widow both told the author that Sunderland's motives were influenced by colour.

Thankfully, issues of colour were extremely rare in rugby league and Billy, although not immune from the virus, suffered very little from it over his long career. However, even in the 1950s black players were still a shade exotic in Lancashire, Yorkshire and Cumberland – exotic enough to prompt an article in the *Rugby Leaguer* of 19 December 1953 entitled "Billy Boston, MacBailey and McArthur". It began, "The coloured boys are going to make history this season. There's Billy Boston shining like a beacon for Wigan, and McDonald Bailey having his big fling before the arc lights." Its main concern, however, was the startling debut of Wally McArthur for Rochdale Hornets against Salford on 12 December, the same afternoon that Billy had excelled against Liverpool. McArthur, a seriously quick Aboriginal winger, whose colour had probably prevented him from representing Australia in Olympic sprinting events, had drawn a crowd of over 10,000 to see just how good he was. He did not score any tries, but did land three goals and went on to play with distinction for the Hornets and subsequently, Salford, Workington Town and Blackpool Borough.

Four days later MacDonald Bailey, a 32 year-old West Indian, one of the fastest men in the world and an Olympic bronze medallist, made his long awaited debut for Leigh in a game staged under the club's new floodlights. This was a major news event in view of Bailey's world-wide celebrity. Leigh's opponents were Wigan and the home side's enterprise was rewarded with a crowd of 17,000. Billy was unable to play as the Army had other things for him to do and Leigh won 11–3, with Bailey scoring a try but ending the game limping, and never played. At Bailey's age and with his total lack of experience, logic should have told those involved that he would never have made a rugby player.

There was nothing gimmicky about Billy Boston, who made his third appearance for Wigan in a 31–7 rout of Swinton on 2 January at a fog-shrouded Central Park. His performance illuminated the stadium for, despite the ball running his way only four times, he ran in his first hat-trick in his new sport. For the first two it was devastating speed which got him over at the corner. "The third was a real smasher", according to the *Wigan Observer*. "Boston took a pass from Cunliffe after a passing movement deep in the Wigan half and then made the Swinton defence look cheap in a dash of 75 yards in which he showed bewildering change of pace and an acute body swerve. Lawrenson, who went in to tackle him, was left just grasping at the empty air. If Boston can get permission from the War Office he must be a possibility for the tour. There is no telling how good Boston is going to be for at the moment he is not match fit. Yet he can come along and make a clever and experienced player like Johnny Lawrenson look like a raw beginner. Boston looks like being a winger (that is, if Wigan keep him as a winger) in the Ellaby and Van Heerden tradition, or, to bring matters to the present day, in the manner of Warrington's Brian Bevan. He has speed, physique, swerve and side-step, as well as a good pair of hands. When his defence has tightened up he will be the perfect footballer."

After just three first team games and one for the reserves Billy had made a big enough impression to be compared to some of the game's greatest wingmen in Alf Ellaby, Attie van Heerden and the inimitable Brian Bevan and was being put forward as a possible Lion for the summer tour of Australasia. It was all heady stuff, but Billy had more than enough on his plate with his Army commitments to worry about such prospects. He would certainly have questioned the *Wigan Observer's* comments about not being match fit. He was after all a PTI in the Royal Signals, played rugby union two or three times a week, and indulged in whatever other sports were available. He could hardly have been any fitter. Indeed, Billy confesses that he was always amazed at how little training he did at Wigan compared to his days as a rugby union player. On the other hand, he happily asserts that "In rugby union you hardly had the ball in your hands as a threequarter. Often enough you could have gone for a smoke behind the posts. When I got into rugby league, I suddenly found the ball was in your hands a lot more and I realised that was something I could do with."

The Army continued to have first call on Billy's services and on 9 January he figured in Northern Command's 12–11 win at Birkenhead Park. A local *Sports Pink* reported: "Such is Boston's drawing power that a party of Wiganers went to see him in action at Birkenhead Park in preference to the Liverpool City versus Wigan match." They were well rewarded. *The Times* reported: "The Army owed nearly everything to Boston, a rugby league centre. His strong, relentless running produced the first two tries before the interval by Hancock and Jackson and afterwards Boston himself went over before Hancock crossed again." Billy's Commanding Officer denied him the chance to play against Workington Town the following week, insisting that he be fit for the semi-final of the Army Cup, which took place on the Monday, although Billy was allowed to attend Central Park on weekend leave.

The cancellation of a military fixture at Cambridge University enabled Billy to figure in his first Rugby League Challenge Cup-tie on 6 February, when Warrington amateurs Latchford Albion were beaten 40–20 in a mud bath, although the conditions did not stop Billy from scoring twice, one a magnificent 90 yard effort after scooping up a loose ball. On Thursday 11 February, Billy and four other Royal Signals were in the Army team which defeated the Territorial Army 23–8 at Aldershot in an excellent, open encounter. Billy scored four tries, two of which were interceptions from halfway, while the real stunner was a 70 yarder from an opening created by fellow league player Brian Gabbitas.

Five days later Billy was back at the Aldershot Military Stadium for the Army Cup Final (Home Command). The Signals eventually despatched the Royal Army Medical Corps 27–0, but had a hard fight of it from the medics, who lost their hooker after half an hour and defended heroically before shipping 19 points in the last 20 minutes. Billy was well held in the first half, but cut loose in the second to score twice, while Phil Jackson also grabbed two tries with Jimmy Dunn claiming three goals and a try. Billy's mother and two of his sisters attended the game, his mother raising a few officers' eyebrows after the game by ordering him to leave the field to have his bruised hand treated. There was no let-up for the Royal Signals' stars, five of whom were in the Army XV which beat British Police 16–15 at Northampton, just two days after the Army Cup Final. On Wednesday 24 February Billy played his fifth game in 13 days in the Army's 11–3 win over the Civil Service at Chiswick.

Three days later it was back to rugby league for a fixture with Batley. Billy's mother and sister Helena were at Central Park as the club's guests and "saw him at his best", according to the *Wigan Observer*. Both Wigan wingers, the other being Brian Nordgren, bagged four tries, but one of Billy's stole the show as "he sidestepped his way through the Batley defence as delicately as a cat might pick its way along a shelf loaded with china ornaments".

A major disappointment followed for Billy and Phil Jackson, who were selected as centre partners for the Army versus Royal Navy Inter Services fixture at Twickenham on 6 March. Billy had desperately wanted to win his Army cap, but had been denied it the pervious season when his current centre at Wigan Jack Broome got the nod ahead of him. This time Billy had to withdraw because of a pulled muscle sustained against Batley and Jackson went down with flu. Another talented rugby league player, Syd Lowden, a Lance-Bombardier in the Royal Artillery, took Billy's place, while another Artilleryman, Second Lieutenant J.N.D. Chapman, replaced Jackson.

The Great Britain touring team to Australasia was due to be selected after a second tour trial at Swinton on Wednesday, 10 March. Phil Jackson had played in the first trial at Leeds and was rated as having a good chance of winning a place in the squad, while there was a great deal of support for Billy to be included, despite his lack of experience. Anyway, the matter was beyond their control and the pair were occupied far away in Hanover, where the Royal Signals were playing the Rhine Army champions, the South Wales Borderers, in the Army Rugby Cup Final. Billy scored the opening try of a tight game, which the Signals won 11–6. A perfect day was capped by the news that Billy and Phil had indeed been selected for the Lions tour.

However, there was still plenty of action ahead of Billy before he could think too closely about Australia and New Zealand. On 18 March he was in an Army XV which lost 9–8 at Bedford – a low profile affair compared to what faced him two days later at Central Park. Wigan, who since the New Year had risen up the league to sixth place, had been drawn at home to league leaders Halifax in the third round of the Challenge Cup, a game which was declared all-ticket and drew a massive 43,953 through the turnstiles. It was certainly the biggest game of his rugby career in either code to date and gave him an indication of just how tough a game rugby league could be at the highest level. Halifax won the scrums 31–20 and were dominant in the forwards and half-backs, while former Wigan winger Dai Bevan "fulfilled his mission in blotting Boston out of the match". Halifax won much more easily than the 2–0 score-line indicated. Welsh full-back Tuss Griffiths kicked the crucial goal from near touch after a penalty was awarded when Billy played the ball, from which Nat Silcock ran in front of Harry Street, thereby obstructing the Halifax defence. The *Wigan Observer* noted, "This play-the-ball was preceded by an incident which may be described as a touch of psychological warfare when a Halifax player addressed a remark to Boston. This remark was in the worst possible taste and may have been made more by way of design than of accident for it had the effect of putting Boston temporarily off his game".

Another big occasion followed on 27 March when Billy finally won that coveted Army cap, starring in a 16–3 win against the RAF at Twickenham. The Army forwards excelled and the whole XV "really came into their own and gave a brilliant exhibition of rugby", according to *The Times*. Billy scored the fourth and final try for his side, supporting a 40 yard dash by Phil Jackson, who sent him careering over at the corner flag. A week later Billy was back at Twickenham, scoring yet another try for the Army in a 27–0 thrashing of the French Army. His last major game of rugby union followed on 10 April, when he earned a Yorkshire Cup winners' medal as the Royal Signals beat Roundhay 17–3 at Otley before a crowd of 5,000. Billy scored the vital try just before half-time cashing in on an astute cross-kick by Jimmy Dunn, who contributed a couple of penalty goals and a conversion, with other tries coming from Jackson and skipper SQMS Rees. Lifting the Yorkshire Cup ('t' owd tin pot') was to gain the holy grail of rugby union in that county and the Signals had to dispose of some of the best XVs in the county on their way to the final.

Billy was allowed to gain more rugby league experience when the Army released him to play in Wigan's last four games of the season, which were completed in just seven days. Three of them were lost, including a fixture at Keighley, which was the first defeat Wigan had ever suffered against that club. More eye-opening for him, however, was his first experience of a Wigan versus St Helens derby on Good Friday. Because of the religious significance of the day, Christian bodies had persuaded the clubs to stage a short silence in the middle of the field "while spectators stood bare-headed in a devotional attitude". The 35,000 fans must have wondered where the Easter goodwill had vanished. Saints' Welsh forward Ray Cale and Wigan's recent signing from Warrington, Jim Featherstone, were sent off as strong-arm tactics dominated. An irate spectator made an effort to attack the referee, who was protected by Ken Gee and in the kafuffle a police sergeant was bowled over. To cap it all, two fire engines were summoned to quell a fire on the popular side. Billy managed to score a try amid the mayhem.

The RFL organised an international match at Odsal between Great Britain and France on 27 April and Billy was brought in on the right wing with Phil Jackson as his centre. Britain won 17–8 and Billy had the satisfaction of claiming his first try in representative rugby league, giving his side the lead seven minutes from time after sterling play by Ken Traill and Jackson.

The countdown to the Lions tour was approaching fast, but Billy still found time to show his younger brother Herbie around Wigan at the beginning of May. Herbie was firmly in Wigan's sights but they were not alone, as Leigh had made a firm offer to him the previous week. On 3 May Billy and his three Wigan team-mates, who had also won tour selection – Ernie Ashcroft, Jack Cunliffe and Nat Silcock – were each presented with a £25 cheque by club chairman Joe Taylor for spending money on tour.

## 1953–54 (From Billy Boston's debut)

Wigan finished 7th in the League: P36, W23, L12, D1, For 688, Against 392
Boston scored 14 tries for Wigan, plus 1 in representative rugby league

| Date | Opponent | Score | Boston | Crowd | |
|---|---|---|---|---|---|
| 21 November | **Barrow** | 27–15 | 1T | 18,247 | |
| 28 November | Rochdale H | 21–9 | dnp | 6,603 | |
| 5 December | Workington T | 10–21 | dnp | 12,411 | |
| 12 December | **Liverpool City** | 55–10 | 2T | 6,221 | |
| 19 December | Widnes | 10–5 | dnp | 6,333 | |
| 25 December | **Salford** | 5–0 | dnp | 13,249 | |
| 26 December | St Helens | 4–14 | dnp | 23,718 | |
| 1 January | **Warrington** | 12–17 | dnp | 22,048 | |
| 2 January | **Swinton** | 31–7 | 3T | 10,360 | |
| 9 January | Liverpool City | 18–5 | dnp | 983 | |
| 16 January | **Workington T** | 12–2 | dnp | 12,371 | |
| 23 January | **Belle Vue R** | 47–2 | dnp | 10,748 | |
| 30 January | Swinton | 15–3 | dnp | 9,000 | |
| 6 February | Latchford Albion | 40–20 | 2T | 9,011 | Cup 1 |
| 13 February | **Latchford Albion** | 41–2 | dnp | 8,139 | Cup 1 |
| 20 February | Belle Vue R | 23–7 | dnp | 2,852 | |
| 27 February | **Batley** | 45–0 | 4T | 14,109 | |
| 6 March | **Bradford N** | 15–10 | dnp | 26,120 | Cup 2 |
| 20 March | **Halifax** | 0–2 | | 43,953 | Cup 3 |
| 27 March | **Widnes** | 31–12 | dnp | 10,145 | |
| 3 April | Batley | 10–7 | dnp | 4,500 | |
| 7 April | **Whitehaven** | 32–10 | dnp | 9,062 | |
| 10 April | **Oldham** | 2–7 | dnp | 17,982 | |
| 13 April | Keighley | 10–20 | | 5,047 | |
| 16 April | **St Helens** | 8–14 | 1T | 35,090 | |
| 17 April | Leigh | 16–22 | | 11,436 | |
| 19 April | Salford | 14–10 | 1T | 9,717 | |

## Boston's representative matches:

| Date | For | Opponent | Score | Boston | Venue |
|---|---|---|---|---|---|
| 27 April | Great Britain | France | 17–8 | 1T | Odsal |

# 4. On tour with the Lions

Billy and the 1954 Lions made history in more ways than one in a tour which set many precedents and records. Some were unwelcome and damaging to the sport of rugby league. However, on a personal level Billy's Australasian adventure brought him huge success and enhanced his already burgeoning reputation. Billy became the youngest British tourist to date. The previous youngest Lion had been Alan Edwards, like Billy a spellbinding wingman and a Welshman, who had gone on the 1936 tour, celebrating his 20th birthday in May. Billy would not celebrate his 20th birthday until 6 August, when the 1954 tour was almost over. For a young man who had been desperate not to leave Angelina Street in Tiger Bay barely a year ago, Billy was now keen to see what the other side of the globe was like.

The Lions party consisted of the following 26 players: Ernie Ashcroft (Wigan), Billy Boston (Wigan), Jim Bowden (Huddersfield), Brian Briggs (Huddersfield), Alf Burnell (Hunslet), Ted Cahill (Rochdale Hornets), Frank Castle (Barrow), Jack Cunliffe (Wigan), Duggie Greenall (St Helens), Geoff Gunney (Hunslet), Tommy Harris (Hull), Gerry Helme (Warrington), John Henderson (Workington Town), Phil Jackson (Barrow), Lewis Jones (Leeds), Tom McKinney (Salford), Terry O'Grady (Oldham), Charlie Pawsey (Leigh), Alan Prescott (St Helens), Ray Price (Warrington), Nat Silcock (Wigan), Ken Traill (Bradford Northern), Drew Turnbull (Leeds), Dave Valentine (Huddersfield), Jack Wilkinson (Halifax) and Dickie Williams (Hunslet).

Billy's fellow Welshman Williams, a cerebral, red-haired stand-off, was the tour captain, and his club colleague Ashcroft was vice-captain. Both had toured in 1950, as had Cunliffe, Helme and Traill. The party included five Welshmen, the three others being Harris, Jones and Price, two Scots – Turnbull and Valentine – and a solitary Irishman, McKinney. The tour managers were Hector Rawson (Hunslet) and Tom Hesketh (Wigan). Billy was far-and-away the least experienced player in the party and was regarded as something of an outsider for the tests. He was one of four wingers, the exceptionally fast Frank Castle and prolific Drew Turnbull being the likely test wingers in most pundits' opinion. The fourth winger, Terry O'Grady, was just four months older than Billy, but had been in Oldham's first-team since 1951. Billy and Terry were room-mates for most of the tour.

As with all touring parties, the critics were not all in unison. There was widespread disbelief that the three leading teams, Halifax, Warrington and St Helens, were only called upon to supply four players between them. There was also some surprise at the inexperienced nature of the party – six players were aged under 22 and another four under 25. Major surprise omissions were scrum-halves Billy Banks of Huddersfield and Stan Kielty of Halifax, while many thought Barrow stand-off Willie Horne might have been captain of the Lions. Overall, however, most pundits gave the party the thumbs up and rated them a good bet to retain the Ashes. A notable sceptic regarding Billy was Jim Brough, who was not too happy about the blind-side props, hookers and particularly the wingers. He wrote in the *Yorkshire Evening News:* "The wings, a moderate lot, are the weakest section of the team. Boston we know so little about. O'Grady, like Turnbull, is a straight runner with little or no idea of beating the full-back. Castle requires acres of room for speed is his only asset. I would have taken Rose of Huddersfield." Brough, a former England rugby union full-back as well as a rugby league Lion in 1928 and 1936, noted that 10 of the 26 selected were former rugby union players. In the same newspaper, Arthur Haddock was more upbeat and wrote: "Everyone who has watched Boston says he is good. Yet I cannot help thinking he is a lucky fellow, untested as he is in rugby league football... and untried even in top-class rugby union. But I sincerely hope he fulfils the expectations of him."

As a single man Billy would receive £3 a week while on tour plus £20 on arrival in Australia, while married men were allowed £3 per week for their wives and 10 shillings per week for each child. However, a considerable incentive for all the touring party was a share of 30 per cent of the tour profits.

The British party made history by flying to Australia. All previous Lions' tours had been made by sea. Although obviously more time consuming, importantly the sea journeys had allowed players recuperative time after a long domestic season. Nagging injuries could be eased or eradicated, players had the time to build up fitness and team spirit would be galvanised. Billy's party was not allowed that luxury. They departed from London Airport on 13 May and immediately hit a snag, when fog caused the plane to divert from Rome to Nice, where the Lions spent their first night. It took four days and three nights to reach Sydney. Their first fixture was scheduled for 19 May, the day after they arrived in Australia. Billy was on the right wing for that opening game, a 29–11 victory against Western Districts at Bathurst.

With Phil Jackson at the start of the tour.

He got off to a flying start with a couple of tries from 70 yards and 60 yards out. Billy recalls: "That first try was a bit like my first for Wigan 'A'. I scored more or less the first time I got the ball but really I didn't have to do much. I think it was Alf Burnell who put me away." Billy's centre partner Lewis Jones booted seven goals. Both would go on to take Australia and New Zealand by storm.

Billy, as the first black Briton to tour, was a huge centre of attraction to the public and to the press. Typical of many articles was one, which appeared in *Australia Magazine*. Perhaps politically incorrect in today's climate, it was headlined "Billy Boston. Everyone in Australia, it seems, wants to see the first coloured man to be chosen in a British League side. He hopes we don't make a fuss of him." It continued, "Billy Boston is a lad of 19, with exciting promise as a rugby league player. He is tough, quick-footed, schooled to withstand jarring dumps in an uncompromisingly rugged game. When he runs with the ball he is very entertaining. Many players of his potential greatness appear through the years. A few vindicate hopes placed in them. Most fade disappointingly. But Boston is coloured, the first dark man ever to be chosen in a British rugby league team to play overseas, and in the minds of some Australian officials who will entertain his team this season that has become more important than his embryonic skill at the game. Clubs who have matches against the British team in Australia have taken the unprecedented step of asking for Boston to play against their team. They realise he is a drawcard.

Before the British team flew off to Australia letters urging that Boston be included in certain games arrived in England from Australian officials. All of which upset Boston, normally an easy-going character unperturbed by minor mishaps like a stiff punch on the nose. He told me so in an exclusive interview for A.M.

'I wish Australians wouldn't make such a damned fuss of me,' he said. 'I've been lucky. I've got a long way to go. I got the tries. But they were laid on by better players than me. I hope the Australians will drop this attitude of wanting a spectacular show from me every time I play. I'll just play my normal game and play when I'm picked just like the other fellas in the team. I want to ignore those letters practically demanding I play in all the big games'.

If Boston can reproduce his club form in international football his normal game should be more than good enough to satisfy the most demanding fans. For Boston is a strong, resolute attacker, a dashing ball-carrier who is undisturbed by tacklers who clutch hopefully at his torso without trying to knock him down, copybook style. Brainy, despite his inexperience, he is a resourceful all-weather footballer with an instinctive positional sense, and often shows dramatic speed in bursting through openings. He can sidestep off either foot and is a quick runner, but his aim with tackles is a little wild … He is 5 feet 10½ inches tall, has a faintly coloured face, a love of gay entertainment, and weighs 13 stone 7 pounds stripped. After a short while the men who play with him forget he's coloured, so light is his copper tinge. He has black hair like steel wool. He may become a player people will recall long after he quits.

Boston shows surprising guile on the field, but off it he quickly reverts to his true age. He doesn't smoke but he likes a beer and has a reputation, which suggests a boisterous sense of fun. He bites his nails. He likes Frankie Laine, Nat King Cole and Billy Daniels records and can play a useful game of cricket – an all-rounder who bats third man down and bowls fastish. Later on he will probably play cricket in the Lancashire League. His appetite fits his vast enthusiasm for living… [Billy added] 'I wasn't much good at lessons. Too interested in playing sport to care about that. I do everything right-handed: bat, bowl, write, hold me beer – all in me right mit'."

The Lions did not have a happy time in the opening stages of their tour. In the game at Bathurst they conceded 26 penalties as the referee caned them at the play-the-balls, a problem which beset them for the remainder of the tour and which would lead to frustration and fisticuffs on several occasions. The first six games brought three defeats and a draw, one of the worst openings for any Lions squad. Billy only played in two of those six games, his second appearance coming against Sydney, when he scored a try in a 32–25 reverse. Drew Turnbull suffered a badly torn thigh in the third fixture at Wagga Wagga and never played again on tour.

So poor was the British performance that the tour managers took the drastic action of bringing in Ross McKinnon, a Kangaroo tourist back in 1937, to coach the side at Coogee Oval in the week leading up to the first test match. The decision caused uproar in the Australian press and back home in England, but the managers wanted McKinnon to iron out the play-the-ball problems and to get the players' fitness up to scratch. It should be remembered that the Lions took no coach/trainer with them on the early post-war tours but in pre-war years had always hired a local trainer – usually Dave Murray.

In the week before the test match Billy was named as one of five threequarters in a 15-man squad, but was left out of the team when it was decided to play Lewis Jones on the wing, primarily for his goalkicking. An even bigger surprise was the omission of skipper Dickie Williams. In the event Australia completely overran Great Britain at the Sydney Cricket Ground on 12 June, running up a record 37–12 victory. Britain had held their opponents to 12–12 after 50 minutes, but collapsed completely in the last half hour. Of particular significance to Billy, Britain's left winger Frank Castle sustained a badly gashed leg, which prevented him from playing again in Australia. His injury, coupled with Turnbull's, meant that Billy and Terry O'Grady would be the only two regular wingers available.

Following the test debacle at Sydney, the Lions embarked upon a tour of Queensland, winning all their fixtures in that state and building a sequence of 10 consecutive victories. The fortunes of the tourists, at least in a playing sense, were truly turned around. Billy played in eight of those successes, rattled up 22 tries and left fans clamouring to see more of his startling talent. He began with a try in a comprehensive 34–4 rout of Brisbane at the Exhibition Oval and followed five days later with a hat-trick in a thrilling 34–32 defeat of Queensland at Brisbane Cricket Ground.

The day following the Queensland triumph saw Britain beating Wide Bay 60–14 at Maryborough. Billy bagged four tries but was outscored by O'Grady who ran over for five, while Jack Cunliffe landed nine goals. He had few chances to run in a 28–7 win against Mackay "but displayed fine talent in scoring his only try", while Lewis Jones was the game's star and claimed 16 points from two tries and five goals. It was a tough game and Brian Briggs became the first Lion to be sent off 14 minutes into the second half after swinging a punch. A timekeeping error brought the game to an early close after 72 minutes, probably denying the British a bigger victory.

By this stage Billy and Terry O'Grady were certainties for the second test team but had to bear a heavy load, as injuries piled up. Britain were reduced to fielding stand-off Dickie Williams and hooker Tommy Harris on the wings for the game at Cairns and forwards Nat Silcock and Brian Briggs at Rockhampton. In between those fixtures Billy and Terry appeared in a 39–13 trouncing of North Queensland at Townsville, both scoring four tries.

On 3 July Britain faced Australia at Brisbane in the second test – a real make-or-break affair for the success of the tour, against a side that was cock-a-hoop after the pummelling they had inflicted on the Lions at Sydney. The teams for Billy's first test match were:
*Great Britain:* Jones, Boston, Jackson, Ashcroft, O'Grady, Williams (captain), Helme, Prescott, McKinney, Bowden, Silcock, Pawsey, Valentine.
*Australia:* Clive Churchill (captain), Brian Carlson, Alex Watson, Noel Hazzard, Noel Pidding, Bob Banks, Keith Holman, Duncan Hall, Ken Kearney, Roy Bull, Norm Provan, Kel O'Shea, Mick Crocker.

Australian writer Jim Mathers summed up the game in *Truth* thus: "England today shook the very life out of Australia like an enraged bloodhound tearing to pieces an innocent rabbit to win the second rugby league test match by the paralysing score of 38 points to 21 before a crowd of 45,000 stunned spectators. Australia were definitely and completely humiliated by a team which in the first test... looked like a bunch of jaded 'no hopers'."

The 1954 Lions squad. Back: Cahill, Turnbull, Boston, Wilkinson, Henderson, Cunliffe, McKinney; standing: O'Grady, Bowden, Traill, Silcock, Pawsey, Gunney, Briggs, Prescott; seated: Greenall, Jones, Ashcroft, Rawson, Williams, Hesketh, Jackson, Valentine, Castle; front: Burnell, Harris, Price, Helme.

Britain's victory was even more emphatic than the scoreline suggested as Australia claimed eight points in the last few minutes, when the game had long gone from them. The Lions' leading lights were undoubtedly reinstated captain Dickie Williams, rampaging second-rower Charlie Pawsey and Lewis Jones.

Jones landed 10 goals and scored 20 points to set new British test records. Eddie Waring reported in the *Sunday Pictorial:* "Two of his goals were dropped efforts from positions that looked impossible. Jones outplayed, out-kicked and out-manoeuvred Clive Churchill, who was cat-called by his own supporters." Billy also impressed Waring, who wrote: "Bill Boston claimed he had scored in the first half when the referee ruled he had knocked on. Boston reckons it cost him a fiver, which an English supporter offered him if he scored a hat-trick." The incident occurred after Billy had beaten everyone else to a smart kick to the in-goal area by Ernie Ashcroft. Billy did, however, score two crucial tries as Britain deliberately took play out to their wings. Tom Goodman noted: "They played a lot to Boston's right wing. The bouncing six-footer, weaving and side-stepping, was a constant menace and Pidding could not handle him." Billy's first try came after 27 minutes and took his side into a 12–5 lead. His Royal Signals' colleague Phil Jackson worked the oracle when he slipped Billy a reverse pass on his own side of halfway. Churchill tried to cut Billy off but slipped as he approached the winger, who raced the remaining 40 yards to the goal-line. His second try was decisive, as Australia had climbed back to trail 19–13 early in the second half. It was the result of some classic British back play from a scrum on the home '25'. Helme moved the ball to Williams, who passed to Ashcroft and doubled round him for a return pass, which never came. Instead Ashcroft's deliciously feinted a pass to Williams, but kept the ball and went hard through a gaping hole in Australia's defence. He shipped the ball to Jackson, who gave Billy a clear run to the line and Britain were out of sight at 24–13.

Billy could hardly have had a more satisfying introduction to test rugby. J.E. Knowling, the secretary of the New Zealand Rugby League, attended the game and said: "I wanted to see this English team before I returned home to prepare for their tour. I was pleased to see them playing so well, when given room to do so. Boston is a most interesting young player, and Jones has a wonderful boot."

The day after the test match Billy and five of his test colleagues turned out in a 25–14 win against Toowoomba. Billy provided the highlight of the game with a wonderful 50 yard try in the first half, at the end of which Britain trailed 9–7. A scintillating try by Duggie Greenall seven minutes after the break saw Britain take control and clock up a ninth consecutive victory. Four days later, Billy put on a virtuoso performance in a 44–14 trouncing of Northern New South Wales at Grafton. He scored six tries, four of them being crammed into a 13-minute spell in the second half. Tom Goodman, of the *Sun-Herald*, described his performance as "high class and thrilling". His first try in particular was a gem in which "the Wigan wing shed one desperate tackle after another in a spectacular 70-yard dash that took him clean through the Northern defence", according to another local scribe. Billy was also involved in what almost became a riot. Early in the second half he was tackled near the touchline and at the ensuing play-the-ball a Northern forward kicked recklessly at him. Lions prop John Henderson immediately sought retribution on the offending player and an all-in brawl developed, the worst of the tour so far, according to reporters. Spectators who had been allowed to watch from the touch-lines were involved in the fracas and police had to intervene to calm matters down.

If the affair at Grafton had been ugly, it was nothing compared to the Lions next match, against New South Wales at the Sydney Cricket Ground on Saturday 10 July. It was a week before the third and deciding test. Britain with an injury list of 10, fielded only three of their intended test side. Billy and Terry O'Grady were among the rested men, forwards Jack Wilkinson and Brian Briggs taking their places, while a third forward, Geoff Gunney, was drafted in at full-back and two hookers were fielded in the front row. New South Wales fielded eight of the men who would play in the third test.

The game, played in pouring rain, provoked an absolute furore. Jim Mathers of *Truth* summed up matters as well as anyone: "Scenes unprecedented in the annals of all sport took place yesterday before 27,000 stunned spectators on the Sydney Cricket Ground when, after an unbridled frenzy of rioting on the field in which nearly all the players of England and New South Wales... became embroiled, the referee, followed by the players, walked off the field." The Lions were trailing 17–6 when the referee, Aub Oxford, abandoned the game in the 65th minute and ordered all the players to leave the field after a final huge brawl. Ten minutes earlier he had sent off Ray Price for using insulting language to him and a touch-judge. It was true that there had been plenty of fisticuffs and an unpleasant undercurrent throughout the game, but the players were nonplussed when the game was abruptly brought to a conclusion. Several were pictured walking off smiling and arm-in-arm despite the altercations. At the subsequent inquiry Mr Oxford remarked: "From the time I sent Price off, I knew it was going to be impossible to restore order," which begged the question, why did he wait so long? British observers were decidedly of the opinion that the refereeing was far too weak.

Although Billy did not play, he was involved in the aftermath. A Reuter's report ran, "An ugly scene developed outside the British team's dressing-room after the match had been abandoned. Price climbed through a window on to a verandah of the dressing-room, and was quickly surrounded by about 30 spectators. Heated words were exchanged, and Boston jumped through the window to support Price, and it appeared as though blows would be struck. To the accompaniment of jeers, boos and shouts of 'Get back to England', Dickie Williams took both players by the arms and bundled them back into the dressing-room. Price gesticulating wildly, tried to return to the verandah, but was eventually calmed down". Ironically, the three Lions who were being told to get back to England were all Welshmen!

An inquiry into the game by the general committee of the NSWRL was held on the following Monday. The upshot was the severe cautioning of Lions Alf Burnell and Ken Traill and of Harry Wells, the NSW centre. The judiciary suspended Ray Price until 1 August.

The deciding test match for the Ashes took place at the scene of the recent mayhem on the Saturday following the abandoned game, when Britain were quoted as 7 to 4 on favourites by the bookies. Overnight rain made the pitch more treacherous than it appeared to the crowd of over 67,000, which got full value for its money. Tom Goodman was happy to report, "It wasn't all good football but it was a real test match – one of the most gripping I have ever seen. It was close, gruelling and thrilling, and there were some spectacular tries. Referee [Darcy] Lawler rarely had to speak to a player for unnecessarily hard play. There were no nasty 'incidents'." Billy was on Britain's right wing but failed to score. He told Goodman: "Three times in the second half I thought I was through, but each time, when I tried to move infield, I lost my footing". The Australians had clearly pinpointed Billy as a danger and Clive Churchill had made it his business to get up quickly onto him throughout the first half. Britain looked likely winners early on after snatching an 8–0 lead and both sides scored four tries but in the end Australia were good value for their 20–16 victory. Billy's first tilt at the Ashes had ended in defeat.

Australia had taken warmly to Billy Boston. They recognised a star when they saw one. Remarkably, he had scored 25 tries in 11 games in Australia, failing to score only in the final test. His reputation preceded him to New Zealand and he did not disappoint.

Britain arrived in New Zealand minus two injured Lions, full-back Ted Cahill and winger Drew Turnbull, who were flown home from Australia, the latter bearing a confidential report by the tour managers to Bill Fallowfield about the abandoned game against New South Wales. Billy did not play in the opening game, a hard fought 14–4 victory over a Maori XIII at Whangarei. It was a costly 80 minutes for Britain as Frank Castle, playing his first game since the opening Ashes test, was again crocked and played no further games on tour, leaving Billy and Terry O'Grady as the only functioning wingmen for an itinerary which still held a dozen fixtures in a period of 29 days. Prop John Henderson broke a hand in the Maori game and was also ruled out of action for the rest of the tour.

Britain entered the first game against New Zealand at Auckland with two test debutants in the pack, hooker Tommy Harris and second-rower Geoff Gunney. Although the day remained fine the notorious Carlaw Park pitch was a slimy, treacherous mess. However, it did not stop Billy from turning in a prodigious performance. In the very first minute Phil Jackson stole an interception, streaked clear and held his nerve to send Billy a perfect pass and the winger ambled over for a try converted by Lewis Jones. Twenty minutes later Billy extended his side's lead to 8–0 after O'Grady had torn up the middle before lofting a pass to Billy who ran hard to the corner flag. In the 34th minute the game was effectively over when Billy completed a remarkable and authentic hat-trick. Ashcroft initiated it with a slick inside pass to O'Grady who ate up a lot of ground before handing on to Wilkinson. 'Wilkie' saw Billy out to the right and gave him a good, quick ball and no one could get near him as he dashed for his third try. Jones converted and New Zealand's only reply in the first half was a 38th minute penalty goal from skipper Jimmy Haig. Six minutes into the second half New Zealand pulled back to 13–4 when Des White landed another easy penalty goal but that was as near as the Kiwis were to overhauling a rampant British side for which Pawsey and Valentine were magnificent forwards. By the 67th minute the Lions were coasting at 24–4 as a result of a blistering four minute spell that brought tries to Ashcroft after 63 and 67 minutes, and Harris after 64 minutes. New Zealand finally scored a try after 72 minutes through Bond, a scrambled effort at which Pawsey protested too loud and long to the referee causing an irate section of the crowd to shower the field with stand seat cushions, not that Charlie would have been too worried by a few cushions. Billy ended the scoring with his fourth try in the last minute following good work by Wilkinson and Valentine.

A 27–7 win was just the fillip that Britain needed and Billy had made history by emulating the British test try-scoring record set by Jim Leytham, who was also a Wigan winger, against the Australians at Brisbane in 1910.

Three days later Britain romped to a 61–4 win against Wellington. Billy bagged another hat-trick and a local reporter wrote that "the crowd was not disappointed with his clever jinking and speed". O'Grady with four tries and Jones with 11 goals were also impressive.

On 31 July Britain went into the second test at Greymouth without the injured Ashcroft and Pawsey, but were still favourites to win, especially as the ground was firm and the weather fair. Victory looked likely when they led 7–0 after seven minutes, Jones landing a penalty before Duggie Greenall and O'Grady developed a mesmeric move from a scrum almost on the British line, which ended with the winger jumping out of two tackles for a brilliant try, converted by Jones. Greenall also created a try for Wilkinson in the 22nd minute with a finely judged punt which eluded full-back Des White. Britain deservedly led 12–8 at the break, White having landed four penalties for New Zealand. The second half was a complete reversal, however. The New Zealand forwards took control and tempers began to fray. Britain eventually succumbed 20–14 and the series was levelled. Billy had to leave the field for five minutes after injuring his hand in a try-saving tackle on the Kiwi loose-forward Alister Atkinson and the *New Zealand Herald* noted, "Boston, although starved, was dangerous" and added, "the only failure in the New Zealand backs was Vern Bakalich, who was bettered by Boston". Both sides scored two tries, but Des White landed seven goals to Lewis Jones's four.

Billy celebrated his 20th birthday on 6 August and received a cake with the appropriate number of candles. However, a better present came his way the following day as he rewrote the record books on a saturated pitch at Canterbury, when the Lions hammered their hosts 60–14 despite losing skipper Dickie Williams after just 20 minutes. Billy scored two first half tries after fine runs which left the opposition trailing, the second of which brought his try tally to 34 for the tour and equalled the record set by Salford winger Tom Danby on the 1950 tour. Two more tries in the second half took his haul to a Lions tour record of 36, amassed in a mere 15 appearances. With seven games left of the tour Billy looked set to boost the record even higher but did not add a solitary touchdown, missing four of the remaining fixtures and failing to score in his last three outings.

On 14 August the deciding test was held at Carlaw Park. The Auckland Rugby League was hoping for a 30,000 crowd. However, conditions were so utterly dreadful that just over 6,000 hardy souls braved the elements. The *New Zealand Herald* observed: "Conditions could not have been more dismaying. Sixty-knot squalls, bearing rain in the second half, lashed the ground. Sawdust along the grandstand touchline deepened rather than lessened the problem of adequate footholds. Elsewhere, the water lay like a glaze." In the circumstances the play was remarkably good although there was also an excess of rough stuff – an alarmingly recurring feature of the New Zealand leg of the tour. Britain clinched the series with a 12–6 victory, having scored the only tries of the test in the first quarter through Price and O'Grady. Jones kicked a couple of goals to give the Lions a 10–6 interval lead and his fine penalty into the teeth of the gale was the only score of the second half.

Billy did not have any real opportunity to shine, but enjoyed a good tussle with test debutant Jim Austin. However, more of a trial to him was a member of the crowd. Billy remembers: "There was this bloke who was really getting on my nerves. He was screaming 'you black this, you black that'. He carried on like that all through the first half and I took note of him and where he was standing. I thought I would be spared all that rubbish in the second half because I would be on the other side of the field. I was wrong though because he swapped sides too and carried on yelling abuse until the end of the game. I had had enough of him by then and went over the fence at the final whistle to sort him out. It was probably a good job that he got away. Later on that day I arrived back at the hotel where we were staying and who should be propping up the bar near the doorway with a pint in his hand but that idiot! Well, I saw red and sent him flying. When he had collected his senses and cleared off, I went and sat on the hotel steps to wait for the police to arrive, but fortunately they never did. That sort of racist behaviour was very rare in my experience of rugby league. Folk in Wigan and rugby league in general have always treated me respectfully and problems with colour have been few and far between."

The final fixture of the New Zealand tour was against Auckland just two days after the test match and Carlaw Park was in parts six inches deep in mud. Billy and Lewis Jones "played splendidly", according to one newspaper, but the game was a real brute. Mike Brett, in the *Auckland Star*, wrote: "The merit of Auckland's 5–4 win was overshadowed by the toughness of the play. British pressmen rated the game as the dirtiest of the tour – far worse than the called-off match against New South Wales." Britain lost Nat Silcock, playing on the wing again, after 38 minutes, when he was sent off after an altercation with Auckland second-rower Doug Richards-Jolley. Jack Wilkinson followed Silcock to the dressing-room a few minutes after half-time after another set-to with Richards-Jolley. The penalty count favoured Auckland 19–6 and Auckland's test full-back Des White was hospitalised with a ruptured stomach following a savage tackle by Duggie Greenall. Silcock and Wilkinson subsequently received one month bans from the NZRL Council. It was an unhappy ending to the Lions' sojourn in the land of the long white cloud.

Billy and his team-mates completed the tour by returning to Australia where a further three games were played in just five days. Billy played in the first, a potentially explosive return fixture against New South Wales. He created the first try with a 60 yard run after fielding a wayward kick by Clive Churchill, cleverly skipped round Ross Kite and Churchill, and took Merv Lees's tackle before passing inside to Dave Valentine, who touched down. Jones kicked three goals and Britain were sailing along serenely with a 9–3 lead when Billy received an injury to his left elbow in bumping Kite into touch and was forced to retire. Reduced to 12 men for an hour Britain fell away and lost 35–15. Billy missed the remaining games in Canberra and Maitland. The first, a 66–21 rout of Southern District, was notable for Lewis Jones's haul of 15 goals, which enabled him to set a points scoring record for any tour of Australia, surpassing French full-back legend Puig Aubert's 236 points set in 1951. The second, a 28–22 reverse against Newcastle Coalfields, saw Jones bag another 13 points to stretch his record to 278 points but was another bad-tempered, brawling affair. By that stage in the tour Britain had lost all four of their wingers to injury and most of the tourists were eager to return to home and hearth in England.

The Lions arrived at London Airport on Friday 27 August around 9.30 in the morning to be greeted by a party of RFL officials led by Bill Fallowfield. Later in the day the Wigan contingent arrived at Wigan North West Station, where a considerable crowd had assembled. A local reporter noted that all four players had put on weight, Billy having now attained 14 stone 12 pounds. Nat Silcock tipped the scales at 17 stone 7 pounds. Ernie Ashcroft had the thrill of seeing his twin baby daughters for the first time.

Billy had come home with his reputation sky high, five test matches to his credit and the new record-holder for tries on a Lions tour. When he had landed in Australia he recalls: "I was so green that Charlie Pawsey and some of the other players had to show me how to play the ball properly in hotel corridors." Pawsey was in no doubt as to Billy's worth. After the tour he wrote in his *Manchester Evening News* column: "It is the tendency for the young and innocent who have been honoured with tour selection to become blasé and to take their future into their own hands. On this trip there were no 'know-alls' and I could not help but admire the modesty, almost nonchalance, of record scorer Billy Boston. Billy, always a favourite with the crowd, particularly the children, took the blaze of honour in the same easy stride with which he took his tries. Let us give credit to the centres who served Boston so well without underestimating in any way the invaluable part played by the boy in most of the tour's successes. It was indeed a magnificent performance to beat Tom Danby's record."

# The 1954 Lions tour

Tour record: P32, W21, D1, L8, Abandoned 1, For 919, against 532
Boston scored 36 tries

| Date | Opponent | Score | Boston | Crowd | Venue |
|------|----------|-------|--------|-------|-------|
| 19 May | Western Districts | 29–11 | 2T | 5,218 | Bathurst |
| 22 May | Newcastle | 10–11 | dnp | 22,825 | Newcastle |
| 25 May | Riverina | 36–26 | dnp | 10,000 | Wagga Wagga |
| 29 May | Sydney | 25–32 | 1T | 50,889 | Sydney |
| 30 May | Southern Districts | 17–17 | dnp | 15,434 | Wollongong |
| 5 June | New South Wales | 11–22 | dnp | 55,518 | Sydney |
| **12 June** | **Australia** | **12–37** | **dnp** | **65,884** | **Sydney** |
| 14 June | Brisbane | 34–4 | 1T | 20,041 | Brisbane |
| 19 June | Queensland | 34–32 | 3T | 29,002 | Brisbane |
| 20 June | Wide Bay | 60–14 | 4T | 5,912 | Maryborough |
| 22 June | Mackay District | 28–7 | 1T | 5,860 | Mackay |
| 24 June | Cairns District | 39–18 | dnp | 6,545 | Cairns |
| 27 June | North Queensland | 39–13 | 4T | 8,360 | Townsville |
| 29 June | Central Queensland | 21–12 | dnp | 5,200 | Rockhampton |
| **3 July** | **Australia** | **38–21** | **2T** | **46,355** | **Brisbane** |
| 4 July | Toowoomba | 25–14 | 1T | 13,310 | Toowoomba |
| 7 July | Northern NSW | 44–14 | 6T | 7,201 | Grafton |
| 10 July | New South Wales+ | 6–17 | dnp | 27,333 | Sydney |
| **17 July** | **Australia** | **16–20** | | **67,577** | **Sydney** |
| 21 July | Maoris | 14–4 | dnp | 1,728 | Whangarei |
| **24 July** | **New Zealand** | **27–7** | **4T** | **22,097** | **Auckland** |
| 27 July | Wellington | 61–18 | 3T | 3,103 | Wellington |
| **31 July** | **New Zealand** | **14–20** | | **4,240** | **Greymouth** |
| 4 August | South Island | 32–11 | dnp | 1,154 | Dunedin |
| 7 August | Canterbury | 60–14 | 4T | 1,544 | Canterbury |
| 9 August | North Island | 42–7 | dnp | 2,448 | New Plymouth |
| 11 August | South Auckland | 26–14 | dnp | 1,683 | Hamilton |
| **14 August** | **New Zealand** | **12–6** | | **6,186** | **Auckland** |
| 16 August | Auckland | 4–5 | | 4,949 | Auckland |
| 18 August | New South Wales | 15–35 | | 21,035 | Sydney |
| 21 August | Southern District | 66–21 | dnp | 3,253 | Canberra |
| 22 August | Newcastle Coalfields | 22–28 | dnp | 9,585 | Maitland |

+ Match abandoned after 56 minutes

The Wigan team that lost 8–7 at Leigh on 30 October 1954. Back: Boston, Nordgren, Broome, Griffin, Mather, McTigue, Armstrong; front: Featherstone, Bolton, Parr, Platt, Cunliffe, Street.

Passing to Mike McGillicuddy against Workington Town.

# 5. 1954-55 Wigan top try-scorer

Billy's tour of Australasia had been profitable in terms of gaining vital experience in his new game and it had also brought him and his colleagues a bonus of £392 each, their 30 per cent share of the tour profits, which amounted to a record £34,000. One thing which was in short supply for Billy, however, was rest. He was still in the Army, albeit for only 11 days, and had to quickly return to Catterick. It was worse for Nat Silcock though, who, amazingly, was pressed into service on Wigan's right wing at Liverpool City the day after he returned from the tour, while Ernie Ashcroft was drafted back into action for the home game against Keighley on 4 September. That game was won 44–2 but was notable as it marked the first team debut at stand-off of a prodigious talent in Dave Bolton, a 17 year-old local.

Wigan won four of their first five fixtures. However, they were so anxious to get Billy back into the side that they despatched coach Ted Ward on a 244 mile round trip by car to Catterick to collect him in order that he could play against Rochdale Hornets on 6 September – a Monday evening game which went Wigan's way 12–9, thanks to a 75th minute match-winning try by second-rower Norman Cherrington. Five days later, before 24,000 fans, Wigan crashed out of the Lancashire Cup at Leigh in the first round with Billy appearing at left centre. The following Wednesday he was demobbed and finally got a short holiday with a trip home to Cardiff before returning to civilian life in Wigan.

Wiganers' expectations of Billy were high before he went on tour. His exploits in Australia and New Zealand only served to heighten them. Wigan folk were used to watching good rugby and great rugby players. Their club had enjoyed several golden ages and arguably no other club had down the years commanded such esteem and prestige in the game. Wigan was still one of the sport's most prestigious names, but over the past couple of years the team had flattered to deceive. From 1945 to 1952 Wigan had been the main power in the game, winning the Championship in 1945–46, 1946–47, 1949–50 and 1951–52 and the Challenge Cup in 1948 and 1951, as well as being losing finalists in 1946. They had contested the Lancashire Cup Final in seven consecutive seasons, losing only the first in 1945, and they had lifted the Lancashire League Championship in 1945–46, 1946–47, 1949–50 and 1951–52. It was a wonderful team, brimming with outstanding backs such as Martin Ryan, Johnny Lawrenson, Jack Hilton, Gordon Ratcliffe, Ted Ward and the fantastic half-back pairing of stand-off Ces Mountford, "the Blackball Bullet" from New Zealand, and Tommy Bradshaw, a local who played for Great Britain against New Zealand in 1947 and had been a Lions tourist in 1950. The forwards were a veritable 'Who's Who' of packmen, the foremost of them being Joe Egan, an extraordinarily gifted hooker and leader, and his gargantuan prop partner Ken Gee. The pair were cornerstones of the Lancashire, England and Great Britain packs during this halcyon period and fellow internationals George Curran, Billy Blan, Bill Hudson and Les White were just some of the mighty men who ensured that the team's dazzling array of backs got the protection and ammunition they required.

By the time Billy had joined Wigan, the club's star had dimmed. In 1952–53 the club had slumped to 11th in the league, but had risen to seventh in 1953–54. However, the nearest the team had come to lifting silverware was losing to St Helens in the 1953 Lancashire Cup Final. When Billy returned from touring at the start of the 1954–55 season only Jackie Cunliffe, Ernie Ashcroft and Brian Nordgren, a forceful and prolific winger from New Zealand, remained of the super-successful old guard, although Nat Silcock, Jackie Broome and Harry Street had also enjoyed participating in the latter stages of those happy days. Ken Gee had announced his retirement from playing just three games into the new season and the Wigan board had magnanimously made him a Life Member of the club. Times were certainly changing at Central Park. For many, the acquisition of Billy was seen as evidence of the directors' determination to elevate the club to its former glory, but it was going to take a little longer than they probably anticipated. Billy could not be expected to transform the side. He had, after all, just turned 20, was a stranger to the town, had been separated from his family, who were 200 miles away, was clearly regarded as a winger and, usually, wingers do not transform sides.

Billy would hardly have recognised Central Park when he arrived back there following the tour. During his absence the famous old Dutch Barn Stand, which had been erected in 1911–12, had been demolished and massive ground improvements were in progress. A new stand, which included 800 seats, had replaced the Dutch Barn and work had begun on restructuring the Kop end. The directors took some criticism from fans for investing in bricks and mortar rather than in more Billy Bostons, but they correctly realised that such investment would eventually produce rich dividends. They needed to maximise income as well as reconstruct the team. Wigan's home league crowds had averaged 22,901 in 1949–50. By 1953–54 they were down to 14,837, as the game suffered from the downturn in sporting attendances since the boom in the period after the war. Wigan had been the second best supported club behind St Helens in 1953–54, but their falling attractiveness as visitors to opposing grounds could clearly be seen in the statistic that they trailed Saints, Warrington, Halifax, Oldham, Leeds and Huddersfield in the attendance ratings.

When the 1954–55 season began there were four Welshmen besides Billy at Central Park. His brother Herbie was playing in the 'A' team, Ted Ward was the first team coach and Peter Clubb, a former Ebbw Vale rugby union centre, and Roy Williams, a former Llanelli forward, were also on the club's register. Billy recalls: "When I came to live in Wigan I shared lodgings with Ted Ward and Roy Williams in Douglas Road – three Welshmen together. Our landlady, Mrs Toy, looked after us. I remember mornings used to be a case of 'first out, best dressed', as we all grabbed each other's stuff. When I was in the Signals I had been a Physical Training Instructor, but now I was in Civvy Street I began working as a labourer for the firm of Mr Webster, the Wigan chairman".

Although the 1954 Lions tour was already history, the repercussions of rough play, especially from the abandoned game against NSW and some of the later matches in New Zealand, were still being felt. The Rugby League Council met at Manchester on 13 September and after a three-hour meeting announced that six players had brought discredit to the game and were to be placed on a black list. The players in question had seriously jeopardised their chances of future international selection. It later transpired that a further three names could be added to the list. The Council then shot itself in the foot by declining to name the miscreants, thereby possibly implicating any of the 26 Lions.

The matter was particularly disturbing because the first Rugby League World Cup was scheduled to be held in France later in the autumn and the squad was to be selected on 30 September. By then 10 of the Lions squad had declared themselves unavailable for the World Cup and a further 13 top quality contenders had followed suit. A few of the declining Lions obviously pre-empted the selectors' decision to blacklist them, but many of the refusniks may simply have been unwilling or unable to accept the paltry financial terms of £25 per man, plus a £10 bonus for winning a tournament, which would involve three weeks away from home and therefore an actual loss of income. Billy did not fall into any of those categories. He was certainly not on the black list, had done passably well financially over the past year or so and was raring to win selection for the historic event.

Billy gave the selectors a timely nudge five days before their decisions were due with his first try of the season in a 20–11 home win against Bradford Northern, scoring at the corner flag festooned by two shattered defenders and having a second try disallowed after a 45 yard dash. When the selection committee announced the World Cup team on Thursday 30 September, Billy was duly named as the right wingman in a team which read: Jim Ledgard (Leigh); Billy Boston (Wigan), Phil Jackson (Barrow), Mick Sullivan (Huddersfield), Frank Kitchen (Leigh); Willie Horne (Barrow) captain, Gerry Helme (Warrington); John Thorley (Halifax), Sam Smith (Hunslet), Bob Coverdale (Hull), Don Robinson (Wakefield Trinity), Geoff Gunney (Hunslet) and Dave Valentine (Huddersfield) vice-captain. The five other squad members were Billy Banks and Ronnie Rylance (both Huddersfield), Ally Naughton (Warrington), Alvin Ackerley (Halifax) and Johnny Whiteley (Hull). That evening Billy, together with Dave Valentine, experienced his first television interview when he appeared on BBC's *Sportsview* and was questioned about the World Cup prospects by Eddie Waring.

Only five of the 1954 Lions had been selected for the World Cup party and in the event only three of them actually made the trip to France. Willie Horne, who declared he had asked the selectors not to pick him, immediately withdrew and was replaced as stand-off by Leeds's Gordon Brown, leaving Dave Valentine to the captaincy. On 6 October Alvin Ackerley had to withdraw because he could not get three weeks off work and Huddersfield hooker Harry Bradshaw took his place.

Still Billy's priority was the challenge of helping Great Britain to win the World Cup and his form with Wigan in the weeks leading up to the tournament was excellent. In the three games prior to the departure of the squad he rattled up six tries, including one in an 18–12 win at Whitehaven that was marred by a constant downpour. Conditions were dreadful but Billy made light of them when Whitehaven full-back John McKeown launched a 25-yard drop-out after Brian Nordgren had failed to convert a penalty. Billy dashed forward to gather the greasy ball and went full speed for the line, beat Harrison with a sparkling side-step and dived in at the corner before McKeown could nail him. The *Wigan Examiner* reported: "A very sporting Whitehaven crowd gave Billy Boston a wonderful ovation as he left the field after scoring a superb try five minutes from the end. Whitehaven officials stated that it is a long time since anything like it had been seen there. Boston was applauded all the way that he was walking to the dressing-room, which is a considerable distance from the playing pitch." The following week a letter from "Rugbyite" appeared in the *Rugby Leaguer* endorsing a view about Billy which was becoming ever more prevalent: "When a crowd stands at the players' exit to cheer an opposing player he must be great. This, of course, was 'Gentleman Boston', the man who took time off to crack jokes back at the crowd, and to sign scores of small boys' autograph books."

Billy's last game before the start of the World Cup was Wigan's first ever encounter with the newly formed Blackpool Borough club at Central Park on 23 October. Borough were smashed 39–2. Billy weighed in with the last three tries in the 61st, 70th and 74th minutes, while he also made a try for Jackie Broome. Ike Fishwick, Borough's teak-tough hooker, unfortunately suffered a shoulder injury tackling Billy, which put him out of action until Christmas Day and enabled Wigan to win the scrums 33–19. Of more concern to Billy, however, was his own ankle, which was damaged during the victory. It was not a serious injury, but it was bad enough to preclude him from being able to travel with the World Cup party to France and with an 18-man squad there was no point in taking anyone who was not absolutely 100 per cent fit.

Geoff Gunney was in the same predicament having picked up an injury playing for Hunslet at York on the same afternoon as Billy hurt his ankle. The injured pair were replaced by Leeds's David Rose and York's Basil Watts. History shows that Great Britain went on to glory in France while Billy was left in Wigan ruing his bad luck.

Billy's ankle may have kept him out of the Great Britain side but he was, somewhat controversially, allowed to play for Wigan at Leigh the day before Great Britain opened their World Cup campaign with a 28–13 win against Australia in Lyon. Billy opened the scoring after two minutes, finishing off a classic 65 yard move initiated by scrum-half Tommy Parr and full-back Don Platt. Leigh, however, won a cliff-hanger 8–7 with a try by full-back Jack Lowe three minutes from time. A fortnight later, Wigan had their revenge at Central Park, winning 8–6. Almost 16,000 attended despite some diabolical conditions, which meant a waterlogged pitch, and the novel counter-attraction of the World Cup final against France in Paris being shown live on television.

Wigan fielded their new signing Don Hayward at blind-side prop, a compatriot of Billy, who had played union for Pontypridd and Newbridge before emigrating to New Zealand for a couple of years, having won a dozen caps for Wales. Billy won the game for Wigan with the only two tries of a grim struggle in the mud. Brian McTigue initiated the first in the 12th minute. Ernie Ashcroft developed the move by kicking forward for Billy to follow up, kick on again and win the race to the line. The second on 27 minutes followed a magnificent run from Don Platt, who threw the ball inside to Billy. Lowe was waiting for him near the corner but Billy crashed through his tackle to score just inside the flag.

They were the last tries Billy claimed for over a month as Wigan struggled with a difficult run of matches. After a good 20–15 win at Barrow, Wigan went down 9–5 in their first home defeat of the season against league leaders Oldham in a fine, clean game before over 21,000 fans. Many of the crowd were sheltered for the first time by the completed roof at the Kop end of the ground.

December opened with two tough games against Halifax, the first at a rain drenched Thrum Hall, where a violent wind blew from corner to corner. The aerial conditions were so tricky that the goalposts swayed throughout the 80 minutes and only one successful goalkick accrued from 11 attempts. Wigan introduced debutants Mike McGillicuddy, a £1,000 signing from Widnes at stand-off, and hooker Bill (Sos) Sayer. Halifax fans were, however, much more interested in who their trialist left centre, a tall, handsome black man, was. The trialist was no stranger to Billy. It was Johnny Freeman, his childhood friend and former team-mate with the Cardiff International Athletic Club. This was to be the first of many momentous encounters between the two Tiger Bay boys. Billy broke the deadlock in the 35th minute when he burst brilliantly down the wing, threw an inside pass, which went to ground, but was tapped cleverly on by McGillicuddy to Broome who claimed a stunning try. Tuss Griffiths landed a penalty for Halifax after 56 minutes and the score remained 3–2 until the last seconds when Platt scored Wigan's second try to give Wigan a 6–2 success. Wigan thus became the first Lancashire club to win a league fixture at Halifax since April 1952, a victory which gave them fourth place in the league table.

Wigan had struck a period of playing in very wet and cold conditions and the *Lancashire Evening Post* reporter Eric Thompson revealed that Wigan's policy to ensure that their players did not catch 'flu was to make sure they took two capsules of halibut oil a day and had courses of sunray treatment. That treatment might have warded off the germs, but it did not stop Halifax exacting quick revenge on 11 December, when Wigan went down 9–3 at Central Park. Both sides scored a try, but Griffiths kicked three goals for Halifax which proved decisive, as Nordgren missed seven shots and Cunliffe two at goal, goalkicking being a recurring problem for Wigan. Billy again had his hands full trying to get the better of Dai Bevan and the local paper noted that a private feud appeared to have developed between the pair. On one occasion Billy showed considerable vigour in tackling Bevan, who clearly showed his resentment and Billy "was for some reason cautioned by the referee". Billy recalls: "There was no feud or problem between me and Dai Bevan. Sometimes people see things that aren't there. Mind you, I don't think too much of players who just spend their time on top of their opponents. There's no skill in that tactic. Anyone can do that. It just spoils the game."

Things soon perked up for Billy, who received a travelling clock from the Wigan Supporters' Association at Ince Public Hall in recognition of his record-breaking performance for the Lions. He picked up his second hat-trick of the season in a comfortable victory over Liverpool City before Christmas Day brought Wigan their biggest spree of the season with a 50–7 thrashing of Salford. Don Platt scored a hat-trick, a rare achievement for a full-back in those days. Billy also took the eye with a couple of successful goal-kicks, the first of only seven he landed in his career. He also grabbed two tries and the *Wigan Observer* noted: "Boston was another Wigan attacker who was in excellent form. His touch line runs thrilled the crowd and when Boston was running in possession there was usually an ominous buckling about the Salford defence." Two days later Wigan succumbed 19–7 at St Helens. Tries by Duggie Greenall and Eric Ledger, both converted by Joe Ball, put St Helens 10 points up within four minutes and Wigan, losing the scrums 29–24 and missing six shots at goal, were never in the game. Billy "had few chances in attack, but his defence was sound".

Wigan began 1955 in fifth place in the league behind Warrington, Oldham, St Helens and Leigh. New Year's Day pitted them against top dogs Warrington at Central Park. The crowd of almost 29,000 saw Wigan won 18–6 in a wonderful performance on a rare dry pitch. It was the first time that Billy had shared the same playing field as Brian Bevan, who many good judges deemed the greatest winger to have played rugby league, an opinion endorsed by Billy. On this occasion Bevan was the only Wire player capable of taking chances, scoring both their tries. Billy gave his opposing winger, Stan McCormick, another great player, a really torrid time in both attack and defence, while he opened the scoring with a lovely try in the 15th minute after Street and Hill had got him away.

An easy double against Belle Vue Rangers brought Billy a last minute goal in a drab, fog-ridden game at Belle Vue and a hat-trick of tries in the return match at Central Park. It was to be the last game Wigan played against the Rangers, who disbanded later in 1955. Two tries at Widnes followed in a narrow victory, but Billy suffered a knee injury in an equally tight home win against Workington Town, when Wigan's new hooker Jack Richardson appeared to have solved their problems with scrum possession in taking the strikes 26–11.

Billy visited a specialist in Leeds to try to sort out his damaged knee, but was not fit for Wigan's most important game of the season, a first round Challenge Cup tie at Oldham on 12 February 1955. By now Wigan had risen to third in the table, while Oldham were second. Watersheddings was simply not big enough to house all those enthusiasts who wanted to see the tie of the round. For the all-ticket match Wigan fans took all 7,000 of the tickets allotted to them, but were mortified by the result of a titanic encounter – 5–2 to Oldham.

Wigan's only achievable target for the season was now a place in the top four and a shot at the Championship. Nine league games remained to be played and by the time the weather allowed them to restart operations against Swinton on 5 March Billy had recovered from his knee trouble. Swinton conceded four tries to him as they were crushed 29–2. Billy scored one try from 70 yards out, two from half-way and for the fourth crashed over at the corner from a Dave Bolton pass. A one point defeat at Barrow, when Nordgren missed an easy 77th minute conversion of a McTigue try, did not seem too damaging when Warrington were beaten 13–9 a week later. To Wigan followers this was the match of the season and Warrington's first home defeat in two seasons. It was Billy who did the damage, finishing off a superb break by Broome to give his side a 5–4 interval lead. His second try was "the reward of a magnificent touch-line run in which he beat three opponents by sheer speed and elusiveness". A 71st minute try by Tommy Parr, converted by stand-in skipper Jack Cunliffe took Wigan to an unassailable 13–4 lead before Brian Bevan grabbed a debatable try in the 75th minute to put some gloss on the score for Warrington.

March ended disastrously for Wigan with a 7–7 draw at Swinton, when Billy did not receive a second half pass until the 72nd minute and then it was forward. April began even more disastrously with a 26–0 shellacking at Oldham, although Billy came out of it with glowing references. The *Wigan Examiner* stated: "Those people who have had doubts about the defensive ability of Wigan's ace winger, Billy Boston, need have no fears after Wigan's overwhelming and humiliating 26–0 defeat by Oldham at Watersheddings for, if Boston had not shown remarkable speed and football intelligence, Oldham could quite easily have inflicted a far greater defeat. When the extremely fast and fit Oldham backs, prompted by a virile pack, had bewildered the rest of the Wigan team, Boston often found himself facing as many as three or four opponents. That happened on at least half a dozen occasions, and Boston was beaten only once! All those Wigan supporters who travelled to Oldham must be settled in their own minds that Boston is a great defensive player as well as a brilliant attacker and if he takes care of himself, this lad can certainly become one of the rugby league greats... Only Brian Bevan can be classed with him." Wigan had been so woeful that Billy had only handled the ball twice.

Mercifully, Wigan got back to form in the Good Friday derby against St Helens. Two wonderful defences dominated the game and kept more than 33,000 fans on tenterhooks. Saints' half-back Peter Metcalfe kept his side in the hunt with six goals from six attempts, while Jack Cunliffe landed five for Wigan. The only tries of the game went to Wigan, Dave Bolton going over after 11 minutes, followed four minutes later by Billy, who beat Don Gullick to a clever short kick to the corner by Cunliffe. The rest of a tingling game was try-less, although one highlight was Billy's brilliant overhauling of Bill Finnan to prevent a score.

Salford and Blackpool Borough were despatched and Wigan went into the final game of the season at Rochdale on Monday 18 April requiring a victory to clinch fourth spot in the table. If Billy was hoping for a first Championship Final, his fellow winger Brian Nordgren was hoping that this would not be his last game for Wigan, because he had qualified as a barrister and was leaving for home in New Zealand as and when Wigan's season ended – and end it did. Hornets played above their station and won 12–7. Nordgren scored Wigan's only try – his 312th in 294 games for the club. He also played most of the game with a fractured thumb, an unhappy ending to a great career. Wigan were left hoping that Halifax did not win their last three games, all to be played within five days. It was a forlorn hope as the Thrum Hallers won the lot and pushed Wigan down to fifth on points averages.

Billy had finished top of Wigan's try-scorers with 31 in 31 games, pipping Nordgren who had claimed 26 and kicked 73 goals. Thirty-one tries in a season was a good effort, but this was a period in which wingers in particular were expected to get hatfuls of tries and Billy was only 10th in the leading try-scorers lists, way behind Huddersfield's Lionel Cooper on 66 and Brian Bevan on 63. His season was not yet over, however. On Monday 9 May Billy guested for Huddersfield against Hunslet at Fartown in a testimonial match for Lionel Cooper. He gave the Yorkshire fans an indication that they may be observing someone who would become just as good as, or even better than, their great Lionel. Billy scored five tries that evening. His final engagement of the season followed ten days later in France when he represented Wales at centre in a 24–11 loss to a France 'B' side in Nantes.

# 1954–55

Wigan finished 5th in the League: P36, W26, L9, D1, For 643, Against 328
Boston scored 31 tries and 3 goals for Wigan

| Date | Opponent | Score | Boston | Crowd | |
|---|---|---|---|---|---|
| 14 August | Hunslet | 10–9 | dnp | 9,700 | |
| 21 August | **Hunslet** | 16–6 | dnp | 14,275 | |
| 25 August | Bradford N | 0–11 | dnp | 13,764 | |
| 28 August | Liverpool City | 26–16 | dnp | 4,858 | |
| 4 September | **Keighley** | 44–2 | dnp | 15,077 | |
| 6 September | **Rochdale H** | 12–9 | | 16,007 | |
| 11 September | Leigh | 10–21 | | 24,000 | LC1 |
| 18 September | Keighley | 24–7 | dnp | 4,565 | |
| 25 September | **Bradford N** | 20–11 | 1T | 18,319 | |
| 2 October | Workington T | 20–28 | | 11,993 | |
| 9 October | **Widnes** | 35–5 | 2T | 12,850 | |
| 16 October | Whitehaven | 18–12 | 1T | 5,831 | |
| 23 October | **Blackpool B** | 39–2 | 3T | 5,396 | |
| 30 October | Leigh | 7–8 | 1T | 13,203 | |
| 6 November | **Whitehaven** | 28–5 | | 8,370 | |
| 13 November | **Leigh** | 8–6 | 2T | 15,954 | |
| 20 November | Barrow | 20–15 | | 9,381 | |
| 27 November | **Oldham** | 5–9 | | 21,244 | |
| 4 December | Halifax | 6–2 | | 8,363 | |
| 11 December | **Halifax** | 3–9 | | 15,876 | |
| 18 December | **Liverpool City** | 27–6 | 3T | 7,333 | |
| 25 December | **Salford** | 50–7 | 2T, 2G | 11,085 | |
| 27 December | St Helens | 7–19 | | 26,537 | |
| 1 January | **Warrington** | 18–6 | 1T | 28,778 | |
| 8 January | Belle Vue R | 21–9 | 1G | 2,557 | |
| 22 January | **Belle Vue R** | 30–3 | 3T | 9,132 | |
| 29 January | Widnes | 11–7 | 2T | 8,020 | |
| 5 February | **Workington T** | 14–9 | | 18,158 | |
| 12 February | Oldham | 2–5 | dnp | 22,354 | Cup 1 |
| 5 March | **Swinton** | 29–2 | 4T | 8,156 | |
| 12 March | **Barrow** | 11–12 | 1T | 16,222 | |
| 19 March | Warrington | 13–9 | 2T | 21,629 | |
| 30 March | Swinton | 7–7 | | 7,500 | |
| 2 April | Oldham | 0–26 | | 15,127 | |
| 8 April | **St Helens** | 16–12 | 1T | 33,461 | |
| 11 April | Salford | 24–2 | 2T | 6,966 | |
| 16 April | Blackpool B | 17–8 | | 4,482 | |
| 18 April | Rochdale H | 7–12 | | 11,659 | |

## Boston's representative matches:

| Date | For | Opponent | Score | Boston | Venue |
|---|---|---|---|---|---|
| 19 May | Wales | France 'B' 11–24 | | | Nantes |

**International appearances in 1955**

Other Nationalities 33 England 16 at Wigan, 12 September 1955. Back: Price, McKinney, Kelly, Clues, Thorley, Bath, Bevan; front: Lynch, Banks, Valentine, G. Moses, Boston, Jones.

Wales team versus France 'B', 19 May at Nantes. This was Billy's only appearance for Wales.
Back: Daniels, Boston, Thorley, Winslade, Owen, Tierney, Davies;
front: G. Moses, Banks, Goldswain, Emmitt, Harris, Thomas.

# 6. 1955-56 Upheaval

Although Billy had been a Wigan player for more than two years when the 1955–56 season came round, he had not yet experienced a rugby league season from beginning to end. For the first time he was coming fresh to a new campaign after playing top grade rugby union and rugby league continuously since the late summer of 1953. There was much to look forward to, including possible inclusion in the approaching test series against New Zealand, while Wigan were hopeful of getting back on the trophy-winning trail and an improvement on their previous season's league finish of fifth. League crowds at Wigan had bucked the downward trend in the game in 1954–55, rising to an average of 15,316 and the better facilities had helped to increase gross receipts at league fixtures by £6,174. All that was required now was for the team to perform to its full potential – given a few tweaks.

Billy was unable to foresee how much change and drama would touch his life over the coming months...

The pre-season activity began on 6 August when Wigan staged their annual public practice match at a bone-hard Central Park. A crowd of 2,539 turned out to see Billy's side of Cherry and Whites defeat the Blues 40–28. These games usually entailed the first team forwards combining with the reserve team backs and vice versa, while also allowing for likely new candidates to show their talents. Billy certainly showed his by grabbing five tries. His brother Herbie, a replacement on the Blues team in the second half, also got a try but the most significant aspect of the afternoon was the appearance of a gangling young trialist in the Blues side. The *Wigan Examiner* recognised his potential, "A likely looking centre threequarter who played for the Blues in the first half attracted attention. He has ability and pace and both took and gave passes with perfection." Suffering a cut knee, the newcomer switched to the wing in the second half, but had clearly done enough and was signed immediately after the game for a paltry £150. The *Examiner* added, "The club's supporters will await his further appearances with interest... [He] is well-built for a centre or wing threequarter."

The man in question was St Helens born Eric Ashton, who was not quite six months younger than Billy. The names Boston and Ashton were to become inextricably linked and their friendship would thrive until Eric's death in March 2008.

In the week following the practice match Wigan reported a rush on season tickets, the most expensive of which cost £4 and the cheapest 35 shillings (£1.75), while boys could watch for the entire season for seven shillings and six pence (37.5p). Among the other newsworthy items was the transfer listing of test loose-forward Harry Street at £3,000. Billy had earned praise for his cricketing skills. Wigan RLFC had beaten Westhoughton CC by five wickets, Billy hitting an outstanding 58 out Wigan's 142 runs.

On 13 August Wigan hosted Warrington in the annual charity match for the Wardonia Cup and lost 19–10 before a crowd of 14,593. Brian Bevan grabbed a couple of tries for the Wire, but Billy had to be satisfied with two near misses after scintillating efforts. He had more luck the following Saturday when the season proper opened with a 52–5 drubbing of Dewsbury. A new play-the-ball law had been introduced, allowing the acting half-back to get as close as he could to the man playing the ball, instead of standing a yard away. All other players had now to retire three yards behind the men at the play-the-ball, the previous law having stipulated just one yard. It made no difference to Billy, who blitzed Dewsbury with seven tries to equal the club record set by Johnny Ring (twice – in 1925 and again in 1927) and Gordon Ratcliffe in 1947. The *Wigan Examiner* trilled: "It was a joy to watch this natural footballer beating opponents close to the touch-line, swerving and side-stepping without losing pace and scoring after runs of anything from 35 to 75 yards. It was the finest performance any Wiganer has ever shown, for, with one possible exception, the tries were not made for him." Normally Eric Ashton, making his first-class debut on the left wing, and scrum-half Tommy Parr might have expected a little more press coverage for their efforts in claiming two tries and four goals each. Nor did anyone notice that Billy's fifth try in the 49th minute was his 50th for the club in his 42nd appearance.

Billy was at it again on the following Tuesday enjoying a pleasant evening at Blackpool where Wigan won 31-6. This time he crossed for four tries, the last three between the 56th and 62nd minutes. On 27 August Wigan faced Warrington at Central Park again in the first round of the Lancashire Cup. At half-time Wigan led 9–0 and by the 65th minute extended their lead to an apparently unassailable 15–0. Then the wheels fell off as Warrington rallied mightily to reduce the deficit to 15-13 with one minute remaining and snatched the game 16–15 at the death with a breathtaking try from Jim Honey.

A couple of tries came Billy's way in a scratchy 17–9 home win against perennial strugglers Liverpool City and that was followed by a 15–2 defeat at Halifax. Wigan did click in the next game, a 36–11 rout of Wakefield Trinity at Central Park, with Billy rattling up a hat-trick of tries in the 45th, 59th and 67th minutes, for one of which "he had the audacity to side-step two opponents over the line in order to touch down behind the posts."

Wigan as a team may have been misfiring, but Billy had piled up 16 tries in six games and the representative selectors could not ignore such form. He was picked on the left wing for Other Nationalities against England at Central Park on Monday 12 September. The 1954 World Cup had disrupted the normal post-war international programme in which an annual European Championship had been contested between England, France and Wales, with the Other Nationalities joining in from 1949 onwards. Unfortunately for Billy, the European Championship ended after the 1955–56 season and he was denied the chance to win caps for Wales. It was considered that by 1955 Wales were not strong enough to compete and consequently Welshmen were eligible for the Other Nationalities. Billy thus had the opportunity to play in what was considered one of the best threequarter lines to have been gathered together in rugby league history – Brian Bevan (Warrington), Tommy Lynch (Halifax), Lewis Jones (Leeds) and Billy Boston. His old sparring partner from Boys Clubs union internationals, Mick Sullivan, was on England's right wing, partnered by another familiar character, Phil Jackson.

Eighteen thousand fans entered Central Park in glorious sunshine, but shortly before half-time a tremendous cloudburst sent them rushing for cover and created a treacherous surface for the remainder of the game. It did not perturb the Other Nationalities one iota and certainly not Lewis Jones, who was simply Merlinesque. Jack Bentley wrote in the *Daily Dispatch:* "Time and again Jones shot past Jackson with ridiculous ease, aided by a baffling change of pace and remarkable acceleration. He kicked six goals, scored a try for good measure, and gave Boston what must have been three of the easiest tries he has ever scored. Boston and Jones... looked a ready-made wing pair for Great Britain, for their defence was also good. Boston missed Sullivan on the England right wing only once." Other Nationalities triumphed 33–16, Billy's tries coming after 17, 27 and 35 minutes. The second was his 100th in first-class rugby league and it had taken him only 68 matches to achieve this. No one had ever accomplished that feat as quickly, even the great Bevan taking 84 matches. It was a fabulous achievement and prompted the *Wigan Examiner* to declare: "When Wigan are visitors people are asking, 'Is Boston playing?' just as they used to do in the case of Jimmy Leytham, Jim Sullivan and other great Wigan players of the past."

Whether it was the cloudburst which gave Billy a severe case of cold or not, he was lucky to miss Wigan's next outing, a 13–6 defeat at Featherstone. The New Zealanders had done their homework on Billy for their visit to Central Park on 24 September. He was marked mercilessly and only received one touch of the ball in the first half, which ended at 7–7, Eric Ashton having scored all Wigan's points. By the 60th minute Wigan trailed 15–10, Norman Cherrington having scored Wigan's second try. Then, according to the *Rugby Leaguer*, came "one of the finest tries ever scored on the ground. This was by Billy Boston, who is fast reaching the heights attained by the club's 'past masters'. He came in-field, took a pass from the scrum, and left behind him all would-be tacklers to score a brilliant try after an exciting 50 yards dash." The Wigan crowd's thunderous ovation subsided in time to watch Ashton's conversion bounce in off a post to equalise at 15–15. Ashton repeated the dose when his 72nd minute match-winning penalty cannoned in off the post and Wigan had recorded a famous victory, 17–15.

Wigan's Jekyll and Hyde form continued four days later when they travelled to London to play Huddersfield in a new tournament, the ITV Floodlit Trophy. The second half was shown live on television, albeit only in the south, and the *Wigan Examiner* described it as "a match, which must have thrilled the southern television viewers, but brought little credit to Wigan, whose defence was not of the highest order". Ernie Ashcroft sent Billy in for an early try, but thereafter it was all Huddersfield, who won 33–11.

Barely a month of the new season had elapsed and already Wigan were out of two competitions. It was not at all what the Wigan board and fans had expected. However, Billy continued to thrill the fans, however indifferently his team performed. His 22nd try of the season at Wakefield in a 21–10 win on 1 October brought him a wonderful ovation as he left the field at Belle Vue. Trinity had switched centre Don Froggett, a renowned tackler, to mark him, but Don put his shoulder out in the first half. Billy's wonder try, a 75 yarder, "the like of which has probably seldom been seen at Belle Vue", came on 38 minutes. Ernie Ashcroft threw a long pass to Billy near the Wigan '25', and the *Wigan Examiner* wrote: "Boston was quickly racing at full speed and side-stepping opponents before getting into the open. It seemed that he would have a clear run of 30 yards to the line but Fewster had cut across from the other wing. Boston stopped as the Wakefield player got near to him, side-stepped quickly and went on to score unopposed."

Great Britain called Billy up for the first test against New Zealand at Swinton on 8 October in a classic threequarter line that read Boston, Jackson, Jones and Sullivan. The Kiwis surprisingly offered scant resistance, going down 25–6, despite the fact that Great Britain lost second-rower Don Robinson after only nine minutes with a fractured fibula. Billy also retired for 10 minutes with an injury to his right foot and was clearly in some distress when he returned. It did not prevent him from claiming a tremendous try, however, when Britain mounted a devastating barrage of three converted tries in the last 12 minutes. Billy's was the first of them. Loose-forward Peter Foster grabbed a loose ball and passed to Jeff Stevenson, who got stand-off Ray Price away on a dazzling zigzag run past four defenders. Price shot out a beautiful pass for Billy, who had managed to keep up with play, to take on an inside burst and touch down under the posts. Britain's other points came from Jones's five goals, two tries from Sullivan and one each from Jack Gundy and Jack Wilkinson.

Billy switched back to the left wing on 19 October when he represented Other Nationalities against France in a floodlit international at Leigh. Despite a wet evening a brilliant match ensued. The French played some dazzling rugby, but were not steady enough in defence to stop Other Nationalities winning 32–19. The victory gave Other Nationalities the European Championship and Billy received his first winners' medal as a rugby league player. Lewis Jones again starred, kicked four goals and put Billy in for two tries in the first half, while there were also tries for Bryn Goldswain (two), Bevan, Lynch, Ray Price and Harry Bath. Sadly, it was the last international game ever played by the Other Nationalities.

Billy, not all that thrilled to be playing on the left wing rather than his favoured right, remembers: "Brian Bevan was on the right wing and before the game I noticed that my opponent was a little bloke of about 5 feet 4 inches or 5 feet 6 inches at most [André Ducasse of Bordeaux], who I thought would be easy to swat off in the tackle. Bev's opponent was André Savonne, who was built like a brick wall! I sidled up to Brian and said to him, 'You know, I'm really glad you're a better right winger than me!' Oddly enough though, I later played a test against Savonne and he was as soft as anything. It was one of the easiest games I ever had. That little winger Ducasse gave me far more trouble than Savonne."

Returning to domestic rugby Billy helped Wigan to their first win, 14–10, at Leigh since 1949 with a super try in the 58th minute, cantering over from half-way after coming inside in support of a typical break by Jack Broome. The following week the Central Park faithful got full measure as Billy blasted Whitehaven with five tries in a 29–2 success. The *Wigan Examiner* reported: "This great natural footballer, with assets of speed and weight, fairly shook the Whitehaven defence. Three of his five tries must have astonished his opponents for the average player would have made little headway in the same circumstances. He not only got through against strong opposition and close to the touch-line all the way, he plunged over the line with two players trying to bar his way. It was a remarkable display of powerful, courageous running."

Wigan won their fifth game in a row at Rochdale on 5 November, but it was a bad afternoon for Billy, who sustained a broken bone in his hand. It caused him to withdraw from Great Britain's team for the second test against the Kiwis at Bradford and effectively cost him further caps against New Zealand and France in December because of his lack of match fitness.

Billy was out of action for a month during which Wigan lost three out of four fixtures, including a traumatic 48–23 walloping from Oldham at Central Park. During that time they dropped from second in the league to sixth, behind St Helens, Bradford Northern, Warrington, Halifax and Featherstone Rovers. Billy was, despite his month-long lay-off, still top of the league's try-scorers with 31, one more than Bradford's powerful New Zealand winger Jack McLean.

Wigan enjoyed a successful December, winning five and drawing one of their six matches before crashing to a 40–5 defeat at Barrow on New Year's Eve. Billy, however, went through a lean patch, claiming only three tries during the period and not looking anything like the player he had been before his hand injury. On 2 January he was shifted to the left wing to mark Brian Bevan in the home derby with Warrington. There was a lot of good rugby played, but Wigan went under 14–6. The crowd was enthralled by the Boston-Bevan contest, which ended level at one try each. Billy retained his place on the left wing for Widnes's visit to Central Park, for which six tons of straw had been placed on the pitch as frost protection. Widnes in losing 21–8 "put up an uncommonly good fight", according to the *Wigan Examiner*, which also noted, "Boston gave an indifferent display and lacked his customary pace and determination in attack".

Wigan's board was so anxious about Billy's form and increasing weight that, according to Eddie Waring's column in the *Sunday Pictorial*, they put him into Turkish baths and required him to play at centre in the 'A' team against St Helens in a friendly fixture. Billy responded by scoring four tries and putting winger Bobby Chisnall over for another.

Billy's "indifferent" form may well have had something to do with his personal life. He had plenty on his mind apart from rugby league. The *Wigan Examiner* of Tuesday 31 January 1956 ran a story headlined "Billy Boston Weds in Secret". Billy had married "pretty 19 years old shop assistant, Miss Joan Rudd, of Somerset Road, Norley Hall Estate, Pemberton at St Cuthbert's Roman Catholic Church, Pemberton" on the previous Saturday. It was certainly a no-fuss affair. Half an hour before the wedding took place few people knew anything about it and there were only a handful of people present. Wigan secretary Jack Wood and coach Ted Ward told the press that they had known nothing about it. By the time the ceremony was over, however, news had leaked out and reporters and photographers were quickly on the scene. Billy wore a dark grey suit and a white carnation. Joan, in a blue dress, carried a spray. Herbie Boston was the best man. There was no honeymoon, just a quiet reception for family members at their new home in Swan Meadow Road, Poolstock, in which, coincidentally, Nat Silcock had previously been housed. The house belonged to the Wigan rugby league club, but Billy and Joan bought it from them.

Billy turned out later that afternoon at right centre at Central Park, where Wigan beat Salford 28–22 in a friendly. The crowd of 6,500, now mostly probably aware of Billy's new marital status, cheered wildly when he scorched 60 yards for a try in the 72nd minute – the last score of the match.

Joan recalls: "Billy and I met on a blind date. My mother warned me not to go on it! One of my girl friends, Barbara Ashurst, was going out with Billy's fellow lodger Roy Williams, another Welsh player with Wigan, and it was her idea. Barbara and Roy ended up married and Roy became a solicitor. Billy and I have certainly had some fun down the years but the run-up to the wedding was a bit of a love-hate relationship. I remember once having a tiff with Billy and throwing the ring away in some grass. It was dark and the pair of us ended up scrabbling about on the ground looking for it. A policeman, who was pretty well known in the area, but whose name escapes me now, found us and must have wondered what on earth we were up to. But he ended up on his hands and knees too until we found the ring. I remember the wedding day was very cold and there was snow on the ground that night. Members of my family stayed the night at the new house. They all slept upstairs and Billy and I only had a blanket on the sitting room floor. Well, it was so cold that I eventually just had to go upstairs and got into bed with my sister and mum! That was a funny do."

Billy's form recovered following his wedding – just in time for the Challenge Cup-ties. Wigan had signed prop Bill Bretherton from St Helens for £1,500, the same price for which they had sold Harry Street to Leeds a couple of months earlier. They had made renewed attempts to lure Welsh union international stand-off Cliff Morgan north, but had no success. They had, however, signed, in the *Wigan Examiner's* parlance, "another coloured boy" in 22 year-old centre or stand-off Jimmy Foster. Foster was an Aborigine from Adelaide, South Australia, a keen cricketer and a big friend of Wally McArthur, with whom he had played league as a teenager. Billy recalls: "Apart from Herbie – and he never played in the first team – I was always the only coloured player in the teams I represented at Wigan and for Great Britain. It looked like it might be different with the arrival of Foster, but he never made the grade. The business of being the only coloured player in my teams never bothered me but it did make me think about it."

The first round of the Cup pitted Wigan at home to Featherstone Rovers, who were just above them in the table. Bretherton made his debut but it was Billy who won the plaudits in a splendid 24–11 triumph. He scored twice, after 17 and 20 minutes. The first try came direct from a cross-kick by Eric Ashton and the second was a real Boston special. Jack Cunliffe gave him the ball just outside the Wigan '25'. The *Examiner* reported: "He was quickly in his stride and after a deceptive slackening of speed, he suddenly swerved inside and then went all out for the corner to crash over against a concentrated defence. It was a try which warmed the hearts of the spectators." In his next game it was Billy who might as well have been a spectator for the ball never reached the wings, as Wigan went down to their now customary defeat at high-flying Oldham.

The following week Wigan pasted Rochdale Hornets 31–5 and gave debuts to Ken Bird and Jimmy Foster as their left wing pairing. It had taken 200 braziers, burning through Friday night and into Saturday morning, to ensure that the game went ahead. Billy certainly appreciated the efforts of those involved, scoring a spectacular hat-trick in the second half.

Wigan crossed the Pennines to Keighley for the second round of the Challenge Cup, enjoying a pleasant motor coach trip through Whalley, Clitheroe, Gisburn and Skipton, made even more enjoyable on the return as a 12–3 victory put them into the quarter-finals. The game was an all-ticket affair and 3,500 Wigan fans swelled the crowd to 11,947. It proved a lot easier than the score suggested, Keighley having the benefit of a dubious try, while Billy had one disallowed. A reporter remarked, "The Yorkshire club's supporters seemed to get a lot of satisfaction whenever Billy Boston was stopped... Seldom has a team been so overplayed and lost by only nine points". A sour note was the breaking of Wigan prop Alan Armstrong's jaw in the last few minutes.

On 10 March Wigan won 36–9 at Liverpool, with Billy scoring two tries. He had paid his own admission at the turnstiles along with his team-mates and all the Wigan officials, directors and pressmen, "as on previous occasions at Knotty Ash". The poverty-stricken Liverpool club were truly grateful for any help and were particularly gratified to see a dozen coaches turn up from Wigan. Billy demonstrated his sportsmanship "when Jack Wood tackled him, having to turn and tap his ankle to do so. Boston, on returning to his position, patted Wood on the back as a token of appreciation of splendid defensive work." Four days later Blackpool Borough put up a spirited performance at Central Park but went down 26–15. Billy scored four tries, including a magnificent 75 yarder, and might have had six or eight with better service.

Barrow were next up at Central Park before a crowd of over 24,000 and drew a thrilling game 9–9 with Willie Horne reviving the lost art of dropping goals, landing one beauty and just failing to win the match with another attempt. Billy got remarkably few chances, bearing in mind that his opposite number Frank Castle was limping badly throughout the second half. When Billy's chance finally came in the last minute he knocked on after gathering a loose ball. Even so, seven tries in three games within a week was a sure sign that he was right back in form.

The third round of the Challenge Cup attracted a crowd of 29,184 to Central Park for Huddersfield's visit. Wigan put on a scintillating display in winning 24–2. Billy was the first to cross the Fartowners' line, beating three men in a powerful surge before crashing in at the corner flag. Unfortunately, he had brushed the touch-line and the try was disallowed. Even more unfortunately, Billy had hurt his ankle and hobbled back into play before going off for running repairs. In the 21st minute he somehow eluded Johnny Hunter and Austin Kilroy before struggling over at the corner off Broome's pass.

Wigan had qualified for the Challenge Cup semi-finals and Billy was presented with the prospect of a Wembley appearance – the biggest game by far of his career with Wigan. Wigan's opponents were Halifax, as formidable a force as could be imagined at that time. The only rugby league ground capable of housing the anticipated crowd was Odsal Stadium and the date set for the match was 7 April. It was a mouth-watering prospect but Billy's ankle was in bad shape, so bad that he was unable to play in either of Wigan's games leading up to the Odsal clash. It was touch-and-go as to whether he would be ready and able to take the field. Deep down Billy thought he was not fit and he told the Wigan directors so. At training on the Thursday before the game Wigan skipper Ernie Ashcroft was also asked by the directors whether he thought Billy was fit enough for the semi-final and said he thought not. Billy had a late fitness test on the morning of the match and complained that the ankle was not right. However, such was his value to the side, that he was persuaded to play despite his obvious misgivings.

Halifax, several places above Wigan in the league table and in with a chance of taking all four cups, were slight favourites to reach Wembley. They were not taking anything for granted, except, perhaps, that they needed to keep Billy Boston on a tight rein. To that end, they left out the in-form, but inexperienced, Johnny Freeman and reinstated Dai Bevan on the left wing to 'bottle up' Billy. Billy had played five times against Halifax, always marked by Bevan, and had never managed to score a try.

Almost 52,000 fans were treated to a splendidly contested match. David Nicholls, of the *Daily Express,* described it as "a gripping, suspense-laden semi-final, packed with devastating tackling, hard running and near-misses... all taken and given in a fine sporting spirit". Wigan struck first and it was Billy who put the first points on the score-board in the sixth minute. Jack Cunliffe linked up from full-back and gave Billy the ball with plenty of space in which to manoeuvre. He wasted no time in evading Bevan, handed off full-back Tuss Griffiths and surged to the corner, bearing giant centre Geoff Palmer along with him. He had beaten the Bevan bogey at last, but in scoring the try he felt his ankle give. Wigan increased their lead on 20 minutes with a fine penalty by Cunliffe and looked much the livelier side in the first half hour. Halifax levelled on 33 minutes when stand-off Ken Dean dashed over from a scrum before the packs even had time to look up, Griffiths converted and half-time arrived with the score 5–5.

As the game wore on Halifax gained the ascendancy, although they did not take the lead until the 68th minute, when scrum-half Stan Kielty sent Palmer careering through. Four minutes from time Palmer went over again after some bewildering handling by Halifax and at 11–5 down Wigan were as good as out of the running for a Wembley appearance. In the last minute, however, Eric Ashton went over for a converted try, but it was too late to have any bearing on the result as the final whistle sounded almost immediately after the restart. Earlier in the second half Billy's centre partner Jack Broome was injured and the two swapped places, a move which was to have truly unexpected repercussions.

Wigan had lost 11–10 and their Wembley dream had evaporated. They had, however, performed heroically and there was no disgrace in their defeat to an immensely powerful and experienced adversary. That was not apparently how the Wigan board viewed matters. At a meeting the following day to select the team to play at Widnes in a game vital to Wigan's top four hopes they also discussed the semi-final defeat. The upshot was a sensational decision to suspend Billy indefinitely "for disciplinary reasons". Billy was not invited to the meeting and he was only informed about it via a letter from the club. Chairman Tom Brown told the press: "It was unanimously decided to suspend Boston. We have suspended him because of events before, during and after, the semi-final against Halifax. Boston's general attitude since he joined Wigan has not been satisfactory." A *Daily Express* report added: "There have been training troubles too. Wigan rate power man Boston – height 5 feet 10 inches – a fleeter menace if he keeps his weight around 14 stone – about a stone lighter than at present. Boston said last night: 'I have no comment to make at the moment. It is a complete surprise to me. I was not called to a meeting of the directors. I had no idea that I had been suspended'." It was also revealed that Billy had requested to be transfer-listed earlier in the season but had quickly changed his mind.

Billy's Odsal misdemeanours were defined thus. Before the match Billy was missing from the dressing-room 20 minutes before kick-off when the rest of the team were stripped and ready for action. Billy was found outside the ground trying to find Joan, then pregnant, who had come to the match with her father, for whom Billy had procured a ticket so that he could sit with her, Billy being understandably anxious about her condition. The issue concerning the match itself was the view that Billy had been mainly responsible for the defeat because he had not stopped Palmer from scoring the match-winning tries. Finally, the after-match bone of contention was Billy's failure to travel back to Wigan with the rest of the players and officials. Instead, he had gone back to Halifax to see his friend Johnny Freeman, which was in hindsight not too diplomatic a decision.

Billy's version of events runs: "The real cause of the suspension was the directors' wish to deflect blame from themselves for the defeat. They knew I wasn't fit from the start and when I had to move inside to centre there was some bad decision making, because then we had two injured men forming one flank. It was ludicrous. I wouldn't mind so much if they had had the sense to move Eric Ashton into the centre that afternoon after the injuries happened. Eric was bursting to play centre all season, but they kept him on the left wing. I don't see why I should have been blamed for Palmer's tries – he had big overlaps for both of them and there wasn't only me playing. I did the best I could. I admit that I was not ready for action with the other boys 20 minutes before the game but that wasn't unusual for me. I didn't like changing a long time before playing. I just liked to change and get straight on with the game. Besides, I had to make sure Joan was all right."

The charges that Billy's attitude had not been satisfactory and that he had not given his full attention to training were most puzzling. Billy had been at training all week, despite his injured ankle, and desperately wanted to play at Wembley. He had on several occasions been prevailed upon to play when injured, had never balked when asked to play in the 'A' team, to be tested at centre. He had even turned out in the friendly against Salford on the afternoon of his wedding. If that was a bad attitude, there must have been something wrong in the board's view of the world.

As for the aspersions on his performance against Halifax, the facts, as reported in the newspapers, which presumably had no axes to grind, indicate no blame attached to him. The *Sunday Pictorial* wrote: "Boston was the big man for Wigan throughout. First on the wing, and later at centre, the coloured boy was terrific in attack and defence." The *Yorkshire Sports* observed: "Boston just would not be 'bottled up' by anyone". The *Rugby Leaguer*, describing the crucial last stages of the match, noted, "Great though Wigan's defensive play was in this period (and none performed greater feats in tackling than Boston did at this hectic stage) the threatened try had to come."

The directors had indicated that they felt Billy was too heavy and that he had been to blame for Palmer's tries. Billy admits that he always had a problem trying to keep his weight in check, but at that stage in his career he was one of the most formidable forces in the game, whatever his weight. The official match programme listed him at 14 stone 6 pounds, probably a bit heavier than he would have liked. However, as to his failure to stop Palmer, who among the directors would have relished the prospect of stopping a centre who stood 6 feet 1½ inches tall, weighed 15 stone 11 pounds and could shift amazingly quickly, especially if the tackler was carrying an ankle injury and facing an overlap?

Billy's response to his suspension was to tell the press: "I'm finished. I'm selling my Wigan home when this season ends and returning to Cardiff with my wife. I am not going to appeal against Wigan's decision – it's just over for me. I am aggrieved at allegations that I have treated the Wigan club like dirt. I told Wigan beforehand they would blame me if they lost Saturday's semi-final."

Under the RFL's bye-laws, Billy's suspension meant that he missed Great Britain's 18–10 victory over France, ironically at Odsal, on Wednesday 11 April. Workington Town's Ike Southward took his place on the right wing. The following day Billy went down to Central Park to collect some of his personal effects and his losing pay for the semi-final. At that juncture the issue seemed irreconcilable, but Billy's thoughts clarified and on the Friday he submitted a letter to the board saying: "I have been given so much advice by many people who are older and wiser than myself that I decided this was probably the best thing to do. After all, I am only 21 and supporters have more experience of these sorts of things."

Jack Winstanley, the rugby league correspondent for the *Wigan Observer*, who wrote the excellent *The Billy Boston Story* in 1963, recalled in that book: "Actually, Boston has since told me that he was strangely influenced by a mystery Hindley Green lady who wrote to him repeatedly urging him to face the Wigan directors, 'take his medicine' and get back to Central Park. The happy outcome was that at their next meeting, on Monday, 17 April, the Wigan directors, after considering Boston's letter, lifted the suspension. Billy Boston was back in the fold – to the disappointment of a well-known association football club who approached him during his 'nine days in the wilderness'." The club was Wrexham.

Suspension or not, Billy's season was over. His ankle injury needed attention and a specialist in Leeds examined him. He was given a manipulative operation and adhesions, which had formed on his ankle, were removed. Billy was back in training on 20 April.

So Billy completed his third season at Central Park. Wigan had still not won anything in his time with them but they had almost reached Wembley and had again finished fifth in the league, trailing Warrington, Halifax, St Helens and Hull. There was promise in such achievements, but it was still silverware that all at Central Park craved, not near misses. On a personal level Billy had scored 49 tries and finished third in the leading try-scorers behind Jack McLean, who scored 61, and Brian Bevan with 57. No one doubted Billy's playing qualities, even if the recent traumas suggested to some sceptics that his mindset might need adjusting.

## 1955–56

Wigan finished 5th in the League: P34, W22, L10, D2, For 596, Against 402
Boston scored 43 tries for Wigan, plus 6 in representative rugby league

| Date | Opponent | Score | Boston | Crowd | |
|---|---|---|---|---|---|
| 20 August | **Dewsbury** | 52–5 | 7T | 10,865 | |
| 23 August | Blackpool B | 31–6 | 4T | 5,192 | |
| 27 August | **Warrington** | 15–16 | | 23,161 | LC1 |
| 31 August | **Liverpool City** | 17–9 | 2T | 7,776 | |
| 3 September | Halifax | 2–15 | | 14,620 | |
| 10 September | **Wakefield T** | 36–11 | 3T | 12,073 | |
| 17 September | Featherstone R | 6–13 | dnp | 8,000 | |
| 24 September | **New Zealand** | 17–15 | 1T | 19,386 | Tour |
| 28 September | Huddersfield* | 11–33 | 1T | 500 | ITV Trophy |
| 1 October | Wakefield T | 21–10 | 1T | 6,875 | |
| 8 October | Whitehaven | 15–9 | dnp | 4,121 | |
| 22 October | Leigh | 14–10 | 1T | 15,255 | |
| 29 October | **Whitehaven** | 29–2 | 5T | 10,096 | |
| 5 November | Rochdale H | 15–7 | | 13,102 | |
| 12 November | **Leigh** | 11–24 | dnp | 20,286 | |
| 19 November | **Oldham** | 23–48 | dnp | 16,430 | |
| 26 November | Warrington | 4–13 | dnp | 14,320 | |
| 3 December | **Workington T** | 17–14 | dnp | 10,645 | |
| 10 December | Dewsbury | 31–2 | 2T | 2,169 | |
| 17 December | **Halifax** | 9–9 | | 13,260 | |
| 24 December | **Swinton** | 7–5 | | 11,578 | |
| 26 December | Salford | 21–6 | | 4,198 | |
| 27 December | **St Helens** | 8–0 | | 20,924 | |
| 31 December | Barrow | 5–40 | 1T | 9,731 | |
| 2 January | **Warrington** | 6–14 | 1T | 24,387 | |
| 14 January | **Widnes** | 21–8 | | 8,119 | |
| 11 February | **Featherstone R** | 24–11 | 2T | 19,677 | Cup 1 |
| 18 February | Oldham | 5–14 | | 15,137 | |
| 25 February | **Rochdale H** | 31–5 | 3T | 16,382 | |
| 3 March | Keighley | 12–3 | | 11,947 | Cup 2 |
| 10 March | Liverpool City | 36–9 | 2T | 2,339 | |
| 14 March | **Blackpool B** | 26–15 | 4T | 7,961 | |
| 17 March | **Barrow** | 9–9 | 1T | 24,076 | |
| 24 March | **Huddersfield** | 24–2 | 1T | 29,184 | Cup 3 |
| 30 March | St Helens | 7–29 | dnp | 30,793 | |
| 2 April | **Salford** | 39–7 | dnp | 12,990 | |
| 7 April | Halifax | 10–11 | 1T | 51,889 | Cup SF (at Odsal) |
| 9 April | Widnes | 10–2 | dnp | 5,995 | |
| 14 April | Workington T | 14–9 | dnp | 4,494 | |
| 18 April | **Featherstone R** | 11–7 | dnp | 9,757 | |
| 21 April | Swinton | 7–16 | dnp | 6,500 | |

*At Woolwich Stadium, London

**Boston's representative matches:**

| Date | For | Opponent | Score | Boston | Venue |
|---|---|---|---|---|---|
| 12 September | Other Nat's | England | 33–16 | 3T | Wigan |
| 8 October | Great Britain | New Zealand | 25–6 | 1T | Swinton |
| 19 October | Other Nat's | France | 32–19 | 2T | Leigh |

1956 Great Britain versus Australia test at Swinton. Billy fights off two Australian tacklers. Great Britain won 19–0 to clinch the Ashes. Billy scored the final British try.

Billy and Joan on their Wedding day.

Charging forward against Leigh. Jack Broome is supporting Billy.

Billy played cricket in his early
years in Wigan, and was a
successful bowler.

58

# 7. 1956–57 "Trying to stop Boston"

The uproar caused in Wigan rugby league circles by Billy's suspension subsided as the 1956 close season wore on. Billy and Joan were adapting to married life and looking forward to the birth of their first child. Also, Billy had begun to play cricket again. He had joined Highfield Cricket Club, which played in Division 'A' West of the West Lancashire Cricket League. His debut was impressive as he took four Blackrod wickets for 18 runs and caught John Speak in the slips. His second ball took out Bateson's middle and off stumps and Highfield won comfortably without Billy being required to bat. By mid-July Billy was top of the league bowling averages with 18 wickets at a cost of only 6.28 runs each. Among his best performances was his 6/14 against Dalton, while he bagged 6/32 against Orrell RT and hit an unbeaten 31 runs. By the season's end Billy had been the League's most successful bowler, taking 30 wickets for 168 runs (average 5.60) and Highfield had won the championship after defeating Norley Hall in a play-off.

There were a couple of significant changes at Wigan for the new rugby league season. Trainer Maurice Hughes had left to take up a post with Barrow and Joe Egan had returned from Leigh as manager-coach, replacing his former playing colleague Ted Ward, who had decided to return to Wales. Billy grabbed three tries in the Cherry and Whites' 32–31 victory over the Reds in the public practice match on Tuesday 7 August, but did not figure the following day in the inaugural Wigan Sevens tournament, which the hosts won, beating Warrington 16–8 in the Final. Warrington were overcome again three days later when Wigan beat them 16–15 at Wilderspool to take the Wardonia Cup.

The season proper opened at Hull where Wigan went down 16–8 in a thriller. Billy was injured in a tackle in the early minutes and spent the remainder of the game as a limping passenger, having suffered a contusion below the knee. 'TG' (Tom Groves), the *Wigan Examiner* reporter, noted "By the way Wigan had another disadvantage against Hull. As we entered the ground, there was a terrible smell and locals explained that there was a fish manure dump not far away. The wind was blowing the smell towards us. After the game, some of the Wigan players told me that the manure must have been used on the pitch. When they were tackled, the smell was nauseating." A 22–8 home win against Leeds provided a welcome two points, but was a poor game. A wet afternoon produced 47 scrums and "many needless penalties" although Billy scored twice in the second half. His first came via a 40 yard run to the corner, while his second saw him kick the ball over two opponents before retrieving the bouncing ball to score, a ploy not often used by Billy.

An extraordinary 24–0 victory in incessant rain at Workington Town's new stadium, Derwent Park, followed, despite the loss of Bill Bretherton, who was sent off just before half-time for delivering an uppercut to Brian Edgar. The *Examiner* observed that Billy was not as fast as last season, even though he caught the swift-moving Ike Southward in a crossfield run and "shot through the whole Workington side to send Bolton over for a try".

September opened with a first round Lancashire Cup-tie against Oldham, which attracted a crowd of 28,511, and produced a real nerve-jangler. In fact it was so exciting that one man was reported to have chewed away his pipe stem. Unfortunately for Wigan, a 78th minute converted try by scrum-half Frank Pitchford gave Oldham an 18–16 victory and once again Wigan said a quick good-bye to hopes of winning a trophy. Billy was rarely in the game and the *Examiner* lamented, "It was obvious, however, that he is still nowhere near as fast as he can be, and seemed to be carrying too much weight".

Billy was in reality having a bad time. Seven years later Jack Winstanley explained in *The Billy Boston Story*, "One of the best kept secrets of Boston's Rugby League career with Wigan was that it came perilously close to ending in heartbreaking fashion in the early weeks of season 1956–57. Joe Egan had just taken over as Wigan's coach... and he could hardly have been faced with a more monumental headache – his star player wanted to call it a day. Yes, Billy Boston, at 22, was ready to throw in the towel because he thought he was finished, ready for the scrap heap. And undoubtedly the reason was that he still could not rid his mind of the suspension imposed upon him a few months earlier. Outwardly, the dispute was settled when the Wigan directors lifted the suspension on Boston; inwardly it still tormented him.

Billy recalled: 'I felt terrible when that season opened. I wanted to do well but all my movements seemed to be paralysed, and I couldn't get my breath. It seemed as though I had lead weights in my legs and they wouldn't go properly. My confidence and morale touched rock bottom one day when I couldn't even keep up with Joe Egan in a practice run. I wanted to pack it all in but Joe wouldn't let me and drove me on.'

Joe Egan, recalling those dramatic training sessions behind closed doors at Central Park, said 'I knew how important it was for me and the Wigan club to get Boston back into shape. He was right out of condition, mainly from a psychological point of view. All his troubles were mental rather than physical ones and my first job was to convince him that he wasn't all washed up as he thought. I must admit there were some anxious moments in my early days as Wigan coach. I never had any worries about Boston's abilities as a player because that was beyond question. But I was extremely worried about his mental approach to the game. He badly wanted a confidence-booster to make him forget that suspension – which, in my opinion, was nothing short of a disgrace.'

Egan had literally to nurse Boston back to top physical and mental fitness and he spent hours on the Central Park pitch tuning up his dejected player with sprints between the corner flags. Long talks, in which Egan brought all his experience and understanding of other players' troubles to bear, brought Boston out of the cocoon of worry and depression into which all his confidence and great natural talent had temporarily retreated."

The *Wigan Examiner* weighed in with explanations for Billy's lack of form, suggesting that Joan's pregnancy was causing Billy anxiety and that his confidence was shot to pieces. It maintained that there was "a lot of misplaced criticism of Billy Boston" and that instead of criticising him the Wigan crowd should support him. Joe Egan realised that what Billy really needed was a morale booster on the pitch. It came against Widnes on 8 September in a very tame game, when the 40 scrums were described as "annoying and farcical". Wigan triumphed 30–5. Billy had a stormer and scored two typical tries, swatting off Tommy Sale for the first and for the second dashing between two defenders, brushing another off and swerving past the full-back – normal service was resumed. It was reported that Billy had chosen to play without shoulder pads against Widnes "to give him a little incentive to try and swerve past a man rather than bullock into him".

In the succeeding weeks Billy seemed like a new man. Against Barrow he took the ball following a scrum 70 yards out, scorched down the touch-line, beat off two tackles and then outpaced Frank Castle to the corner for a try, which had the Central Park crowd applauding him all the way back up the field. Four tries followed at Liverpool City and another two beauties against Hull at Central Park. For the second he received a pass from Ashcroft well inside his own half. According to the *Examiner*, he then "swerved round Whiteley, handed off Bowman, went round Hutton by sheer speed and then outpaced the persistent Bowman to score near the corner. What an ovation Boston received". On 29 September Billy failed to score in a 9–3 loss at Halifax, having received virtually no passes but he shone in defence, bottling up Freeman. That game was notable for the debut of giant prop John Barton, acquired from Leigh for £1,500. Barton did fit one of the age-old stereotypes of rugby league, when he was waylaid straight out of the pit cage by two Wigan directors coming off his night shift at 6.30am and persuaded to sign for Wigan rather than Warrington.

Billy must have realised his rehabilitation was complete when he turned out for Great Britain against the Rest of the League at Odsal on Wednesday, 3 October. The fixture was a virtual trial for the test team to face Australia in the coming months. Billy's club-mate Dave Bolton was also in the side, which won 26–23. Billy had a field day, sweeping in for four tries. His opposing winger, former All Black Peter Henderson was the only winger who failed to score. Brian Bevan went over for three tries for the Rest, while Mick Sullivan claimed one for Great Britain. If there had been something of an exhibition air about the Odsal game, there certainly was nothing of the sort when Wigan met Oldham at Central Park three days later. Oldham, who went on to win the Championship, were too good again for Wigan and had won the game by half-time when they led 17–5 before finishing 25–13 victors. There was, however, no stopping Billy, who scored all three of his side's tries, a remarkably rare feat in a defeated team. His first, following a wonderful combined movement after 15 minutes, brought him his 100th try for Wigan.

Saturday 13 October 1956 was a red-letter day for Billy. It was the start of his sublime wing-centre partnership with Eric Ashton. Wigan were playing at Leigh. Ashton had so far played all his first team rugby on the left wing, although many astute observers had long called for him to be played at centre. Now the two were paired together and Central Parkers had something special to rejoice in for the next dozen years, while opposition teams, coaches and fans had something extra to worry about. Both were exceptional footballers in their own right, but as a pair they added up to even more than the sum of their parts.

Down the years some people have said Ashton "made" Billy but that is nonsense, as Billy was a great star before the two combined. Others have said Billy "made" Ashton, which is equally silly, as wingers definitely do not "make" centres. What can safely be said is that neither made the other but that they were made for each other – probably in heaven. Anyway, at Hilton Park on that auspicious occasion it looked as if Wigan were heading for a 14–11 defeat with a minute remaining. Eric had scored one of Wigan's tries. Billy had the final word, however, and knocked down a Leigh pass, which John Barton swiftly picked up and returned the ball to Billy, who dashed 60 yards for a try, which levelled the score. Loose-forward Teddy Cheetham converted and Wigan scraped home 16–14.

Billy's next engagement was at Marseilles on Sunday, 21 October, where he appeared for a Rugby League XIII, which very closely resembled a test team, against France. The game, played before a crowd of 20,000, certainly had all the hallmarks of an Anglo-French test match. Jack Bentley summed it up in his *Daily Express* report: "The Entente was decidedly *Uncordiale* at the Stade Municipal... TEMPERS flared. FISTS flew. Rugby League stand-off Ray Price and French full-back André Audy were SENT OFF. Rugby League forwards Don Robinson and Mick Scott were CARRIED OFF. But the lion's tail was defiantly erect at the end for the British produced their best rugby of the game to snatch victory in the last 10 minutes." Billy was opposed by André Savonne and both scored a try. Billy's brought the Rugby League XIII back into the game after they had gone 10-0 down within 26 minutes and came courtesy of some great play from York loose-forward Edgar Dawson. It was, however, scrum-half Jeff Stevenson's wonderful 40 yard try in the 71st minute which won the match 18–17. Audy had kicked four goals for France before he was dismissed and the French tried to bring him back on late in the proceedings but he had to retire when the British lads objected strongly! It was just as well because France had a chance to win the game with a straight 45 yard penalty three minutes from time, which their stand-in kicker, loose-forward Jean Rouqueirol, failed to land. After the game Billy told the press, "You only had to go down and they came into you with fists and boots". He would experience more such incident-packed games in France over the next few years.

Returning to the domestic scene Billy scored Wigan's only try in defeat at Leeds, a game marked by a stunning performance from Lewis Jones. Wigan fans were, however, a little more interested in another Welshman, Rees Thomas, a balding scrum-half signed from Swinton. Thomas was to become a fulcrum in future years for Wigan. His debut was marked by his "rocket-like and accurate passes" although he was also cautioned and his name placed in referee Dickie Thomas's little black note-book. 'Flu kept Billy out of Wigan's defeat at top-of-the-table Barrow, their fourth in five games, as they languished in 18th place in the league. He was back on 10 November for the visit of Blackpool Borough, a victory for Wigan, but of which they made hard work. Billy practically beat Borough on his own with a little help from Eric Ashton. Four tries went into Billy's account. The *Wigan Examiner* was ecstatic about Billy: "Back to his brilliant best. Without Boston the match would have been like Guy Fawkes night without the fireworks."

The following Saturday Central Park played host to a much more prestigious match – the first Ashes test. Wigan's board had been rewarded for their drive to improve their ground accommodation, the capacity now being 48,000 with 17,000 under cover. Central Park had been given its first Ashes test in preference to Headingley, which had hosted tests against Australia in every series since 1921. Surprisingly in view of his outstanding form, Billy, Wigan's sole representative in the British side, had just scraped into the team on the casting vote of the chairman of the 13-man selection committee. There had been a proposal to switch Mick Sullivan to the right wing in place of Billy and bring St Helens' Frank Carlton in on the left wing.

Unfortunately, rain fell throughout the morning of the test reducing the crowd to 22,473. Central Park's greensward was transformed into a muddy morass. Australia were clearly second favourites, having already lost to Leeds, Whitehaven, Warrington and Oldham in their previous 11 tour fixtures. None of which mattered, of course, when it came to the nitty-gritty of an Ashes test. Australia scored first and last but in between were unable to cope with either the mud or the power and guile of their opponents. It was Billy who gained most of the headlines. He had a part in Britain's first try on 19 minutes, which went to left centre Alan Davies and enabled Britain to level at 3–3. Australia went 5–3 up but on 29 minutes Jack Grundy scored after chasing a short kick through by Mick Sullivan and Britain led 6–5. Five minutes before half-time Davies slashed through and, according to George M Thompson in *Yorkshire Sports:* "There was a quick pass to Jackson, then another to Boston. Tyquin had shot back to check the winger, but Boston slipped him, stumbled, and scrambled over the line." Nine minutes into the second half Billy sealed the victory. There seemed little danger when, as the *Rugby Leaguer* reported: "Boston received the ball on the touch-line about the '25' line and weaved in and out of the Australian players to touch down in the centre [of the posts]. Even the hard-boiled press box occupants were cheering at such a magnificent effort." Jim Sullivan, writing in the *News of the World,* joined in the praise: "When Billy Boston raced clean through [the Australian] defence... they were simply dumbfounded. His brilliant effort was the turning point of the match." Full-back Frank Mortimer converted, then landed a penalty and finally improved a try by Mick Sullivan. Britain had well deserved their 21–10 victory.

Wigan got back to winning ways on 24 November with a 17–7 win against Swinton, when Billy's erstwhile centre partner Jack Broome played his last game for Wigan – on the left wing – before being transferred to Widnes. However, Billy's next three Saturdays would all be spent in further tussles with the 1956 Kangaroos.

On 1 December the second test took place at Odsal Stadium, where 23,364 braved another appalling afternoon and the pitch was even deeper in mud than Central Park had been. Britain made just one change, bringing in Derek Turner for his test debut at loose-forward. Australia, shocked by their comprehensive loss at Wigan, made six changes. Britain could have had the game won by half-time, but squandered the chances that came their way. At the break it was 7–7 and around the hour 9–9. At that point the Australian forwards took complete control and tries by props Brian Davies and Roy Bull and a sizzling solo effort by half-back Bobby Banks took Australia to a 22–9 victory. Billy and fellow wing Mick Sullivan hardly got any chance to run.

Billy did not fare any better the following week. The Australians pulverised Wigan 32–4 in a really rough match in which there were "umpteen fights", according to the *Wigan Examiner*. Penalties went Wigan's way, 8–6 in the first half and 7–0 in the second, while the Kangaroos took the scrums 20–17. After half an hour the teams were locked at 4–4, Eric Ashton landing two penalties for Wigan. Thereafter the Australians ran riot. The *Examiner* railed that the referee, Mr Harrison of Horbury, cautioned Aussie skipper Ken Kearney twice and gave Australia at least 10 points. It complained: "Time and again... Billy Boston was obstructed or tackled before he got the ball. Time and again he was pulled back by his jersey as he was running into position to take a pass." It summarised the game thus: "A war cry and a dance, a number of fights, poor refereeing, pathetically weak passing, tries which were not tries and flashes of brilliant football."

The Ashes decider was at Swinton on 15 December. Britain brought in Glyn Moses of St Helens at full-back, Oldham's Syd Little at prop and Hunslet's Geoff Gunney in the second-row, replacing Frank Mortimer, Brian Shaw and Don Robinson. The threequarter line – Billy, Phil Jackson, Alan Davies and Mick Sullivan, plus the half-backs Ray Price and Jeff Stevenson – remained unchanged throughout the series. Australia lacked key forwards Norm Provan, Don Furner and Brian Davies. Britain's main concern was the lack of a recognised goalkicker, which might prove fatal in a close encounter. Under their inspirational skipper Alan Prescott, the side was reported to be so confident that they would score too many tries to worry about goalkicking. That confidence proved to be well founded because Britain scored five tries to none and could have doubled that figure with a bit of luck. A dreadfully disappointing crowd of only 17,529 turned up, but saw a good British performance on another greasy pitch. Australia were unlucky when Billy's opposite number, Des McGovern, dislocated his shoulder in a tackle by Moses going for the corner in the first few minutes. That was counter-balanced when Billy's centre Phil Jackson was concussed and spent most of the game on the wing with Mick Sullivan taking his place.

Britain did not take the lead until the 26th minute when Little scored a try, converted by Davies. By half-time they led 8–0 with a further try from Derek Turner. Gunney claimed the game-breaking try early in the second half, to which Davies added his second conversion, and at 13–0 Britain had effectively recovered the Ashes lost in 1954. Sullivan and Billy finished off the scoring at 19–0 with unconverted tries.

Billy's try in that Ashes decider was the first of 21 he scored in 13 games. Between 15 December 1956 and 9 March 1957 in 10 appearances for Wigan and three tests he never failed to score at least one try – a pretty staggering performance for a man who a few months earlier was on the verge of giving up the game. In this period Billy displayed some of the best form of his career. One of his most memorable tries was scored against Workington Town on 29 December in a 52–5 home win. It came in the last minute and completed yet another hat-trick. Tom Groves, in the *Wigan Examiner,* described it as "the try which has set all Wigan rugby league fans talking". Town scrum-half Sol Roper kicked off after Rees Thomas had scored a Wigan try. "Billy caught the ball on his '25' and set off. A group of Town players were ready for him but he swerved right through them by virtue of his amazing speed. He then cut slightly infield to beat two other opponents and cut back towards the corner as full-back Vickers came hurtling across to try and stop him. For a few seconds it looked as if Vickers would be successful but Boston pulled out a little extra speed from somewhere and Vickers missed him by inches. After this Boston had a clear run to the line – and what an ovation he received!" A prominent national sports writer told Tom Groves that it was the best try he had seen in his 35-year career. Tom had not been watching as long as that "but it was the best and most thrilling run it has been my good fortune ever to see. As soon as the final whistle blew a number of Workington players ran over to shake Boston's hand. A fine tribute!"

The New Year opened with a 20,000 attendance for the local derby with Warrington and a stunning 37–2 victory for Wigan. Eric Ashton scored 13 points and Bobby Chisnall scored a hat-trick on the left wing. Billy scored a try on 30 minutes when he "whizzed between two opponents". The main talking point, however, occurred on the hour, when Wigan skipper Ernie Ashcroft was sent off by Dickie Thomas after an altercation with Brian Bevan, whom he appeared to strike. Bev was roundly booed as Ashcroft walked off, dismissed for the first and only time in a career that had begun in 1942.

Four days later at Whitehaven conditions were atrocious – heavy rain, high winds and a third of the pitch inches deep in oozy mud. Unsurprisingly, there was no score in the first half. Billy broke the deadlock in the 56th minute after Eric Ashton broke through a clutch of players, veered towards touch and threw an inside pass to Billy, who streaked to the posts – the move which was to become the pair's trademark. Ashton converted and Billy killed the game stone dead 12 minutes later when Whitehaven dropped the ball at a scrum and he dribbled the ball through 40 yards of mud to score in the corner. A superb run brought a final try to Norman Cherrington and Wigan had a hard-earned 11–0 victory. As useful as Billy's tries had been, two of his tackles on Whitehaven's tough winger Bill Smith were also match-savers, as Billy crossed to the opposite wing to halt him in his tracks.

At that stage in the season Billy had scored 35 ties and shared the top of the try-scoring chart with Barrow's veteran winger Jim Lewthwaite, Johnny Freeman being third with 28.

Billy was selected for Great Britain against France at Headingley on 26 January. This was the first time that France had been accorded full test match status for games against Great Britain, the European Championship now having been officially abandoned. Moreover, there was to be a full-blown three test series and performances in those fixtures would go a long way to determining who would win places in the Great Britain squad for the second World Cup tournament in Australia in the summer. Dave Bolton was selected for his first test cap and the only other change from the sides which had won the Ashes was the reintroduction of Lewis Jones at left-centre in place of Alan Davies. For a change the playing pitch was in perfect condition and a crowd of 20,221 was treated to a super show from Great Britain. The Lions won 45–12 but the crowd stayed, according to the *Daily Mail's* Derek Marshall, "to revel in the artistry of Lewis Jones, to cheer the magnificent duel between Billy Boston and André Savonne, and to rise as one man to the spectacular scoring run of Alan Prescott". Billy got a late try but Marshall noted, "The Wigan winger had an opponent worthy of him, and had to bring off some spectacular tackles to finish with honours even."

Lewis Jones, with 21 points from nine goals and a spectacular try, broke the Great Britain points-in-a-match record. However, the highlight was skipper Alan Prescott's try on the hour. The 16 stone open-side prop suddenly burst clear 65 yards out and outran all pursuers for an amazing try, Savonne's last-ditch tackle being a yard too late.

Wigan certainly had no problems with their right wing strength, but the left wing had been a source of weakness and a raft of players had been tried there since Eric Ashton's move inside to partner Billy. Jack Broome, Bobby Chisnall, Dave Bolton and Norman Cherrington had played at number five and there appeared a hint of desperation when Wigan turned to fielding a raw rugby union recruit, Bob Turnock, there on 19 January at Rochdale. The following week against Liverpool City they were even more desperate and, with Billy on test duty, Toni Romano, an Italian rugby union forward, was given a trial on the left wing. Romano was an alias, to protect his identity and amateur status, and he never played another first team game for Wigan. The club finally solved their dilemma by signing Oldham's Terry O'Grady, Billy's colleague on the 1954 Lions tour, just before the Challenge Cup signings deadline.

O'Grady made his debut on 2 February in a 32–3 home rout of Whitehaven and bagged three tries, the first an obstruction try, the second a beauty. Billy was not to be outshone, however, and scored three himself, two on a plate from Ashton and the other a wonderful Boston special.

Wigan's most important match of the season followed on 9 February – a first round Challenge Cup tie at Leeds. It was the tie of the round and unquestionably one of the ties of the decade. The gates were closed 20 minutes before kick-off with almost 39,000 fans jammed into Headingley and hundreds of Wiganers locked out. Five trains and over 100 coaches had journeyed from Wigan and so great was the crush at one corner of the ground that the police allowed "women, children and the aged" to come on to the pitch-side. The prelude to the match saw Leeds emerge first, surreally followed by about 1,000 fans, who surged down the corner ramp to spread out around the perimeter. The Wigan team followed the multitude.

From beginning to end the game was a heart-stopper. Leeds grabbed the lead after about 10 minutes when Wigan passing broke down near their own '25' and Lewis Jones quickly toed the ball forward before dribbling 25 yards to score. His conversion was good. A couple of minutes later Billy brought the house down. He was given the ball on the blind-side from a scrum and streaked 75 yards down the touchline, chased by his old Signals team-mate Jimmy Dunn, Jeff Stevenson and Del Hodgkinson. He crossed at the corner and had the presence of mind to run infield 20 yards, but Ashton's conversion failed. It did not seem to matter too much because in the 37th minute he gave Wigan the lead with an even more spectacular try. Again the ball reached him following a scrum. Ashton delivered the pass and Billy smashed Dunn out of the way, wriggled out of Lendill's tackle and went like a bullet for the corner "to a reception from friend and foe alike that must have been heard at Elland Road", according to the *Rugby Leaguer*.

A year later Lewis Jones recalled the score in his autobiography: "Billy must have covered fully 90 yards *en route* and, taking into account the back-to-the-wall circumstances in which it was scored, his try will rank with the greatest I've seen on any rugger ground – league or union."

By that point Wigan had been reduced to 12 men, Dave Bolton having broken his fibula, but they continued to play uninhibitedly. Six minutes into the second half Jones dropped a goal and seven minutes later Hodgkinson scored a try to give Leeds a 10–6 lead. Wigan were not finished, however. Audaciously dispensing of the idea of playing a full-back, they regained the lead when Ashton forced his way over for a 62nd minute try, converted by Don Platt. Three minutes later Leeds snatched the initiative back when skipper Keith McLellan scored a marvellous solo try, taking advantage of an overlap, dummying his way past Platt and O'Grady and turning inside for the winning points. There was a last dramatic twist in the 79th minute when Wigan were awarded a comparatively easy penalty. The *Wigan Examiner* reported, "You could have heard a pin drop", as Ashton booted the ball goalwards. At first it seemed a good kick, but then swerved and passed a foot outside the post. A classic encounter thus went 13–11 to Leeds, who proceeded to lift the Cup, but Wigan were out of yet another competition in the first round.

There was still the Championship to play for, however. Prior to the loss at Headingley, Wigan had won 12 consecutive league fixtures and dragged themselves up to sixth in the table. Losing Dave Bolton for the rest of the season was not going to help their chances of finishing in the top four, but an alarmingly inept 14–5 defeat away to lowly Bradford Northern on 16 February cast immediate doubt on their prospects for success. Billy scored their only try in the ninth minute and was conspicuous for heroics in defence.

Some Bradford fans took exception to his crash tackles as Northern worked some clever overlaps, moving a reader, calling himself 'Fair Play', to write to the *Rugby Leaguer:* "On Saturday, Boston made several hefty but legitimate tackles which did not meet with the approval of the Bradford spectators. As the players were passing through the crowd en route to the dressing room some rather personal and crude remarks were spoken to Boston, who immediately took certain action against the culprit thus causing the police to intervene. This sort of occurrence would not be possible if a dressing room were made in a more suitable position." The Odsal dressing rooms were a long, mountainous hike from the pitch in those days and players had to run the gauntlet of a crowd which could be adulatory or hostile in equal measure.

Billy had by 1957 developed a devastating ability to crash tackle opposing centres who were in danger of creating overlaps for their wing partners. Lots of top class wingers were adept at this smothering manoeuvre apart from Billy. Of course, such tackles had to be performed at exactly the right moment, just as the centre received the ball and before he could release it. However, no other winger met the centre with such velocity and power as Billy could generate. Billy's victims were often dazed and/or winded in such collisions and the supporters of the suffering player were often outraged when their man struggled to get up again. The following Saturday Ray Oddy, in the Bradford weekly paper, *Yorkshire Sports*, wrote: "The boos and jeers from a certain section of the crowd were unjustified against a player who ranks as the most outstanding personality in the game today. No, let's have fair play! Boston was simply applying what ex-Northern favourite Eric Batten used to practice – much to the pleasure of Odsal fans. Batten describes the tackle – so perfectly exploited by Boston – as the 'most brilliant' in the game, and is full of praise for any player who adopts it – whether he be friend or foe. The Northern players, themselves, said after the game, 'What's Boston there for? He was doing quite right'. Seemingly, they can take it – but not a certain section of the crowd."

On Sunday 3 March Billy was in Toulouse for the second test against France. Astonishingly, Great Britain recovered from a 17–2 deficit to lead 19–17 with five minutes remaining. According to the *Daily Express's* Jack Bentley: "Billy Boston, for once, evaded Gilbert Alberti (who climbed on the coloured boy's back whenever the ball looked like moving to the British right) and stormed 45 yards for a 61st minute try". Ten minutes later Lewis Jones intercepted 75 yards out and raced over for the try that gave Britain the lead, converting it himself and bringing his tally for the match to 13 points. In the 75th minute

Billy's side were robbed by, as Bentley complained, "a flagrant piece of biased refereeing which filched victory from Great Britain." A scrum went down 35 yards from the British posts. Bentley objected: "It was the old story... the one that seems to have a bearing on almost every English game in France... The inevitable penalty had to come. 'Put the ball into the French feet', said British skipper Alan Prescott. Tiny scrum-half Jeff Stevenson obliged. 'Don't strike', said Prescott to hooker Tommy Harris – and the little Welshman held off. But 32-year-old French accountant Jean Banneau – refereeing a British international for the first time – had his answer. 'Loose arm', he indicated to Harris. The French hooker was on the ground with the ball behind him, but that made no difference." Gilbert Benausse, the great French stand-off, landed the game-saving penalty. France had won the penalty count 29–11 and the scrums 23–12. It was no wonder that five selectors present recommended that the British boys should be awarded winning pay of £14. Sad to say, the recommendation was rejected by the RFL.

Wigan got back on the winning path with a fine 20–11 victory at St Helens on 9 March after racing to a 17–4 half-time lead. In the 32nd minute Billy scored an unusual try after a Saints player knocked on and fly-hacked the ball straight into his stomach. Billy held on and promptly drove over the line with two defenders wrapped round his legs. It was a rough game with Norman Cherrington being sent off just after the interval and the *Wigan Examiner* complained that Saints were "very vigorous" and that "Karalius, Rhodes and Dickinson could all have been sent off".

A good 20–10 win followed at Huddersfield. The *Examiner* reported: "Boston and Sullivan were in opposition and we saw a sporting and interesting tussle between these two. Neither scored, but on at least three occasions, Sullivan was sent racing away, only to be caught by Boston." Three days later, in dreadful conditions, Billy scored three tries in a smashing 28–7 success at Swinton, his second being his 50th of the season.

Over 22,000 poured into Central Park for Wigan's first home game for seven weeks when Halifax visited on 23 March. Wigan won well enough – 25–9 – to maintain their assault on the top four. However, for the first time in his career Billy had the experience of seeing his opposing winger claim a hat-trick. That opponent was his old friend Johnny Freeman and he was only on the field for about an hour. The *Wigan Examiner* noted incredulously, "Believe it or not that veteran loose-forward, Ken Traill, kept swinging the ball to his left, playing time and again on Boston's wing. You don't often get a team with sufficient temerity to do that. It wasn't Boston who was at fault, but his inside colleagues. On numerous occasions he was left to face two or three men." Freeman scored his third try in the 55th minute, but Billy tackled him hard at the corner in doing so and Freeman went off with a damaged shoulder, returning to the fray later. Billy got some revenge in the 64th minute with a try. The *Examiner* remarked: "Freeman was back on the field but when Boston went hurtling for the corner and left three players lying on the ground, one of them was Freeman. There is nothing funny about trying to stop Boston once he is in his stride. Freeman was helped off the field and did not return."

The following Saturday Wigan faced a crunch match at league leaders Oldham, where the police closed the gates well before kick-off time. Wigan could have won but threw the game away in going down 14–6 to their 12th consecutive loss to the Roughyeds. Ashton and Boston scored the Wigan tries, but four goals from Oldham full-back Bernard Ganley proved the deciding factor. Two days later, on April Fools' Day, Billy's spirits were lifted when he and Eric Ashton were among the 18 players selected for the 1957 Great Britain World Cup squad, while on 3 April he bagged a couple of tries against Bradford Northern on his 100th appearance for Wigan.

A potentially disastrous 13–8 home defeat by Huddersfield saw Billy starved of possession until it was too late. However, Wigan won 26–17 at Widnes in a fierce encounter on 13 April to keep hopes of a top four finish alive. It was reported: "Personality of the game was Wigan wingman Billy Boston. Besieged by autograph hunters after the game, he had to have a police escort to reach the dressing room. Boston collected two brilliant tries after weaving his way through a barrier of opponents, and would have made it three had he played to the whistle. Midway through the second half he broke clear, but halted, thinking there had been an infringement, and was tackled before he realised that the referee was signalling play to continue."

Three days previously Billy had figured in Great Britain's 29–14 success against France in the third test at St Helens. It had been a pretty routine victory with the French scoring their two tries in the last 10 minutes. Billy was rarely in attacking mode and Lewis Jones with seven goals and a try, and Mick Sullivan with two tries, took the scoring honours. More importantly, no injuries were sustained by any of the team, some of whom were suffering the after-effects of inoculations for the World Cup trip.

Wigan beat Leigh 26–9 in a wonderfully open game before embarking on their Easter programme, which would determine whether they gained a place in the Championship play-offs. Good Friday drew a crowd of almost 35,000 for the visit of St Helens and Billy sealed Wigan's 19–11 win with a grand converted try in the 70th minute. The victory left Wigan needing to win at Warrington the following day and at Salford on Easter Monday. Anything less meant they would not qualify. They were soon disabused of their aspirations at Wilderspool where the Wigan supporters were left speechless after a 40–7 hiding. Billy only had the ball three times in the first half and scored his side's only try on the third occasion – his 60th try of the season and 50th for Wigan. He missed the 15–10 defeat at Salford because of blistered feet.

Wigan thus finished sixth in the final table, trailing behind Oldham, Hull, Barrow, Leeds and St Helens. Billy's 60 tries had left him at the top of the leading try-scorers' list, well ahead of Jim Lewthwaite with 51, Johnny Freeman on 48 and Oldham's John Etty on 43. He had also won the *Manchester Evening Chronicle's* Player-of-the-Year award, a trophy won in its first two years by Brian Bevan. He had polled 25,545 votes, the runner-up being his Great Britain captain Alan Prescott with 25,380.

At least the early end to Wigan's season meant that Billy was well rested for the World Cup. He was included in the following squad: Eric Ashton (Wigan), Billy Boston (Wigan), Alan Davies (Oldham), Jack Grundy (Barrow), Geoff Gunney (Hunslet), Tommy Harris (Hull), Phil Jackson (Barrow), Lewis Jones (Leeds), Syd Little (Oldham), Tom McKinney (St Helens), Glyn Moses (St Helens), Alan Prescott (St Helens) captain, Ray Price (Warrington), Austin Rhodes (St Helens), Jeff Stevenson (Leeds), Mick Sullivan (Huddersfield), Derek Turner (Oldham) and Johnny Whiteley (Hull). Hector Rawson of Hunslet and Bill Fallowfield, the RFL secretary, were appointed tour managers. Fallowfield also helped to coach the side.

The squad contained only a couple of surprise selections in the uncapped Eric Ashton and utility back Austin Rhodes. The rest were test-hardened men. Great Britain were favourites to retain the trophy. Indeed many pundits had declared that the 1956–57 British test team was the best the country had produced – a rare accolade and one that is seldom accorded to contemporary teams.

However, this squad of only 18 players faced an itinerary of nine games between 15 June and 27 July, while a few of the players would also be required to play in a couple of other exhibition games. It was not, on closer inspection, anything resembling a holiday. The scope for complications was limitless. Moreover the trip did not just embrace Australia. The party, along with the French squad, was also to visit New Zealand and, most contentiously, South Africa. It might have been worse because at one stage the French had been pressing for a game in Madagascar en route to Australia. French teams were established there, mainly in military centres, and the French Rugby League had aspirations of promoting the game there.

South Africa had adopted apartheid after the National Party election victory in 1948, consolidating into law the racist regime that had beset the country since the nineteenth century. This presented a big problem for Billy. It was a problem that many thought should not even have arisen because they believed that the RFL should not be aiding and abetting such a regime, even if they were trying merely to promote the game in South Africa. To many it beggared belief that the RFL should contemplate going to a country where one of their players would have to live in separate quarters to his team-mates and not be allowed to play in any of the three exhibition games to be staged against the French. Billy had already decided that he would not be going to South Africa.

Some critics were well ahead of the RFL in their prognostications. For example, the editor of the *Rugby Leaguer* wrote on 15 March, 1957: "Make no mistake about it – any British RL team which plays in South Africa will NOT include some of our very finest players such as Boston and Freeman. In other words, our RL authorities would have to truckle to the obscene APARTHEID laws which the South African government applies to all forms of social life, including sport… If we tamely submit to an extension of the colour-bar to our own grand lads, then we are not fit to call ourselves sportsmen". Hardly surprisingly, there was no official response from the RFL, who proceeded as planned.

The British team were to be paid £100 per man for the tour, although some of the RL Council thought the fee should be higher. They were to receive £25 at the start of the trip, £20 in Australia, £5 in New Zealand and the £50 balance on returning to England. There was no mention of any payment for the South African expedition. It was a better deal than the 1954 World Cup squad received, but not much better.

The team left London for Perth on 1 June and arrived in Western Australia on 4 June. The first fixture, a warm-up game on 9 June saw the British crush Western Australia 66–5. Billy ran over for four tries but was upstaged by Mick Sullivan on the left wing, who bagged seven. The game was extremely costly to the Britons, however, as stand-off Ray Price suffered a severe ankle injury, which prevented him from playing again on tour.

Britain moved on to Sydney for the first World Cup match against France on Saturday, 15 June, arriving there in the middle of a drought. The Sydney Cricket Ground pitch was dangerously hard and so 6,000 gallons of water were poured on to it the day before the match took place. Sod's Law prevailed and it rained all Friday night and for much of the following morning turning the pitch into a mud heap. It did not really worry Great Britain though. A crowd of 50,077 got full value for their money from an entertaining match and some of Britain's play in treacherous conditions was almost unbelievably good. France were lucky to get away with only a 23–5 defeat. Mick Sullivan scored two tries and Lewis Jones landed four goals, with additional tries from Jeff Stevenson, Phil Jackson and Billy, who took his try with aplomb after taking a Mick Sullivan kick-through in his stride.

However, the victory again came at a cost. Phil Jackson and Geoff Gunney both picked up injuries and were forced to sit out the next, crucial, game against Australia at the SCG just two days later. Jackson's misfortune allowed Eric Ashton to make his test debut as partner to Billy, the first of a dozen tests the pair would play together over the next six years. Australia won 31–6 before a satisfied audience of 57,955 and everything went wrong

The Great Britain 1957 World Cup squad. Back: Harris, Sullivan, Davies, G. Moses, Rhodes, Price; middle: Turner, Little, Grundy, Gunney, Ashton, Whiteley, Boston; front: McKinney, Jackson, Fallowfield, Prescott, Rawson, Stevenson, Jones.

for Great Britain. Alan Davies was taken to hospital after 15 minutes with a suspected broken leg and Britain did well to restrict their opponents to a 10–6 half-time lead, all their points coming from the boot of Jones. Billy suffered a knee ligament injury midway through the second half and was reduced to a shuffling passenger, although he continued to tackle heroically and before 80 minutes elapsed Britain were reduced to 10 fit men, when Tommy Harris sustained a badly bruised arm. Some critics poured scorn on the British pack, but Phil King wrote in *The People:* "Don't believe those stories that the Great Britain boys let you down. After the match our five-man pack looked like the front end of a tram smash. Alan Prescott had a beautiful shiner. Tommy Harris, who had an ugly facial bruise, had his arm in a sling. Syd Little's nose was broken and his eyebrow badly swollen. Jack Grundy had a stiff arm and a loosened tooth and Derek Turner's nose was lacking two inches of skin. Still they didn't run away!"

Fortunately, Alan Davies' leg was not broken, but his injury was bad enough to end his tour, as was Billy's. The two were flown home early. So Billy's intention not to go to South Africa became somewhat academic and undoubtedly spared the RFL considerable political flak. Britain went on to lose 29–21 to New Zealand in Sydney, while Australia took the World Cup with three wins from three games.

# 1956–57

Wigan finished 6th in the League: P38, W26, L12, For 750, Against 417
Boston scored 50 tries for Wigan, plus 10 in representative rugby league

| Date | Opponent | Score | Boston | Crowd | |
|------|----------|-------|--------|-------|---|
| 18 August | Hull | 8–16 | | 11,511 | |
| 25 August | **Leeds** | 22–8 | 2T | 18,404 | |
| 27 August | Workington T | 24–0 | | 4,516 | |
| 1 September | **Oldham** | 16–18 | | 28,511 | LC1 |
| 8 September | **Widnes** | 30–5 | 2T | 12,545 | |
| 10 September | **Barrow** | 15–26 | 1T | 19,713 | |
| 15 September | Liverpool City | 44–14 | 4T | 1,842 | |
| 22 September | **Hull** | 30–17 | 2T | 19,886 | |
| 29 September | Halifax | 3–9 | | 14,809 | |
| 6 October | **Oldham** | 13–25 | 3T | 27,990 | |
| 13 October | Leigh | 17–11 | 1T | 15,642 | |
| 27 October | Leeds | 7–13 | 1T | 19,654 | |
| 3 November | Barrow | 12–15 | dnp | 9,899 | |
| 10 November | **Blackpool B** | 22–8 | 4T | 10,037 | |
| 24 November | **Swinton** | 17–7 | | 13,218 | |
| 1 December | **Featherstone R** | 19–4 | dnp | 11,632 | |
| 8 December | **Australia** | 4–32 | | 15,854 | Tour |
| 15 December | Blackpool B | 18–9 | dnp | 713 | |
| 25 December | **Salford** | 13–10 | 1T | 6,692 | |
| 29 December | **Workington T** | 52–5 | 3T | 12,390 | |
| 1 January | **Warrington** | 37–2 | 1T | 20,284 | |
| 5 January | Whitehaven | 11–0 | 2T | 3,215 | |
| 12 January | **Rochdale H** | 18–5 | 2T | 13,550 | |
| 19 January | Rochdale H | 19–11 | 2T | 5,654 | |
| 26 January | **Liverpool City** | 20–4 | dnp | 11,289 | |
| 2 February | **Whitehaven** | 32–3 | 3T | 18,316 | |
| 9 February | Leeds | 11–13 | 2T | 38,914 | Cup 1 |
| 16 February | Bradford N | 5–14 | 1T | 5,832 | |
| 2 March | Featherstone R | 9–15 | dnp | 6,500 | |
| 9 March | St Helens | 20–11 | 1T | 18,854 | |
| 16 March | Huddersfield | 20–10 | | 10,708 | |
| 20 March | Swinton | 28–7 | 3T | 6,000 | |
| 23 March | **Halifax** | 25–9 | 1T | 22,303 | |
| 30 March | Oldham | 6–14 | 1T | 19,176 | |
| 3 April | **Bradford N** | 38–5 | 2T | 12,107 | |
| 6 April | **Huddersfield** | 8–13 | | 18,221 | |
| 13 April | Widnes | 26–17 | 2T | 5,732 | |
| 15 April | **Leigh** | 26–9 | 1T | 15,852 | |
| 19 April | **St Helens** | 19–11 | 1T | 34,641 | |
| 20 April | Warrington | 7–40 | 1T | 15,700 | |
| 22 April | Salford | 10–15 | dnp | 8,412 | |

## Boston's representative matches:

| Date | For | Opponent | Score | Boston | Venue |
|------|-----|----------|-------|--------|-------|
| 3 October | Great Britain | Rest of League | 26–23 | 4T | Odsal |
| 21 October | RL XIII | France | 18–17 | 1T | Marseilles |
| 17 November | Great Britain | Australia | 21–10 | 2T | Wigan |
| 1 December | Great Britain | Australia | 9–22 | | Odsal |
| 15 December | Great Britain | Australia | 19–0 | 1T | Swinton |
| 26 January | Great Britain | France | 45–12 | 1T | Leeds |
| 3 March | Great Britain | France | 19–19 | 1T | Toulouse |
| 10 April | Great Britain | France | 29–14 | | St Helens |

**World Cup tour**

| 9 June | Great Britain | W. Australia | 66– 5 | 4T | Perth |
|--------|---------------|--------------|-------|-----|--------|
| 15 June | Great Britain | France | 23–5 | 1T | Sydney |
| 17 June | Great Britain | Australia | 6–31 | | Sydney |

Billy celebrates after scoring a try against France at the Sydney Cricket Ground.
Great Britain won 23–5 in front of a crowd of 50,007.
From left: Jeff Stevenson, Mick Sullivan, Billy Boston, Geoff Gunney.

# 8. 1957-58 Challenge Cup winners

Billy's early return from the World Cup at least brought some relief from his anxiety about Joan, who was expecting their second child in September. It also allowed him to play some cricket with Highfield once his injury had settled down. By the close of the season he had finished second to Orrell RT's J. Bradshaw in the bowling averages, having taken 19 wickets for 101 runs at an average of 5.32.

Eric Ashton arrived home with the World Cup squad on 31 July and forthrightly told the *Wigan Examiner*, "Rugby League will never go in South Africa". The South African public had been unimpressed by the three games played between the British and French World Cup squads, which resulted in victories for the Britons 61–41, 32–11 and 69–11. The exhibition matches, particularly the first, bore little resemblance to real rugby league. Bill Fallowfield was more diplomatic and said, "We would certainly go again if we were invited". Billy got a pleasant surprise when he and the rest of the World Cup squad were awarded a £50 bonus from RFL's £8,500 profit on the tournament. All told, the players received £170 for the tour, including £20 each from the organisers of the South African games.

Wigan were, as usual, hoping to win trophies. However, this time there was genuine anticipation that the team would deliver. League crowds at Central Park in 1956–57 had grossed 319,070 at an average of 16,793, bringing receipts of £30,565 – £9,000 up on the previous campaign. On the back of finances like that it was certainly time that the team did deliver. Don Platt was appointed captain and Wigan began the season as if they might sweep the honours board. They won the Wardonia Cup on 10 August, beating Warrington 15–14 before a crowd of 15,209. Billy scored the first try on 13 minutes sweeping past the Wire defence after a searing break by Dave Bolton. Brian Bevan scored two late tries for Warrington, although by then it was much too late to matter. A notable debutant in the Wigan ranks was local teenager Roy Evans, who played in the second-row, but was destined to become a test loose-forward.

August provided five fixtures within a fortnight and Wigan won the lot. Billy ran in a hat-trick at Swinton in the opening league match and caused another pitch invasion at Widnes. The police had already issued a warning about keeping off the field. However, hundreds of boys ignored it when the final whistle blew, their main focus being to get Billy's autograph. He was a long time getting off the pitch, but earlier on it taken him very little time to whip past three or four Chemics in a dazzling 55-yard dash for his try. On 31 August Swinton offered more resistance in the first round Lancashire Cup-tie at Station Road than in the opening league match, but Wigan progressed to the next round with an 18–10 win.

Wigan's bubble burst at Wakefield where Trinity beat them 23–16. Billy raced in at the corner in the 65th minute from an Eric Ashton break to make the score 18–16. However, his conversion failed and a 74th minute try by Les Chamberlain, converted by Neil Fox, won the match. Billy only got two chances to run and the *Wigan Examiner* lamented that he was obviously yards faster than any opposition player, "yet he was left admiring the scenery". Four days later Wigan went to Leigh for the second round of the Lancashire Cup, which was a typically hard tie, played in very heavy rain. There were 45 scrums and 26 penalties, but no one left early. In the third minute Platt and Ashton got Billy away and with speed and swerve he zipped past three men in a 25-yard run for the opening try of a 12–2 win. One tackle on Billy by Fred Hewitt, Leigh's full-back, was fantastic. Just before half-time Billy got away at a great pace and Hewitt, a small, stocky man, flew into him at such a velocity that the Wigan players were later heard debating why neither player was injured as the collision had been truly shattering. The *Examiner* noted, "The crowd roared its approval".

On 14 September almost 21,000 fans went to Central Park and witnessed an amazing game against Leeds. The *Examiner* described it as "a nerve-tingling and palpitating display of fast, clean and honest-to-goodness rugby against adversity". It began dramatically when Lewis Jones ran clear and was faced by full-back Don Platt, who was so baffled by Jones's movements that he almost did the splits. Jones tripped over Platt's right leg, but scored a try, which he converted. A few minutes later he kicked a penalty and Leeds led 7–0. The unfortunate Platt was stretchered off after the try was scored, his leg badly broken. It was the end of his season. Wigan had to re-jig their backs, moving Bolton to full-back, second-rower Roy Abram to right wing and Billy to stand-off. The effect was amazing. *The Examiner* remarked: "Leeds had their hands full watching the middle of the field. Every time Boston got the ball it was 'hey, lads, hey!' He was tackling ferociously and Leeds could not afford to give him much room."

With Billy bedazzling Leeds, the 12-man Wigan side edged 15–12 ahead and in the 70th minute Billy settled the issue. He put on a one-man demolition act in the middle beating man after man before two tacklers finally brought him down, but not before his right hand had rocketed a pass to Ashcroft, "who went over amid deafening applause". Ashton kicked a magnificent conversion and "the crowd nearly went hysterical". Although Leeds pulled back five points two minutes from time, Wigan held out for a 20–18 triumph in one of the bravest exhibitions at Central Park for years.

Billy's performance at stand-off was so stunning that Wigan kept him there, moving Dave Bolton to scrum-half and bringing the veteran Jack Cunliffe into the full-back role in place of the unfortunate Platt. The captaincy was given to Eric Ashton, still only 22 years old and destined to lead Wigan for almost the rest of his career. The changes galvanised Wigan into a side that won six games in a row and became the talk of the league. Billy and Dave Bolton formed a half-back partnership which terrorised opponents to such an extent that in four consecutive games against Barrow, Rochdale, Liverpool and Hull the pair aggregated 20 tries, with Billy claiming a dozen. There was simply no stopping them and Wigan piled up 195 points in those four victories.

The second of those wins was in the semi-final of the Lancashire Cup at Rochdale, where the Hornets, despite having Asian 'flu in their camp, were fully expected to give Wigan a hard game. Incredibly, Wigan won 52–0, an unheard of result for a semi-final. Tom Groves wrote: "The trio of Bolton, Boston and Ashton must, without doubt, be the fastest and most intelligent combination in the Rugby League. I don't know which of these three Rochdale feared most." Although Billy was wearing the number six jersey one of his three tries was scored from the right wing and one from the left wing – he was all over the place. A *Rugby League Gazette* journalist was highly impressed: "One man who did more than any Wiganer to take the sting out of the Hornets was Billy Boston. Talk about atom bombs, red moons and earth covering rockets – well, Billy was not so devastating, but when he gets the ball – wham!! He got three tries and could have had one or two more, but Billy believes in team-work and the team believe in him. When Billy scores practically the whole team jump at him, and there is no more popular fellow in Wigan rugby today than Billy-oh. That looks as if it will be his name from now on for when he gets the ball the Wigan crowd yell Billy-oh! Wigan have had many stand-off halves, and good ones at that, but the switching of Boston to the No. 6 role has rejuvenated the side and also caused a lot of change in the play. The whole idea of open play has changed and Wigan are going to cause quite a lot of worry to honours rivals this season."

Wigan's least impressive performance in this spell was their 39–11 romp at Knotty Ash, when Billy only scored twice. Tom Groves remarked, "Dave Bolton is "probably the greatest opportunist in the game" but pondered, "I have yet to be convinced that Boston is, in fact, a stand-off. His name might be in that position on the team sheet, but have you observed how often he is at centre when he gets the ball from a scrum and how often he suddenly materialises on the wing?" Both Ashton and Ashcroft often received the ball at stand-off.

Wigan faced a potentially very difficult encounter on 12 October against the redoubtable Hull team at Central Park. It was expected to be a real test for Wigan's developing pack but in the event it was practically a walk-over, as Wigan played heavenly rugby to win 56–8, their biggest victory since they hammered Cardiff 72–5 in 1951. Billy helped himself to four tries, three of them between the 61st and 67th minutes. Bernard McGurrin scored a try in the 65th minute, giving Wigan four tries in six minutes. During that period Hull did not handle the ball at all, except to place it to kick off. Tom Groves described it as "one of the most amazing spells of rugby I have ever seen. So much so that even the Hull players were applauding their opponents." Billy's performance was practically superhuman and caused some wags in Hull to start up a rumour, according to the *Rugby Leaguer*, that "Billy Boston would miss the Lancashire Cup Final owing to a back injury caused through touching down so often against the Boulevarders!"

The Lancashire Cup Final was set for Station Road, Swinton on 19 October. At last Wigan had a chance to win silverware again and they were certainly in the form to do it. The only fly in the ointment was their adversary, Oldham, the current Rugby League champions and Lancashire Cup holders. Moreover, Oldham had beaten Wigan in each of their last 12 meetings, so Billy had never played in a winning side against them. Even so, this was a one-off, a cup final, and the teams were both in prime form, Wigan third in the table and Oldham fourth. The teams for Billy's first rugby league final were:

*Wigan:* Cunliffe, Chisnall, Ashton (capt), Ashcroft, O'Grady, Boston, Bolton, Armstrong, Sayer, McTigue, Cherrington, Bretherton, McGurrin.
*Oldham:* Ganley (capt), Cracknell, Nestor, Davies, Etty, Daley, Pitchford, Jackson, Keith, Vines, Winslade, Little, Turner.

The press had made much of Billy's stupendous form at stand-off and Wigan's attractive open rugby although Oldham, according to the *Wigan Examiner*, were "not much short of being a wonder team". Oldham had danger men everywhere, but their key advantage was thought to be in Bernard Ganley whose goalkicking was deadly, whereas Wigan had for several years been erratic in that department. Oldham had also taken note of Billy's prowess and laid plans accordingly. They were not going to let him run the show and in tough-tackling Frank Daley they believed they had the man to cramp his style. The game was such a big attraction that 42,497 packed into Station Road, more than attended Manchester United's game against Portsmouth down the road at Old Trafford.

They got their money's worth too. After the pre-match formalities, including a rendition of the national anthem played to complete silence, Oldham took the game to Wigan. Ganley swept over for a 12th minute try, which he converted, and on the half hour Frank Pitchford took a pass from Derek Turner to streak in at the corner to give Oldham an 8–0 lead. Despite Wigan's early deficit, the *Rugby Leaguer* reported: "During all this period of Oldham supremacy Boston and McTigue stood out as potential match-winners". Three minutes into the second half Oldham looked to have sewn the game up when Alan Davies beat a couple of defenders after a fluent movement and scored an unconverted try in the corner. However, Wigan were far from finished. McTigue went over near the right corner in the 49th minute and on the hour Terry O'Grady scored a lovely solo try against his old club after chasing his own kick. Jack Cunliffe converted and, at 11–8, Wigan were still in with a chance. The issue was not finally decided until the last minute when Ganley potted a simple penalty goal to give Oldham a 13–8 victory and retention of the trophy.

So Billy's first final had ended in disappointment. Although Wigan had made a close fight of the game, they were definitely second best. Only McTigue had been in the same class as the Oldham pack, although Wigan had won the scrums 24–15. Dave Bolton had been "a bag of nerves" before kick-off, according to the *Examiner*, "but played like three men". Billy had made a few breaks and had put in three good kicks in the first half, but they had all come to nothing. Frank Daley had done a good job on him and "if he missed him, there was always a seething mass of humanity to down him before he got into his stride". Oldham had done their homework and executed their strategy to nullify 'Ossie', Wigan's planned move from scrums that had previously worked so effectively for Bolton, Billy and Ashton.

It was not exactly back to the drawing-board for Wigan. They may have lost their first final since 1953 but they were certainly on the right track. Even so, they were still intent on strengthening the side. They were hot on the trail of Tom van Vollenhoven, the Springbok winger, who had made such an enormous impression in the 1955 series against the British rugby union Lions. Much to the Wigan board's chagrin St Helens got in first and signed van Vollenhoven for close on £8,000. That fee, including £2,900 in tax, was the biggest paid out in rugby league up to then. It was reported that Lewis Jones had received £6,000 from Leeds to turn professional in 1952, although the largest fee ever paid by one rugby league club to another was still only £5,000. Wigan had been involved in both transfers for that fee in 1950–51, selling Joe Egan to Leigh and buying Harry Street from Dewsbury.

In view of the situation in South Africa regarding Apartheid and Billy's eminently understandable refusal to go there a few months earlier, Wigan sounded Billy out about his feelings if Voll were to come to Central Park. Billy told them, "It's OK by me but van Vollenhoven will have to play on the left wing!" Billy and Tom were to become great rivals and something of a mutual admiration society. Although the two rarely came into direct opposition, both being primarily right wingers, there was always increased public interest when the pair played in local derbies.

Despite losing out to Saints over van Vollenhoven, Wigan were not to be outdone and promptly signed Huddersfield's test left winger Mick Sullivan for a record £9,500. Wakefield Trinity, Leeds, Swinton, Oldham and St Helens were all reported to have been in the hunt for Sullivan. Mick declared that no player was worth that amount of money and, anyway, he reckoned that "Billy Boston is the finest winger in the game". Norman Berry, editor of the *Rugby League Gazette*, wrote: "You must remember that Wigan is the hub of the rugby league world. That is an undisputed fact and hardly needs stressing. They are about the only club that could raise such money... and, at the same time, one of the few clubs that can recoup that money via the turnstile."

Sullivan made a poor start to his career at Central Park. For his first training session he ran into terrible conditions driving over the Pennines in his Vanguard car. He lost his way and finished up at Ashton-under-Lyne, finally arriving in Wigan an hour and a half late. His debut against Leigh on 26 October helped draw a massive crowd approaching 28,000 to Central Park. Unfortunately, Wigan put on a very uninspired performance and went down 9–7. Billy played stand-off for the seventh time in a row that afternoon, but after this defeat Wigan dispensed with the experiment.

The test selectors clearly thought that Billy was still a better wingman than a stand-off and picked him at number two for the test match against France at Toulouse the following week. They also thought that Dave Bolton was a better stand-off than a scrum-half. Mick

Sullivan retained his left wing position. Wigan had not had three men in the test team since the second and third Ashes tests of 1954 when Billy had made his start as a test player. Britain won 25–14 in an unusually clean and sporting game for an Anglo-French test. Mick Sullivan scored twice, but the game's highlight was a terrific 75-yard try by loose-forward Derek Turner. Bernard Ganley scored five goals and a try on his test debut and Alan Davies claimed Britain's fifth try. According to Jack Bentley in the *Daily Express*, Billy "just couldn't get into Britain's scoring act. Three times [Jeff] Stevenson bursts and smooth-as-silk Phil Jackson passes gave Billy the ball. Twice he knocked on, the other time he was downed by an obviously forewarned flurry of Frenchmen. But Boston's tackling twice prevented possible French tries."

Wigan's adverse reaction to the Lancashire Cup Final defeat continued with a 21–5 loss at Warrington, which Billy, Bolton and Sullivan missed because of test duty. An easy victory over Liverpool City, when Billy scored two tries and Eric Ashton five, seemed to have stopped the rot, but successive defeats at Leeds and Hunslet set alarm bells ringing.

Billy, Bolton and Sullivan missed the game at Hunslet, being required for the second test against France at Central Park on 23 November. Britain romped to a 44–15 success before a crowd of 19,152 and all three Wigan players scored tries, the outstanding Dave Bolton claiming a hat-trick. Ganley kicked 10 goals from 10 attempts, but missed with his 11th, which would have set a new British test record. The kick was from touch and followed Billy's touchdown in the 78th minute. The try was, as reported by Jack Bentley, "purely by courtesy of the crew-cut Contrastin, who knocked on at Boston's feet, fell flat, and obviously decided with typical Gallic resignation that no useful purpose would be served by getting up and chasing Billy."

Alfred Drewry of the *Yorkshire Post*, a fervent admirer of Billy, was astonished by the performance of his opposing winger, writing: "Raymond Contrastin scored a clear-cut personal triumph over the great Billy Boston. I have never seen anyone handle the powerful Boston with such aplomb. Every time he got the ball (and that was often because there was a Great Britain conspiracy to give Boston a triumph before his own crowd) Contrastin downed him with swift, strong tackles. Boston could not escape. His side-step was not quick enough, and he had not enough pace off the mark to leave his watchdog behind. And, crowning indignity, Contrastin put Boston flat on his back with a hand-off during one of the French winger's infrequent runs."

Following the game Billy told Jack Bentley: "I've lost confidence and pep. I reckon it's with playing stand-off. I'm still waiting for the ball as I did then. I'm worried about it. I'm down to 13 stone 13 pounds, my lowest weight for three seasons, but I'm not moving as fast as I did at 15 stone"

If Billy was despondent after the test match, things were about to get worse. He returned to action with Wigan for their home game against Wakefield Trinity on 30 November. In the 20th minute Ashton got Billy away and Billy went hard for the line. Tacklers hit him from both sides as he went down a couple of feet short before reaching out to touch down. The referee, Mr Flanagan of Keighley, disallowed the effort, but Billy did not get up. An ambulance was summoned and Billy went off to hospital. He had chipped a bone in his shoulder and would miss the next six games. Wigan lost three of those games and by the New Year they were in that familiar league position – fifth, and just out of the play-off positions. Two new men from faraway places had made their debuts in Billy's absence. Fred 'Poensie' Griffiths, a South African full-back, had first appeared in the first team on 14 December against Widnes, while Italian forward Tony Rossi made his debut a fortnight later against Blackpool Borough. Billy would only play twice in the same side as Rossi but

Griffiths, after a slow start, would become a marvellous, goalkicking match-winner for Wigan over the next five years.

Billy's return on New Year's Day was a dramatic affair. Warrington led 13–7 at Central Park at half-time, Billy having scored Wigan's only try with a typical barnstorming try at the corner, taking two men and the flag with him. The *Wigan Examiner* remarked that he was "clearly only half-fit but trying all the time and made the sparks fly on one or two occasions." Wigan still trailed 13–12 after 70 minutes when the half-fit Billy made Warrington glad that he was not fully fit. From a scrum Rees Thomas scuttled down the blind-side and put Bernard McGurrin through a gap. McGurrin threw a high pass to Billy, "who took it above his head and thundered over at the corner. The crowd really roared and Boston was besieged by his colleagues". Cunliffe struck a fine conversion and then a penalty goal before Bill Sayer sealed the game at 22–13 in the 77th minute.

Three days later Wigan won an exciting game 16–8 at Halifax, despite losing the scrums 20–16 and the penalties 20–10. Halifax had been unbeaten in 10 games and were keen enough to pay £150 to have the Thrum Hall pitch cleared of snow. There was much amusement when snow started to slip off the stand roofs and onto onlookers. Late in the game, however, after McGurrin had scored a 68th minute try, the referee, Tom Watkinson, had to get the police to stop boys from throwing snowballs at him and Eric Ashton, who was attempting to take the conversion. The *Examiner* decided that Billy was "now looking trim and fit again". He certainly had appeared so in the 28th minute when Roy Evans made a wonderful break before throwing a grand pass to Billy, who outpaced all opposition in a 50 yard run for a try. Mick Sullivan, playing regularly at left centre, also scored a truly fantastic try, causing 'Delwyn', the Halifax correspondent of the *Rugby Leaguer* to drool, "Wigan were magnificent and their three-quarter line played better than any combination seen at Thrum Hall for a number of years".

Billy claimed his 25th try of the season for Wigan in a 22–10 home success against Rochdale Hornets, who had not won at Central Park since 1915 – 43 straight defeats. It had been another of those joint enterprises with Eric Ashton, which the Wigan supporters were becoming used to seeing on a regular basis. Fred Griffiths kicked beautifully – five goals from six shots – on his second appearance. Wigan arranged a friendly against Salford 'A' on 18 January and selected Billy and Ernie Ashcroft at centre. Ashcroft was making his first appearance as an 'A' teamer and had been listed at £1,250 after over 500 appearances for the club. Griffiths kicked eight goals in a 37–5 victory but it was Billy who "stood head and shoulders above everyone else as far as class goes", according to the *Examiner*. His tearaway runs caused havoc early on and he scored three tries, two from the left wing, where he ended up, having injured his shoulder again.

Oldham visited Wigan on 1 February, drawing a crowd of 30,754. However, the promised classic did not materialise. The only try of the match fell to Oldham's Syd Little in the 43rd minute after Wigan had led 6–2 at half-time. Cunliffe and Ganley each kicked three goals and Oldham's 9–6 victory was their 14th in a row over Wigan. It was a brawling affair with Wigan suffering in the face of deficits in the scrums, 12–23, and penalties, 18–20. Neither Billy nor Terry O'Grady got any chance to run on the wings, but Mick Sullivan had plenty of involvement, the *Examiner* warning that "Sullivan's hard, head-high tackling leads to losing of tempers and makes him a marked man for retaliation." After the game Oldham were installed as 4–1 favourites by the bookies to win the Challenge Cup, with Wigan, St Helens and Hull at 6–1.

Wigan's tilt at Wembley began with a 39–10 home win over Whitehaven on a straw matted pitch. Billy scored twice and "was a constant source of danger, and time and again

The Great Britain team which played France on 2 March 1958 in Grenoble.
Back: Ganley, Turner, Goodwin, Owen, Davies, Jackson, Little, Boston;
front: Stevenson, Sullivan, Prescott, Bolton, Harris.

he sent players sprawling in his dashes for the line." Sullivan, now repositioned on the left wing outside a rejuvenated Ernie Ashcroft, claimed a hat-trick. The following week Billy bagged four tries in a 24–0 rout of Hunslet in dreadful, muddy conditions. Those tries brought his tally for the season to 32, level with Mick Sullivan in joint second place, six behind the try chart leader Johnny Freeman, whose season had been ended by injury two months earlier.

On 22 February Wigan attracted a post-war record crowd of 26,924 to Belle Vue for their second round Challenge Cup tie against Wakefield Trinity. It proved a hard, tough game in which Trinity worked wonders to keep out superior opponents. Eric Ashton had a blinder, as did the whole of the Wigan pack. It was Ashton who opened up the Trinity defence in the sixth minute with a beautifully judged grubber kick to the corner and, as the ball slowly crossed the line, Billy won the race to touch down. The *Wigan Examiner* observed, "Wakefield must have wished that Boston was not playing, for in trying to stop him two of their players were knocked out!" It was 5–5 at half-time, but then tries by Ashton and Ashcroft carried Wigan through to the third round 11–5.

Billy had another big date on Sunday 2 March, when he represented Great Britain in the third test against France at Grenoble. The 1958 Lions squad for Australia and New Zealand was due to be selected on 22 March and good performances from the British boys in Grenoble would probably seal seats on the plane for the antipodes. In fact there was very little doubt among the pundits that the whole team was probably already pencilled in for the tour, with the possible exception of test debutant prop Stan Owen of Leigh, who would be able to make his late claim for a place.

Six of the tour selection committee attended the match, as well as the tour coach Jim Brough and tour manager Tom Mitchell. Britain came back from 7–0 down to lead 23–9 with 10 minutes to go in a ferociously fought game. Billy scored Britain's third try and there were others for Stevenson, Sullivan, Turner and Prescott, while Ganley booted four goals. It had been a sterling performance by Britain who were caned 26-2 in the penalty count and

79

lost the scrums 29-15. One critic wrote, "This Britain outfit, unbeaten this season, MUST be the backbone of our test side in Australia this summer".

The Lions tour may have been exercising Billy's mind, but the only thing of immediate concern to him on the field of play was Wigan's third round Challenge Cup tie at Oldham on 8 March. He still had not played on a winning team against the great men from Watersheddings, who had already beaten Wigan twice that season. This tie would be a humdinger, the victors likely Wembley finalists, and once again Watersheddings was not big enough to take all who wanted to see it. Wigan quickly sold all 7,000 of their allotted tickets and a capacity all-ticket crowd of 22,496 squeezed into the ground on a bitterly cold afternoon. Occasional driving snow made conditions even more daunting. It would be fair to say that Wigan's 8–0 victory ranks very high in the list of great triumphs in the club's history. It finished Oldham's seemingly inviolable hoodoo over the Central Park men at the 15th attempt. Wigan won only 11 of the 29 scrums but their pack was on top form in the loose and in defence, McTigue and Barton being titans. McTigue put Wigan ahead in the third minute, driving over wide out for Cunliffe to add a superb conversion. The score remained 5–0 until the 78th minute. Then Thomas, Bolton and Ashton contrived to get the ball to Billy 30 yards out for his only real chance of the match. The *Wigan Examiner* reported, "Boston took the ball on the burst and left Etty and Cracknell standing by the sheer speed at which he was off the mark. When he got to Ganley – standing about five yards from the touch-line – he wiggled his hips to turn inside, but promptly cut outside and left Ganley grasping fresh air. He touched down in the corner." Billy was immediately engulfed by jubilant Wiganers. When the game ended he was chaired from the field and had to be rescued by the police.

A week later Wigan were given an almighty scare at the seaside where Blackpool Borough restricted their visitors to four Jack Cunliffe penalty goals and an 8–2 lead as the game entered its closing minutes. Billy finished Borough off, however, taking a pass from Thomas on the blind-side of a scrum, thundering down the flank and stepping out of two tackles before racing 20 yards for the only try of the game, converted by Cunliffe.

If winning matches by scoring vital tries was a qualification for gaining a tour berth, Billy was certainly delivering the goods. However, doubts about his place began to emerge when he was asked to play in the second tour trial at Headingley on Wednesday 19 March, three days before the 13-man selection committee was to choose the touring party. He and fellow Welshman Stan Owen were the only members of the winning Great Britain team at Grenoble who were required to appear in the tour trial. They were both in the White XIII which went down 41–18 to the Green XIII. George M. Thompson in the *Yorkshire Observer* wrote, "Boston... is the surprise choice, but, apparently, the selectors desire to check whether he is in that form which made him such a triumph on the last tour." Gus Risman, in his *Empire News and Sunday Chronicle* column, commented, "One or two selectors are not sure that Britain's strongest winger has found that extra yard of pace since his shoulder injury lay-off."

On the day of the selection committee meeting Billy played for Wigan against Halifax at Central Park. It was a pity that they did not see his 41st minute try, which broke the 2–2 half-time deadlock. Billy latched on to a reverse pass from Ashton, juggled with the ball, wriggled out of Garfield Owen's tackle and raced 50 yards for a great try. Wigan won the match 20–8, but had to rely on a late burst of 13 points in the last 11 minutes. Since New Year's Day, when he had returned from his shoulder injury, Billy had played in 10 games for Wigan and scored in nine of them – 14 tries in total. That was clearly not good enough for the tour selectors. They left Billy out of their squad. He was not the only shock omission, however. Also missing were two of the greatest goalkickers in the world in Bernard Ganley and Lewis Jones, while Oldham scrum-half Frank Pitchford was also overlooked, until Jeff Stevenson pulled out a few days after selection.

For many critics and for most followers of the game Billy's omission was a mystery as well as a shock. Back in January the *Daily Herald's* Allan Cave discussed the possible make-up of the touring party in *Rugby League Gazette* and proclaimed: "For the wings there are Billy Boston (Wigan) – of course – and Ike Southward (Workington) on the right and Mick Sullivan (Wigan) and Johnny Freeman (Halifax) on the left as outstanding candidates for the four places". Three months later, in the same publication, Cave wrote: "I'm convinced that the Billy Boston v Bill Wookey Leeds duel decided in favour of the Workington Lancastrian; which means that Workington send both their wingers; Ike Southward had been a cert for weeks. The Boston omission will be talked about for years. On form there's none to compare with the Wigan wonder Welshman, but he's gone off at the wrong time. But there's ample time for Billy to thrust himself back to the international forefront. Australia are glad Boston is not going, but they are wondering among themselves just how well off for wingers we are that we can afford to leave out this world-beater-on-his-day!"

The four wingers selected were Southward, Wookey, Frank Carlton of St Helens and Mick Sullivan, while Wigan also provided Eric Ashton, Dave Bolton and the uncapped Brian McTigue. Bill Wookey was a real outsider until the tour trial at Headingley, when he played well opposite Billy, but had the advantage of playing in a much superior side on the day. Only two of the Whites won tour places – Warrington full-back Eric Fraser and Carlton – while no fewer than eight of the Greens did. A fairly typical reaction was that of David Swallow of the *Rugby Leaguer* on 28 March 1958. He raged: "With all due respect to the men picked, I think to leave out Jones, Boston and Pitchford is football folly. Boston admittedly is out of form and fitness at the moment, but he is the best wingman in the game today... The lad from Tiger Bay has had a raw deal."

When asked as to why he was not selected, Billy remains as perplexed as everyone else. He says "It may have had something to do with the 1954 tour, when we were 'bad lads' and there was all that fighting and trouble. I think I was fit enough and I was still scoring plenty of tries."

According to Jack Winstanley, in his book *The Billy Boston Story*, Billy had not been too hopeful of going on tour. Winstanley wrote: "I do believe that events off the field in the first week of March 1958, when Great Britain beat France at Grenoble (Boston scored one try and Jim Brough accompanied the team in an official capacity), had something to do with his omission from the touring party. Certainly I remember talking to Boston at the first tour trial played in a snowstorm at Swinton. I personally regarded him as a certain choice for the tour – after all, he was in possession of Britain's right wing position at the time – and it therefore came as a surprise when he told me he would be lucky to get even a trial for the tour."

Phil Jackson was very candid about the affair in his biography *A Prince among Centres*, written with Keith Nutter in 2005. He wrote "When we played the third test against France in March 1958, Bennett Manson of Swinton was part of the management team. Known to us as Barney, he would make the trip to Australia in 1958 as business manager. He had absolutely no idea how to treat people, especially how to deal with and talk to high-spirited young athletes. He was, to put it bluntly, a miserable old bastard and there is nothing good I can say about him. I was the captain (sic) of that team for the game in France and he never came and spoke to me about the game at all. He didn't discuss tactics or anything, which I found very strange but I realised he wasn't a likable man anyway so I didn't bother about it. The hotel where we were staying was quite old and had a lift that had gates made of wrought iron and they could be opened at the bottom gate when the lift was making its way up to the top floors. This of course brought the lift to a shuddering halt. Not long after we arrived back at the hotel after the game, which we had won comfortably with Billy Boston grabbing a try if my memory serves me correctly, a few of the boys were in the foyer and naturally in high spirits. They weren't out of control or anything but we had drunk a few beers and were generally just having a good laugh. In came Barney with his big Macintosh coat and trilby hat on. He marched straight across the foyer without saying a word to anybody and then he proceeded to go up in the lift to his room. Mick Sullivan (who was always a real prankster) opened the gate at the bottom and of course the lift stopped between floors with Barney in it. Well, we were all in stitches and Barney must have recognised Billy Boston's laugh and we could hear him shouting and bawling. He screamed at the top of his voice, 'I KNOW YOU DID THIS BOSTON, I KNOW IT'S YOU!' Well we all had a good laugh of course and thought the matter was closed because we heard nothing more about it. A few weeks after that game, the squad to tour was announced with one notable omission – Billy Boston. Billy was probably the best winger going around at that time and his non-selection was obviously due to Barney blaming him for the affair with the lift. And poor Billy wasn't even guilty."

Whether Phil Jackson is right or wrong will remain debatable, but Barney Manson was a member of the 13-man tour selection committee. In 1959 Mr Manson wrote a book *Another Battle for Britain*, about the 1958 tour and simply stated, "Omission of stars Lewis Jones and Billy Boston were on form and for no other reason."

Manson's tour co-manager Tom Mitchell, who was not a selector, wrote in his memoirs in 1998: "The wing berth was there for Billy Boston's taking but [in the tour trial] Bill Wookey flew past him, not just the once, and then overtook him from behind in a straight chase along the touch-line. As someone in the Council Chamber, not me, said, 'What is the point of having trial matches if you reject what you have all just seen?'… Of course, I wanted Boston but he didn't make the trip – he sauntered through the pre-tour trial match, Bill Wookey caught him from behind and surprisingly he did not get a majority vote."

There was the prospect of consolation for Billy on the Saturday following his tour selection disappointment. He would have the opportunity of playing at Wembley, if Wigan could get past Rochdale Hornets at Swinton in the Challenge Cup semi-final. On the face of it, Rochdale should not have been too much of a problem. Wigan had annihilated the Hornets 52–0 in the semi-final of the Lancashire Cup and Rochdale were 22nd in the league table. Hornets had not read the script, though. They were aided by some diabolical conditions and Wigan coach Joe Egan noted in his *Sunday Express* column: "This slog in the slime was a test of stamina rather than football skill. The water on the surface and firm ground underneath added up to a greasy, treacherous surface on which players could not turn quickly or even run with certainty." The game was not one for back play and the *Daily Express* reporter, David Nicholls, described the game as "this thud in the mud". Nonetheless the closeness of the score kept everyone on tenterhooks to the end. Wigan took the lead with a Cunliffe penalty on 38 minutes. A minute later came the only classic rugby of the tie, when Thomas took a tap penalty and ran with the ball, passing to Bolton, who handed on to Ashton. The Wigan skipper ran 60 yards, drew the full-back and sent Sullivan flying in at the flag. The only score of the second half went to Hornets when winger Ferdi Corsi took advantage of a fortuitous bounce to score in 57th minute. Billy and the other backs hardly touched the ball in Wigan's 5–3 victory but they had got to Wembley, so who cared?

The Easter programme was something of an anti-climax with decisive defeats at St Helens and Oldham, where O'Grady was sent off. Billy moved to right centre for the game at Watersheddings and to left centre for home victories over Swinton and Salford. He was back on the wing for Wigan's game at Huddersfield on 16 April, scoring twice in a 31–11 win. Huddersfield played their speedy second-rower Ken Bowman on the left wing to counter Billy, but it was their scrum-half, Tommy Smales, who gave him most trouble. The *Wigan Examiner* reported: "[In the second half] Smales tackled Boston in a hard manner and was flung away in an equally hard way. Smales then got up and struck Boston in the face. For the first time ever, I saw Boston retaliate. 'It's all a bit thick', said Boston afterwards. 'I have been punched up and down the field in the past and never retaliated. I have never been cautioned (sic) or had my name taken before. I wouldn't have minded if this had been an accident, but he deliberately struck me. The first time I retaliate, I have my name taken'." The referee, Dickie Thomas in fact booked both Smales and Billy.

Billy was thereafter booed every time he had the ball but was undeterred and scored a good try in the corner in the 62nd minute. Mick Sullivan, captain for the day against his old club, had a great game and he and Billy must have given Albert Rosenfeld, the record try-scoring winger of Huddersfield's 'Team of All the Talents', much pleasure as he watched them from the Fartown stand.

Billy's form in the run-up to the Cup Final must have given the tour selectors some misgivings. He scored in five consecutive games and Wigan won their last six league games to finish 5th yet again. His last try of the season, his 41st for Wigan, came in an exciting but rough 23–14 win at Leigh, where he sustained a leg injury and ended up limping badly in the last few minutes. Wigan took the sensible precaution of leaving him out of their final league game at Rochdale.

On 10 May Wigan met Workington Town in the Challenge Cup Final. Town were a fine side, had finished third in the league and beaten St Helens in the Championship semi-finals. They were thus in with a chance of achieving a Cup and Championship double. It was their third Wembley appearance in seven years, having beaten Featherstone in 1952 and lost to Barrow in 1955.

For Billy there was a little added spice in the fact that Town's tourist wingers, Southward and Wookey, were both to play. However, Ernie Ashcroft had broken a rib at Barrow on 19 April so Billy took his place at left centre, which allowed Terry O'Grady to fill in on the right wing. Teenage loose-forward Roy Evans had played in all the previous Cup-ties, but was deemed unfit by the doctor after suffering from a heavy cold and was replaced by Bernard McGurrin.

Wembley was blessed with fine weather, although there was a tricky breeze which some thought might trouble the goalkickers. The teams were:
*Wigan:* Cunliffe, O'Grady, Ashton (capt), Boston, Sullivan, Bolton, Thomas, Barton, Sayer, McTigue, Cherrington, Collier, McGurrin.
*Workington Town:* McAvoy, Southward, O'Neil, Leatherbarrow, Wookey, Archer, Roper (capt), Herbert, Eden, Key, Edgar, Thompson, Eve.

Wigan dominated the opening proceedings, Jack Cunliffe firing a 45-yard penalty attempt wide after five minutes, while Billy had several tilts at the Workington defence. After 10 minutes, however, Town went ahead entirely against the run of play, when the outstanding Brian Edgar surged through a gap before releasing Ike Southward on a 40-yard run to the line, leaving Mick Sullivan in his wake. Southward added the conversion and Wigan were five points adrift. They were soon level again. Sullivan had pole-axed Harry Archer with a stiff-arm tackle, captured brilliantly by several photographers' lenses, causing the Cumbrian stand-off to leave the field for 10 minutes. While Archer recovered some of his senses Wigan unfolded a stunning movement, which brought an overlap, after Cunliffe had joined the threequarters. Cunliffe drew in Southward before setting Billy free. Billy hared for the line, avoiding Cec Thompson's diving tackle and resisting a challenge from Jock McAvoy. It seemed as if Billy might make it to the line, but he decided instead to send out a pass to Sullivan, who almost strolled over wide out for his 50th try of the season. A super conversion by Cunliffe levelled the game at 5–5 after 17 minutes.

Wigan pressed constantly and went ahead in the 28th minute when Lance Todd Trophy winner Rees Thomas wound his way through from close range before sending John Barton crashing over for a try near the posts, easily converted by Cunliffe. Sol Roper retaliated with a good run for Town, but Billy's smothering tackle snuffed out the danger. Five minutes before the break Southward landed a straightforward penalty goal and Wigan went back to the dressing-rooms 10–7 up, having also won the scrums 10–7.

The second half was less entertaining, but immensely tension-packed and absorbing. Town had no luck, Edgar being another victim of a high tackle early in the half and playing the remainder of the game concussed, while Andy Key suffered an ankle injury that effectively finished his career. Wigan gained the decisive score they craved in the 50th minute when Brian McTigue conjured a piece of magic, dummying and then shooting over near the corner flag to stretch the lead to 13–7. A 61st minute penalty from Southward brought Workington back to within striking distance and as the game entered its death throes Wigan almost lost the Cup. With eight minutes remaining Southward was set free around Wigan's '25' and scorched down the touch-line before crossing near the corner flag. It seemed a certain try but somehow, miraculously, Norman Cherrington dislodged the ball from Ike's grasp as he hit him with a desperate last gasp flying tackle. On such incidents are Challenge Cups won and lost. Cherrington's effort ensured that Wigan lifted the trophy for the first time since 1951 and that Billy had his first winners' medal in rugby league.

Wigan's 13–9 victory had been hard earned. 'Red Rose's' summary in the *Lancashire Evening Post Football Pink* ran: "Wigan and Workington did not disappoint all the thousands at Wembley and all the millions watching them on the television screens, in a Rugby League Cup Final today which was superior to most of the post-war finals. Wigan just about deserved their win, which reflected on the whole their superiority. They dominated most of the attack throughout, with some brilliant play in the first half. But Workington never gave in until the final whistle and in the finish Wigan were glad to emerge the winners after a dour second half struggle. McTigue was the man-of-the-match with his brilliant second half try for Wigan, but in the backs Boston caught the eye in many of his bursts."

Jack Nott (*News of the World*) wrote: "True, two Workington players had to receive attention. True, Wigan occasionally employed the stiff arm tackle. But do not let anyone kid you. This was a tough game, a robust game. But a clean game. And Wigan, always ready to attack and forever searching for a breach, deserved to win it."

Like all Challenge Cup winning teams Wigan returned to a heroes' welcome on the Monday after the Final. They were, however, minus Eric Ashton, Dave Bolton, Brian McTigue and Mick Sullivan, who were already on their way to Australia with the 1958 Lions. Crowds estimated at 50,000 greeted the rest of the team on its nine-mile tour of the district in an open-top bus and the mayor, Councillor Oliver Bowers, gave them the time-honoured civic reception. It was at the town hall reception that Billy learned that his 21 month-old daughter Christine had suffered an accident at the weekend at their home in Swan Meadow Road. He was rushed home by car to see her, but on finding she was not seriously injured he was able to return to the celebrations, which by then had moved on to Central Park.

Triumphant at Wembley: McTigue, Cunliffe, O'Grady, Thomas, Collier, Ashton, McGurrin, Sullivan, Cherrington (obscured), Bolton, Boston, Barton; front; Sayer.

Billy had appeared at Wembley with a heavily bandaged right knee. He had suffered strained ligaments in the game at Leigh 17 days prior to the Final and it was touch-and-go as to whether he would be fit for Wembley. Jack Bentley (*Daily Express*) revealed after the game: "Not until just before the kick-off was he certain to tread that lush green turf. Even then it required a pain killing injection... the best kept Rugby League Cup secret for years... No wonder he fingered that gold medal so lovingly and grinned so hugely." Billy could not in his wildest dreams imagine that he was to become a six-time Wembley finalist, but that is what fate had in store for him. This was just the start.

## Season 1957-58

Wigan finished 5th in the League: P38, W27, L11, For 815, Against 430
Boston scored 41 tries for Wigan, plus 2 in representative rugby league

| Date | Opponent | Score | Boston | Crowd | |
|------|----------|-------|--------|-------|---|
| 17 August | Swinton | 28–5 | 3T | 10,750 | |
| 21 August | **Workington T** | 35–11 | 1T | 16,687 | |
| 24 August | **Huddersfield** | 25–7 | | 18,293 | |
| 28 August | Widnes | 28–11 | 1T | 10,999 | |
| 31 August | Swinton | 18–10 | | 8,000 | LC1 |
| 7 September | Wakefield T | 16–23 | 1T | 13,843 | |
| 11 September | Leigh | 12–2 | 1T | 12,763 | LC2 |
| 14 September | **Leeds** | 20–17 | | 20,808 | |
| 21 September | Whitehaven | 16–6 | | 5,897 | |
| 28 September | **Barrow** | 48–5 | 3T | 11,171 | |
| 1 October | Rochdale H | 52–0 | 3T | 9,720 | LCSF |
| 5 October | Liverpool City | 39–11 | 2T | 2,527 | |
| 12 October | **Hull** | 56–8 | 4T | 22,601 | |
| 19 October | Oldham | 8–13 | | 42,497 | LC Final (at Swinton) |
| 26 October | **Leigh** | 7–9 | | 27,630 | |
| 2 November | Warrington | 5–21 | dnp | 13,491 | |
| 9 November | **Liverpool City** | 44–5 | 2T | 10,744 | |
| 16 November | Leeds | 5–17 | | 18,687 | |
| 23 November | Hunslet | 17–25 | dnp | 8,000 | |
| 30 November | **Wakefield T** | 23–10 | | 18,353 | |
| 7 December | Workington T | 3–8 | dnp | 4,380 | |
| 14 December | **Widnes** | 18–5 | dnp | 17,855 | |
| 21 December | Hull | 5–37 | dnp | 14,154 | |
| 25 December | Salford | 14–7 | dnp | 6,737 | |
| 26 December | **St Helens** | 9–12 | dnp | 33,449 | |
| 28 December | **Blackpool B** | 30–13 | dnp | 14,122 | |
| 1 January | **Warrington** | 22–13 | 2T | 14,267 | |
| 4 January | Halifax | 16–8 | 1T | 13,706 | |
| 11 January | **Rochdale H** | 22–10 | 1T | 14,096 | |
| 1 February | **Oldham** | 6–9 | | 30,754 | |
| 8 February | **Whitehaven** | 39–10 | 2T | 16,650 | Cup 1 |
| 15 February | **Hunslet** | 24–0 | 4T | 10,855 | |
| 22 February | Wakefield T | 11–5 | 1T | 26,924 | Cup 2 |
| 8 March | Oldham | 8–0 | 1T | 22,496 | Cup 3 |
| 15 March | Blackpool B | 13–2 | 1T | 3,277 | |
| 19 March | **Whitehaven** | 28–6 | dnp | 10,273 | |
| 22 March | **Halifax** | 20–8 | 1T | 19,366 | |
| 29 March | Rochdale H | 5–3 | | 28,597 | Cup SF (at Swinton) |
| 4 April | St Helens | 7–32 | | 29,171 | |
| 5 April | Oldham | 7–19 | | 15,031 | |
| 7 April | **Swinton** | 26–7 | 1T | 14,905 | |
| 12 April | **Salford** | 42–2 | 1T | 14,095 | |
| 16 April | Huddersfield | 31–11 | 2T | 6,185 | |
| 19 April | Barrow | 25–12 | 1T | 6,293 | |
| 23 April | Leigh | 23–14 | 1T | 12,100 | |
| 26 April | Rochdale H | 12–4 | dnp | 4,590 | |
| 10 May | Workington T | 13–9 | | 66,109 | Cup Final (at Wembley) |

## Boston's representative matches:

| Date | For | Opponent | Score | Boston | Venue |
|------|-----|----------|-------|--------|-------|
| 3 November | Great Britain | France | 25–14 | | Toulouse |
| 23 November | Great Britain | France | 44–15 | 1T | Wigan |
| 2 March | Great Britain | France | 23–9 | 1T | Grenoble |
| 19 March | Whites | Greens | 18–41 | | Leeds |

86

# 9. 1958-59 Challenge Cup encore

Having lifted the Challenge Cup and reached the Final of the Lancashire Cup in the previous season, Wigan were looking to do even better in 1958–59. Crowds had continued to rise, an aggregate 340,324 having attended Wigan's league fixtures for an average of 17,912 – the club's best since 1951–52.

On the playing front the RFL had decided on another change to the play-the-ball laws. From now on if the dummy-half was tackled, having run with the ball from the play-the-ball, a scrum was to be formed. The intention was to open up play and stop the creeping barrage which sometimes blighted the game. It was also agreed that live televising of 10 league fixtures would be allowed.

Billy had lost his Lions try-scoring record over the summer. The Lions had famously won the Ashes and his club colleague Mick Sullivan had claimed 38 tries on tour – two more than Billy had scored in 1954. Mick had also pushed Billy off the top of the try-scorers at home in 1957–58 with 51, while Billy had finished fifth on 43. Regaining his test status and topping the try charts would give Billy a rare challenge, but would not be easily achieved.

He began the season by scoring a try from right centre in the Cherry and Whites' 31–30 defeat by the Blues in the public trial match on 2 August and helped his winger Terry O'Grady to four tries. The following week O'Grady got another hat-trick playing outside Billy, when Wigan won 29–21 at Warrington in the Wardonia Cup. Billy had "a storming first half" and sped for a try from half way after snapping up a loose ball. Later that week Billy was in the Highfield CC team which won the Salter Cup, beating Norley Hall at Poolstock. Billy took one wicket for 41 runs, as Norley Hall were bowled out for 101 in reply to Highfield's 130–7.

The rugby season proper commenced with a visit from Hunslet on 16 August. Wigan won 18–13 but the local press described the game as "a washout as a spectacle". Billy claimed Wigan's first try of the season in the 45th minute, after backing up an amazing burst by Frank Collier from his own '25', but it took two late penalty goals from Jack Cunliffe to secure two league points. Billy claimed a wonderful try at Halifax the following Saturday. Thomas, McGurrin, Chisnall and Ashcroft all handled from a mid-field scrum before Billy got possession and ran diagonally for the corner, outpacing all opposition. Wigan led 12–7 at the break, but collapsed to lose 25–12. Two days later worse followed with a 24–12 loss at Whitehaven. A bright note was the return of Don Platt in the second-row after recovering from his broken leg. The game marked Terry O'Grady's last match for Wigan. He was sold a few weeks later to Warrington for £2,250 – the same as Wigan had paid Oldham for him.

Wigan welcomed back their four tourists for the first round Lancashire Cup tie at Swinton on 30 August. They were particularly happy that Eric Ashton was back – he partnered Billy at centre – and the *Wigan Examiner* noted, "Ashton was like the switch which sets everything else going." Wigan won 31–12 and Billy profited from a jarring tackle by Cunliffe on a Swinton player to scoop up the dislodged ball and race 70 yards to score. Barrow were then hammered 49–16 at Central Park, Ashton scoring three tries and Griffiths eight goals. Billy scored twice, the second a dazzling solo effort, but finished with a slight arm injury. He probably wished it had kept him out of Wigan's next game – a 34–15 drubbing at Hull.

Billy had played the first six games of the season at right centre, but for the crucial second round Lancashire Cup-tie at Oldham on 16 September he was moved to stand-off and Dave Bolton was shifted to scrum-half. Shades of the Lancashire Cup Final defeat of the previous year! It probably came as not much of a surprise to the 20,534 folk jammed into Watersheddings that Oldham again beat Wigan. Bill Sayer did not score Wigan's only try until the 77th minute in a comprehensive 19–7 defeat. Tom Groves maintained that Wigan needed a settled half-back combination and that Billy was not getting the chances he deserved. He baldly stated: "Boston did his best but is not quick enough off the mark to be a good stand-off." Whether Tom was right or not, the game at Oldham was the last time Billy would ever start a game at stand-off.

Wigan selected Billy for the right wing for the home game against Featherstone on 20 September, although that probably was not the reason why the local Labour MP Alan Fitch turned up at Central Park with Hugh Gaitskell, the Labour Party leader. Billy certainly put on a good show for them with "three swashbuckling tries" and was "a constant menace". Fred Griffiths landed eight goals in Wigan's 46–5 win, but exceeded even that performance the following week when he kicked nine goals from 10 attempts in a 24–10 home success against Swinton. Wigan won their third game in a row at Rochdale on 4 October, although the next-to-bottom Hornets gave them another stern struggle. Wigan owed much to Billy for their 23–16 win. The two tries he scored were both sensational affairs, the first over 70 yards and the second over 50 yards with bemused men left prostrate behind him.

Wigan entered a disappointing period beginning with a humiliating defeat at Featherstone, when Billy and Mick Sullivan barely caught sight of the ball. Billy got more ball in the game against Whitehaven a week later, running in a hat-trick in a 39–16 win. However, things were not going well for Wigan, who listed Don Platt and Bernard McGurrin and splashed out £6,666 for Leigh centre Keith Holden. Ernie Ashcroft went to Huddersfield on a £1,500 transfer, leaving only Jack Cunliffe as a representative of the previous golden age of Wigan rugby. There was also still the problem of finding a satisfactory pairing at half-back with three scrum-halves being tried in Terry Entwistle, Wilf Jeram and Rees Thomas. Tom Groves, obviously keener on Thomas than the others, wrote: "Of course, he's slow, but he has the experience, the guile, a remarkably accurate pass and he is the best tackler on Wigan's books... Spectators must learn that they cannot always have perfection!"

They certainly did not have perfection at Headingley on 25 October. Holden made his debut and Wigan went down 17–8 before more than 23,000 fans. The *Wigan Examiner* was not at all happy and complained about "a poor side who are blackening the proud name of Wigan by unsavoury tactics when they are up against superior footballers." Brian McTigue was sent off for an uppercut on the Leeds hooker after 65 minutes but the *Examiner* claimed that "lots worse escaped" and that Wigan had "a mania for stiff-arm, high tackles". It was strong stuff. Billy had a problem of his own. Leeds had brought in an 'A' team winger, Lewis Garside, for the injured Delmos Hodgkinson. Garside carved his own niche in rugby league history by becoming only the second man to score a hat-trick when facing Billy. The *Examiner* explained: "But Boston wasn't to blame. On the contrary, he was the best Wiganer on view, but too often (as in the game against Whitehaven) he was left facing two or three opponents. When Garside got the ball, all he had to do was run. When Boston got the ball in attack, he was always faced with overwhelming odds. It is to his credit that he did not shirk the task."

At this point in the season Wigan were languishing at 13th in the table having already lost five league matches and seen Oldham take the Lancashire Cup for the third successive year. The general consensus in the game was that Wigan had better threequarters than any other team, but that the forwards were not playing to their potential. Things had to improve quickly if Wigan were to achieve any sort of success in 1958–59. Improve they did – remarkably. By Christmas Wigan had lost just two of their next nine fixtures and Billy had found a rich vein of form, scoring 15 tries in that period.

Leigh were beaten 26–12 at Central Park on 1 November and this time it was Wigan's turn to turn the other cheek as Leigh, fired up by Stan Owen, applied over-vigorous tactics. The following Saturday Wigan went down 29–21 in a thrilling game at Hunslet despite two splendid tries by Billy in the first 20 minutes. On 15 November Central Park was chosen for the first of the BBC's televised rugby league matches. Hull were the visitors and the crowd was down on expectations to 15,451. The identity of the televised matches was supposed to be a secret until the day of the match, but pretty well every supporter in Wigan and Hull knew a week before. Anyway, Wigan certainly put on a good show for the supporters and the second-half television audience. The television watchers had missed Billy's 21st minute try following smart work from McTigue, Bretherton and Bolton, and a fabulous 75 yarder from Griffiths 10 minutes later. The highlights of the second-half were two runaway tries by Holden, while Billy ended the scoring in the 76th minute when he stole the ball from an opponent 10 yards out to give Wigan a 31–7 victory.

An even better show unfolded at Barrow the following week, where Wigan won 23–17 in inflicting Barrow's first home reverse of the season. Billy was irrepressible. On 20 minutes he laid on a try for Sullivan after "a crossfield run from a scrum brought gasps of amazement from Barrow supporters." Then in the second-half he bagged another couple of tremendous tries. For the first, on 55 minutes, he took Ashton's pass 30 yards out, easily beat the speed merchant Frank Castle and ran through full-back Tommy Dawes. Five minutes later Ashton again released him down the touch-line and Billy beat off the attentions of four defenders to touch down. One particularly interested spectator at Barrow was Tommy Gentles, the diminutive South African rugby union test scrum-half whom Wigan had just signed, hoping to solve their half-back problem. It was Gentles's first view of a rugby league match. His remark to the *Wigan Examiner* was an understated, "Rugged, wasn't it?" The *Rugby Leaguer* got more out of him: "He said, 'I am very impressed by the speed at which the ball is passed between the threequarters, and the running of several players was terrific'. He was especially taken up with Billy Boston and said he thought that it was about the best exhibition of wing play he had ever seen – this is saying a lot, he himself having played against the great van Vollenhoven in South Africa."

Wigan gained a super 19–7 win against Oldham on 29 November, fully satisfying the crowd of almost 25,000. Billy was "always a thorn in Oldham's side" and scored Wigan's first try to level the score at 5–5 in the eighth minute. He crashed in at the corner after a splendid bout of passing between McTigue, Collier, Sayer, Thomas and Ashton. However, it took nine points in the last nine minutes to finish off the Roughyeds. December opened with a 22–7 success at high-flying Swinton, where "McTigue was the most constructive player on the field and Boston was the most devastating." Billy reached the 200 try mark for Wigan after 22 minutes with the first of two tries after taking a long pass from Holden and then beating two men in little space. Three minutes later he got an even better 201st. The ball was moved from wing-to-wing before Billy rushed past or through Doughty, Moses and Hayes to the corner.

Halifax were Wigan's next victims, going down 27–7 at Central Park on a soft pitch in what Wiganers term a "Billinge rain". Billy had a heavy chest cold but was again in fine form, claiming tries in the 8th and 39th minutes and having a third disallowed. He was once again marked by his old friend Johnny Freeman, who was back in the game after a year out with injury. "Freeman had little opportunity on attack and had the unenviable task of trying to stop a rampaging Boston," according to the *Wigan Examiner*. It was also noted that Keith Holden was beginning to make a difference to the stiffness of Wigan's defence.

On 20 December Wigan appeared on television again at Oldham in a wonderful game, the only drawback being the reduction in the crowd from capacity to 15,217, giving the anti-television critics further ammunition to ban the practice of showing live matches. Among other things, viewers saw Bernard Ganley become the first man to reach 100 goals for the season as Oldham led 13–7 at the break. They missed Billy's 25th minute try, however, when from Wigan's first scrummage heel, Thomas and Bolton got him away. Billy crashed past John Etty and Ganley in his own inimitable style. Wigan had bad luck when a try by Holden was disallowed at a crucial point and lost John Barton through injury on the hour. Oldham retained second place in the league to St Helens with their 21–18 win. At one point Billy supported Rees Thomas on the blind-side of a scrum and Tom Groves wrote: "A try seemed imminent but Ganley tackled the winger from the front. Trying to stop Boston like that is almost suicidal, but the full-back managed to hold on. I admired his courage."

Christmas Day brought Salford to Central Park. The main attraction was Tommy Gentles' first team debut and the scrum-half put in a steady performance in a 31–14 victory before unfortunately suffering a bad knee ligament injury. However, Fred Griffiths and Billy overshadowed him. Billy made a try for Dave Bolton and scored a hat-trick. The *Examiner* reported there was no stopping "bustling Billy Boston, whose fiery touch-line bursts knocked the seasonal stuffing right out of Jones, his opposite number, and full-back Arthur Gregory." Billy's three tries brought his season's tally to 28, one fewer than Tom van Vollenhoven, who led the try-scorers, and one more than Brian Bevan, who was seemingly indestructible.

The Boxing Day fixture at league leaders St Helens therefore had added spice as Billy and Voll appeared on the same pitch for the first time, albeit on opposite sides of the field. Billy was still up against a South African though as Saints had imported another Springbok star winger in Jan Prinsloo. The crowd of almost 30,000 saw a typically rugged derby, which was full of interest and tension. Wigan led 5–3 and 9–8 but Saints won the game in the 70th minute when Prinsloo, barging over at the flag, claimed the crucial try, which was converted by Peter Fearis. Prinsloo had a fine game, catching Billy once when he seemed clear away for a try. The South Africans had a good day all round because Fred Griffiths scored all of Wigan's points and van Vollenhoven grabbed Saints' two other tries in the first half. Billy and Holden both had tries disallowed.

Good wins at Leigh and at home against Warrington took Wigan fans into the New Year in an optimistic frame of mind, their team having gone from mid-table to the fringe of the top four over the past couple of months. On 3 January against Wakefield Trinity Billy filled in at right centre for the injured Eric Ashton and for the first time was entrusted with the captaincy. Wigan won 22–5 and the local press noted that Billy "skippered the side well". It was Billy who brought Wigan back from a 5–2 deficit on the half hour. He and Rees Thomas got Chisnall away and the little winger kicked ahead. Billy shot after the ball, which evaded Trinity full-back Frank Mortimer, and hacked it on twice before snatching it up to cross for a superlative try. It is often forgotten that Billy took the captain's role for several years whenever Ashton was missing and that he was effective, popular and successful in the job.

Wigan's good fortunes in this period owed much to the improvement in two vital spheres – goalkicking and possession from the scrums. Fred Griffiths was proving the answer to the long-standing kicking problem, passing the century with the first of nine goals in a 36–18 win against Liverpool City at Knotty Ash on 24 January. In the hooking stakes Bill Sayer was developing into one of the game's best ball-winners, as well as being a lively customer in the loose. Wigan's pack, coincidentally, was usually now entirely Wigan-born players.

By the time the Challenge Cup came round Wigan were installed as 4–1 favourites to lift the trophy, despite the fact that no club had ever retained it in the Wembley era. St Helens, at 9–2, and Oldham, at 6–1, were the next most favoured teams but had been drawn together. On 21 February, Leeds, at 16–1, were attractive visitors to Central Park, drawing 31,614 to the turnstiles, the biggest crowd of the first round ties. Griffiths kicked a 13th minute penalty for Wigan but, according to the *Sunday Express's* Jack Paul, a minute later "bustling Billy Boston knocked on 10 yards from the Leeds line... and you could almost hear Wigan's confidence gurgling down the plug-hole, and the Cup holders began to scratch and scrape." Wigan struggled to put Leeds, minus the injured Lewis Jones, away in a dour but exciting game, despite being the better side and enjoying a 24–16 scrum advantage. In the 68th minute they secured a 10–5 lead when Brian McTigue pirouetted majestically and scored in the corner. Griffiths clinched Wigan's 12–5 victory with a 74th minute penalty.

Billy had better luck the next week with two tries, both courtesy of Ashton, in a 29–11 home win against Blackpool Borough. He could have been playing for Wales against France in Toulouse instead but, because of the imminent birth of his and Joan's third child, he had asked to be left out of the selectors' considerations. Whether or not that had any bearing on his non-selection for Britain's test team against the French at Headingley on 14 March and for the return at Grenoble on 5 April will remain a mystery. Basically, the selectors stuck with the men who won the Ashes down under in 1958 and retained Ike Southward on the right wing for both games. Ike was transferred from Workington to Oldham for a world record £10,650 on 11 March, the same day that Wigan sold their own winger Bobby Chisnall to Widnes for a more modest £2,000.

Four days before those transfers Wigan, by now third in the league, took on fourth-placed Hunslet in the second round of the Challenge Cup before a crowd of 32,007 at Central Park. The anticipated tough tie did not materialise as Wigan's pack took complete control and the Parksiders were vanquished 22–4. Eric Ashton was involved in all the scoring movements. In the 20th minute he and Dave Bolton released Billy on full power from 20 yards out. No one stood a chance of stopping him although there survives a classic photograph of Hunslet scrum-half Kevin Doyle making a valiant but vain attempt, flying horizontally through space, only to clutch thin air, as Billy is already past him in the act of scoring. Billy added a second, game-breaking, try on 40 minutes to give his side a 12–4 lead. Brilliant handling by Bolton sent Ashton racing down field and, as Billy Langton challenged him, he sent a perfect pass to Billy. Although seemingly hemmed in near touch, Billy effortlessly proceeded to evade a flying tackle by Hunslet winger Boland before romping over and round to the posts.

On 14 March, while four of his colleagues represented Great Britain at Headingley, Billy captained Wigan to a smashing 32–3 home rout of a "gutless" Leeds, grabbing a 64th minute try off a cute pass from Sayer. It proved a very satisfying week for Billy, whose third daughter Karen was born on 18 March.

Three days later the third round of the Challenge Cup took Wigan to Halifax, where the ground record was shattered with 29,153 people shoehorned into Thrum Hall and ticket-less thousands locked out. Eric Ashton confided to the author more than 40 years later that of all the Cup-ties Wigan were involved in during his captaincy this was the one he was most worried about beforehand. In the event there was only one team in it. Dave Bolton ripped in for an interception try after 11 minutes and four minutes later Ashton mesmerised a couple of defenders before putting Billy over for his 40th try of the season. Two minutes after the break McTigue and Ashton completely spread-eagled the Halifax defence before Billy went in at the corner to make it 13–0.

Neither Billy nor Wigan were finished yet. The *Yorkshire Evening News* 'Special Representative' wrote: "Sensation of a sensational match came after 58 minutes when

Boston scored a superlative try to complete his hat-trick. Receiving from Thomas 40 yards out, Boston cut inside, picked himself up from three semi-tackles, and hurled himself over in the corner. Immediately scores of Wigan supporters swarmed onto the pitch to embrace Boston, who was lost under a cloud of red and white scarves and rosettes." Mick Sullivan finished the rout at 26–0 with tries in the 65th and 74th minutes as Wigan proceeded to the semi-finals. Amazingly, Wigan lost the penalty count 21–9 and the scrums 24–8.

Six days later, on Good Friday, it was clear that Cup fever was engulfing the town of Wigan. A ground record for Central Park was established when over 47,000 passed through the turnstiles for the clash with table-toppers St Helens. That crowd was also the highest ever to have watched any ordinary British league fixture and remains so. Nor were the spectators disappointed for the game was a thrill-a-minute affair. Wigan led 14–0 after 55 minutes and looked home and dry. However, four tries by Saints in the last 17 minutes almost stole the game before Wigan edged home 19–14. It was no game for wingers, Billy being well policed, while Sullivan and van Vollenhoven had a rare tussle. Duggie Greenall broke his arm, causing him, prematurely as it turned out, to contemplate retirement.

In Ashton's absence, Billy took his place at centre and captained the side again in a tough game at Workington on Easter Saturday. He was the best of Wigan's backs in a 13–5 success. His late try, after a typically determined run from Holden's long pass, clinched Wigan's victory. A couple of routine big wins for Wigan against Salford and Rochdale preceded the semi-finals, although there was nothing routine about one of Billy's two tries against the Hornets, when he jinked past six opponents in bewildering fashion before touching down under the sticks.

The semi-final on 11 April pitted Wigan against local rivals Leigh at Swinton. By now Wigan were down to 6–4 with the bookies, while Leigh, 21st in the league, were 6–1 outsiders. However, in muddy conditions, Leigh proved just as obstinate as Rochdale had the previous year. It was "a forwards' day", according to the *Wigan Examiner*, and there was precious little of a spectacular nature to cheer almost 28,000 anxious fans on the ground and the myriad viewers of *Grandstand*, who were witnessing the first ever televised Challenge Cup semi-final. The viewers missed the only score of the first half, which came after 14 minutes. Billy laid the platform for it, taking an inside pass from Ashton on the burst and slicing between the Leigh centres before being stopped 30 yards later. The ball was swiftly switched to the left wing via Rees Thomas, who fed Mick Sullivan. His swerving corkscrew run left Derek Hurt, Joe Hosking and Gwyn Davies in his wake, as he claimed a try worthy to take any side to Wembley. Mick had done the damage that took Wigan through to the final, but he was himself badly damaged, having no recollection of anything after the 33rd minute, when he was concussed. Spectators had to tell the Wigan players to retrieve Sullivan from the field at half-time, as he wandered aimlessly on his own '25', unaware of what was happening. The only other score of the game was a simple penalty by Griffiths for obstruction after 57 minutes, although Billy would probably have scored with a late interception if the ground had been dry. The final score of 5–0 flattered Leigh, who never looked like scoring a try, and rued their inability to land any of their six penalties.

Wigan were now faced with the exciting, but daunting, prospect of attempting a Cup and League double. Four league fixtures remained to be played between 15 and 27 April. St Helens were already virtually assured of finishing top, but there was to be a real scrap for the three remaining top four places involving Hunslet, Oldham, Swinton, Wakefield Trinity and Wigan. Billy, Ashton and Griffiths scored tries in a nerve-jangling 15–12 win at Blackpool and a week later were even harder pressed at Wakefield in a genuine four-pointer. Billy opened the scoring with a bizarre try in the eighth minute. Neil Fox says that every time he and Billy begin reminiscing about the old days that try bubbles to the surface: "A really quick pass was thrown to Billy about 30 yards out. It went straight into his midriff and bounced out again about four yards in front of him. Billy just automatically collected it up in a flash but everyone knew he had knocked it on, apart from Denis Davies, the referee, who was obviously unsighted. The crowd was screaming blue murder and Billy hesitated, waiting for the whistle to blow because he knew it was a knock-on. Mr Davies waved 'play on'. So Billy did and ran on to touch down. Billy always says to me, 'Neil, I did stop, didn't I? It wasn't my fault, was it?' He's right, of course." It did not get any better for Neil whose pass to John Etty in the 39th minute went to ground at Billy's feet. Billy grabbed the ball and sprinted 65 yards for another try to give Wigan a 10–2 lead. In the end Wigan sneaked home 13–12, but the crowd of almost 22,000 was very unhappy and Mr Davies had to have a police escort from the field after being struck by spectators. It had been a hell of a struggle and was Wigan's first win in a league game in Yorkshire for a year.

Billy was moved to left centre for the final home league game of the season against Workington Town on 25 April – a must-win fixture. Although the conditions were dreadful Wigan played magnificently to win 31–16, scoring nine tries. Billy revelled in his partnership with Ashton and both registered hat-tricks. Two days later, in a Monday evening match, Billy had the responsibility of skippering the side at Widnes. The top four spots were to be decided by that evening's fixtures and if St Helens lost at Oldham and Wigan beat the Chemics, Wigan would take the Lancashire League Championship. The stakes were certainly high and to say the game was tense was an understatement. The *Wigan Examiner* described the encounter as "not a classic but exciting". Watched by a crowd of over 17,000, Widnes were five points up in the first five minutes. Wigan responded on the half hour when Billy's excellent long pass sent Mick Sullivan belting over wide out for an unconverted try. Four minutes after the break Dave Bolton claimed a bobby-dazzler of a try. Griffiths converted and added a penalty and Wigan ran out 10–5 winners. Oldham defeated Saints 15–14 and Wigan's cup was apparently overflowing. They had the Lancashire League Championship and had finished second in the league.

Wigan had won 15 games in a row and since Boxing Day had won 20 out of 21 fixtures. They had recently thrashed Hunslet, their opposition in the Championship semi-final. They looked a good bet to reach the Championship Final with a mouth-watering clash against St Helens in prospect. There were 23,254 fans at Central Park for the clash with Hunslet and Billy and his team-mates were warmly applauded before kick-off, when they received the Lancashire League Championship trophy and their winners' medals from Bill Cunningham, the vice-chairman of the RFL. That was as good as it got for Wigan, however. Hunslet led 3–0 at half-time and devastated Wigan with a 17 points scoring spree in 13 minutes in the second half to win 22–11. Their fans sang their famous anthem *We've swept the seas before, boys*, and their team thwarted Wigan's dreams of the double.

Prior to the Hunslet game, Joe Egan had taken his team to Blackpool for several days to tone up and they returned there on the day after losing to the Parksiders. They had plenty to ponder over, as well as some injuries to tend, particularly those sustained by Mick Sullivan and Fred Griffiths, while skipper Eric Ashton had missed the Hunslet defeat. Egan decided not to announce his team to meet Hull at Wembley until the Thursday before the game. One thing not in doubt was that Billy would be playing. Unlike the previous year, he was in fine fettle for the Final. En route to Wembley he had scored five of Wigan's 13 tries and was hungry to get some more. The Wigan players were on £50 to win – less tax, of course. Hull were reported to be on £60 a man for victory.

Despite the Hunslet debacle Wigan were 6–4 favourites to win and were not short on confidence. Nor were the estimated 20,000 Wigan fans that went to London for the Final. Thirteen special trains and 200 coaches helped ferry them south and two charter planes flew parties down from Blackpool. The *Lancashire Evening Post* reported: "One stalwart enthusiast struggled down busy Wallgate this morning to catch a special train. He perspired in the hot sunshine as he pushed a barrow loaded with crates of beer – each bottle having a red and white ribbon tied around the neck". The *Wigan Observer* reported after the match: "Wigan followers spent plenty of money in London... Withdrawals from Wigan banks soared to £150,000."

At Wembley the pitch and weather conditions were perfect for the players, who entered the arena before 79,811 spectators. The *Wigan Observer* reporter noted: "Both teams had been kept waiting in the dressing rooms tunnel for 10 minutes – probably the most nerve-wracking period of all as far as the players are concerned. Billy Boston relieved the tension for the Wigan players by bursting into song."

The teams for Billy's second Wembley appearance were:

*Wigan:* Griffiths, Boston, Ashton (capt), Holden, Sullivan, Bolton, Thomas, Bretherton, Sayer, Barton, Cherrington, McTigue, Evans.
*Hull:* Keegan, Watts, Saville, Cooper, Cowan, Matthews, Finn, Scott, Harris, J. Drake, Sykes, W. Drake, Whiteley (capt).

Wigan were on top from the outset and by half-time had run up an unassailable 20–4 lead. Ten minutes into the game Ashton applied his scalpel to Hull's defence and opened up a huge space for Holden to exploit, finally side-stepping nonchalantly past Arthur Keegan for a try under the posts, which Griffiths converted. Three minutes later Hull replied with a Keegan penalty goal. On 22 minutes Bolton pilfered a wayward Hull pass and quickly shifted the ball to Sullivan, who sailed away from the Hull pursuit in a 60-yard dash to the goal-line for another converted try. On the half hour another 60-yard try unfolded as McTigue shattered the defence before sending Bolton on his way. Griffiths added his third conversion. Two minutes later Keegan's second penalty reduced the arrears to 15–4, but five minutes before half-time Billy delivered the killer blow. Again Bolton was involved, ripping through several defenders before somehow despatching a high pass to Billy, who was able to almost saunter over for Wigan's fourth converted try – his 53rd of the season.

Hull's defence stiffened in the first 20 minutes of the second half. Billy made a couple of dangerous runs and produced a try-saving tackle on Brian Saville, while Sullivan was held on his back over the Hull line. Holden almost had Billy in at the corner, but a valiant tackle by Johnny Whiteley stemmed the danger. Whiteley had to retire with a badly cut head although, typically, he returned to the field within minutes, head swathed in bandages and blood streaming down his face. Keegan potted two more goals in this period to reduce Wigan's lead to 20–8, but Hull were finished when McTigue picked up a bobbling pass from Bretherton to touch down on the hour. It enabled Wigan to set up a new record score at Wembley, beating the 22 points claimed by Halifax against York in 1931, Griffiths adding the goal. Ten minutes later Ashton, gliding towards the half-way line, flicked an inside pass to Bolton, who punted long to the corner. The ball appeared to be going dead but Billy gave chase, shot past Keegan and as Eric Thompson observed: "There was great excitement as the ball sped towards the dead-line, but with a determined dive Wigan's sepia streak just managed to get the touch down." For a change, Griffiths missed the conversion and Hull finally claimed a try from Tommy Finn in the 72nd minute, to which Keegan added the goal. Wigan still had the last word, however, when Griffiths banged over a 78th minute penalty to make the score Wigan 30 Hull 13.

One of Billy's two tries at Wembley that beat Hull.  Arthur Keegan cannot stop him.

Eric Thompson's summary of the game on the front page of the *Lancashire Evening Post's Football Pink* stated in bold type: "Hull's dreadnought pack more than met their match from the Wigan six at Wembley today and their backs were completely outclassed in a record Wembley score from a cracking Wigan side. Wembley nerves had a lot to do with Hull losing this game but they cannot make that entirely their excuse. Wigan were their masters from start to finish and were always the more confident side. Hull's first half handling and covering mistakes, plus a lot of knock-ons, let Wigan's slippery backs – of whom Dave Bolton was outstanding – in for a hatful of tries. In the second half Wigan continued to cash in and McTigue earned himself the title of the best forward on the field. Wigan could be justly proud of their team today and they fully deserved the hero's homecoming on Monday, after putting on such a spectacular attacking exhibition."

It was only after the match that it was revealed that Eric Ashton had played with pain-killing injections and was scheduled to have a cartilage operation the following Friday. The club and some co-operative pressmen had described his injury as "strained ligaments" in the weeks leading up to Wembley in order to prevent Hull from realising the seriousness of Eric's injury. It was an almost exact replica of Billy's predicament in the previous year's Wembley triumph.

So Billy's and Wigan's season had ended in the best possible manner. He had won two major medals and enjoyed an injury-free season. His 54 tries had tied him with Brian Bevan in second place in the league try-scoring lists, eight behind Tom van Vollenhoven. Wigan had again increased their attendances, grossing 361,688 for their 19 league matches, with an average of 19,036, their best since 1950–51. Just as importantly, the rugby league they had played was in the finest traditions of the club – fast, open, inventive and entertaining.

## 1958–59

Wigan finished 2nd in the League: P38, W29, L9, For 894, Against 491
Boston scored 54 tries for Wigan

| Date | Opponent | Score | Boston | Crowd | |
|------|----------|-------|--------|-------|---|
| 16 August | **Hunslet** | 18–13 | 1T | 17,261 | |
| 23 August | Halifax | 12–25 | 1T | 11,690 | |
| 25 August | Whitehaven | 12–24 | | 5,831 | |
| 30 August | Swinton | 31–12 | 1T | 15,018 | LC1 |
| 6 September | **Barrow** | 49–16 | 2T | 17,288 | |
| 13 September | Hull | 15–34 | | 15,349 | |
| 16 September | Oldham | 7–19 | | 20,534 | LC2 |
| 20 September | **Featherstone R** | 46–5 | 3T | 14,798 | |
| 27 September | **Swinton** | 24–8 | | 19,321 | |
| 4 October | Rochdale H | 23–16 | 2T | 8,466 | |
| 11 October | Featherstone R | 6–13 | | 5,300 | |
| 18 October | **Whitehaven** | 39–16 | 3T | 14,418 | |
| 25 October | Leeds | 8–17 | | 23,221 | |
| 1 November | **Leigh** | 26–12 | | 20,363 | |
| 8 November | Hunslet | 21–29 | 2T | 12,500 | |
| 15 November | **Hull** | 31–7 | 2T | 15,451 | |
| 22 November | Barrow | 23–17 | 2T | 9,157 | |
| 29 November | **Oldham** | 19–7 | 1T | 24,782 | |
| 6 December | Swinton | 22–7 | 2T | 13,500 | |
| 13 December | **Halifax** | 27–7 | 2T | 14,854 | |
| 20 December | Oldham | 18–21 | 1T | 15,217 | |
| 25 December | **Salford** | 31–14 | 3T | 17,606 | |
| 26 December | St Helens | 9–13 | | 29,465 | |
| 27 December | Leigh | 25–15 | | 11,931 | |
| 1 January | **Warrington** | 24–16 | | 23,142 | |
| 3 January | **Wakefield T** | 22–5 | 1T | 18,877 | |
| 24 January | Liverpool City | 36–18 | 1T | 3,283 | |
| 31 January | **Liverpool City** | 45–7 | 3T | 13,316 | |
| 7 February | **Widnes** | 7–11 | 1T | 19,693 | |
| 14 February | Warrington | 18–5 | dnp | 11,914 | |
| 21 February | **Leeds** | 12–5 | | 31,614 | Cup 1 |
| 28 February | **Blackpool B** | 29–11 | 2T | 12,728 | |
| 7 March | **Hunslet** | 22–4 | 2T | 32,007 | Cup 2 |
| 14 March | **Leeds** | 32–3 | 1T | 18,682 | |
| 21 March | Halifax | 26–0 | 3T | 29,153 | Cup 3 |
| 27 March | **St Helens** | 19–14 | | 47,747 | |
| 28 March | Workington T | 13–5 | 1T | 7,275 | |
| 30 March | Salford | 38–15 | 1T | 13,616 | |
| 4 April | **Rochdale H** | 38–0 | 2T | 17,806 | |
| 11 April | Leigh | 5–0 | | 27,906 | Cup SF (at Swinton) |
| 15 April | Blackpool B | 15–12 | 1T | 2,106 | |
| 22 April | Wakefield T | 13–12 | 2T | 21,900 | |
| 25 April | **Workington T** | 31–16 | 3T | 13,555 | |
| 27 April | Widnes | 10–5 | | 17,389 | |
| 2 May | **Hunslet** | 11–22 | | 23,254 | CH SF |
| 9 May | Hull | 30–13 | 2T | 79,811 | Cup Final (at Wembley) |

# 10. 1959–60 Championship triumph

During the 1959 close season Billy had a novel experience. He played rugby league in the land of his fathers for the first time. A consortium of businessmen from Birmingham and Swansea thought it would be a good idea to promote rugby league in Wales. They consequently offered to put up £2,000 to stage three games between St Helens and a Welsh XIII in Llanelli, Pontypool and Cardiff at the end of May. It seemed like a good idea at the time but, as often was the case in rugby league's incursions into Wales, it all went wrong. The businessmen promised to lodge the £2,000 with the RFL two weeks before the first game on Whit Monday, 18 May. However, when no money had reached the RFL a day or so before that date, Bill Fallowfield took the

only option open to him and called the exercise off. The money finally materialised, but not before, on the Friday morning, the Welsh media had been told the games were cancelled.

Billy had been invited to play for the Welsh XIII and amongst his colleagues were Tommy Harris (Hull), John Thorley, Brian Sparks, Johnny Freeman (all Halifax), Dai Moses (Salford), Gordon Lewis (Leigh), Don Devereux (Huddersfield), Terry Robbins and John Griffiths (both Hunslet). Unfortunately, two of the players of most interest to Welsh rugby union followers were unavailable through injury – St Helens' Tom van Vollenhoven and Llanelli's former darling, Lewis Jones.

The first game at Stebonheath Park, Llanelli was played in a heat wave and local railway officials announced record Whitsuntide traffic to local resorts. The previous announcement of the tour's cancellation combined with the tropical conditions restricted the crowd to around 3,500 rather than the hoped-for 10,000. Saints beat the Welsh XIII 44–28. Billy scored twice and "had his countrymen excited with his display", according to the *St Helens Newspaper*. Two days later Saints repeated their victory by 35-19 at Pontypool Park before a crowd of barely 1,000 in impossible deluge conditions. This time Billy, playing left centre, claimed three tries and was "the most forceful of the Welsh three-quarters". The final game, on Saturday, 23 May at Cardiff's Maindy Stadium, enjoyed ideal conditions. However, the Welsh public were clearly not enamoured of the exhibition nature of the games, and only 3,217 spectators bothered to attend a game which Saints again won 47–31. Billy had the satisfaction of bringing the house down in his home town with two of his characteristic blockbusting specials.

Joe (J.R.) Jones, who acted as organisational and publicity agent for the tour and had been a player with Hull in the 1940s, wrote: "Where their own compatriots were concerned, they simply revelled in the cavalry charge sorties of Billy Boston who made a dramatic 100 mile an hour car dash down from Wigan in response to the promoters' desperate plea for his services. Boston was very much the strong man of the Welsh XIII on this tour, and indeed I shudder to think of the points tallies the Saints would have run up had they not had to deploy a good measure of their resources to deal with – not always successfully – his tank-like charges down the middle."

There was, as usual, some cricket too for Billy. Of special interest to Wiganers was a game played at Poolstock on 19 July, which raised £100 towards a new children's playing field. Billy knocked up 51 runs out of a Rugby League XI's 208 but a Poolstock local XI beat his side by three wickets.

Off the rugby field there was trouble brewing at Central Park. The Wigan players were unhappy about pay. They wanted £7 for losing rather than the £5 on offer. The board offered them £6, which the players promptly rejected and went on strike shortly before the public trial match was due to be played. The Wigan board declared that their players were the best paid in the league and it had cost Wigan £20/10 (£20.50) every time a player took the field. They argued that they had paid out a record £12,700 in wages during 1958–59, although they did not labour the point that Wigan had also made a profit of £6,405 on the season. Mick Sullivan was nominated to be the players' spokesman and it was his job to tell the board that their terms of £10 a win and £5 a draw or defeat (£3.50 after tax) were hardly worth playing for when it came to away trips, especially when players had to take time off work. The dispute lasted several days before an agreement was reached. The players did not gain the desired £7 losing pay across the board. They only got it for long distance fixtures at Barrow, Whitehaven and Workington and for their six trips into Yorkshire. There must have been some eyebrows raised among the Wigan players when Leeds announced their playing terms for the season of £13 for a win, £10 for a draw and £7 for a defeat – home or away. Even the RFL gave the referees a rise, from £5 to £7.

When normal service was resumed Wigan won the annual sevens tournament and then took the Wardonia Cup with a 31–22 victory against Warrington on 8 August before a bumper crowd of 18,701. Billy set the crowd alight with a wonderful try in the 25th minute, swerving both ways in a run from his own half, beating four men in the process. The following Saturday Wigan's league campaign opened with a 21–14 defeat at Wakefield. Billy made his mark with a scintillating second half try from his own half and two minutes later went over again, only for the referee to rule a forward pass. However, he picked up a toe injury, which caused him to miss a scratchy home win against Widnes. He was back for a 37–6 mauling of Swinton on 22 August when he and Eric Ashton, who bagged eight goals and two tries, put on a spectacular show of threequarter play. It was Billy's 13th appearance against Swinton, who must have become heartily sick of him as he scored his sixth hat-trick against them. Tom Groves observed: "Boston seems to be able to adapt himself to any type of game, but Ashton and Cherrington [who scored Wigan's remaining two tries] are obviously more at home in the open style."

Four days later Wigan played in an extraordinary game at Leigh, which was very rough and full of incident. Frank Collier suffered for his own sins and for everyone else's apparently, when he was sent off on the hour. Wigan were 7–0 down, but recovered to lead 22–7 before a pass from Tommy Gentles to Mick Sullivan was intercepted by Welsh winger Lionel Emmitt. He raced a way for a 70th minute try which turned the game and Leigh earned an improbable 22–22 draw. Wigan next embarked on their annual assault on the Lancashire Cup with a first round home tie against Rochdale Hornets, who were undefeated in the league. Their new coach was Jim Sullivan, Wigan's biggest Welsh icon until Billy arrived to rival him for that title. Jim's Hornets put up a good show and managed to prevent Billy from touching the ball for 25 minutes. They could not contain Dave Bolton, though, or Ashton, who plundered another 18 points in a 39–20 win.

Wakefield Trinity came to Central Park for the return league fixture on 5 September, attracting a crowd of close on 24,000 and once again they were too good for Wigan. Although Wigan won the scrums 19–6, they were 18–9 down by half-time and had Keith Holden hobbling on the wing from the seventh minute. It was a very robust game and Eric Clay dished out 10 cautions, although surprisingly no one was dismissed. Billy moved to centre in the second half and it was his 62nd minute try which started a Wigan rally. Evans almost had Bolton over but from the play-the-ball McTigue's long pass enabled Billy to hurtle over. For the next few years games against Trinity were going to be among the highlights of Billy's career and leave indelible memories for followers of both clubs.

Wigan bounced back within a couple of days to wallop Salford 39–15 in the second round of the county Cup. Billy contributed two tries but sustained a groin injury that kept him out of the semi-final on 15 September, when over 30,000 saw a humdinger against Warrington at Central Park. In one of the most exciting cup-ties imaginable Warrington sneaked a 15–13 victory through a last gasp drop-goal from centre Jim Challinor. Billy was given the all clear by a specialist to resume against Leeds at Headingley, where Wigan stunned the Loiners to win 29–13.

Billy played one of his finest games that afternoon as Wigan won at Leeds for the first time in over seven years. Early on he overhauled the flying Springbok, Wilf Rosenberg, in a 60 yards chase and the *Wigan Examiner* remarked: "Boston was here, there and everywhere, but it is a pity that there is not more teamwork. There should be more results to show for his hard work". Billy provided two more thrilling tries – the 300th and 301st of his first class rugby league career. The first, on the half hour, saw Evans releasing Ashton, who gave that classic reverse pass to Billy around halfway. Billy strode round Pat Quinn and outpaced Rosenberg for a great try. Six minutes from time, he followed a feint and dash by Bolton, took his pass and charged 70 yards beating Quinn and Tomlinson for a score that brought rapturous applause.

Billy's groin trouble kept him out of a shock home defeat by Rochdale on 26 September, when Hornets won at Wigan for the first time since 1915. He returned for another defeat at Warrington. Brian Bevan stole the show with a hat-trick in the Wire's 16–6 win. Wigan played themselves to a standstill and the *Examiner* complained about them being "in a bog of inability and rank bad luck". Billy had a slice of that bad luck and when the referee disallowed him a try "the winger was so disgusted that he slammed the ball to the ground". Wigan's start to the league campaign had been too bad to be true and with only three wins and a draw from eight games they languished at 20th place in the table.

However, matters perked up the following week when Billy ran Whitehaven ragged for three tries in a 31–12 home victory. It began a seven-match winning run, despite Billy missing the next three of them. He was happy about missing the first, a splendid win at Hull, albeit by only one point. Billy had been selected for Great Britain in the first test against Australia at Swinton on 17 October, along with fellow Wigan players Ashton, Sullivan, Bolton and McTigue. His main rival for the right wing berth, Ike Southward, had sustained a serious eye injury and Billy came back into the test arena after missing the last seven Great Britain matches. Billy and his team-mates were summoned to train at Blackpool on the Thursday and Friday before the game, although the RFL did not bother to appoint a coach. They did, however, raise winning pay from £14 to £15 and upped the fee for a draw from £8 to £10, but losing pay was held at £8.

Despite his injuries Billy had claimed 13 tries in nine games for Wigan and the British team started as favourites, the Kangaroos having lost to Leigh, Lancashire and Yorkshire in their 10 fixtures so far. History also favoured Great Britain, as Australia had never won a test at Swinton. The players were presented to Lord Derby, the president of the RFL, before the game, which was watched by a crowd of 35,224. By half-time Britain were 12–4 behind and by the hour it was 20–4. Britain had no answer to the scintillating Australian centres, Reg Gasnier and Harry Wells, who between them scored all their side's tries, nor to the guile and power of stand-off Brian Clay, while the only British forward to match the Kangaroos was Brian McTigue. Australia finally won 22–14. Billy, who was penalised when streaking clear from an interception in the first half, claimed Britain's first try in the 70th minute after chasing a kick from Bolton up the middle before dribbling to the posts to touch down. It had certainly been no dream return to test rugby for Billy. He had also been badly knocked about and was suffering from fluid on the knee and a badly swollen elbow, which kept him out of the Wigan line-up for three weeks.

Billy returned to the Wigan side on 7 November, captaining a weakened team from left centre and inspiring a 38–3 rout of Hunslet. Five days later the test selectors left him and Eric Ashton out of the team for the second test, although Ashton was recalled when Alan Davies dropped out. The team was comprehensively culled, eight changes being announced. Two days after the announcement, Billy had a golden opportunity to prove the selectors wrong, when the Australians drew a crowd of 24,466 to Central Park for their game against Wigan. After some early fisticuffs the match became an enjoyable spectacle with both teams displaying tremendous defence. By half-time Wigan led 6–2, thanks to three penalties from Fred Griffiths to one by Brian Carlson. By the 65th minute both sides had added a further penalty and Wigan led 8–4. It was at that point that the Boston-Ashton machine clicked into gear and finished off the Kangaroos.

From a scrum Roy Evans made a 20 yards dash towards the right flank and served Ashton, who punted the ball forward. Full-back Keith Barnes moved to cover the kick, but the ball bounced capriciously away from him. For Billy, however, it was a perfect bounce. He gathered the ball up, cut inside the despairing Don Parish and sprinted the last 30 yards for an inspirational try, converted by Griffiths. A few minutes later Billy almost repeated the effort, but then Ashton delivered the killer blow in the 75th minute with an even more spectacular try. A scrum went down on the Douglas Stand side. Bolton and Holden interpassed as the ball moved to the left, then Ashton flashed inside to take a reverse pass from Bolton and swerved to the left. Sullivan made to come inside for Ashton's pass but was too quick, so Ashton held on and went like a bat from hell to the left corner flag, taking two Australians with him for a score which put Wigan out of sight at 16–4. Carlson converted his own last minute try to make the final score 16–9.

Four Wigan players took part in Britain's nail-biting 11–10 victory over Australia at Headingley on 21 November, but Billy was absent, captaining Wigan against Hull at Central Park. Billy, playing left centre, had a stormer, scoring twice and making a try for his winger Syd Fenton. His first try on 65 minutes followed a wonderful move from a scrum by a rejuvenated Rees Thomas, with Billy taking his inside pass before cantering to the posts. Twelve minutes later Billy picked up a more characteristic try, bursting between two hesitant tacklers and racing 50 yards to touch down. Hull were so demoralised that they resorted to kicking a last minute penalty goal, despite being 24–0 down.

On 28 November Billy led Wigan at Halifax, Ashton being troubled by a shoulder injury. By now Wigan had risen to ninth in the league on the back of seven consecutive victories and were expected to hammer 24th placed Halifax. It was Billy's 200th game for Wigan and he scored a try in the 55th minute after collecting a Thomas kick and "allowing nothing to stop him". He set a good example as skipper and saved another try by turning Palmer on his back but Halifax caused a big shock by winning 21–20, with Johnny Freeman scoring twice. The game proved to be Rees Thomas's last for Wigan and within days he was granted a free transfer, resulting in a return to his former club Swinton.

Wigan had signed another Welsh scrum-half, Brian Scrivens, from Newport rugby union, paying him £3,000, the same figure that Billy had received, but without quite the same results. Scrivens drew a crowd of 4,000 to Central Park for his 'A' Team debut against Liverpool City on the day Wigan lost at Halifax. However, he ultimately proved no more successful than Tommy Gentles.

Wigan got back on the winning track with a fine 27–7 win over Oldham in frightful cold and rain, but faced even worse conditions at Workington the following week, when Billy was again skipper and Scrivens made his first team debut. The only scores of the game, on a pitch of even parts of mud and sand, were tries by Cherrington and Fenton in the first 10 minutes. The *Wigan Examiner* reported: "Boston showed much thrust, but his attacking was excelled by his defensive ability. Although he did on occasions tackle a shade too low and then rely upon his brawn to ground his man, he was always to the forefront and was rarely caught napping." No doubt Billy would have preferred to be at Wigan that afternoon, where Britain retained the Ashes with an 18–12 third test win. He had been selected in the 'shadow test team', along with fellow future Hall of Famers, Alex Murphy and Vince Karalius, which certainly said something about the strength of the national XIII 50 years ago.

Wigan's year ended with victories against Blackpool, who simply could not deal with Billy's power-packed straight running, and at Salford, with an exciting and controversial home defeat by St Helens sandwiched in between. When the New Year dawned Billy had claimed 19 tries, including one for Britain, and was well behind van Vollenhoven, Prinsloo and Bevan in the try-scoring stakes. Wigan were eighth in the league, handily placed for a top four challenge but with some undercurrents of dissatisfaction in the camp.

New Year's Day brought a brilliant 34–5 home win over Warrington before a crowd of more than 25,000. Billy led a very under-strength side in a tremendous performance. He claimed the last points of the game in the 63rd minute, when the ball was kicked to the left flank. Billy chased, gathered and scored – it appeared as simple as shelling peas – at least that was the way Billy sometimes made difficult things look. The *Wigan Examiner* wrote: "Boston directed operations very well but try as he would he could not get his left wing partner Mick Sullivan over for a try." Mick had only scored nine tries for Wigan so far, plus two for Yorkshire, and although he had played in all three Ashes tests he had failed to score – the test selectors worked in mysterious ways.

Wigan failed to win any of their next three games. Billy had to carry on playing at centre and fulfilling the captain's role, as Eric Ashton struggled with his shoulder injury and some personal disillusionment. Hunslet beat Wigan 15–10 in front of the television cameras on 2 January. Wigan fielded the same under-strength team that had worked the oracle the previous day against Warrington, but Hunslet were disinclined to surrender an unbeaten home record against club sides which stretched back over 30 games and almost two years. The following week Workington Town inflicted a shock 11–7 defeat on Wigan, a game that saw Jackie Cunliffe make his 447th and last appearance for Wigan. Jackie represented the last link with Wigan's fabulous team of the immediate post-war period and had recently been given a cheque for £1,000 to mark his 21st season with the club. The game was also notable as the first that Wigan played under new rules that abolished the tap penalty and advantage at scrums. Contrary to expectations, the effect of the revised rules was more rather than fewer scrums, which also took longer to complete.

A 7–7 draw at Whitehaven on 16 January provided Mick Sullivan with a timely try, his first in 14 games for the club, but the dropped point left Wigan in 13th place in the league and in real danger of falling out of the chase for a top four spot. Matters were not improved when the bombshell burst that Eric Ashton had been transfer listed at his own request at a world record £13,000. Barrow were reported to have offered Wigan £8,000 and there was press speculation that Eric was headed for his hometown club St Helens. Keith Holden was also unsettled and considering a transfer request. With the Challenge Cup ties on the horizon Wigan countered these developments by buying veteran centre Duggie Greenall from St Helens for £1,000 and Leeds full-back-cum-centre Pat Quinn for £1,500. Tommy Gentles went in the opposite direction to Headingley and Billy and his colleagues must have thought that Wigan had installed perpetually revolving doors. In the event Greenall only made three appearances for Wigan and Quinn only a couple.

Greenall made his debut in an unlikely centre pairing with Billy in a 12–10 home success against Leigh on 23 January. It was Billy's last game of the season as a centre. He left his mark by masterfully sending Mick Sullivan over for tries in the 17th and 42nd minutes, but he almost gave Leigh a draw in a sensational finale. Six minutes from time Billy tackled a Leigh player and referee Eric Clay penalised him. No one knew why and Billy obviously disagreed. The *Wigan Examiner* asserted: "He probably began to say so, but Sullivan pulled him away." Leigh scrum-half Brian Fallon took the kick amid a cacophony of booing and sent the ball wide.

Thankfully, things began to settle down at Central Park. Eric Ashton came off the list and returned to action in a 43–3 humbling of Barrow at Central Park on 6 February. Billy was able to return to the right wing and flashed over for a hat-trick, while Mick Sullivan went one better with four tries. The *Examiner* happily noted, "Boston used his tremendous strength to advantage and the defenders were often skittled flat on their backs".

The Challenge Cup first round threw up a really tricky tie for Wigan – Hunslet at Parkside. Hunslet were several places above Wigan in the league and practically unbeatable at home. If Billy and his team-mates were to complete a Wembley treble Hunslet was as tough a hurdle as they were likely to encounter – and so it proved. There were 8,000 Wiganers among the crowd of almost 18,000 and they were treated to a nerve-tingling cup-tie staged in slippery, heavy conditions. Wigan took the lead with a Griffiths penalty in the 10th minute and 10 minutes more elapsed before Billy scored Wigan's solitary try. It was a fantastic effort. Norman Cherrington, the game's star forward, broke through inside his own half and veered out to the right wing, feinting to pass on three occasions as he crabbed sideways. Hunslet's South African winger Ron Colin came inside to tackle him but, quick as a flash, Cherrington slipped a pass to Billy, who was now unmarked. Billy raced forward 15 yards and thundered through full-back Billy Langton and then outran Colin to touch down near the posts. Bafflingly, Griffiths fluffed the conversion. 'Enthusiast', writing in the *Rugby Leaguer*, had a word of comfort for Langton, saying, "The Hunslet full-back should not be too despondent, because it takes a lot to stop the sepia streak!" Griffiths stretched Wigan's lead to a precious seven points with a 31st minute penalty, but Hunslet hit back hard within two minutes, when Colin claimed a converted try. At 7–5 the result remained in the balance until the 77th minute when Griffiths potted his third penalty to give Wigan a greatly deserved victory. Dave Bolton had spent the second half concussed on the wing but Wigan's forwards had been magnificent and Billy's charges had been tremendously damaging. At the final whistle the referee, D.T.H. Davies, had to be escorted from the field – it had definitely been an old-fashioned cup tie.

Wigan's next two games were against Leeds, unhappily two-thirds of the way down the table, both at Central Park. The first, on 20 February, was a league fixture and was marked by a horrible afternoon and a mud heap of a pitch. As a cup rehearsal it proved little, as

Wigan won 9–0 in a poor game, in which Pat Quinn made his debut at full-back against his former club. Leeds lost stand-off Horsman for threequarters of the game with a jaw injury. An unusual feature of the encounter was Billy's excellent touch-finding with penalties in the absence of Fred Griffiths. Tom Banks, in the *Empire News and Sunday Chronicle*, reported: "The two men who struck me as having their minds on yesterday's game more than on Saturday's Cup-tie were Billy Boston and Dave Bolton. Billy got two tries in the first half, and could have easily finished up with six. His first was when he used his 15 stones to block-bust his way through three tackles with only a yard of running space from the touch-line. His second came when Evans obligingly played him on by knocking up an Eric Ashton pass."

If the league match, which was televised, had disappointed the 14,871 crowd, the second round Challenge Cup tie a week later completely enthralled its 33,388 onlookers. Lewis Jones was at his mercurial best for Leeds, who rocked Wigan to the core. Wigan led 9–4 at half-time, courtesy of a try by Keith Holden and three goals from Griffiths. As the game entered its death throes Leeds had established an 11–9 lead and Wigan looked out of the Cup. Wigan had provided precious few chances for Billy and Mick Sullivan on the wings. However, the crowd exploded into spasms of ecstasy when McTigue and Bolton finally unleashed Sullivan, who screeched past three desperately covering Loiners to squeeze in at the corner flag for the winning try. Griffiths's brilliant conversion gave Wigan a 14–11 victory. If ever there was 'a close-run thing', this had been it. According to Tom Glover, there were only five seconds of time remaining when Sullivan touched down to give Wigan their 12th consecutive Challenge Cup tie success.

The flu kept Billy out of Wigan's next game, a 7–0 win at Rochdale with practically a reserve side. He was better for a fine televised 11–10 league win at Oldham, 5–2 favourites to win the Cup, on 12 March, though, scoring a devastating try in the eighth minute to give Wigan the lead. After receiving a pass from Griffiths in midfield, he shrugged off Vince Nestor's tackle from behind and shot forward 20 yards to be met by an attempted low tackle by Bernard Ganley. He wriggled free and outpaced the covering defenders to score a try that confirmed he was as big a threat as ever, even if the test selectors had still picked him as 'shadow' right winger to Ike Southward for the test in Toulouse the previous Sunday, a game Britain lost 20–18 and in which Norman Cherrington had made his test debut.

Wigan were drawn against Hull, their victims at Wembley the previous year, in the third round of the Challenge Cup. The tie, at The Boulevard, drew 25,000 through the turnstiles and was undoubtedly the most attractive of the round – on paper. Wigan, now 7–2 for the Cup, were slight favourites against the Airlie Birds, whom the bookies rated at 4–1. In the event the game was a damp squib. At least it was for Wigan and the 7,200 fans who followed them to East Yorkshire. Hull had won 10 games in a row and were hell bent on revenge for their Wembley humiliation. They got it with a 12–8 victory, clinched in the last two minutes when a try by winger Jack Kershaw triggered a pitch invasion, which took several minutes to clear. It was certainly an unlucky 13th cup-tie for Wigan, whose dream of a third consecutive Wembley final was shattered.

Billy, too, was shattered. He had received a severely bruised hip. It was bad enough losing at Hull, but his injury had forced him to withdraw from Great Britain's test against France at St Helens the following Saturday. His excellent form had finally convinced the selectors to reinstate him as Britain's right winger and now he had lost his long awaited opportunity. Billy had several treatment sessions in a bid to be fit, but had to concede defeat, telling the *Daily Express* reporter Jack Bentley: "I want to play very much but I can't risk getting another knock and breaking down. It's not fair on the other lads." At least he had the consolation that he was no longer in the international wilderness and could reasonably hope to figure in Great Britain's plans for the 1960 World Cup.

Wigan still had plenty to play for. They were fifth in the table on 42 points as they entered April, a long way behind leaders St Helens, on 57 points, and Wakefield on 52, but only two points behind both Featherstone and Hull. On 2 April Wigan visited Widnes and drubbed them 42–9, Billy bagging six of their 10 tries, a remarkable feat on a ground notorious for making visiting teams work hard for any reward. There was simply no stopping Billy, who might well have ended up with eight or nine tries with a little more luck. The *Widnes Weekly News* reporter Ron King drooled: "The Wigan player to hit the headlines was, of course, Billy Boston, whose six magnificent tries had the ground in an uproar. Boston was in his best form. Thundering down the wing, leaving a shattered disconsolate trail of defenders behind him, the winger certainly provided the thrills that the fans love." Dave Bolton also put in a wonderful performance in his first appearance as Wigan's full-back in Fred Griffiths's absence.

A week later Billy performed an unprecedented feat by scoring another six tries in a whopping 58–6 annihilation of Dewsbury at Central Park. He set Wigan on the way to the rout by scoring their first three tries between the 12th and 22nd minutes. Dave Bolton, again at full-back, helped put him in for three of his touchdowns. Billy had played just three games against Dewsbury and had amassed an incredible 15 tries in those appearances. Dewsbury full-back Ken Bosworth scored all Dewsbury's points from penalty kicks, one of which was from eight yards inside his own half and earned a rapturous round of cheering from an amazed crowd. Tom Glover said it was the longest goal he had ever seen kicked at Central Park and even the prodigious Jim Sullivan would have been proud to have landed such a monster. The win over Dewsbury lifted Wigan into the top four at the expense of Hull, who were busy beating Oldham in the Challenge Cup semi-final.

Billy claimed his 40th try of the season in a vital 11–0 win at Barrow but drew a blank at Knowsley Road on Good Friday, when Wigan went down 12–4 to St Helens. Saints produced the only two tries of the game, both dazzling affairs, by Tom van Vollenhoven after 17 minutes and Alex Murphy eight minutes later to lead 10–2 at half-time. Billy had the crowd of 31,846 on tenterhooks early on with a bewitching run from his own half, beating three tacklers and coming inside the full-back before falling to Jan Prinsloo's crucial last gasp tackle. Saints clearly regarded Billy as their main threat and repeatedly gang-tackled him.

The following afternoon Wigan went to Knotty Ash, as did the Lord Mayor of Liverpool and the city's police band. Liverpool put on a brave show for their Mayor, but were stuffed 39–20 with Billy shaking off three tackles for his first try and racing over 50 yards for his second. Billy followed that on Easter Monday with one of his greatest tries in a 38–13 home mauling of Salford. A bumbling Wigan were losing 10–7, when Billy's masterpiece turned the game in the 53rd minute. Salford second-rower Stott was going over Wigan's line for a try, which might have finished Wigan off, but failed to gather the scoring pass. The *Wigan Examiner* described what happened then: "The ball came loose, Lyon picked up and swung out a long pass to Boston. The winger was in his own '25' and he whizzed round Baines. He was soon in his stride but it looked as if Hartley would catch him, but Boston handed off the loose-forward and beat the full-back before going over at the corner for a wonderful try." The *Liverpool Echo* told it somewhat differently: "Salford easily weathered the Wigan attacks until Boston got the ball on his own line and went on a length-of-the-field touch-line run in which he beat five opponents to score in the corner." Whether the *Examiner* or the *Echo* gave the more accurate description is a moot point. What is certain is that it was a lulu of a try and one that is invariably in the mix when Billy's greatest scores are debated.

Wigan needed to win their last two games at Swinton and Blackpool to ensure that they had a chance to qualify for the Championship semi-finals and had also to hope that Featherstone would lose one of their last two games. Billy was having trouble with a hamstring but volunteered to play against Swinton, who were overcome 16–14 on 23 April. His injury was aggravated and he had to undergo daily heat treatment, causing him to miss the final league fixture at the seaside on 30 April. Wigan duly despatched Blackpool 30–7 with Brian McTigue the chief executioner. At the same time Featherstone went down 15–11 at Leeds and Wigan were assured of fourth place and a semi-final engagement at runaway leaders St Helens, who were also the current champions.

There was immense interest in the semi-final and Knowsley Road was bursting at the seams with more than 32,000 fans expecting fireworks. Saints had only lost three of their 38 league games, had done the double over Wigan and finished 13 points clear of them in the table. They were expecting to win, especially as Wigan had to re-jig their back division, fielding Mick Sullivan at stand-off and the peripatetic Dave Bolton at scrum-half. Sullivan was playing opposite Alex Murphy and everyone expected that their clash would be explosive. So it proved. There was niggle between the two from the start and both were sent off after a stand-up stoush in front of the main stand after 37 minutes. Their departure brought Billy into the centre, while Ashton went to stand-off, with second-row flyer Geoff Lyon going to right wing. Saints moved Vince Karalius from the pack to stand-off but he came a poor second to Ashton, who dictated play brilliantly. Another key feature was Wigan's forward dominance in the loose and tight. Saints had to play Jim Rose at hooker for his first game of the season in place of Bob Dagnall and Wigan won the scrums 27–14.

The first half was pretty claustrophobic with little open play and large dollops of roughness. Nonetheless it was riveting. Austin Rhodes and Fred Griffiths exchanged penalties in the first 18 minutes, but it was a lovely piece of centre play from Ken Large that sent van Vollenhoven scorching to the posts for the opening try after 27 minutes. Rhodes's conversion gave Saints a 7–2 lead, but a minute after the dismissals Billy struck. McTigue, Griffiths, Barton and Collier paved the way and there was no stopping Billy from tearing over wide out. Harvey Stead wrote in the *Daily Express:* "In Billy Boston Wigan had a shock trooper St Helens couldn't contain. Only twice did Billy get the attack signal, once in each half; twice he stormed through the Saints' defensive line, leaving opponents straggling, for decisive tries." Two penalties from Griffiths gave Wigan a 9–7 lead before Billy's second try decided the issue in the 61st minute. It was a startling effort, which began when Griffiths broke away near the Wigan goal-line and linked with Ashton. The Wigan skipper strode forward elegantly, slowed suddenly and appeared to almost wait for Billy to come up on his inside. Time seemed to stand still and only Billy appeared to be moving. Van Vollenhoven made a jaded attempt to stop Billy but was brushed aside, as were a couple of other defenders. Griffiths's conversion gave Wigan a 14–7 lead. Saints' only reply was a penalty from Rhodes and two minutes from time John Barton steamrollered over from 15 yards for a final converted try which gave Wigan a 19–9 win, one of the club's most famous victories over their greatest rivals.

Billy was eagerly looking forward to his first, and as history shows, his only Championship Final appearance. Wigan's opponents, a fortnight after the shock win at St Helens, were Wakefield Trinity, who had smashed Hull 38–5 at Wembley the previous Saturday. Trinity had plenty of style and steel and were many people's favourites to complete a magnificent double. Wigan, however, were a very confident side and believed their form was good enough to see off Wakefield. Odsal Stadium was the venue with a crowd limit of 80,000, which was not really expected to be tested by the RFL, police and ground authorities. However, the game excited quite amazing interest. Every coach proprietor in Wigan had to put up 'fully booked' notices and at least 15,000 Wigan fans trekked to Bradford. All the crowd estimations fell short of the 83,190 that greeted the two sides – a record for the Championship Final or any of its successors. It was certainly the biggest crowd before which Billy had yet appeared. The two sides which descended the vertiginous slopes from the dressing-rooms to the Odsal pitch just before 3pm on a balmy afternoon were:

*Wigan:* Griffiths, Halliwell, Boston, Holden, Fenton, Ashton (capt), Bolton, Barton, Sayer, Collier, McTigue, Lyon, Evans

*Wakefield Trinity:* Round, Smith, Skene, Fox, Etty, Rollin, Holliday, Wilkinson, Oakes, Vines, Firth, Chamberlain, Turner (capt)

Mick Sullivan had received a two match ban for his dismissal at Knowsley Road, so Wigan had decided to continue with Billy at centre and Ashton and Bolton at half-back for the final. Reserve players Frank Halliwell and Syd Fenton filled the wing berths in a strange looking back division. The only forward missing was Norman Cherrington, who had fractured his ankle against Halifax almost two months earlier. His replacement Geoff Lyon had been one of the major discoveries of the season. After the preliminaries, when Billy and the other players were presented to Lord Derby, Wigan were set back on their heels within two minutes of the kick-off. Glorious handling brought the opening score to Trinity right winger Fred Smith and Wakefield had three points on the board before thousands of spectators had managed to get past the turnstiles. During the early exchanges Billy made one of his bone-shaking crash tackles on Neil Fox much to the outrage of the Trinity masses. A few minutes later Fox had to move out to the wing where he spent the next 68 minutes hobbling. Almost half a century later there are many folk who will recall that Billy's tackle did the damage, but Neil maintains that nothing untoward caused his injury and certainly not that tackle. He did it trying to go between Billy and Halliwell, whose knee caught him on his thigh. It was a pure accident.

While Wakefield certainly suffered because of Fox's incapacity, the critics were unanimously convinced that even a fully powered Trinity would ultimately have been overwhelmed, because Wigan were simply masterful in the forward exchanges, where Collier, Barton and McTigue played the games of their lives.

Wigan threw everything at Trinity in the first half but by the 40th minute they had a lead of only 4–3, courtesy of Fred Griffiths's boot. Billy had twice made barnstorming breaks, once beating six men, but had been stopped heroically by Gerry Round, who had also thwarted Halliwell and Fenton with superb tackles. Just before Eric Clay was ready to blow for half-time Billy finally wrecked the Trinity defence. McTigue, Ashton and Lyon carved through the Trinity ranks before Billy took a sweet reverse pass from Bolton to break clear before leaving Round standing and wondering where he had gone. Griffiths's touch-line conversion sent Wigan in at the break leading 9–3. There was no way back for Wakefield, who shipped a further 18 points without reply in the second half. Two cracking tries by Ashton and one each from Bill Sayer and Billy, plus three more Griffiths goals made the final score 27–3. Billy's second try on 68 minutes was a real spectacular, as he intercepted Wakefield passing and swept unchallenged over half the field to touch down under the bar.

Lewis Jones observed in the *News of the World:* "What a fine player is Boston, going to centre for this game, his performance emphasized what I have always said – If Great Britain can afford to discard this man, we must have a gold mine of backs. Boston's thrusts were a constant menace and but for some brilliant last ditch tackles by Round, Wakefield would have faced heavier arrears at half-time than six points." The *Rugby Leaguer* added:

"Billy's name was on everyone's lips after the game. He certainly surprised many by that fine turn of speed after the interception, which led to his great run-in. It has also to be recalled that Billy did more than his share of chasing around so that late try spurt once again showed that he has the stamina and that the training schedule at Central Park is the real thing."

Billy's season had concluded on a high note. For the third year in a row he had picked up a winners' medal in a major final. His form towards the end of the campaign had been sensational lifting him to second place in the try-scoring chart with 47 – seven fewer than Tom van Vollenhoven and seven more than third placed Brian Bevan. Wigan were in danger of re-establishing themselves as the game's glamour team and there was talk that soon enough they may be capable of lifting all four cups in a season. They had drawn an aggregate 309,944 attendance to their home league matches at an average of 16,313, while their five other home games had aggregated 127,652, with an average of 25,530.

Billy's season ended on 28 May with an appearance at Hull in a testimonial match for Tommy Harris and Brian Cooper. A Humberside XIII met an All Stars XIII, selected by Roy Francis, the Hull coach. Billy and half a dozen other Wigan players joined Brian Gabbitas, Lewis Jones and Jeff Stevenson in the All Stars side, which won 72–57, in a game that obviously descended to pantomime depths when referee Charlie Appleton failed with two kicks at goal. A crowd of 10,000 clearly had some fun though and Billy certainly did. The *Hull Daily Mail's* headline proclaimed, "Boston scores four tries and then declares!" Billy came off at half-time to be replaced, ironically enough, by Ike Southward.

Scoring in the 1960 Championship Final.

## 1959–60

Wigan finished 4th in the League: P38, W28, L10, For 828, Against 390
Boston scored 46 tries for Wigan, plus 1 in representative rugby league

| Date | Opponent | Score | Boston | Crowd | |
|---|---|---|---|---|---|
| 15 August | Wakefield T | 14–21 | 1T | 17,000 | |
| 19 August | **Widnes** | 16–12 | dnp | 21,740 | |
| 22 August | **Swinton** | 37–6 | 3T | 20,254 | |
| 26 August | Leigh | 22–22 | | 18,743 | |
| 29 August | **Rochdale H** | 39–20 | 1T | 19,198 | LC1 |
| 5 September | **Wakefield T** | 19–27 | 1T | 23,774 | |
| 7 September | **Salford** | 39–15 | 2T | 19,963 | LC2 |
| 15 September | **Warrington** | 13–15 | dnp | 30,637 | LCSF |
| 19 September | Leeds | 29–13 | 2T | 16,425 | |
| 26 September | **Rochdale H** | 8–18 | dnp | 14,905 | |
| 3 October | Warrington | 6–16 | | 18,940 | |
| 10 October | **Whitehaven** | 31–12 | 3T | 15,184 | |
| 17 October | Hull | 9–8 | dnp | 10,808 | |
| 24 October | **Liverpool City** | 17–6 | dnp | 7,761 | |
| 31 October | Dewsbury | 35–7 | dnp | 2,600 | |
| 7 November | **Hunslet** | 38–3 | | 14,408 | |
| 14 November | **Australians** | 16–9 | 1T | 24,466 | Tour |
| 21 November | **Hull** | 24–2 | 2T | 10,883 | |
| 28 November | Halifax | 20–21 | 1T | 8,539 | |
| 5 December | **Oldham** | 27–7 | | 19,678 | |
| 12 December | Workington T | 6–0 | | 1,868 | |
| 19 December | **Blackpool B** | 47–3 | | 7,051 | |
| 26 December | **St Helens** | 7–19 | | 33,197 | |
| 28 December | Salford | 20–13 | 1T | 8,337 | |
| 1 January | **Warrington** | 34–5 | 1T | 25,760 | |
| 2 January | Hunslet | 10–15 | | 8,000 | |
| 9 January | **Workington T** | 7–11 | | 12,726 | |
| 16 January | Whitehaven | 7–7 | | 6,236 | |
| 23 January | **Leigh** | 12–10 | | 17,686 | |
| 6 February | **Barrow** | 43–3 | 3T | 14,369 | |
| 13 February | Hunslet | 9–5 | 1T | 17,956 | Cup 1 |
| 20 February | **Leeds** | 9–0 | 2T | 14,871 | |
| 27 February | **Leeds** | 14–11 | | 33,388 | Cup 2 |
| 5 March | Rochdale H | 7–0 | dnp | 4,909 | |
| 12 March | Oldham | 11–10 | 1T | 16,366 | |
| 19 March | Hull | 8–12 | | 25,000 | Cup 3 |
| 26 March | **Halifax** | 18–12 | dnp | 8,858 | |
| 2 April | Widnes | 42–9 | 6T | 9,013 | |
| 9 April | **Dewsbury** | 58–6 | 6T | 10,884 | |
| 11 April | Barrow | 11–0 | 1T | 4,944 | |
| 15 April | St Helens | 4–12 | | 31,846 | |
| 16 April | Liverpool City | 39–20 | 2T | 2,470 | |
| 18 April | **Salford** | 38–13 | 1T | 15,955 | |
| 23 April | Swinton | 16–14 | | 11,993 | |
| 30 April | Blackpool B | 30–7 | dnp | 3,850 | |
| 7 May | St Helens | 19–9 | 2T | 32,094 | CH SF |
| 21 May | Wakefield T | 27–3 | 2T | 83,190 | CH Final (at Odsal) |

## Boston's representative matches:

| Date | For | Opponent | Score | Boston | Venue |
|---|---|---|---|---|---|
| 17 Oct | Great Britain | Australia | 14–22 | 1T | Swinton |

# 11. 1960–61 World Cup victory

Billy continued to indulge in his cricketing activities for Highfield during the close season of 1960, doing plenty of damage with his bowling. His best performance of the season was 9/28 against Winstanley Park. He also took part in an interesting encounter for Wigan RLFC on 17 July, when they met a West Indies Amateur XI at Poolstock in aid of Brian McTigue's testimonial fund. Billy failed to take any wickets and conceded 17 runs as the West Indies XI piled up 235/5. He scored 13 not out in Wigan's reply of 84/4, Fred Griffiths top scoring with 40 runs.

Although Billy's thoughts had probably not yet turned to his own possible testimonial year, he was just about to turn 26 and was already a veteran of almost seven years as a rugby league player. In that period of time he had played 225 games for Wigan and piled up 279 tries. People were already talking of him as one of the game's all-time greats. In his domestic life he was now the father of three daughters and had gone from labouring to being an employee of the General Post Office working on line-testing.

One of Billy's unfulfilled ambitions was to play in a World Cup winning team for Great Britain and the autumn of 1960 might fulfil that desire, as for the first time the World Cup was to be staged in England. A good few of the Wigan side were regarded as near certainties or at least possibilities for the Great Britain World Cup squad. The problem was that there were only 18 places in that squad, so good form in the early weeks of the season was a pre-requisite, with a World Cup trial set for St Helens on 12 September, just one month into the season.

Wigan's pre-season public practice match took place on 30 July before a crowd of 5,037, which saw Billy score two tries and a goal as the Cherry and Whites beat the Blues 44–25. The highlight was a bizarre conversion taken by Frank Collier that hit one post, bobbled along the bar before hitting the other post and dropped over for a goal. After that it was impossible for the players to take the game seriously. Wigan started their season by winning the annual sevens, now christened the Silcock Cup, before a crowd of 14,659 at Central Park. Billy and Mick Sullivan were the star men, both scoring in all three rounds. Leigh were beaten 10–8, Widnes 19–3 and Oldham 18–11 in the final, with Billy scoring twice in the final. The Wigan VII was Ashton, Fenton, Sullivan, Bolton, Boston, Sayer and Lyon. Billy missed the Wardonia Cup match, on 6 August, his 26th birthday, because of the death of an aunt. Wigan pulverised Warrington 31–8 at Wilderspool.

Among the changes at Central Park was the introduction of sprint coach Percy Breckell, while the board had ordered a new set of special plastic tracksuits, which were designed to help the players reduce weight.

The opening league fixture on 13 August provided Wigan with a 44–0 stroll against Barrow at Central Park. The *Wigan Examiner* match report was headlined "Right Wing Pair Shatter Barrow". Billy scored four tries and Eric Ashton bagged three to send an early message to the World Cup selectors. Billy's four were scored between the 30th and 48th minutes. His first was a fabulous affair. Barrow kicked off after Griffiths had landed a penalty. Billy caught the ball on his '25' and the *Examiner* reported: "He beat the man nearest to him before swerving to the wing and, in a superb dash along the touch-line, he beat Grundy, Roper, Woolveridge and Dawes to score at the corner. On each occasion he seemed to have no more than inches in which to beat his man – and it was his power, allied to speed, which got him through... For a period straddling half-time Billy Boston was irrepressible and some of the Barrow players considered it was a wonderful achievement if they stopped this jet-propelled winger." The following Wednesday evening Billy skippered the side at Leigh as Ashton was suffering from fibrositis. In a thrilling game, which was won 25–9, Billy caused Leigh all sorts of problems. The *Examiner* noted: "He made a great impression on the Great Britain selector present by his powerful and speedy running. On his present form Boston is probably the greatest winger in the world."

On 20 August Billy was moved to left centre for the trip to Hull, despite being reported to still be suffering from a kick to his abdomen in the Leigh game. It did not seem to bother him as Hull were smashed 30–9 and he collected a hat-trick. The Boulevard gateman had initially refused scrum-half Brian Scrivens entry because he could not prove his identity. The disappointed Hull fans probably wished that gateman had stopped the rest of the Wigan side from entering the ground, particularly Billy, who was in fantastic form. Tom Groves wrote: "He is a more mature winger. He has the natural talent, the speed and the power. It may be thought that Vollenhoven is a little faster, or that some other winger is a slightly better defender, but taken all round he is the best equipped wingman in the game."

Two days later Billy claimed his third hat-trick in four games in a 25–11 home victory over Whitehaven. Much stiffer opponents on 27 August were Oldham, who attracted a crowd of more than 26,000 to Central Park for a first round Lancashire Cup tie. In the end Wigan won comfortably enough 19–5 but not before much bad blood had been spilled. Referee Jack Senior issued 27 penalties – 15–12 to Wigan – and there were 45 scrums, 30–15 to Wigan, but he did not send anyone off until six minutes from time, when Mick Sullivan and Frank Pitchford were marched.

A dreadful high tackle by Alan Davies on Dave Bolton in the 17th minute was the spark for trouble. Tom Groves wailed, "It is a long time since I have seen Wigan players, particularly acting captain Boston, so incensed". Billy received a bang on the head and cut his mouth and tongue when tackling Ike Southward and he did not know much about what was going on. However, he did get involved in some of the bother that ensued. Groves observed: "What happened was that Boston and another Wiganer pointed at Davies and were obviously threatening him. Thereafter there were a number of scuffles between these players. Said Billy this week: 'All that arm-waving and shouting is not the thing and I wouldn't have done it had I known properly what was happening. I only had a vague idea of what was going on and I remembered thinking that we were losing and then looked up at the score-board to see that we were winning easily. I didn't see any of the tries, apart from the last one, when I sent Keith Holden in, but even then Charlie Winslade charged me just as I was passing the ball and shook every bone in my body. I don't know what happened when I tackled Southward earlier in the match, but my mouth and tongue were cut and I have not been able to eat anything until yesterday'. If Billy had known what he was doing, then his attitude would have been discreditable, but that sort of action is in fact foreign to his normal nature."

Billy reverted to the right wing when Ashton returned for a 24–12 win at Barrow on 1 September, putting in a series of barnstorming dashes before playing the ball to himself in the 75th minute and charging 30 yards for a try. Two days later Wigan won by exactly the same score, 24–12, at Blackpool, but were given a much harder time by Borough on their narrow pitch than expected. It was Billy, with yet another hat-trick, who made the ultimate difference. After two minutes he picked up a Blackpool fumble and beat three men to score from halfway; on the half hour he surged forward on to a kick by Bolton, took it on the bounce, went between Gee and Foster and rounded Lowe; finally in the 55th minute he claimed the last try of the game from an interception 50 yards out, again slicing between

Billy scoring against Whitehaven on 22 August 1960, leaving John McKeown in his wake.

two defenders and rounding Lowe. With 14 tries in seven games Billy shot straight to the top of the try-scoring lists, while Wigan were top of the league and only they and Halifax remained unbeaten.

Things were certainly going Billy's way because he was selected for the right wing spot in the Great Britain side to meet the Rest of the League on 12 September in the World Cup trial. Ashton, Sullivan, Barton and McTigue were also in the team while Frank Collier was in the Rest's second-row. However, Billy's and Wigan's paths were quickly to become bumpy.

On 7 September Wigan went to St Helens for a Lancashire Cup second round tie and lost 7–4 before 27,000 enthralled fans, to suffer their first defeat of the season. Austin Rhodes scored the only try of the match after seven minutes following some classic interplay between Murphy and Huddart. The Wigan pack was outplayed in a hard but unspectacular affair. It was hard even for the touch-judges, one of whom, Mr J. Tyrer, pulled a muscle and was replaced by an official from the crowd after 17 minutes. Billy threw a forward pass to Frank Halliwell, which cost his side a try, and then dropped an inside pass from Ashton from which he would probably have scored. Even so, Billy was the man-of-the-match. The *Wigan Examiner* purred: "He was nothing short of magnificent. Time and again he streaked through the middle beating man after man in glorious runs, but the St Helens defenders covered well and crowded in on him. Yet Boston remained the supreme figure on the field." Fred Griffiths hurt a thigh and Billy took the touch kicks, some of which were massive ground makers drawing the crowd's admiration.

Billy's touch kicking was again excellent in the home league game against Hunslet on 10 September and his 43rd minute try, when he effortlessly broke three tackles, was the game's highlight. However, Wigan lost again, 23–17, and Billy picked up a leg injury, which kept him out of the World Cup trial two days later. The selectors met at Manchester on Wednesday, 14 September and Billy was delighted to learn that he was one of the 18 man squad for the tournament, which would open on 24 September with games between Great Britain and New Zealand at Odsal and Australia and France at Central Park. The Great Britain squad was:

Eric Ashton (Wigan) captain, Billy Boston (Wigan), Jim Challinor (Warrington), Alan Davies (Oldham), Eric Fraser (Warrington), Bobby Greenough (Warrington), Tommy Harris (Hull), Vince Karalius (St

Helens), Brian McTigue (Wigan), Alex Murphy (St Helens), Frank Myler (Widnes), Austin Rhodes (St Helens), Brian Shaw (Hunslet), John Shaw (Halifax), Mick Sullivan (Wigan), Derek Turner (Wakefield Trinity), Johnny Whiteley (Hull) and Jack Wilkinson (Wakefield Trinity).

Billy's form was so outstanding that it would have been almost impossible for the selectors to overlook him. The major surprise was perhaps the inclusion of stand-off Frank Myler in preference to Billy's team-mate Dave Bolton, while Bobby Greenough and Austin Rhodes were also outsiders, whose versatility probably weighed heavily in their favour. The big surprise was Britain's gamble in picking only eight forwards – most pundits had assumed the party would include nine forwards and nine backs. All three of the game's finest loose-forwards – Karalius, Turner and Whiteley – had been included, along with two hookers – Harris and John Shaw. That did not leave the selectors with much room for manoeuvre if things went awry.

On the Saturday preceding the World Cup Wigan went to Whitehaven and were whacked 14–2, their third loss in a row. If that was a bad blow for the club and its supporters, Billy suffered an even worse blow. Just after half-time he got away on a storming run but suddenly pulled up in agony. He had severely torn a muscle in his thigh. Thereafter he was practically immobile and left the field with about eight minutes remaining. It could not have happened at a worse time. Within three days, Tuesday, 20 September, the final nominations had to be registered for the World Cup squads. Billy and the other Wigan World Cup squad members were obliged to miss Wigan's win over Rochdale Hornets on Monday 19 September, but there was no way that Billy could have played anyway and the selectors were put in a real quandary as to whether to register Billy for the tournament. They were prepared to allow him to miss the game against New Zealand but what if his injury persisted? How could Britain be expected to cope with only 17 men in the squad?

In the event they gave Billy the nod and excused him from attending training at Hunslet and three days pre-match residence at a Leeds hotel. Instead he had treatment at Wigan and hoped to be fit for the second game against France at Swinton on 1 October.

Britain decided to field Bobby Greenough, usually a stand-off, in Billy's place against the Kiwis and won less convincingly than the 23–8 score suggested, while Australia just edged out France 13–12. Britain's players were being paid £20 for a victory, £13 for a draw and £10 for a loss and were to receive a £25 bonus if they won the competition. None of this really mattered to Billy, who was reliving his previous World Cup nightmares. In 1954 he was forced to withdraw through injury without even getting to France. In 1957 he had at least got to Australia and played in two games, but was again injured and forced to return home early. Third time lucky? Perhaps not, it seemed. Billy had told the press at Odsal that he expected to be fit for the French game and when the team was announced for it he was indeed on the right wing, while Tommy Harris and Derek Turner had been left out in favour of John Shaw and Brian Shaw.

However, while training at Swinton he failed to last more than 10 minutes when testing his fitness. He realised that he was definitely not sufficiently recovered and Britain drafted in Jim Challinor to play on the right wing. Britain managed well enough without Billy and Eric Ashton, who went down with a throat infection. They hammered France 33–7 and thereby set up a World Cup decider at Odsal against Australia, who defeated New Zealand 21–15 at Headingley.

Billy trained at Wigan on the Tuesday before the game against Australia, had an injection into his leg and survived a 90 minute training session, which included a soccer match, at Hunslet on the Thursday and was declared fit to meet the Australians in what was

112

**The 1960 World Cup**

Billy tackles Reg Gasnier against Australia at Odsal. Derek Turner is behind Billy.

Scoring in the same match.

effectively the World Cup Final on 8 October. Less fortunate were full-back Eric Fraser and back-rower Johnny Whiteley, who were both ruled out with knee injuries. At least Billy's World Cup hoodoo was broken and he had a chance to finally be a member of a World Cup-winning side. Odsal Stadium was not at its best for this crucial game. Rain had fallen throughout the week and it rained again on the morning of the match and then returned half an hour before kick-off.

The pitch was an ocean of mud and there was consequently not much hope of an open game for the 32,773 crowd which braved the conditions or for the millions at home watching it on BBC's *Grandstand*, accompanied by Eddie Waring's less than dulcet tones. Australia were clearly worried about Billy's presence and switched 14 stone Brian Carlson from the right wing to the left to mark him. Australia were unfortunate to be missing their outstanding loose-forward Johnny Raper through injury. The teams were:

*Great Britain:* Rhodes, Boston, Ashton (capt), Davies, Sullivan, Myler, Murphy, Wilkinson, J Shaw, McTigue, B Shaw, Turner, Karalius
*Australia:* Barnes (capt), Boden, Gasnier, Wells, Carlson, Brown, Muir, Beattie, Kelly, Parcell, Mossop, Rasmussen, Hambly

From the start it was clear that no one would be taking any prisoners and that the French referee Edouard Martung was in for a busy 80 minutes. Murphy and Muir had an altercation at the second scrum and after 10 minutes Wilkinson and Parcell had a set-to. By then Britain had taken the lead after Rhodes landed a very good penalty from near touch in the sixth minute. George M. Thompson noted in *Yorkshire Sports,* "Boston soon showed he was going to be a menace to Australia, having two short, penetrative bursts and then easily beating the shadowing Carlson." Britain had most of the play but there was constant trouble for Monsieur Martung and his touch-judges as the mud and mayhem made mischief. The game was won and lost in the 10 minutes before half-time and Billy drove the first nail into Australia's coffin. Wilkinson, Brian Shaw, Turner and Karalius made inroads into Australia's defence, stretching it to breaking point. Karalius then delivered a beautiful long pass to Ashton, who got clear and served Billy, who side-stepped and brushed past an opponent before slamming the ball down left-handed near the corner flag for the opening try. Rhodes booted a tremendous conversion and Britain led 7–0. Billy made two more sterling attempts to burst the Australian defence before the ball was smartly switched to the left in the 78th minute and culminated in Alex Murphy sending Mick Sullivan scorching 35 yards to the corner, outpacing three pursuers in the process.

At 10–0 down and in such vile conditions Australia were never going to make up that deficit. The second half was fought out with increasing fury and brutality but Australia finally scored on 70 minutes, when Brown made a lovely, elusive mid-field run before parting to Carlson about 20 yards out. Billy attempted to tackle him but the mud got the better of him and Carlson touched down wide out. There was no more scoring and Great Britain triumphed 10–3. Billy and his team had deserved their victory and the £45 per man that accompanied it. The press, however, was vitriolic about the nature of the game. Tom Longworth, of the *News Chronicle*, railed, "This was Rugby League in its ugliest form", while the *Yorkshire Post's* Alfred Drewry complained, "The Odsal match was quite the nastiest it has been my misfortune to report". Derek Marshall wrote in the *Daily Mail:* "The game produced a sustained brand of viciousness I hope never to see again. In the second half the need to halt an opponent seemed to be exceeded by the desire to hurt him, so that every tackle was accompanied by a battery of blows... How players avoided serious injury is a mystery. How referee Edouard Martung managed to finish the match without sending anybody off is a miracle." He was generous to Billy, however, writing: "Britain's gamble of playing Billy Boston paid off handsomely. He threw the Australian defence into a panic whenever he had the ball, and romped over for Britain's first try."

Returning to more mundane matters with Wigan, the period of the World Cup had seen new developments. The club itself had stated to the RFL that it would no longer offer any facilities for live televising of league matches at Central Park, the board being of the persuasion that it caused a drastic reduction in attendances. Prop forward Bill Bretherton had been sold to Swinton for £1,500 and whole groups of directors had been on trips to Wales in pursuit of a winger or yet another scrum-half, depending on which rumour was going the rounds. However, no more Welshmen appeared at Central Park. Wigan's fortunes slumped in the weeks following Billy's return from World Cup duty. On 15 October Leigh won 17–15 at Central Park. Before kick-off Billy received a mounted cricket ball from Mr Elliott, the chairman of Highfield CC, in recognition of that 9/28 performance against Winstanley Park in the summer. There was also a pre-match presentation to Brian McTigue – a cheque for £1,100 for his testimonial, the largest in Wigan's history. Billy was not his usual self against Leigh, appearing not fully fit. He was not. His thigh was still a painful problem and he missed Wigan's 11–6 – three tries to none – defeat at St Helens, when two sensational touchdowns from Alex Murphy put the skids under Wigan.

Eric Ashton was having a bad time too – injuries and illness seemed to be dogging him. His latest misfortune was damaged knee ligaments, which required an operation and put the onus of captaincy on Billy from Bonfire Night to Boxing Day. His spell in charge began well enough with a hard-earned 10–3 win at Hunslet, where Mick Sullivan scored a wonder try. Mick played left centre to the newly signed 1958 Lion Frank Carlton, who cost Wigan £5,000. Carlton was a very classy wingman and with Billy, Ashton, Holden, Sullivan and Carlton all available for the three-quarters, Wigan fans began to wonder how they could all be kept sweet.

On 12 November at Wakefield Wigan lost their sixth game in eight outings and were then very hard pushed to sneak a 16–11 home win against Blackpool, who swarmed all over Billy whenever he was in possession, but could not prevent him from scoring one try and putting Carlton over for another. A defeat at Widnes, where Harry Dawson lifted a wonderful 40-yard penalty goal out of the mud to win the game 5–3 six minutes from time, was followed by a good win at home against Hull. This in-and-out form continued with a home defeat by Swinton and a victory at Workington on Christmas Eve. However, Billy was absent firstly through bronchitis and then through a gashed knee sustained in training. By that time Keith Holden had been transferred to Oldham for £6,666, Norman Cherrington had been listed at £8,000 and soon Mick Sullivan joined him on the list at £11,000. Central Park appeared to the outside world to be in turmoil.

Billy's international rehabilitation had continued at Bordeaux on 11 December. Great Britain had beaten France 21–10, after trailing 7–5 at the break, and the *Daily Express* headline declared "Boston Bounce Flattens France". This game was unusual on two counts – Billy did not score and, for a welcome change in tests in France, there were no brawls or controversial incidents. Jack Bentley reported: "Billy Boston, Wigan winger who has never been on a losing Great Britain side in France, proved Britain's lucky mascot... when he sparked two great tries for their first test victory in France since Boston last played here – in Grenoble, March 1958. Try no.1 came in the 31st minute as France led 5–0. Big Billy grabbed a loose French pass, powered 30 yards then turned the ball inside to stand-off Frank Myler. The Widnes lad handed it on to second-row man Derek Turner, and then backed up brilliantly to take a return pass and go behind the posts... Try no.2 came after 60 minutes when Britain had edged ahead at 8–7 but were being penned in their own half by furious French tackling. This time Boston went inside as acting half-back and after a play-the-ball thundered through three tackles before hooker John Shaw and scrum-half Alex Murphy took over to get centre Neil Fox in at the corner." Billy was the only Welshman in the test team although he did have his club colleagues Mick Sullivan and debutant John Barton playing alongside him.

Meanwhile, Wigan had plummeted from top of the league in September to 12th in the league table as Christmas approached. Wigan chairman Bill Gore told the press: "Something will have to be done. We can't let the slide go on like this. Team spirit is practically nil." Wigan had already lost eight league games, and could not afford to lose more than two more if they were to even reach the top four to defend their Championship title. They were a long way behind the joint leaders Warrington, Wakefield Trinity and Leeds.

A huge boost for Wigan came on Boxing Day against Salford with the return of Eric Ashton, who had been sorely missed. Billy benefited with two tries, while Frank Carlton claimed his first hat-trick for Wigan in a 47–6 success. Over 28,000 turned up at Central Park on 2 January for the fixture against Warrington. Mick Sullivan, already in dispute over wages with Wigan, got caught up in the traffic jam and turned up just minutes before kick-off, provoking Joe Egan into leaving him out of the team. Wigan led 5–0 at half-time. However, Billy and Ashton blundered in the 57th minute in failing to field a kick through by Laurie Gilfedder and were mortified when Brian Bevan raced through to gleefully fall on the ball for a gift try and Wigan succumbed 10–5.

Fortunately, Wigan's form recovered dramatically beginning with a dogged but exciting game at Swinton. The lead changed hands six times before Wigan won 12–10, a 72nd minute try from Carlton sealing the victory. At the final whistle a spectator spat at the referee and another threw a punch at Ashton. On 21 January Billy and Eric put on virtuoso performances in a 45–3 home demolition of Hull KR. Both scored four tries and Ashton added six goals for a tally of 24 points. With his second touchdown Billy reached the landmark of 300 tries for Wigan.

The following week Billy was in Great Britain's side for the return against France at St Helens. He had a new centre partner in Mick Sullivan, but Mick was now a St Helens player, having been transferred for a world record fee of £11,000. On a very muddy pitch Britain won an excellently contested test 27–8. Eric Fraser booted six goals and tries were scored by Alex Murphy, who got two, Billy, Brian Shaw and left wing debutant John Stopford. Billy's try gave Britain an 18–3 lead in the 31st minute and was an easy romp to the line from an intelligent 20-yard pass from Frank Myler. Billy also got over the French line in the second half. However, he was adjudged to have lost the ball in touching down.

On 4 February Wigan beat Liverpool City 20–7 at Central Park. Liverpool must have taken great satisfaction from preventing him from scoring for up to that game Billy had made ten appearances against them and scored tries in every one, for a total of 23. Billy was, in fact, embarking on a pretty lean spell as far as try-scoring was concerned, his next 11 games for Wigan yielding only five tries for him, and they were gathered in just two games. For most of this period Billy was employed in the centre alongside Ashton and even though his scoring rate plummeted he was providing the goods for Wigan, whose season was now turning round for the better. Wigan's resurgence came, perversely, at a point when they struggled to field a settled threequarter line after having had an embarrassment of riches in that department. With Sullivan and Holden gone, their problem was exacerbated when Carlton sustained a bad shoulder injury against Liverpool. Billy and Eric thus had even more responsibility thrust on their broad shoulders. Typically, they remained unbowed.

Wigan entered the Challenge Cup at 9–1, their longest odds for some time and rated longer shots than St Helens at 5–2, Wakefield and Warrington 5–1, Leeds 7–1 and Oldham and Swinton 8–1. For the third consecutive year Wigan were drawn against Leeds. The tie at Headingley on 11 February attracted a crowd of 32,746 despite some atrocious weather. Apart from the gale, which blew throughout, and a pitch resembling a paddy field, Wigan faced a host of problems. Billy entered the match anxious about a recurrence of his thigh problem, Eric Ashton looked like death warmed up as he fought the effects of a streaming cold and Dave Bolton had been in-and-out of hospital all week with a rash and septic leg. Leeds were, incidentally, top of the league. In the face of all this Wigan put up an amazing performance in, according to the *Wigan Examiner,* "a grim and epic struggle for supremacy". Leeds took the lead in the ninth minute, when Derek Hallas claimed a try just before Billy could get to him and on the half hour Lewis Jones kicked a penalty goal. Frank Collier was concussed and did not know where he was for 15 minutes of the first half. Wigan showed great courage, stamina and ability to restrict Leeds to a 5–0 interval lead.

Dave Bolton opened the Leeds defence up in the 48th minute to send Jeff Bootle over for a try, but Wigan's Wembley aspirations seemed to have been scuppered when hooker Bill Sayer was sent off for tripping on 57 minutes. Ashton's leadership, Billy's awesome defence and Brian McTigue's nous kept Wigan in the game and eight minutes from time they were rewarded. Fred Griffiths landed one of the goals of his life from a penalty three yards infield and into the teeth of the gale. It earned Wigan a 5–5 draw and £30 per man.

The replay on the following Wednesday afternoon drew 40,033 fans to Central Park. It was the first of nine consecutive games in which Billy was to figure in the centre. While Wigan's astonishing 32–7 victory delighted their fans, for neutrals and Loiners the game was an anticlimax. The result was beyond any doubt well before half-time, when Wigan led 21–2. Ashton and McTigue were towering figures. Ashton became a dejected figure, however, when he was sent off for the first time in his career in the 62nd minute after a set-to with giant Leeds forward Jack Fairbank at a play-the-ball.

Billy was altogether too much of a handful for Leeds. As early as the second minute he whizzed past Fred Pickup, swerved past two more defenders and sent Ashton over with a lofted pass for the first try. Ten minutes later Billy hurtled over at the corner after a swift bout of passing and two minutes from time he bludgeoned his way through for his second try to end the scoring.

Wigan's run of six matches without defeat came to a halt at Thrum Hall three days later when Halifax beat them 17–10. The feature of the game was Garfield Owen's fearless tackling of Billy, who constantly broke the midfield defence, while Billy was also frustrated and incredulous when the touch-judge ruled out a try he and everyone else believed he had scored perfectly legitimately. On 25 February Wigan had another fearsome challenge, when they went to Wakefield in the second round of the Cup for an all-ticket match. A post-war ground record of 28,681 shoehorned itself into Belle Vue, a figure that would have been much higher if the authorities had been more lenient on the permitted capacity. Wigan lacked suspended hooker Bill Sayer, but his stand-in Jack Gregory won the scrums 22–20. It was a gruelling, unspectacular cup-tie, again played in dreadful conditions. Wigan were reported to be on £35 to win while the Trinitarians were on £46. There was a solitary score after 11 minutes and it went to Wigan, when Griffiths landed a simple penalty after Ken Rollin was penalised at a scrum. Thereafter Wigan's forwards throttled Trinity's efforts to open out play. Billy made a magnificent try-saving tackle on Harold Poynton and twice Jan Prinsloo broke clear only to fall tamely to tackles by Griffiths. Billy got Fenton over late in the proceedings, but the winger was unable to ground the ball. However, 2–0 might just as well have been 20–0 for Wigan, who were soon installed as 2–1 favourites for the Cup after they drew Salford at Central Park in the third round.

Wigan embarked on a run of five home matches on 4 March with a 24–5 beating of Widnes. For a change the weather was spring-like. Billy captained the side in the absence of Ashton, who had been suspended for his fight with Fairbank, the RFL's Disciplinary Committee having used film evidence – from the BBC – for the first time ever. Billy put in a sensational performance, moving the *Wigan Examiner* to say: "There will be many bruised chests and shoulders among the Widnes players who took part in the stopping, or attempted stopping, of Billy Boston. Billy scored three tries and had the crowd cheering as time and time again he went barging through, much to the consternation of the Widnes defenders." He also helped his winger Syd Fenton to two tries.

Billy again led the side in the third round cup-tie against Salford, which attracted an attendance of 29,110 on a beautiful afternoon. Salford gave Wigan a shock to lead 5–4 at half-time but Billy, Griffiths and Bolton tore huge gaps down the middle in the second half and Wigan eventually cruised into the semi-finals with a 22–5 victory.

Successes against Wakefield Trinity, Oldham and St Helens, which brought an aggregate crowd of 87,000 to Central Park, followed. Those victories pushed Wigan back into the fight for a top four spot. As usual the most satisfying was that against St Helens on Good Friday, which drew a massive crowd of 45,899. Wigan established a half-time lead of 7–2, Ashton claiming a try and two goals for Wigan against a penalty goal by Austin Rhodes. Saints unfortunately lost Vince Karalius through injury after 19 minutes. Wigan clinched a 12–2 win in the 65th minute with a fabulous try from Norman Cherrington, who dummied 40 yards out, shot through a gap, punted over Rhodes, caught the ball on the first bounce and scored under the posts. Billy and Mick Sullivan were in direct confrontation in the centres – a genuine titbit for the game's connoisseurs. Reports say the two pals blotted each other out and that Mick tackled brilliantly – and mostly low! The following afternoon Wigan performed dismally at Warrington, who were inspired by former Wigan favourite Nat Silcock. They were lucky to lose only 17–0 and defeat effectively ended their chances of finishing in the top four.

On Easter Monday Billy returned to the right wing for the visit to Salford. He also captained a very under strength side which included three debutants in full-back Tommy Vose and half-backs Johnny Phillips and Frank Parr. Scrum-half Parr would go on to make more than 300 appearances for the club. He was soon in trouble for his feeding of the scrums and Billy had to listen to the referee issuing him with his first warning, immediately after which the boyish number seven proceeded to score a gem of a try. Billy was not to be upstaged, however, and sizzled over for two wonder tries of his own. For the first he began 30 yards out, swerved past two men and left four on the turf in the space of a few yards, all having failed to force him into touch. The second saw him feint to run wide of the full-back, only to completely deceive him by jumping over his outstretched arms. They were Billy's first tries in six matches.

Wigan's opponents in the Challenge Cup semi-final were Halifax at Swinton on 15 April. The two teams had met at Wigan the previous week, but Billy and many top men from both teams had been rested, so not too much store was set on Wigan's 19–12 victory. The semi-final was declared all-ticket and the second half was televised on BBC's *Grandstand*. For those with long memories it was just five years since that momentous other Challenge Cup semi-final between the clubs at Odsal which had such strong repercussions for Billy. Only three of that 1956 Wigan team turned out at Swinton – Billy, Eric Ashton and Dave Bolton – while only one man from the Halifax team appeared – Billy's nemesis at Odsal, Geoff

Palmer. This time Wigan were clear favourites. Halifax were 11th in the league and Wigan eighth, although Wigan's form since the New Year had been outstanding with only three defeats in 17 games.

The weather was glorious and Wigan served up a performance that warmed their supporters' hearts. In truth Halifax were never really in the hunt after Wigan took the lead in the 15th minute, when Bolton, the star of the match, created a try for Jeff Bootle, converted by Griffiths. Halifax responded with a goal from Owen but on 32 minutes a kick by Bolton bounced wickedly for Owen and Freeman and Billy came through like an express train to touch down just before the ball went dead. Griffiths converted again and Wigan led 10–2 at half-time. Three more tries went Wigan's way in the second half. Carlton dived in spectacularly at the corner on 44 minutes; Billy spread-eagled the defence in the 63rd minute in finishing off a tremendous 70-yard movement involving Griffiths, Bolton and Bootle; Bolton grabbed the last, swerving electrically away from Williams and Freeman. Halifax gained tries on 53 and 71 minutes through Freeman and Scroby but Wigan were in no way flattered by their 19–10 win.

Wigan won the scrums 24–16 and there were only 15 penalties. The *Yorkshire Post's* Alfred Drewry paid a telling tribute to Wigan's style: "The great thing about the victory that took Wigan to Wembley for the third time in four years was the way it was achieved. Their bold, adventurous rugby, played with a swashbuckling air by gifted players eager to give full rein to their talents was a joy to watch. It put to shame the safety-first school who hold that the first principle of the game is not to make mistakes." For Billy, perhaps, the ghost of Odsal 1956 receded a little into the distance.

After qualifying for Wembley, Wigan completed their league programme by winning their last four games in just eight days. In the second of those fixtures at Hull KR's Craven Park, when Wigan triumphed 31–12, they played so superlatively that the Rovers fans cheered Wigan off at full-time. Billy claimed one of his specials in the 44th minute. Rovers were attacking just inside the Wigan half when the ball popped loose and went straight into Billy's hands. The *Wigan Examiner* wrote: "Boston erupted into action, swerved away from the full-back and then outpaced three or four opponents with such ease that he was slowing down 20 yards before he reached the line." The *Liverpool Echo* added: "In the opinion of old followers of Wigan there has never been such an ovation accorded to a visiting player as that when Boston scored one of his characteristic tries. Billy himself looked astonished as he walked back to the centre to the great round of applause." At Rochdale three days later Billy plundered two more tries in a 37–5 win. His second, courtesy of Ashton, showed him to be "too powerful for Trevor Simms, who did, however, once tackle him in full flight and earned a big ovation!"

Wigan finished fifth in the league table, which Leeds topped with 60 points, five points clear of Warrington and Swinton. St Helens took the last play-off spot with 54 points, followed by Wigan, Leigh and Wakefield Trinity all on 52 points and Oldham on 51. It had been one of the tightest struggles for the top four that anyone could remember.

Wigan's consolation was a fortnight off before they met St Helens at Wembley on 13 May. Saints had no rest and went down to Leeds, the eventual champions, in the semi-final. The prospect of a Saints versus Wigan Cup Final had huge numbers of fans salivating in anticipation. The press referred to it in terms such as "the match of the century" and were forecasting "the greatest ever Wembley final". There was no question that Wembley would be sold out and it was. Of course, the Wigan and St Helens supporters would not give a fig about the quality of the spectacle, as long as their team won. Both sides were packed with test men, personalities and match winners. Wigan were, if anything, slight favourites because of their superior experience of Wembley and because of their pack's power, while their threequarters were also physically bigger than their counterparts. St Helens believed their superior pace and fitness would swing the issue. Wigan, as had become customary, spent several days in preparation at Blackpool, while Saints decamped to Southport.

It was Billy's third Wembley final and once again he was playing with an injury. This time he had damaged his shoulder in training, but the secret was well kept. To balance it out Billy's direct opponent was Mick Sullivan, who had his own secret injury – a slightly displaced bone in his foot.

The teams for the 1961 Challenge Cup final were:

*Wigan:* Griffiths, Boston, Ashton (capt), Bootle, Carlton, Bolton, Entwistle, Barton, Sayer, McTigue, Collier, Lyon, Evans

*St Helens:* Rhodes, Vollenhoven, Large, McGinn, Sullivan, Murphy, Smith, Terry, Dagnall, Watson, Vines, Huddart, Karalius (capt)

When Wigan arrived at their London headquarters in Hendon on Thursday 11 May, Eric Ashton told the press: "We're hoping it stays fine and warm. All the lads want it that way". Their wish was certainly granted because on the great day a sun-soaked Wembley sweltered in over 80 degrees. If nothing else, it was the hottest cup final on record. However, the hoped-for spectacular did not materialise, although the game never lacked interest because of its intensity and the closeness of the score. The first half hour saw Wigan in the ascendancy but unable to turn their superiority to significant advantage. Griffiths fired them into the lead with a splendid long-distance penalty goal in the fifth minute but it was Saints who claimed the first try on 33 minutes, when Murphy tore on to Huddart's pass, after the second-row had majestically forced a gap. Billy made a desperate effort to get to Murphy but to no avail. A couple of minutes later Rhodes landed a tremendous penalty from near half-way and Wigan went in at half-time 5–2 down. Billy had a pain-killing injection for his troublesome shoulder as the players tried to cool down in the dressing-rooms. His duel with Mick Sullivan was a stalemate. Eddie Waring wrote in the *Sunday Pictorial:* "Billy Boston had not a lot of chances, nor had Sullivan, and they had one 'dust-up' in the first half". Lewis Jones commented in the *News of the World:* "Class cancelled out class in the wing duel between Boston and Sullivan, and also with regard to stand-off halves Bolton and Murphy."

Wigan could have turned the game on its head in the opening 10 minutes of the second half, but the gods were clearly on Saints' side. Frank Carlton touched down in the corner, but referee Tom Watkinson ruled a forward pass. Griffiths kicked a fairly simple penalty after 44 minutes to make the score 5–4. A minute later a couple of St Helens defenders were deemed to have been too rough in tackling Billy and Griffiths hit the post from wide out from the resultant penalty. Had the ball bounced in instead of out, Wigan would have led 6–5 and changed the whole complexion of the game. Billy then got a rare chance to run. He left Rhodes lying on the touchline turf and plunged for the corner, where he was met with avalanche force by Cliff Watson and, as Brian McGinn helped finalise the tackle, the corner flag went down in the flurry of bodies and limbs and the touch-judge ruled no-try. Billy was adamant that he had scored and that it was not he who knocked down the flag. On such trifles is the Challenge Cup sometimes won and lost.

The decisive action came around the hour and it was won by arguably the greatest try in the history of the Challenge Cup. Certainly, there have been no more spectacular tries and no one present at Wembley or who watched the television coverage, will be able to erase the image of *that* try by Tom van Vollenhoven from their memory banks. It began

Billy fights off three St Helens defenders at Wembley (Courtesy Alex Service)

innocently enough almost on the St Helens goal-line as Wigan spilled the ball. Huddart grabbed it and before the crowd knew what was happening Ken Large was away and interpassing down the touchline with Vollenhoven. Large fairly sizzled past two coverers and served Voll near half-way. Carlton was left in the slipstream and when Griffiths came to challenge him, the ball was sent back to Large. Ashton was bearing down on the flying centre but not quickly enough to stop him returning the ball to his winger, who scorched away from all pursuit to score under the sticks. Rhodes's conversion was followed by a 40-yard penalty goal and Saints were safely home at 12–4, although Griffiths reduced the deficit to 12–6 with a last minute penalty for Wigan.

Desmond Hackett, a popular columnist on the *Daily Express* – not a rugby league writer – was very impressed with the 1961 Cup Final. He commented: "There was one man from Wigan, name of William Boston, who looked like that character in Popeye who sinks battleships with his fist. And I hope Mr Boston does not think I am trying to be funny. It is well known that Hackett, the People's Friend, is respectful to athletes, particularly when they look like Mr Boston, weigh 15 stone, and are described as 'a strong determined runner'. Another Wigan man who frightened me to death was Brian McTigue, who is all of 16 stone. A St Helens player barged into him and down he went straight as a board. The St Helens man I mean. It struck me as odd that though they went for each other like mad bulls they still finished up as they started with 13 men apiece... And if you want to know how all this alarming stuff compares with rugby union, ask Alex Murphy, of St Helens, who [recently] played at Twickenham for the RAF. He will tell you: 'Compared with this Cup Final, playing at Twickenham is kids' stuff'."

Compared to the rapturous welcomes for the 1958 and 1959 Cup-winning sides and the 1960 Championship winners, the reception accorded to Billy and his colleagues of 1961 was muted. Only a few hundred fans – mostly children and teenage girls, according to the newspapers – lined the 500 yards stretch from the railway station to the town hall, where a reception was held for the team. At the town hall coach Joe Egan declared, "Our players are disappointed but not down and they will soon be back on top again". Joe was not to know it but he was shortly in for an even nastier shock than merely losing a Cup Final.

A few days after Wembley Billy and several of his Cup Final team-mates and opponents played in a benefit match at Salford for 19 year-old Oldham hooker David Goddard. He had been paralysed following a neck injury. Over £400 was raised for David Goddard.

Although Wembley was a disappointing end to Wigan's campaign, the season had been successful for Billy. Apart from a third Challenge Cup Final appearance, he was a World Cup winner and one of only six players to score more than 30 tries in the season. He was third in the try-scorers with 37. Two Springboks led the way – Tom van Vollenhoven with 59 and Wilf Rosenberg of Leeds with 44, Brian Bevan on 35 and Bobby Greenough and Alex Murphy 31 each.

The Wigan team around 1960. Back: Evans, Griffiths, Barton, McTigue, Sayer, Collier, Halliwell; front: Entwistle, Cherrington, Boston, Ashton, Bootle, Carlton.

Racing away from Workington Town half-back Sol Roper

**1960–61**

Wigan finished 5th in the League: P36, W26, L10, For 689, Against 334
Boston scored 35 tries for Wigan, plus 2 in representative rugby league

| Date | Opponent | Score | Boston | Crowd | |
|---|---|---|---|---|---|
| 13 August | **Barrow** | 44–0 | 4T | 17,030 | |
| 17 August | Leigh | 25–9 | | 21,397 | |
| 20 August | Hull | 30–9 | 3T | 15,669 | |
| 22 August | **Whitehaven** | 25–11 | 3T | 19,694 | |
| 27 August | **Oldham** | 19–5 | | 26,140 | LC1 |
| 1 September | Barrow | 24–12 | 1T | 4,539 | |
| 3 September | Blackpool B | 24–12 | 3T | 8,000 | |
| 7 September | St Helens | 4–7 | | 27,000 | LC2 |
| 10 September | **Hunslet** | 17–23 | 1T | 17,677 | |
| 17 September | Whitehaven | 2–14 | | 4,092 | |
| 19 September | **Rochdale H** | 14–5 | dnp | 8,252 | |
| 15 October | **Leigh** | 15–17 | | 20,577 | |
| 22 October | St Helens | 6–11 | dnp | 20,989 | |
| 5 November | Hunslet | 10–3 | | 9,500 | |
| 12 November | Wakefield T | 7–12 | | 18,224 | |
| 19 November | **Blackpool B** | 16–11 | 1T | 10,575 | |
| 26 November | Widnes | 3–5 | | 5,675 | |
| 3 December | **Hull** | 22–15 | 1T | 9,011 | |
| 17 December | **Swinton** | 4–16 | dnp | 12,684 | |
| 24 December | Workington T | 11–10 | dnp | 4,446 | |
| 26 December | **Salford** | 47–6 | 2T | 13,687 | |
| 2 January | **Warrington** | 5–10 | | 28,257 | |
| 7 January | Swinton | 12–10 | | 11,730 | |
| 21 January | **Hull KR** | 45–3 | 4T | 8,770 | |
| 28 January | Oldham | 15–5 | dnp | 9,325 | |
| 4 February | **Liverpool City** | 20–7 | | 8,043 | |
| 11 February | Leeds | 5–5 | | 32,746 | Cup 1 |
| 15 February | **Leeds** | 32–7 | 2T | 40,033 | Replay |
| 18 February | Halifax | 10–17 | | 11,297 | |
| 25 February | Wakefield T | 2–0 | | 28,681 | Cup 2 |
| 4 March | **Widnes** | 24–5 | 3T | 15,448 | |
| 11 March | **Salford** | 22–5 | | 29,110 | Cup 3 |
| 18 March | **Wakefield T** | 25–9 | | 21,904 | |
| 25 March | **Oldham** | 15–8 | | 19,965 | |
| 31 March | **St Helens** | 12–2 | | 45,899 | |
| 1 April | Warrington | 0–17 | | 17,500 | |
| 3 April | Salford | 32–5 | 2T | 7,600 | |
| 8 April | **Halifax** | 19–12 | dnp | 17,025 | |
| 15 April | Halifax | 19–10 | 2T | 35,118 | Cup SF (at Swinton) |
| 19 April | **Workington T** | 22–0 | | 9,275 | |
| 22 April | Hull KR | 31–12 | 1T | 11,802 | |
| 25 April | Rochdale H | 37–5 | 2T | 2,883 | |
| 27 April | Liverpool City | 19–6 | | 999 | |
| 13 May | St Helens | 6–12 | | 94,672 | Cup Final (at Wembley) |

## Representative matches:

| Date | For | Opponent | Score | Boston | Venue | |
|---|---|---|---|---|---|---|
| 8 October | Great Britain | Australia | 10–3 | 1T | Odsal | World Cup |
| 11 December | Great Britain | France | 21–10 | | Bordeaux | |
| 28 January | Great Britain | France | 27–8 | 1T | St Helens | |

# 12. 1961–62 Beating the Kiwis

During the 1961 close season the Wigan fans had been expecting big news. They were sure that Wigan would be announcing a major signing, or even signings, from South Africa. A couple of the directors had been there for a considerable time towards the end of the previous season, although no details had yet emerged. Nor would they. There was big news, however, of an unexpected nature. On 2 June Wigan announced that coach Joe Egan would be leaving the club when his contract expired on 6 August. Joe, who had been a Wigan star as a player, and was popular with fans and players, was not jumping ship. He was being pushed. Three Wembley appearances and a Championship title within the last three years was evidently not enough for the Wigan board. When asked why Joe Egan was being released, chairman Bill Gore commented: "It's like everything else at Wigan. They want new faces. Joe has been with us five years, and that's a long time". Joe said: "I have felt a little uncomfortable at Wigan for the last 12 months, but I couldn't put it down to anything in particular. There have been differences of opinion, but they have been sorted out in a normal way. There has been no personal animosity."

On 19 June Egan joined Widnes on a three-year contract, enjoying great success there, including another Challenge Cup win in 1964. On 3 July Wigan brought in their 'new face', except that it was the very old and familiar face of Jim Sullivan. Sullivan, coach at Rochdale Hornets for the last couple of years, was just about the only man Wigan followers would accept in place of Joe Egan. Unfortunately for Jim, approaching 58 years of age, he contracted pneumonia shortly after agreeing to join Wigan and was consequently out of action for six weeks, until the new season had got well under way. Johnny Lawrenson, a former star threequarter at Central Park, took over as caretaker coach, assisted by Eric Ashton, who had spent the close season recuperating from a throat operation. Billy recalls: "Jim hardly had any time as coach while I was at Wigan. He was strong in all his ways and said what he meant. What I liked about him was that he treated everyone alike. He didn't pamper the stars or have favourites."

The appointment of Sullivan had prompted Wigan to dispense with sprint coach Percy Breckell, as the directors reckoned Jim could cover that sphere. They and their new coach had also decided to have a panel of 20 first team players for each game, instead of 17 the previous season – with two on reserve and five in the 'A' team. The economics of this seemed viable as pre-season ticket sales had rocketed to £4,740, the best since 1952–53.

Billy was raring to go and had been joined at Central Park by a clutch of his compatriots. Wigan had signed centre Alan Jones and back-rower Bob Hodson, who had been successful rugby union players at St Luke's College, Exeter. Jones had also played for London Welsh and Hodson for Newport. Another Welshman, Tony Austin, a black 19 year-old winger from Billy's old club, Cardiff IAC, had the unenviable task of facing Billy in the public trial match on Saturday 5 August. If the crowd of 5,856 thought a new Boston had been discovered, they were wrong. Billy scored three tries in the Blues 43–38 win over the Cherry and Whites and Austin was described as "very slow" by the *Wigan Observer* reporter, never to reappear. The *Wigan Examiner*, incidentally, had folded during the close season.

Two days later Billy scored two tries as Wigan beat Oldham 19–13 in the final of the annual sevens tournament, which drew a crowd of 14,000 to Central Park. Wigan used eight men in the tournament: Boston, Ashton, Bootle, Jones, Bolton, Lyon, Sayer and Cherrington. On 12 August Wigan beat Warrington 26–10 in the Wardonia Cup before a crowd of 17,451. The *Wigan Observer* noted, "Only Boston and Griffiths seemed able to lift

Wigan's game above the ordinary" but added, "It is abundantly clear that Boston – versus top-class opposition at any rate – is not now fast enough to run in long distance tries. For a man of his weighty proportions, that is no surprise but it seems to me that Wigan are going to have to contrive to bring Boston into their attacks for much shorter blasts of 30 or 40 yards. In such circumstances – say when he is given the ball at full speed 30 yards out – Boston is still the game's biggest wing menace."

Wigan opened the season proper on 19 August with a useful 19–9 win at Huddersfield, a game punctuated by 41 scrums and 40 penalties. Billy scored Wigan's first try of the season in the 13th minute when, according to Jack Winstanley, "He slipped inside Breen and sort of skidded over the try-line with two men round his ankles." Eric Ashton was ferried back to Wigan Infirmary by taxi with a suspected broken leg. Fortunately, it turned out to be not so serious. As usual Billy had to fill in for him as right centre and captain for the next game, a 31–5 romp against Blackpool, when he scored two tries. Back on the wing against Hunslet on 26 August, Billy "produced two tries and some stout defence and... stopped Firn from scoring a try with a fearful tackle right on the Wigan line." Hunslet were crushed 44–11 and scored eight of their points in the last five minutes.

Billy plundered another couple of tries in a splendid 30–18 win at Workington in the first round of the Lancashire Cup. He was clearly in great form and the Workington crowd loved his play. Jack Winstanley noted, "He still moves with breathtaking power that only the surest of tackles can hope to stop". For his first try he slipped inside and took a perfect pass from Griffiths before making light of Syd Lowden's attempt at a tackle. The second came after he intercepted a high pass 55 yards out. This time he almost strolled to Lowden to draw him into the tackle and then whipped round him on the outside. Winstanley commented: "Pretorious made a gallant effort to stop Boston at the corner flag – but once the Wigan winger has got so far, almost all hope is gone. And so it was with Pretorious".

After bagging seven tries in the opening four fixtures, Billy finally failed to get on the scoresheet in a 20–0 win at Leigh on 6 September. It was a rough, tough game on a rain-soaked pitch but it was notable because Jim Sullivan appeared "on active duty on the bench for the first time", the *Wigan Observer* reported.

Billy was not the only Wigan winger in the limelight at this time. Syd Fenton was transferred to Barrow for £1,500, but Wigan had introduced yet another exotic character to rugby league in Chuck Wiseman, an American gridiron footballer, who had caught their attention when he had appeared in a rugby union sevens tournament in Wigan the previous April. He had been representing an American Air Force VII from Chicksands in Bedfordshire and had run in five tries. Wigan obviously saw him as a possible star in the Billy Boston mould. Certainly his three 'A' team trials brought in the crowds – 5,116 saw him score twice on his debut, a 36–5 win over Workington Town 'A', while there were 3,020 for Leigh 'A', when he scored again. However, Wiseman was discarded after his third trial game and in 1962 signed for Blackpool Borough, where he and Brian Bevan formed one of the most unlikely pair of wingers in the game's history.

Wigan went down to their first defeat of the season at home to a super-fit, close marking Swinton side on 9 September. Billy was starved out of the action, receiving just three passes as the Lions won 13–6. Three days later he saw more of the ball at Blackpool, scoring twice in a 33–8 win and was again on the scoresheet in a home victory over Leigh on 16 September, which drew a crowd of more than 20,000. It was a pretty robust derby encounter and Billy was twice lectured by referee Eric Clay, first for a tackle on South African left winger Ken Boonzaier and then for apparently throwing the ball down after being penalised. 'Sergeant Major' Clay also cautioned Wigan's Roy Evans and Leigh's Stan

Owen and Don Platt. Wigan won 25–6, Stan McLeod made his debut at left centre and Billy rampaged over to score in the 67th minute more or less ignoring Chris Landsberg, another South African, who was clinging on to his shirt collar. Poor Landsberg also lost his four front teeth during the game.

After the Leigh game Wigan stood proudly at the top of the league, but were suddenly faced with a major dilemma. Jim Sullivan had been in charge at Central Park for the Leigh game. That evening he went out for a stroll with his wife and suffered a seizure after returning home. He was admitted to the Christopher Nursing Home in Wigan for the second time in three months. His coaching career was at an end. Jim's latest venture with Wigan had effectively only covered 10 days and four games. Moreover, by a wicked quirk of fate, Wigan's next game, the following Thursday, saw Wigan go down 9–5 at Widnes in the second round of the Lancashire Cup to a Joe Egan inspired side.

That defeat proved to be Wigan's last for five months as the team launched a record-breaking run of success. Billy's form matched Wigan's, beginning with a brace of tries in a 45–0 whitewashing of Liverpool City. The test selectors clearly had their eyes on Wigan for Billy, together with Ashton, Bolton and the entire front row of Barton, Sayer and McTigue, were chosen for the first test against New Zealand at Leeds on 30 September. A great surprise was the omission of Mick Sullivan, who had not missed a Great Britain test since his debut in the 1954 World Cup, Warrington's Terry O'Grady displacing him.

In the meantime Wigan had splashed out £9,000 to bring Oldham's test centre Alan Davies to Central Park, establishing another all-international three-quarter line in Boston, Ashton, Davies and Carlton. Just as significantly they had replaced Jim Sullivan with another Welshman, Griff Jenkins, as their new coach. Jenkins, a notable pre-war winger at Warrington, had coached at Swinton, Oldham and Halifax. Billy says, "Griff Jenkins was more flamboyant than Jim Sullivan. He was full of himself, a very confident sort of man and, of course, he had a lot of success at Oldham, especially against Wigan!"

Great Britain began the test match at Headingley like a whirlwind. They were 8–2 up within the first quarter and seemed likely to overwhelm the Kiwis. Billy made his presence felt with the first try. From a midfield scrum the ball quickly reached Ashton, who veered out to the wing. It was the old party-piece, as Billy moved inside to receive Eric's flip pass and raced straight through to the posts for a try converted by Austin Rhodes. Shortly afterwards Rhodes ripped 40 yards upfield, developing a majestic back-line movement which ended with Alex Murphy sprinting for his side's second try. Then the wheels fell off. By half-time New Zealand led 14–8 and were 19–8 ahead by the hour at which point Britain made their only gesture of defiance. It was Billy who briefly raised the crowd's enthusiasm, when he surged over for a typical blockbusting try at the corner flag. However, by full-time New Zealand had soared to a record-breaking 29–11 victory. It was a major shock, the Kiwis having been very lacklustre in their games before the test and basically written off by the press. Alfred Drewry in the *Yorkshire Post* moaned, "A case could be made out for dropping all the Great Britain players, except perhaps Boston". Jack Paul commented in the *Sunday Express,* "It was left to Ashton and Boston to supply the class and danger", while another reporter concurred, saying, "The Ashton-Boston wing was the only bright spot in a dismal Great Britain setting."

Billy picked up a knee injury during the test, which kept him out of Wigan's next game. Ironically, it was against the New Zealanders on 7 October. The game marked Alan Davies's first team debut and was Griff Jenkins's first game in charge of the team. The crowd of 25,483 was the biggest of the Kiwi tour and almost 9,000 more than the first test attendance. Wigan handsomely achieved what Britain had failed to do and won 28–6, although Jack Winstanley noted that there was "too much fighting, too little football".

Returning to the fray in a 28–8 stroll at Rochdale, Billy helped him self to two superb second half tries. Barton, Cherrington and Griffiths opened up the way for his first when, according to the *Wigan Observer:* "He hurtled for the corner via Evans and Unsworth – Boston being probably the only winger who could have scored such a try." The second, six minutes later, followed a scrum near the right wing, from which Ashton engineered a beautiful arcing run from Billy to the posts.

Unsurprisingly, there were swingeing changes to the Great Britain team for the second test at Odsal on 21 October. Billy retained his place, as did Bolton and McTigue, while Roy Evans received his first test call-up, but Barton, Sayer and Ashton were discarded, Eric Fraser replacing him as captain. However, Eric was restored, to his centre spot, if not the captaincy, when Frank Myler pulled out injured. The selectors saw the error of their ways by reinstating Mick Sullivan to the left wing and replaced Barton and Sayer with St Helens players Abe Terry and Bob Dagnall.

A crowd of 19,980 saw Great Britain square the series with a comfortable 23–10 victory on a soft pitch. There was some good rugby and Wigan players provided three of Britain's five tries, Bolton, Evans and Ashton all claiming one, while Sullivan scored the other two. Neil Fox kicked four goals, including a monster penalty from 55 yards. Billy failed to score, but claimed a great deal of attention from swarms of Kiwis intent on stopping him. In what was, according to press reports, essentially a tame game, Billy livened matters up. Kiwi manager Colin Siddle got on his high horse and complained about "Billy Boston's challenge of Jim Bond which had the tourists' little ginger stand-off almost bouncing on the Odsal turf after taking the full force of Billy's bulk at top speed." Billy got ticked off by referee Eric Clay and Siddle ranted: "I don't care if you print it. Boston should have been sent off. We don't come 13,000 miles for that."

No one else appeared to be too upset about the incident and in the following week's *Rugby Leaguer* Cyril Briggs wrote: "There was some comment both during and after the match about Billy Boston's bouncing tactics. Now when Boston gets going there are very few players in the league who can stop him. When one or two Kiwis bounced off Boston when they went into the tackle they were knocked out of the way. No doubt this was not relished by the Kiwis. But there is nothing wrong in the way that Boston goes for the line. The great Boston runs have been the subject of a lot of comment over the weekend and there has been a rare old argument about the best way to halt his progress. The usual manner adopted to stop Boston is to collar him in his first few yards. Let him get into his stride and then you are asking for trouble because he can break tackle after tackle. Jack Wood, the former Leigh and Liverpool City player, had the happy habit of going for the ball, which Billy tucks firmly in his arm. And Wood sometimes succeeded, especially when the coloured winger was a long way from the line. Tackling the ball and not the player has been recommended by several leading stars. And if you don't want to feel Boston's shoulder charge, or one of his piston-like knees, then have a go at trying to take the ball from him – but you must try and avoid the hand-off!"

The British selectors were happy enough with the performance at Odsal to announce an unchanged team for the decider at Swinton on 4 November, although in the event Abe Terry pulled out injured and was replaced by Workington Town prop Norm Herbert.

Wigan travelled to Swinton on the Saturday preceding the test match and exacted revenge for their home defeat by the Lions seven weeks earlier. Their 7–4 win was hard earned after a torrid, thrilling, value-for-money clash. Both teams defended like dervishes and Billy was on top form in both attack and defence. He proved the match-winner with the only try of the game in the 24th minute. Swinton forward Ken Roberts broke away from his own line and in an attempt to bypass Ashton and Boston threw a long high pass towards winger Bobby Fleet. The ball seemed to hang in the air and Billy nipped in and dashed 35 yards for a try which stunned the 19,000 crowd.

The attendance for the Swinton test the following week was not much bigger at 22,558, but they got equal value for money from an entirely different type of game. Great Britain, after three days toning up at Southport, took the series with a magnificent 35–19 win in a game replete with astonishing combined movements and brilliant individualism. Alex Murphy played one of his greatest games and there were no weak links in the British side, which ran in seven tries through Sullivan who claimed two, Herbert, Dagnall, Ashton, Fraser and Murphy, Fox adding seven goals. Billy did not score. Indeed, he spent a lot of time in touch on the end of desperate gang-tackles by the Kiwis. The *Rugby Leaguer* reported, "Every time Billy got the ball a great cheer went up", while the *Daily Express* wrote of Billy, "No player can have roused a crowd more by beating more opponents in his rumbustuous runs and yet not have had a try to show for his efforts."

What Billy did have to show for his afternoon's exercise was £15 winning pay, plus £3 for time at Southport, and a spanking brand new gold watch. The brewers Mackeson, in an early incarnation of sponsorship, had organised a competition for the Kiwi tour games in which the side scoring most points against the tourists would be presented with inscribed gold wristwatches. Like most players Billy was keen to possess such an item but thought his chance had gone, when he missed Wigan's 28–6 win over the New Zealanders, Jeff Bootle playing in his place. However, Eric Ashton's try for Britain, followed by Neil Fox's touch-line conversion, had taken the score to 30–15, causing some of the British boys to jump for joy. Jack Paul commented in the *Sunday Express:* "Boston didn't get a try, hard as his colleagues tried to put him in, but he was still smiling at the end after some great efforts. 'Billy B gets the last laugh', he beamed at me, 'I was the only regular at Wigan who wouldn't have got a watch because I didn't play against the Kiwis. They were all laughing at me. Now it's me who's laughing'." Billy recalls, "At the end of the game I went over to the front of the stand and put two fingers up to the Wigan players who were at the game, and especially to Jeff. They all thought they were going to collect the watches at Mackeson's reception that evening in Manchester and now they had another think coming!"

Wigan continued their winning ways with an important 16–10 success at top-of-the-table Workington Town on 11 November. Billy's 50th minute try, after some characteristic combination with Ashton, gave his side daylight and Norman Cherrington's try four minutes from time clinched the two league points. Barrow were routed 39–3 at Central Park, where Billy sustained double vision early on after being poked in the eye. He still managed a try, which took his points tally for Wigan to 999. He duly passed the 1,000 points mark at Whitehaven on 25 November with the first of two tries in a 26–6 victory. The landmark try arrived in the 53rd minute after a back-line move on the Whitehaven '25'. The *Wigan Observer* reported: "Boston took the ball on the burst and three Whitehaven defenders found themselves keeping company with the ground as Boston brushed them aside." For his second try he latched on to Ashton's inside pass and "with unquestionable power and authority, more or less ignored two tackles to score."

Against Rochdale on 2 December Wigan were looking groggy and losing 5–3 to the Hornets at half-time. The weather was dreadful and the Central Park faithful were wet and worried. Then Billy, who had roared over for their only try in the first half, brightened them all up with two tries which took Wigan into an 11–5 lead and turned the game upside down.

From a scrum on the '25' Bolton and Ashton worked one of their familiar run-around moves before Billy thundered on to Ashton's pass. Jim Parr, Ken Parr, Johnny Fishwick and the giant Fijian winger Joe Levula were all ready and waiting for Billy, but need not have bothered turning up. Billy was just unstoppable as he smashed his way through for the 400<sup>th</sup> try of his career. His hat-trick try soon followed but that was a walk-over, courtesy of Ashton, and Wigan won 22–5. Two tries in a 31–11 home thrashing of Whitehaven followed and Billy had scored in eight consecutive games for Wigan, a tally of 14 tries.

Billy's scoring surge ended at Halifax on 16 December on a murky afternoon, when Wigan scraped a 7–4 win, thanks to an imperious display from Eric Ashton, who claimed the game's only try in the 24th minute. Halifax thus surrendered their unbeaten home record and Wigan notched their 10th consecutive victory. The *Wigan Observer* commented: "Boston had a cosy chat and handshake with fellow Welshmen Johnny Freeman and Colin Dixon before the game started. And all through the game Freeman and Dixon stayed close enough to Boston to make it almost an 80 minutes handshake, with the result that the Wigan winger found himself covered almost as soon as he got the ball." Billy was so well marshalled that on one occasion he resorted to punting over the opposition's heads, "something he rarely if ever employed".

Wigan and the whole of the rugby league then more or less closed down for three weeks as frost, ice and fog wiped out fixtures on a grand scale. It was particularly hard on the clubs, who lost their lucrative Christmas and New Year derbies. When the winter bit Wigan and Wakefield Trinity stood level on the top of the league table with just one defeat each and for the rest of the season they were locked in an absorbing struggle to lord it over each other. Billy too was locked into a struggle to finish as the game's leading try-scorer. When normal service was restored on 6 January, 1962 Billy topped the list with 26 tries, followed by Tom van Vollenhoven with 24, Wakefield Trinity's Jan Prinsloo on 23 and Workington's Ike Southward on 21.

Billy had plenty to look forward to in 1962. Wigan were fancied to win at least one of the major trophies and on the international scene he wanted to play in the French tests and secure a place on the Lions tour to Australasia in the summer. The New Year began with a 39–0 win away to Liverpool City. Billy picked up another couple of tries and the newspapers mistakenly reported that one of them was his 400th. A week later Oldham gave Wigan a much harder time in the best game of the season so far, which Wigan won 16–13 before over 20,000 fans. Frank Carlton stole the scoring honours with a hat-trick and Billy's best work came in defence. The following Saturday at Watersheddings Wigan completed the double after another heart-stopping encounter. They led 4–2 and sealed a 7–2 victory in the 68th minute when Billy appeared in the right centre position on the Oldham '25' with Jeff Bootle racing along outside him. Billy delivered a perfect pass and Smethurst and Parker collided trying to cut Bootle off, while Sims was left on the ground as Bootle touched down. The *Wigan Observer* remarked: "Billy Boston alternated his role between hard-running winger and blockbusting forward." Eric Ashton gave such a fantastic performance that the *Observer* described the match as "Ashton versus Oldham".

On 3 February Wigan had an impressive 25–8 home victory over Workington Town, one of their main rivals in the top four, before another near 20,000 crowd. Billy broke Workington when he gave Wigan a 12–8 lead on the hour "with the sort of try which has become as familiar as his much-sought autograph", according to Jack Winstanley, who continued: "Boston zoomed away after taking a short inside pass from Ashton, blasted clear of Lowden's tackle 15 yards from the line and then tossed aside Pretorious with the same nonchalance that I would flick the ash from the end of a cigarette." Just as graphically, the

*Rugby Leaguer* match reporter, clearly a fan of the television western series *Rawhide*, remarked that this particular try-scoring run reminded him of "one of Mr Faver's cattle stampedes and just as difficult to stop".

Wigan began their Challenge Cup campaign in their accustomed role as 3–1 favourites, with Wakefield at 4–1 and St Helens 11–2. The first round took them to Keighley on 10 February, along with thousands of optimistic fans. Keighley were easily dispatched 25–3 in a game the *Observer* labelled "one long yawn". Keighley were allegedly "niggling and negative" and paid very heavy attention to Billy. Billy only had one chance on attack, shrugging off Smith and Owen to score near the end. The Keighley backs Dudley and Brown were both injured when Billy tackled them but the *Observer* was at pains to state there was nothing wrong with the tackles.

Central Park staged the Great Britain versus France test match on 17 February, drawing a disappointing attendance of 17,277. The British selectors chose a somewhat experimental pack with the forthcoming tour looming, although they retained six of the backs who had seen off New Zealand – Boston, Ashton, Fox, Sullivan, Bolton and Murphy, while bringing in Wakefield full-back Gerry Round. Surprisingly, no Wigan forwards were in the pack, which included three debutants in Barry Simms, Mal Dixon and Terry Clawson alongside the more experienced Abe Terry, Dick Huddart and Johnny Whiteley. Britain played some glorious football in the first half, which ended with them leading 13–2. Three tries accrued to Huddart, Ashton, who brilliantly used Billy as a foil, and Sullivan, while Fox landed two goals. Unfortunately, Britain seemed to switch off in the second half, while the French definitely switched on and ran out 20–15 victors. It had been a real Jekyll-and-Hyde performance by the British and undoubtedly cost several forwards dearly in the quest for tour places. It was Billy's 25th test match.

Billy must have been relieved to have been playing in a better side two days later on the same ground, when Wigan trounced Halifax 27–6. Billy picked up a try but Frank Carlton outshone everyone with a four try spree, including a sensational 70-yarder. Following the win against Halifax, Wigan's 17th on the trot, they went to Wakefield Trinity on 24 February. This was undoubtedly the biggest game of the season so far, involving the top two teams. Trinity had won 23 games in a row before improbably drawing 0–0 at Batley the previous Saturday. Wigan had dropped only two points in 22 league games, while Trinity had dropped three in 21 matches. Something had to give and 27,614 fans wanted to see it, Trinity's biggest attendance since the war. Even that was an underestimate as hundreds climbed over the walls when the gates were locked. Although almost continuous drizzle fell the game was a cracker. Trinity, relying on their backs, struck a 9–0 lead only to see Wigan, making it a forward game, level at 9–9 just after the break. Five minutes from time Wigan led 11–9, thanks to Carlton's try and four goals from Griffiths. At that point Neil Fox won the match after brilliant support play brought him a last-gasp try to which he added the conversion. Trinity deserved their 14–11 success and Wigan's winning run ground agonisingly to a halt. The *Wigan Observer* admitted that on the day, "Ashton and Boston did not carry their usual threat," while Fox and Skene were "a near perfect pair".

Dewsbury went to Central Park on 3 March for the second round of the Challenge Cup on an unbelievable bonus of £60 a man. They were never going to get it and duly collapsed 50–2. Billy and Carlton both registered hat-tricks and Griffiths booted 10 goals and grabbed a try. It was the fourth and last time Billy played against Dewsbury and in those four games he rattled up 18 tries – seven, two, six and three, respectively.

Next up for Billy was a trip to France for Great Britain's return test in Perpignan on Sunday, 11 March. This time the selectors played safer and fielded no debutants. Wigan provided Billy, Ashton, Bolton, Sayer, McTigue and Evans to the side. The result was just as bad as it had been at Wigan, however. On a lovely spring afternoon Britain subsided to a 23–13 defeat, despite the tonic of a seventh minute 65-yard interception try by Eric Ashton. The British forwards were ineffective, losing the scrums 24–17, and affording the backs little opportunity to shine. The game was effectively over by half-time when France led 21–5. Wingers Billy and Mick Sullivan hardly had any running chances and Billy's major contributions were a couple of tackles, which stopped almost certain French tries. He and his fellow tour hopefuls would have an anxious 11 days wait before the tour selectors convened at Leeds on Thursday 22 March.

Wigan got back to winning ways in the league with convincing home wins against Widnes, 21–5, and Wakefield Trinity, 28–9. The latter drew an astonishing crowd of 30,674, who regarded it as a rehearsal for a third round Challenge Cup tie at Wakefield just five days later. Trinity put out a very under-strength team, however, while Wigan also missed a smattering of regulars, including Billy, who, it was reported, was suffering from "a chest injury caused by the buckle of a shoulder harness."

Three days after Wakefield were beaten, Billy was elated to learn that he had been selected to tour with the 1962 Lions. Moreover, he was to be accompanied by his club-mates Eric Ashton, Dave Bolton, Frank Carlton, Roy Evans, Brian McTigue and Bill Sayer. All seven had to quickly refocus their attention on the small matter of the cup-tie at Wakefield on 24 March. Interest in the tie was astronomic and it had quickly been declared all-ticket with a capacity of just over 28,000. Wigan believed a crowd of 50,000 would have attended had they received a home draw and there were suggestions that the tie should be moved to Odsal so that all those who wished to see it could be accommodated. At least those without tickets were able to watch the second half live on television on the BBC's *Grandstand*.

Wigan fell back on their old ploy of moving Eric Ashton to stand-off and Billy to right centre, although he wore the number 2 jersey. Billy was up against Trinity's great match-winner Neil Fox and he gave him a tough time, the *Wigan Observer* noting that Fox "had butterfingers as a result". Jack Paul in the *Sunday Express* agreed, "Boston made it a miserable day for Trinity's powerful centre Fox, who time and again either lost the ball in Boston's beefy tackles, or mishandled as the Wigan lad charged in." However, Harold Poynton outplayed Ashton and the Wigan pack could not master Trinity's. The only first half scoring was a penalty each to Fox after 12 minutes and Fred Griffiths after 33 minutes. Wigan nosed ahead two minutes into the second half with a bizarre 30-yard drop-goal from Ashton. The *Observer* reported: "Time and hearts seemed to stand still as the ball cannoned off one upright on to the other and then dropped on to the crossbar before going over." Several of the Trinity players thought that the ball had dropped infield and in vain besieged the referee. Seven minutes later Trinity won a scrum inside the Wigan '25' and Keith Holliday and Brian Briggs opened up the way for winger Fred Smith to dive full length to the corner for the try which won the match 5–4. It had been a torrid, bruising and excruciatingly exciting Cup-tie but Wigan were in truth flattered by the score and their Wembley adventure was brought to a juddering halt.

Wigan recovered sufficiently to crush Hull KR 40–16 two days after their exit from the Challenge Cup, playing some spectacular rugby with seven of their eight tries originating from their own half, but were then held to a 5–5 draw at Barrow. Billy moved to centre for the next three games, performing brilliantly in an excellent 18–11 win away to Cup semi-finalists Hull KR. Rovers found it impossible to stop him apart from in groups and some of his cover tackles were breathtaking. He claimed Wigan's third try in a typically belligerent

A friendly game of bowls with Eric Ashton and Frank Carlton.

style, exploding on to an inside pass from Griffiths and bulldozing Bob Harris and Cyril Kellett. On 4 April Wigan went down 12–10 to Joe Egan's rising Widnes side in diabolical conditions at Naughton Park. Vince Karalius played a storming game against the Wigan pack and Billy was restricted to a try in injury time, the *Wigan Observer* declaring it as "a tribute to his fitness that he summoned enough energy to run as fast as he did to outpace the Widnes defence." Billy's last game in his spell at centre was a 41–3 home thrashing of Huddersfield, who clearly had their Challenge Cup semi-final against Hull KR on their minds. Billy and Ashton were both outstanding, each claiming a try and providing their wingers, Carlton and McLeod, with half a dozen between them. The *Sunday Express's* Alan Dixon described Billy's try beautifully: "Boston galloped in with a daisy chain of Huddersfield tacklers around his neck".

The three points dropped against Barrow and Hull KR had jeopardised Wigan's push to finish top of the table, with Wakefield Trinity now only two points behind them, but with two games in hand. Wigan could not afford to lose any more games and had to hope Trinity lost at least one. Wigan began this quest with a 23–15 home win against Warrington on Wednesday 11 April. The 18,000 crowd saw an error-strewn encounter, which the now-beginning-to-be 'old firm' of Ashton and Boston lit up, Billy taking the game out of the Wire's reach with two early tries in the second half and Eric finishing them off with a late decisive touchdown. The Good Friday derby at Knowsley Road attracted an attendance of 29,615 and was, according to the *Wigan Observer,* "a truly great game... which would have made an unforgettable Wembley final". Wigan needed a point from the match to take the Lancashire League Championship but, naturally enough, Saints made it hard for them. Van Vollenhoven, Sullivan and Briers grabbed tries for Saints with only one in reply from Davies as Wigan went in at half-time 11–9 down. Fortunately, Fred Griffiths was in immaculate form with the boot and his fourth goal levelled the scores. Frank Carlton finally put Wigan ahead around the hour mark with a fantastic 80-yard try. Griffiths converted and added a penalty, when Murphy's tackle on Bolton was adjudged too rough and Wigan led 18–11. Murphy made it a jittery finale for Wigan when his towering up-and-under in the 72nd minute allowed Rhodes to dive in at the corner for a converted try. Wigan hung on for an

18–16 victory and Billy was able to add his second Lancashire League Championship winners' medal to his growing collection. Wigan's joy was doubled when they heard that Leigh had beaten Wakefield Trinity 10–6, enhancing their chances of finishing top.

The following afternoon saw an almost equally pulsating game at Wilderspool on a paddy field of a pitch. Warrington looked good as they took the first five scrums only for Bill Sayer to take the next 13 and his overall superiority of 27–20 counted a great deal to Wigan's 16–10 success. So did Billy's power and presence of mind. It was Billy who gave his side a 6–4 half-time lead with a 34th minute try. Griffiths was tackled just short of the Wire line, but Billy rushed to acting half-back and plunged through Gilfedder and Conroy to score. Frank Carlton, in possibly the best form of his career, scored a corking try to give Wigan an 11–6 advantage, although it was left for Billy to kill off Warrington's challenge as Wigan produced some majestic rugby. McTigue handled three times in a movement, assisted by Cherrington, Bolton and Ashton, before Billy zoomed past Edwards and Conroy to hurtle over at the corner for his second try. Henry Tomlinson wrote in the *Evening Chronicle:* "The passing build-up to Boston's second half try would have looked magnificent on dry land. In the mud it seemed almost miraculous that the ball was so well held."

Easter Monday brought Salford to Central Park on a red-hot afternoon, which marked Billy's 300th appearance for Wigan. He celebrated by claiming a couple of Wigan's 10 tries, the first after 20 minutes being the highlight of the match. "Parr, McLeod, Davies and Ashton handled in a jet-propelled double-scissors move which ended with winger Billy Boston thundering over behind the posts," according to the *Daily Express*. Billy did not get much chance to thunder the following Saturday, when 32,597 expectant fans filed into Central Park for the return fixture against St Helens. Wigan won 12–3 but the game was a sometimes slap-dash, sometimes heated affair between two lethargic teams, who constantly dropped the ball. Billy, Ashton and Bolton all received test caps before the game, when the Lancashire League Championship trophy was also presented to Wigan's skipper. Billy did not get much else as the *Rugby Leaguer* commented: "It hadn't proved a good day for the wingers and chances were few and far between for the flankers, though Saints were finding that one man wasn't enough to stop Boston (one occasion it needed five!)." Wigan's 12–3 win might have been much bigger had they taken their chances.

Wigan's final league fixture took them to Salford on Monday, 30 April. They were dead level with Wakefield Trinity at the top of the league, both teams having dropped just seven points. Wigan's points difference was slightly better than Trinity's, however, so even if both teams won their last game – Trinity were at home to Featherstone – Wigan would finish first. Defeat for either would leave the other on top of the table. Billy also had a target. Tom van Vollenhoven had scored six tries for St Helens against Blackpool on 23 April, thereby knocking Billy off the top of the try-scoring lists, with 45 tries to Billy's 44. Salford crumbled and the *Wigan Observer* remarked that the game soon became "Salford versus Billy Boston". Billy responded to Voll's six of the previous week by scoring seven tries in the 12th, 19th, 25th, 43rd, 49th, 66th and 70th minutes. The last two were exceptional. The first unfolded when Ashton picked up a Salford kick near his own line. Billy developed the movement, handing off Les Bettinson and leaving Jackie Brennan mesmerised as he cut inside to the posts after a dash of 80 yards. His last try was of the more explosive type. Getting up full steam, he simply blasted Price, Bettinson and Clare out of his path. Billy thus equalled his own, Gordon Ratcliffe's and Johnny Ring's joint club record but the Wigan section of the crowd was desperate for him to claim an eighth try. He had already had one disallowed for stepping in touch and late on it seemed as if he would take the record when he was almost over from a scrum. It was ironic that a Wiganer, Jackie Brennan, was the man who prevented Billy from getting the ball over as he grimly held on to his arm.

Wigan's 49–8 victory over Salford meant that Wakefield's 17–9 win against Featherstone was too slight to affect the top placings, although it had been a desperately close run thing between two truly outstanding teams. They had finished with identical records, winning 32, losing three and drawing one of their 36 fixtures. Wigan's scoring average was marginally superior, however, earning them top spot. Wigan had scored 885 points, while conceding 283, giving them both the best attacking and defending records in the league. Trinity had scored 822 points and conceded 288. Wigan were also the best supported team in the league, pushing their average crowd up from 16,876 to 17,370. It was a clear tribute to the quality of their rugby for this Wigan side had finished with a better league record than any Wigan side in the past.

The Cherry and Whites had played eight games in 26 days in April, winning all but the first. If they felt that was arduous they were certainly not alone. Wakefield had played 10 in 23 days, while the two other top four sides, Huddersfield – 9 games in 26 days – and Featherstone with 10 in 26, were equally, if not more, fatigued. Before the Championship semi-finals Billy and Fred Griffiths had played in 12 games in 36 days.

Even allowing for fatigue and injuries, Wigan were expected to dispose of Huddersfield in the semi-final, thereby setting up a classic Odsal final against Wakefield Trinity. Most of the 24,665 fans who assembled at Central Park for the clash against the Fartowners on a rainy evening on 5 May could envisage nothing else. Huddersfield, also Challenge Cup finalists, would surely have Wembley preying on their minds. Wigan certainly looked capable of winning when Frank Parr skipped through for the opening try after only seven minutes and Griffiths's conversion gave them a 5–0 flying start. Thereafter, though, Wigan failed to claim any more tries and the scoring had finished by the 51st minute, when Huddersfield had bagged three, led 13–11 and carried on to record a famous victory. Jack Bentley wrote, "A Huddersfield fan, still limp from this tense, tingling thriller... told me: 'I would never have believed it could have happened in a thousand years' ...Championship outsiders Huddersfield displayed more spirit, purpose and ideas than an international-packed Wigan outfit who started like a house on fire but finished ragged, tattered, tacticless and defending desperately." The *Wigan Observer* used expressions such as "pitiful" and "pathetic" to describe Wigan's display on a "catastrophic evening" and proffered the excuse that the team had a bout of "touristitis". All of which was a little over the top. Nevertheless, it had been a dreadful way to end such a wonderfully entertaining season.

No doubt Billy was as fed up as the most disappointed Wigan fan but it had hardly been his fault. It meant no second Championship final appearance for him and he would never get another shot at the top four play-offs. The season had been one of his greatest on a personal level. He had scored in 27 of the 40 games he played for Wigan, a remarkable ratio. He had topped the try-scoring lists with 51, five more than Tom van Vollenhoven, while Frank Carlton finished third with 38. The Wigan three-quarter line had been a thing of beauty, piling up well over a century of tries. Billy had led the way with 49, Carlton contributing his 38, Ashton 24 and Davies 21, while McLeod, Bootle and Lyon had also added to the tally. Although no one could have anticipated it, no player would score 50 tries again in a season until Bradford Northern's Ellery Hanley gathered 55 in 1984–85. No winger would beat Billy's 51 tries in a season until Widnes's Martin Offiah rattled up 60 in 1988–89. Although there were undoubtedly still some tremendous wingers in the game, Billy and van Vollenhoven being the tip of the iceberg, the golden age of wingmen was slipping away.

## 1961–62

Wigan finished 1st in the League: P36, W32, L3, D1, For 885, Against 283
Boston scored 49 tries for Wigan, plus 2 in representative rugby league

| Date | Opponents | Score | Boston | Crowd | |
|---|---|---|---|---|---|
| 19 August | Huddersfield | 19–9 | 1T | 8,416 | |
| 23 August | **Blackpool B** | 31–5 | 2T | 13,073 | |
| 26 August | **Hunslet** | 44–11 | 2T | 16,385 | |
| 2 September | Workington T | 30–18 | 2T | 9,235 | LC1 |
| 6 September | Leigh | 20–0 | | 13,191 | |
| 9 September | **Swinton** | 6–13 | | 27,437 | |
| 12 September | Blackpool B | 33–8 | 2T | 2,300 | |
| 16 September | **Leigh** | 25–6 | 1T | 20,345 | |
| 21 September | Widnes | 5–9 | | 16,745 | LC2 |
| 23 September | **Liverpool City** | 45–0 | 2T | 8,173 | |
| 7 October | **New Zealanders** | 28–6 | dnp | 25,483 | Tour |
| 14 October | Rochdale H | 28–8 | 2T | 5,210 | |
| 28 October | Swinton | 7–4 | 1T | 19,000 | |
| 11 November | Workington T | 16–10 | 1T | 7,300 | |
| 18 November | **Barrow** | 39–3 | 1T | 13,109 | |
| 25 November | Whitehaven | 26–6 | 2T | 3,189 | |
| 2 December | **Rochdale H** | 22–5 | 3T | 9,005 | |
| 9 December | **Whitehaven** | 31–11 | 2T | 7,627 | |
| 16 December | Halifax | 7–4 | | 6,846 | |
| 6 January | Liverpool City | 39–0 | 2T | 1,783 | |
| 13 January | **Oldham** | 16–13 | | 20,616 | |
| 20 January | Oldham | 7–2 | | 16,105 | |
| 3 February | **Workington T** | 25–8 | 1T | 19,841 | |
| 10 February | Keighley | 25–3 | 1T | 9,617 | Cup 1 |
| 17 February | Hunslet | 34–12 | dnp | 5,000 | |
| 19 February | **Halifax** | 27–6 | 1T | 10,310 | |
| 24 February | Wakefield T | 11–14 | | 27,614 | |
| 3 March | **Dewsbury** | 50–2 | 3T | 16,542 | Cup 2 |
| 14 March | **Widnes** | 21–5 | | 15,923 | |
| 19 March | **Wakefield T** | 28–9 | dnp | 30,674 | |
| 24 March | Wakefield T | 4–5 | | 28,254 | Cup 3 |
| 26 March | **Hull KR** | 40–16 | 1T | 19,445 | |
| 29 March | Barrow | 5–5 | | 4,267 | |
| 31 March | Hull KR | 18–11 | 1T | 12,440 | |
| 4 April | Widnes | 10–12 | 1T | 10,844 | |
| 7 April | **Huddersfield** | 41–3 | 1T | 15,002 | |
| 11 April | **Warrington** | 23–15 | 2T | 18,004 | |
| 20 April | St Helens | 18–16 | | 29,615 | |
| 21 April | Warrington | 16–10 | 2T | 11,013 | |
| 23 April | **Salford** | 46–12 | 2T | 15,095 | |
| 28 April | **St Helens** | 12–3 | | 32,597 | |
| 30 April | Salford | 49–8 | 7T | 4,700 | |
| 5 May | **Huddersfield** | 11–13 | | 24,665 | CH SF |

### Boston's representative matches:

| Date | For | Opponent | Score | Boston | Venue |
|---|---|---|---|---|---|
| 30 September | Great Britain | New Zealand | 11–29 | 2T | Leeds |
| 21 October | Great Britain | New Zealand | 23–10 | | Odsal |
| 4 November | Great Britain | New Zealand | 35–19 | | Swinton |
| 17 February | Great Britain | France | 15–20 | | Wigan |
| 11 March | Great Britain | France | 13–23 | | Perpignan |

# 13. 1962 Ashes victory

Despite the double defeat by France in February and March, the British selectors resisted the urge to play any tour trials. That was probably much to Billy's relief in the light of his travails of 1958. No fewer than 12 of the 13 players who figured in the defeat at Perpignan were included in the tour party, indicating that the selectors were wise enough to know that the odd poor show should not count against proven performers. This time, too, Billy had no real injury worries during the season and, anyway, how could even the doziest selector ignore his brilliant form? Twelve of the tourists came from the top two sides – seven from Wigan, five from Wakefield. As usual there were some shock inclusions and omissions. Among the more surprising omissions were backs Frank Myler (Widnes), Ken Gowers (Swinton) and Frank Pitchford (Oldham), while Johnny Whiteley (Hull) was perhaps the most notable forward overlooked. Wigan would have provided a complete threequarter line if Alan Davies had been chosen, as many believed should have been the case. The centres provided two real bolters in Featherstone's Gary Cooper and Castleford's Peter Small, neither of whom had won even a county cap. The Huddersfield prop Ken Noble and Hull KR's second-rower John Taylor were the surprise choices in the forwards, while prop Jack Wilkinson was pleasantly surprised to find himself on tour again at the ripe old age of almost 32. Jack and Billy were the only 1962 Lions who had also toured in 1954. This time Billy was the only Welshman in the party, alongside 12 Yorkshiremen, 10 Lancastrians and three Cumbrians. Twelve of the party had toured down under before, making it one of the most experienced Lions squads in history.

The tour manager was Wakefield Trinity chairman Stuart Hadfield, a successful coal and fuel distributor. His assistant manager was former paratrooper Arthur Walker, Rochdale Hornets' chairman, who ran a packing case manufacturing company. Colin Hutton, the Hull KR coach and a former goalkicking full-back for Widnes and Hull, was the team's trainer-cum-baggage man. For reasons beyond comprehension the RFL could not bring itself to officially designate him as the coach. Teams were to be selected by Hadfield, Walker, Eric Ashton and Derek Turner, the captain and vice-captain. The tour would start with a game in Perth on 20 May and the final fixture would fall on 31 August. Twenty-one games were scheduled for Australia, nine for New Zealand and three games for South Africa.

The latter raised the same issues for Billy that had surfaced in 1957. If anything, the situation in South Africa had deteriorated as apartheid strengthened its grip under President Verwoerd. The country had just left the Commonwealth and the United Nations was calling for sanctions against South Africa. Nothing had changed for Billy – he would still have to live, eat and lodge separately from his tour colleagues and would not be allowed to play with or against whites. There was no way Billy would be going to South Africa. The desperately sad part of this story was the ludicrous stance the RFL, under Bill Fallowfield, took. They obviously knew that they were once more putting Billy in an embarrassing position and grossly offending many other people within the game, who had called for the South African section of the tour to be cancelled. There was one major complicating factor in the equation – rugby league was being developed in South Africa and two rival organisations were involved. The Lions were to play against teams from Rugby League South Africa (RLSA), while Wakefield Trinity were to tour the country before the Lions, playing against National Rugby League (Pty) Ltd sides. The beguiling prospect of establishing rugby league in South Africa clearly blinded RFL officials to the humanitarian and moral issues. South Africa was already out of the Olympics and FIFA at this time.

The 1962 Lions party was: Eric Ashton (Wigan), Dave Bolton (Wigan), Billy Boston (Wigan), Frank Carlton (Wigan), Gary Cooper (Featherstone Rovers), Brian Edgar (Workington Town), Roy Evans (Wigan), Eric Fraser (Warrington), Don Fox (Featherstone Rovers), Neil Fox (Wakefield Trinity), Laurie Gilfedder (Warrington), Norm Herbert (Workington Town), Dick Huddart (St Helens), Brian McTigue (Wigan), Alex Murphy (St Helens), Ken Noble (Huddersfield), Harold Poynton (Wakefield Trinity), Gerry Round (Wakefield Trinity), Bill Sayer (Wigan), John Shaw (Halifax), Peter Small (Castleford), Ike Southward (Workington Town), Mick Sullivan (St Helens), John Taylor (Hull KR), Derek Turner (Wakefield Trinity) and Jack Wilkinson (Wakefield Trinity).

Australians and New Zealanders who remembered Billy from his trips down under in 1954 and, briefly, in 1957 were looking forward to seeing him again in 1962. Raymond Fletcher, alias Ramon Joyce, wrote in the *Rugby Leaguer* a month before the tourists departed: "Ever since 1954 the player Australian fans have been longing to see again is Billy Boston. They just couldn't believe it when he was left out of the 1958 tour party. Well, now they are going to see him again, though they will hardly recognise him as the 19-year-old panther like athlete who swivel-hipped his way to a record total of tour tries. But I reckon the big 'new' Bouncing Billy will be just as great a favourite."

Billy and the British party flew out of London on 15 May and arrived at Perth via Singapore two days later. However, the tour manager, the five Wakefield Trinity men and Ken Noble were not on the plane. They still had the unfinished business of the Championship Final to resolve on 19 May. Of the seven only Noble was left smiling at the game's conclusion, Huddersfield having sensationally upset Trinity 14–5 at Odsal. Delays en route caused them to arrive several days late on 25 May. By then the Lions had already fulfilled two fixtures.

Six of the Wigan contingent took part in the first game against Western Australia on Sunday 20 May in Perth, the odd one out being Frank Carlton, who had a stomach complaint. With Gerry Round still being in England and Eric Fraser suffering from a back problem, Billy was required to play full-back – the first time he had done so since his days in rugby union. While the people of Perth were delighted to see the Lions, they were equally delighted to see the rain that accompanied them, having suffered a drought for the last nine months.

The Lions won 39–12. Jack McNamara, the *Manchester Evening News* reporter, commented: "The game could hardly be taken seriously. The local team – weak but enthusiastic – used spoiling tactics, and the strong wind sweeping off the Swan River was a further complication." The usual problems of tourists with local referees arose, particularly at the scrums. Billy, Ike Southward and Mick Sullivan all had tries, which seemed fair, disallowed. Typically Alex Murphy got cautioned for undiplomatic remarks to the referee after Sullivan was denied his touch-down, although Mick did score three legitimate tries. Billy grabbed one try and there were others for Southward and Eric Ashton, who both claimed two, and Dave Bolton, while Ashton booted six goals. McNamara wrote of Billy, "Boston was dashing, if somewhat unorthodox, as a full-back". Certainly, some of his barnstorming runs put the wind up the Western Australians who became increasingly unwilling to tackle him. Brian McTigue won a clock and Bolton an electric razor as the best forward and back respectively.

For the second fixture three days later against Riverina at Wagga Wagga all seven Wigan players took the field, the only time on tour that this occurred. Billy moved to right wing, with Gary Cooper taking over at full-back. Billy's old Royal Signals partner Phil Jackson, who had emigrated a few years earlier, coached Riverina. The local inhabitants were almost as grateful for the Lions' visit as had been those at Perth for rain followed the Lions to the district for the first time in three months. McTigue and Huddart were far too effective and damaging for the home team, Don Fox and Bolton combined beautifully at half-back and Bill Sayer won the scrums 32–12. Eric Ashton was the dominating player, however, his three tries and five goals being just a partial contribution to his all-round excellence. Billy collected a couple of tries and was also outstanding in Great Britain's 34–7 victory. A reporter wrote: "This was Boston at his best – moving in attack with the force and pace of a runaway hay wagon, and covering and tackling faultlessly. On this show, there must be no doubt about him making the test side." Another writer observed, "Boston had a good game and... ran with his customary verve". Cooper, Sullivan and Fox were the other British try-scorers.

The Lions moved on to Sydney, where they were based at the Olympic, a hotel, run on very basic lines, on Moore Park Road, opposite the Sydney Cricket Ground. Training took place at the Show Ground, which was adjacent to the SCG. It was all very handy. By now the remaining members of the tour party had arrived, although only Gerry Round was included in the team for the first Saturday game which was the first real test for the British boys. This was on 26 May against Sydney, a side that contained plenty of test class players. More than 57,000 Sydneysiders crushed into the SCG hoping to see the local side hammer the Poms. The first half gave them cause for satisfaction as the Lions struggled for cohesion. Sydney led 5–0 at the break, second-rower Elton Rasmussen barging over for the only try, while full-back Don Parish added a penalty, but missed four other shots at goal. The second half saw a complete reversal of fortunes and after 70 minutes Britain led 21–5 on the back of some fabulous play.

Huddart set them on their way in the 43rd minute with a weaving run to the posts for a try, which Laurie Gilfedder converted. Eight minutes later Billy put the Lions in front when after intense pressure "he dived over like a tank" from a play-the-ball, Gilfedder again converting. Brian Edgar rampaged through for two more tries, one of which was converted, before Billy swept over for his team's final try. Winger Mike Cleary scored two tries in the last ten minutes for Sydney, Parish improving one of them, but the Lions 21–13 success was pretty emphatic.

There was no rest for the wicked or for Billy, who along with Dick Huddart, was called upon to play in his fourth out of four games for the Lions at Bathurst on the day after the Sydney game. Britain, led for the first time by Derek Turner, won 24–10 against Western New South Wales, scoring six tries. Billy did not score, but he played a prominent role in the victory. He went close to scoring several times, once losing possession over the line and also dropping the ball close to the line after gathering a loose ball at high speed. Stars of the match were half-backs Don Fox and Harold Poynton.

Billy and Dick Huddart tuned out for the fifth game in a row on 2 June against New South Wales before a crowd of 60,016 at the SCG. It was one of the most sensational games in which Billy would ever participate and one to rival in infamy the previous two games against New South Wales. The 1954 game, which Billy had watched from the stands, had famously been abandoned because of brawling. The 1958 fixture had seen four men sent off but at least had been completed. This 1962 sequel ended up with six dismissals, including Billy, who had never previously been sent off, and clearly, by all accounts, should not have lost that proud record. In between the mayhem, the Lions played magnificent rugby to win much more decisively than the 33–28 score-line suggested and sent out a loud message that Australia were in for a tough time in the Ashes series.

By half-time the Lions were 23–14 ahead, thanks partially to Bill Sayer's 11–2 pull over Ian Walsh in the scrums, but more especially to a delightfully powerful and open style of play which brought five tries to Ashton with two, Turner, Sullivan and Neil Fox, who added four goals. NSW pulled up to 23–16 before the real rumpus blew up. It had been a pretty robust affair already and referee Cliff Brown had dished out several warnings, including three to Derek Turner. In the 54th minute Brian Edgar was being battered and Billy stepped in to protect him. The fracas escalated and Billy and NSW's flier of a winger Ken Irvine were dismissed, neither having had a previous warning. The game proceeded with Ashton completing his hat-trick and Cooper grabbing Britain's seventh try, while Fox took his goals tally to six. It was 33–23 when a scrum erupted near the Lions' '25' five minutes from full-time. Following the ensuing 'blue' or 'Donnybrook', as the Australians refer to such altercations, Mr Brown sent off the remaining wingers Mick Sullivan and Mike Cleary and Lions hooker Bill Sayer and NSW prop Billy Wilson. Talk about closing the stable door after the horse has bolted! Johnny Raper scored the last try of the game for NSW, to which Don Parish added his eighth goal. Reports noted, "Both teams shook hands amid cheers as they left the field".

Billy thus became involved in what must surely be a unique event, at least in first class rugby league – the sending off of all four wingers. He was hard done by. Mr Hadfield said: "I do not think the referee had any control at all. The trouble could have been avoided if he had given the players a good talking to early on. The sending off of Billy Boston was completely unnecessary. Boston had dashed in to separate players who were punching." Billy recalls: "It was the first time I had ever been sent off and I don't understand why. I was only trying to protect Brian Edgar. Suddenly Mick Sullivan appears out of nowhere. I said, 'What are you doing here?' No answer - then Boomph!... and there's a real scrap, which ends up with me and Irvine sent off. And I really never did anything."

Billy and the other dismissed players had to appear before the NSWRL Judiciary Committee within a few hours of the final whistle. He and Irvine were severely cautioned, which basically meant a slap on the hand. The remaining quartet were all suspended until Tuesday, which meant that the only one to suffer in real terms was Cleary, who missed a club game. None of the Lions would have played in their next game at Newcastle on the Monday in any case. Phil King, the rugby league correspondent for *The People*, agreed that Billy should not have been sent off, saying: "For my money, he was terribly unlucky because he only went in to prevent more trouble when Edgar was tackled". After the tour, in *Windsor's Rugby League Annual and Lions Tour Souvenir*, King recalled: "At the Judiciary meeting... I found the scene in a passage at the NSW League's Club very intriguing. Australia's test selectors were already in session in an adjoining room... Billy Boston was standing at the ready... and the other five 'send-offs' were sitting together on a couch. They reminded me of naughty schoolboys. At the near end Ken Irvine looked cheerful enough, but Billy Wilson, sitting next to him, looked grim and unhappy with an ugly bruise under his left eye and a trickle of blood on his cheek. Bill Sayer sat in the middle nonchalantly reading a paper, and at the far end Mick Sullivan and Mike Cleary were laughing and joking like long lost pals. On the field, they had been fighting like tigers. Now they were calm and in hand-shaking mood. Ah well, that's rugby football. It's a man's game, after all."

It did not come as a great surprise to some people when Cliff Brown retired from refereeing midway through the season.

Billy finally got a rest after playing in five games in 15 days. He and most of the probable test team remained in Sydney while the Lions visited Newcastle, going down 23–18 to their first defeat of the tour. John Shaw and Jack Wilkinson were sent off and Don Fox and Harold Poynton picked up injuries but Ike Southward enjoyed himself with a super hat-trick.

Billy went with 15 other players to Coolangata, near Cronulla for two days pre-test training. The location, near the beach, was ideal and, just as importantly, well away from the hubbub that surrounded the Lions 20 miles away in Sydney. Jack McNamara cabled to Manchester: "War-drums are being sounded here as a fantastic overture of hate to the first rugby league test... in Sydney on Saturday. After the flare-ups against New South Wales and Newcastle, in which five tourists were ordered off, the atmosphere here now is like the eve of Waterloo. Publicity about the two brawls has grown to ridiculous proportions... Local papers are whipping up bloodlust with screaming banner headlines plastered around the city... Nobody can condone the bad behaviour that occurred in both matches and gloss over the spectacular brawls. But, in fairness to the tourists, the brawl in Newcastle was caused by a spectator rushing on to the field and attacking Jack Wilkinson. Looking coolly at both matches, the incidents, while disgraceful, were isolated. Even the opinion of Saturday's test referee, Darcy Lawler, is being sought, which is like asking a judge for his verdict before the case is heard. Lawler is diplomatically reported to have said, 'I'm not expecting any special trouble – just another game'. The tourists are not angels, but are any professional sportsmen? Likewise they are not thugs, which is the impression that could easily be gained here by an outsider. Manager Hadfield told me today: 'It isn't all one-sided. I shall tell them not to start anything, but if anything is started they will retaliate – they're only human beings'. This could hardly be termed an incitement to riot. If Britain win on Saturday without the expected bloodshed it will be like the relief of Mafeking."

The Australians were probably running scared. They had lost the last three Ashes series and had been beaten by Great Britain in the 1960 World Cup. Now they were faced with another outstanding Lions team, whose style, finesse and physicality, particularly in the games against Sydney and New South Wales, announced that they had not come down under to lose. A massive all-ticket crowd of 69,990 filled the SCG and handed over record receipts of £29,576. The teams were:

*Australia:* Parish, Cleary, Gasnier (capt), Hagan, Irvine, Summons, Muir, Parcell, Walsh, Beattie, Rasmussen, Lynch, Raper

*Great Britain:* Round, Boston, Ashton (capt), Fox, Sullivan, Bolton, Murphy, Herbert, Sayer, McTigue, Huddart, Edgar, Turner

The weather was hot and the pitch bone-hard, but there was also a strong wind blowing diagonally across the ground, which was some relief for the players. Billy and the Lions got off to a poor start. After three minutes Australia's stand-off Arthur Summons broke clear down the left side of the field, kicked, regathered the ball and kicked infield again. Billy and Gerry Round were defeated by a perverse bounce and Ken Irvine flashed in to take the ball and dive over for a try near the posts. Don Parish converted and kicked a good penalty a couple of minutes later, when Neil Fox was ruled off-side. At 7–0 to the home side, the crowd was beginning to wonder what all the fuss was about the Lions. They soon found out. By half-time Britain led 9–7, having run in three unanswered tries through Turner after 18 minutes and Sullivan in the 29th and 37th minutes. It would have been worse for Australia if Fox had landed any of the conversions or if Sayer had been able to win more than two of the 12 first half scrums.

The second half became one-way traffic with Britain adding four more tries, all converted by Fox, who also popped over a penalty. Huddart, who won the man of the match award, sailed though for the first after 44 minutes. That was followed by two touchdowns by Ashton in the 57th and 72nd minutes. Billy scored the last British try a few minutes later after good work by Bolton, almost strolling in at the corner as the Australian "defence quit entirely". Australia's sole second half riposte had been a try from Reg Gasnier, converted by Parish, although the ball seemed to pass outside the goal. Australia had been fortunate to escape with only a 31–12 flogging. Heaven knows what the score would have been but for their superiority in the scrums – 17–10 – and penalty count – 20–8.

The Australians simply could not cope with the power and majesty of the British forwards, brilliantly marshalled by McTigue and Turner and so damaging in their running, particularly Huddart and Edgar. Most reports of the game describe the British forwards as "toying" with their opponents. The backs were also much too good for the opposition, the *Daily Telegraph* observing: "Though Murphy had a somewhat quiet game, especially in the last 15 minutes when he hurt his right arm slightly, Bolton, typical of him in test matches, showed such thrust and broke through and made gaps so often that, having straightened his run, overlaps were there. And how well Ashton and Fox supported him on either side and how stringently Boston and Sullivan were always in position for taking passes."

In view of the flak Britain had previously endured about their robust play the Lions were happy to read that the Australian press were quick to praise the cleanness of the first test. It was, however, something of a surprise when Australia's tough guy, scrum-half and vice-captain Barry Muir said on a television interview that he advocated a much more virile approach from his own team, claiming Australia would have won if they had used tougher tactics. He added, stating the blindingly obvious, "I think we should tackle, tackle, tackle".

Billy did not figure in any of the Lions' four games following the first test match, which brought four more victories within seven days, including close fought matches against Brisbane, 16–14, and Queensland, 22–17, at Lang Park. Derek Turner was sent off late in the latter match after a spat with Australian test prop Dud Beattie. The following day Turner took it out on Toowoomba, scoring a hat-trick in a 36–12 win. Britain had left Sydney for an 18-day tour of Queensland, involving eight fixtures. They were billeted in ropey accommodation, primarily the Australian Hotel in central Brisbane and later on in even worse hotels in the further flung parts of Queensland. Players were also suffering from blistered feet and aching legs as a result of firm pitches.

On 20 June Billy made his first Queensland tour appearance at Rockhampton in a 55–8 massacre of Central Queensland. He played at centre along with Peter Small, but was substituted by Neil Fox after receiving a knock on the knee in the first half. With the second test only 10 days off there was no point in risking further damage to his knee. Frank Carlton had a field day, scoring four tries as the temperature hovered around the 80 degrees mark. Billy was one of seven players who had the good fortune to be excused from travelling up to Cairns for the game against Far North Queensland. Instead he, Ashton, Fox, Sayer, McTigue, Bolton and Murphy were despatched to Townsville for three days rest and recuperation, plus a little training on the beach under Ashton. The team that went to Cairns won 33–31, thanks to a last minute try from Round, converted by Gilfedder.

Britain decided to field their potential test team against North Queensland at Townsville on Sunday 24 June – just six days before the second test. Billy had a brilliant game, scoring four tries in a 47–14 success against a pretty strong side. Neil Fox amassed 20 points from seven goals and a couple of tries, while Turner also scored twice, Bolton, Murphy and Gilfedder also touching down. Unfortunately, Turner and Bolton sustained knee injuries, which were to keep them out of the Brisbane test.

After the game against North Queensland Billy and the rest of the test squad travelled to the Gold Coast to prepare for their second clash with Australia. Britain's only changes from the first test were the inclusion of Harold Poynton and Laurie Gilfedder for the stricken Bolton and Turner. Australia dismantled their first test team and fielded the following side: Barnes (capt), Lumsden, Gil, Gasnier, Irvine, Banks, Summons, Beattie, Walsh, Carson, Veivers, Owen, Smith.

There had clearly been panic among the Australian selectors and the press had not been slow to offer criticism after the cataclysm at the SCG. There had been a call to sack the coach Harry Bath, but the Australian Rugby League had instead made him manager-coach. Some Australian players had alleged that Bath was too strict at their pre-test training although Reg Gasnier, the first test captain, had disassociated himself from that charge. It had certainly not been the coach who had missed all the tackles and dropped all the balls. Part of Bath's strategy for the Brisbane test was to pepper Billy with kicks – just why was unclear. Stopping Billy, though, was definitely one of Australia's priorities. If he had been vulnerable under the high ball someone else would surely have noticed in his eight years at the top level of rugby league. Equally, if people believed that his weight was a problem in turning to retrieve low bouncing kicks, Billy had never been found wanting in that area.

Lang Park was packed to the rafters with 34,760 excited spectators, who fully expected their side to put up a better show than they had in Sydney. Australia did perform somewhat better but were still well whacked, the 17–10 score-line not reflecting the Lions' overwhelming superiority. Australia sent two steepling kicks towards Boston early on, but Billy just returned them with interest. They should have had a plan B but persisted with their foolishness. Britain took the lead with a Fox penalty goal after seven minutes and thereafter never looked remotely like losing. In the 18th minute McTigue broke 25 yards before slipping a pass to Huddart who careered from half-way, past Owen, until he was grounded just short of Australia's goal-line by Lumsden. Poynton rushed to acting half-back and flicked out a long bobbling pass to Billy, who snapped the ball up and ambled over for the opening try. Fox's goal gave Britain a 7–0 lead. Seven minutes later Irvine streaked over at the corner after Walsh, Summons and Gasnier had combined in spectacular fashion. Billy put Australia back in their place on 34 minutes after Gilfedder found a gap and served Ashton. Eric knew exactly what to do – he had done it often enough – and passed at precisely the right time to Billy. Irvine and Veivers were swatted away before Billy drove low, taking Summons with him, for a tremendous try at the flag. It was Billy's ninth try in Ashes tests - a record, taking him past the joint holders Mick Sullivan and Brian Carlson.

Britain went in at half-time 10–3 up, but four minutes into the second half Barnes landed a penalty to make it 10–5. It was Barnes who prevented Billy blasting over for his hat-trick barely a minute later with a superb tackle. However, there was no stopping Murphy in the 47th minute, when the scrum-half picked up the ball from a close-in scrum and shot through a dumbfounded defence for the decisive score. Fox converted for a 15–5 lead. Murphy was carried off, however, with 25 minutes left and Australia were spared a greater caning. Ashton moved to stand-off, Billy to centre, Poynton to scrum-half and Huddart to the wing. Ashton coolly dropped a goal and at 17–5 there was no way back for Australia, even against 12 men. Poynton put Sullivan over for a try which film evidence later proved to be legal, but was ruled out by referee Jack Casey and a late converted try by Summons merely made the score look better for the home side.

The Ashes had been retained far more easily than anyone in the British camp had dared hope and the celebrations continued well into the night. However, Billy had to back up the next day at Maryborough against Wide Bay-Burnett, as did Ashton, Huddart and Gilfedder.

Fortunately the local team was easy meat and conceded 20 tries, with Gilfedder collecting 12 goals, as the Lions won 84–20. Billy played left-centre to Frank Carlton who claimed a hat-trick. Billy plundered five tries, the best haul by a Lion on the tour. Ashton, again at stand-off, collected four, Huddart three, Cooper two, and there were also tries for Shaw, Gilfedder and Southward. Prior to the kick-off the British players had been treated to

The 1962 Lions. Back: Cooper, Shaw, D. Fox, Sayer, McTigue, Carlton, Southward, Fraser, Sullivan; standing: Boston, N. Fox, Taylor, Round, Gilfedder, Wilkinson, Evans, Small; seated: Walker (manager), Herbert, Huddart, Ashton, Hadfield (manager), Turner, Edgar, Noble, Hutton (coach); front: Murphy, Bolton, Poynton.

a display of boomerang and spear throwing by some Aborigines. One of them threw a spear 100 yards over the cross-bar, scattering onlookers behind the posts. It is not recorded whether facing Billy or the spear-thrower was more alarming.

The Lions returned to New South Wales with injuries piling up. Don Fox had already been ruled out of action for the remainder of the tour and many players were playing with injuries, when common sense had to be ignored. Billy was having plenty of work and turned out again on 7 July in the Lions' second game against New South Wales at the SCG. It was a back-handed compliment to the Lions that only just over 28,000 attended, according to the Australian press, because everyone expected a British cake-walk, which is more or less what happened. Britain won 20–5 on a wet pitch with Brian Edgar putting on a virtuoso display. Billy did not score, but his mighty surges provided the platform for the first two British tries. It took so many defenders to stop him that from the ensuing play-the-balls the NSW defence was so stretched that Gilfedder and Sullivan had little trouble in crossing for tries. Sayer and Edgar added tries in the second half, Fox converting all four scores.

The following day Billy and the Lions who were able to stand trekked to Wollongong to play against Southern New South Wales. The Lions were so short of bodies that the half-backs were Eric Fraser and Gary Cooper, while Billy partnered Fox in the centres. It was one match too far for the weary Lions who went down 18–10. Arthur Walker was incandescent about the pitch. He declared it was the worst and most dangerous he had ever encountered – "like a ploughed field". The referee told the press that the British players wanted to fight rather than play and a widespread brawl erupted just before the end. Ken Noble scored a try and Neil Fox two goals for Britain, who trailed 8–7 at half-time. Billy's try, his 18th of the tour, was Britain's only second half score.

Britain entered the final Ashes test at the SCG on 14 July with the enticing prospect of becoming the only Lions team to make a clean sweep of an Ashes series in Australia. Billy

144

and his team-mates stood on the threshold of a historic triumph. They were clear favourites when they entered the field before a crowd of 42,104. The walking wounded had been patched up and resuscitated by spending the last few days at Coolangata. The only change to the Lions' winning side in the Brisbane test was the return of Derek Turner in place of Laurie Gilfedder. Australia again chopped and changed their XIII. In perfect weather the two sides were introduced to Robert Menzies, the Australian Prime Minister, before the kick-off. The teams were:

*Great Britain:* Round, Boston, Ashton (capt), Fox, Sullivan, Poynton, Murphy, Herbert, Sayer, McTigue, Huddart, Edgar, Turner

*Australia:* Drake, Lumsden, Gil, Dimond, Irvine, Lisle, Summons (capt), Beattie, Walsh, Carson, Veivers, Rasmussen, Raper

Australia shook Great Britain by taking an 8–0 lead in the first 15 minutes. Skipper Summons, the Australians' third captain in the series, scored a gem of a try in the eighth minute. He ran 60 yards, scooting past Poynton, dodging Round and finally selling Billy a dummy he did not want before crossing at the corner. Seven minutes later Summons instigated the second Australian try after fielding a kick in his own half. Lumsden took his pass and cross-kicked for Frank Drake to take the ball on the full and claim the first try ever scored by a full-back in an Ashes test. Make-shift kicker Ken Irvine converted. Britain responded in the 25th minute with a magical move between Edgar, Poynton and Murphy, which lacerated the home defence before Fox took the final pass to score the try, which he improved. Eleven minutes later Murphy scooped up a loose ball and sent Ashton elegantly sprinting 40 yards to the posts. Fox's conversion gave Britain a 10–8 lead. Fox extended the lead with a difficult penalty and there was still time for Australia to pull back to 12–11 with a try from Irvine.

The second half began explosively and within six minutes referee Darcy Lawler sent off Mick Sullivan for a bad tackle on Peter Dimond. Typically Mick had raced across from the opposite wing after Dimond had gone through tackles by Billy and Turner, which took some doing. Huddart went out to the wing in his place. Ten minutes later Beattie, who was already injured, embroiled Turner in a fight and the pair were sent off. The tackling of both sides was becoming almost murderous but Australia could not unlock the 11-man British defence. With 15 minutes left Britain seemed to have wrapped up an incredible victory when Murphy left everybody standing in a run from half-way straight from a scrum. Fox's goal gave the Lions a 17–11 lead. In the 71st minute Summons came off second best when crash-tackled by Billy and had to be carried off, but returned in time to see Irvine slot a simple penalty from in front of the posts 25 yards out. The game was stolen from the Lions two minutes from time when Summons broke through. Billy set himself to crash the scrum-half down again, but Summons was too wily, ducked under Billy's arms and shot the ball out to Carson, who sent Irvine in at the flag. Amidst palpable tension Irvine landed a fantastic touch-line conversion and Australia had won 18–17. Neil Fox recalled: "When the final whistle was blown, we knew we had been cheated out of winning but credit to Ken Irvine. He did kick that difficult goal to win the game. The last pass for the final try was forward. Billy Boston went up to the referee and told him it was a yard forward. Lawler said 'If it had been three yards forward, I would still have given it!' Still it was nice to run around the field celebrating our Ashes win and again the celebrations continued until the early hours back at the hotel."

The defeat certainly rankled. Stuart Hadfield was particularly scathing about the refereeing of Mr Lawler, who he considered a blatant cheat and said so. Mick Sullivan had also given Lawler a piece of his mind over his dismissal. Turner and Beattie both received cautions from the Judiciary Committee, but Mick was suspended until the end of the Australian season and the Australian Board of Control issued the following statement: "The Board deplored Sullivan's demeanour at the inquiry and particularly his use of filthy language and uncomplimentary remarks to the Board and to the referee. These incidents will be reported by the Board to the team manager and to the English League Council and a full transcript of the evidence will be sent to the English League Council." It almost went without saying that the British team manager endorsed every word Mick said about Mr Lawler, if not the manner he delivered those words.

Britain had lost the scrums 18–10 and the penalties 14–13, Harold Poynton had his thumb broken by a wild kick at a play-the-ball and the Lions had finished with only 11 men. The *Daily Telegraph* was in no doubt about why Britain lost: "[From the point at which they led 10–8] the game really ceased to be a match for the refereeing of D. Lawler became too biased in favour of Australia. Off-side at the play-the-ball, obstruction and the failure of Summons to retire at scrums in the main went unpunished and so hardly surprisingly the tempers of some British players frayed... So what at the outset and even in the early stages had promised to be a good game ended almost in a shambles."

On the Wednesday following the third test the Lions came up against Darcy Lawler again at the SCG in what promised to be an even stiffer examination of their patience and resilience. For the first time Great Britain were to be faced with a club side in Australia and this was no ordinary club side. It was the fabled St George, winners of the last six Premierships, with another five to follow until they were finally deposed in 1967. Many rugby league followers regarded them as stronger than the test team. Interest in the game was huge and a record midweek crowd of 57,895 – 15,000 more than had turned up for the third test – were in the ground to see what would be Billy's last game on Australian soil.

St George put up a stern challenge for the first half-hour, taking the lead after 27 minutes when Eddie Lumsden capitalised on a break by Reg Gasnier to score at the posts, Brian Graham converting. That was as good as it got for the Dragons, however, as the Lions devoured them. By half-time it was 13–5 to Great Britain. Huddart steamed through for the first try, goaled by Fox. Then marvellous passing and combination sent Ashton flashing over at the corner. Unfortunately, the Lions captain ripped ankle ligaments soon afterwards and his tour ended there and then. Frank Carlton took his place and Billy moved into the centre. Billy was matched against Reg Gasnier in the centre and excelled in keeping the great man in check with some terrific tackling. Murphy, playing one of the games of his life, despite injuries, ripped St George apart for the third try, again converted by Fox. The second half was a rout with the Lions roaring through for four converted tries to humiliate the pride of Australia 33–5. It had been a master class. Edgar, Murphy, Billy and McTigue all touched down. Billy's try, after a powerful dash to the corner, was the 49th he had claimed in 29 games in Australia on his three visits. No wonder Australians held him in such awe.

Billy missed Britain's final game in Australia, a 56–13 picnic against Northern New South Wales at Tamworth, in which Neil Fox piled up 32 points and Frank Carlton pocketed three tries. The Lions had performed magnificently in Australia, winning 18 of their 21 fixtures. Billy had figured in 14 games and scored 19 tries, second only to his unfortunate friend and captain Eric Ashton, who had 21 to his name.

The touring party departed from Sydney for New Zealand on 23 July. There was a shock for Billy. On arrival at Auckland airport he was stopped and required to get a visa to enter New Zealand, while his colleagues were waved through without hindrance. Peter Muszkat reported in the *Daily Mail*, "Boston had to fill in a form permitting him to stay for three weeks – the duration of the tour. The form mentioned nothing about colour or birth.

Boston, along with Alex Murphy, is the darling of Kiwi crowds, who admire his strong play". He would have expected a problem entering South Africa, of course, but this was New Zealand, where a large proportion of the population was Maori. Almost half a century later Billy still finds the episode strange: "I just don't get it. When I went to New Zealand in 1954 there was no problem at all and I was waved through, just like the rest of the boys. Why they stopped me in 1962 is beyond me."

Questions were asked in the New Zealand Parliament and a Reuter's report to England soon after the episode ran: "Wellington, New Zealand, Wednesday – The Immigration Minister, Mr Shand, today apologised to Billy Boston, the coloured rugby league player, for embarrassment caused to him by being required to have an entry permit to play in New Zealand with Britain's touring side. Mr Shand also thanked Boston, who was born in Cardiff, for the courteous way he had accepted the situation."

Another Lion with a problem was prop forward Jack Wilkinson, who had been suspended for a month after being sent off in the last game of the 1954 tour against Auckland. The suspension still stood and would have ruled Jack out of all the Lions games in New Zealand if the NZRL had not agreed to lift the ban. The Lions could hardly afford to lose another player. Don Fox was already back in England and Eric Ashton flew back soon after landing in New Zealand. Derek Turner took over the captaincy with Alex Murphy becoming vice-captain. Unfortunately, Murphy had sustained a bad arm injury and took no further part in the tour as a player, departing for home on 4 August. The loss of Ashton and Murphy was almost catastrophic for the Lions, who were now beginning to find it difficult to field a side with 13 fit men. Billy was one of those struggling through pain. His knee had become a big problem and he was able to play in only three of the nine games in New Zealand.

He figured in the opening fixture at Huntley against Waikato on 25 July. Billy played in the centre with Laurie Gilfedder, whose versatility was a real boon to the Lions. With all the half-backs injured, Britain resorted to playing the reserve centres Cooper and Small at six and seven. Fortunately Waikato were totally outclassed and the Lions hardly exerted themselves in winning 59–20. Billy scored two of his side's 13 tries and at one point, according to Jack McNamara, "A wit in the stand yelled, 'Hey, Boston. Come off and give our boys a go'." Another journalist noted: "Boston, the dynamic Wigan winger, who played at centre, was probably the most surprised member of the team. He had a quiet game and was followed all over the field by the diminutive Waikato centre, Brian Porteous. Weighing only 9 stone 2 pounds, he tackled Boston very hard almost every time he tried to break."

Three days later Great Britain went down to a record 19–0 defeat to New Zealand in the first test at Carlaw Park. Billy was ruled out injured and with other notable absentees in Ashton, Murphy and Edgar it was a decidedly uphill battle for the remaining Lions, who resorted to playing Mick Sullivan at scrum-half. The weather was wet and cold, completely different from what had been generally experienced in Australia although it did not reduce the incidence of injuries to the tourists. Billy missed the four games following the test and after a smashing 35–5 win over the Maoris he remained in Auckland when the fit remnants of the party flew to the South Island, winning all three games there in a canter. He returned to action at Rotorua on 7 August and scored one of Britain's 17 tries in an 81–14 massacre of Bay of Plenty. The game, which was more like a practice session, was played on the driest pitch so far encountered in New Zealand. There were hat-tricks for Peter Small, Gerry Round and John Taylor, while Eric Fraser landed 11 goals. However, Mick Sullivan and Norm Herbert picked up injuries, which were to keep them out of the second test.

Billy turned out in the second test in a mud bath at Carlaw Park with his knee heavily strapped. In normal circumstances there was no way that he would have played. By this stage in the tour he was the only winger capable of getting on to the pitch, never mind running up and down it. Peter Small had to play on the other wing and Laurie Gilfedder had to partner Neil Fox in the centre. Norm Herbert and Bill Sayer were missing, allowing Jack Wilkinson and John Shaw to play their only tests of the tour, while Brian McTigue and Brian Edgar were so incapacitated that they could barely raise a trot. In the course of the game Dave Bolton broke his nose and Gerry Round broke his thumb. Unsurprisingly, Britain went down 27–8. It was a sad way for Billy to play his last game in New Zealand. The tour ended in a shambles the following Monday when Auckland swamped the Lions 46–13 at Carlaw Park. Billy was fortunate to miss the debacle, but in truth Auckland, good though they were, were up against a team of walking wounded.

Billy, Brian Edgar, Norm Herbert, Brian McTigue, Gerry Round, Bill Sayer and Stuart Hadfield returned to England, while 17 players, Arthur Walker and Colin Hutton headed to South Africa.

The tour had been exceptionally successful in Australia but the dreadful catalogue of injuries had made the New Zealand section an anti-climax. Even so, Britain's record of 24 victories in 30 games compared favourably with most previous Lions' parties. The quality of their play in Australia had been superlative and they had come within a whisker of being the only Lions team to win every game in a three-match Ashes series. Billy had reinforced his reputation as a world class performer and had again finished as the Lions leading try-scorer with 22 in 17 appearances.

The financial benefits Billy and his colleagues received for touring were a bit better than when he had toured in 1954. Players were still receiving £3 a week for the duration of the tour and received a lump sum of £20 on arrival in Australia. The family allowances had improved, however, from £3 per week for wives and 10 shillings (50p) for each child to £3 and 10 shillings (£3.50) for wives and £1 for each child. With record receipts from the tour the players' share of the profits came to £571/14/9 (£571.74) each, which was a welcome bonus for a man with a wife and three children, although a considerable proportion disappeared in tax and other incidentals.

Billy's stratospheric performances through the 1961–62 season and down under with the Lions earned him the 'Player of the Year' award from *Windsor's Rugby League Annual* and this ringing eulogy: "Billy Boston – toughest centre of our time ... greatest drawing personality in all countries where rugby league is played. Billy the Block-buster... Billy, the bustling, blast-away, brown bomber of the Rugby League. Highest try-scorer of the season, highest try-scorer in a single match (seven against Salford) and highest scorer in Anglo-Australian test history with a total of nine tries. Strong, fearless, tireless and a danger to all opponents, he was chosen by a panel of selected judges across the rugby league areas as the Player of the Year. He is never out of the picture, never a non-trier and is one of the most engaging characters, one of the most likeable fellows, ever to grace the game. The great raking strides, the sheer strength and glowing performances of this wonderful 'panther of the pitch' will be associated in memory as an all-time great, long after he has hung up his boots." Prophetic words.

Billy and his five injured fellow Lions arrived at Ringway Airport in the late evening of 15 August. There was no one from the club to greet them because Wigan secretary Jack Wood had been erroneously informed by London Airport that there were no rugby league players on the flight from New York. The only person there to greet them was Joan Boston "just on the off-chance that Billy would be on board", according to the *Wigan Observer*. The following morning Mr Wood called round to the Bostons' house to tell Joan that Billy had not arrived. He was extremely surprised when Billy opened the door to him.

# The 1962 Lions

Tour record: P30, W24, L6, For 998, Against 464
Boston scored 22 tries

| Date | Opponent | Score | Boston | Crowd | Venue |
|------|----------|-------|--------|-------|-------|
| 20 May | Western Australia | 39–12 | 1T | 2,842 | Perth |
| 23 May | Riverina | 34–7 | 2T | 5,191 | Wagga Wagga |
| 26 May | Sydney | 21–13 | 2T | 57,142 | Sydney |
| 27 May | Western NSW | 24–10 | | 10,000 | Bathurst |
| 2 June | New South Wales | 33–28 | | 60,016 | Sydney |
| 4 June | Newcastle | 18–23 | dnp | 22,750 | Newcastle |
| **9 June** | **Australia** | **31–12** | **1T** | **69,990** | **Sydney** |
| 10 June | North Coast | 33–13 | dnp | 5,240 | Lismore |
| 13 June | Brisbane | 16–14 | dnp | 22,650 | Brisbane |
| 16 June | Queensland | 22–17 | dnp | 29,102 | Brisbane |
| 17 June | Toowoomba | 36–12 | dnp | 10,491 | Toowoomba |
| 20 June | Central Queensland | 55–8 | | 5,000 | Rockhampton |
| 23 June | Far North Queensland | 33–31 | dnp | 4,769 | Cairns |
| 24 June | North Queensland | 47–14 | 4T | 8,278 | Townsville |
| **30 June** | **Australia** | **17–10** | **2T** | **34,760** | **Brisbane** |
| 1 July | Wide Bay | 84–20 | 5T | 4,386 | Maryborough |
| 7 July | New South Wales | 20–5 | | 28,042 | Sydney |
| 8 July | Southern NSW | 10–18 | 1T | 10,527 | Wollongong |
| **14 July** | **Australia** | **17–18** | | **42,104** | **Sydney** |
| 18 July | St George | 33–5 | 1T | 57,895 | Sydney |
| 22 July | Northern NSW | 56–13 | dnp | 9,000 | Tamworth |
| 25 July | Waikato | 59–20 | 2T | 3,461 | Huntley |
| **28 July** | **New Zealand** | **0–19** | **dnp** | **14,976** | **Auckland** |
| 31 July | Maoris | 35–5 | dnp | 3,091 | Wellington |
| 2 August | Canterbury | 26–5 | dnp | 2,500 | Christchurch |
| 4 August | New Zealand XIII | 31–17 | dnp | 5,000 | Christchurch |
| 5 August | West Coast | 66–8 | dnp | 2,758 | Greymouth |
| 7 August | Bay of Plenty | 81–14 | 1T | 1,852 | Rotorua |
| **11 August** | **New Zealand** | **8–27** | | **16,411** | **Auckland** |
| 13 August | Auckland | 13–46 | dnp | 10,444 | Auckland |

Note – The Lions went on to play three exhibition matches in South Africa, beating Rugby League South Africa 49–30 at Pretoria (23 Aug), 39–33 at Durban (25 Aug) and 45–23 at Johannesburg (31 Aug). Billy was not included in the party of 17 players and two officials, which went to South Africa.

Playing for Great Britain

# 14. 1962–63 Wembley and the Great Freeze

The 1962–63 season was a watershed for rugby league in England. Gone was the time-honoured single division, replaced by two divisions for an agreed period of three seasons. Gone too were the old Lancashire and Yorkshire League Championships and in their place came the Western and Eastern Division Championships, staged at the beginning of the season on a league basis over eight fixtures and culminating in top four play-offs. The team that finished top of the First Division would be the Rugby League Champions – a triumph for logic, or so it seemed at the time.

The Western Division passed Billy by. He was not fit enough to play in any of the fixtures and if 1961–62 had been arguably the zenith of his career, the 1962–63 season was something of a nightmare for him. By the time he arrived back in England Wigan had won their annual sevens tournament, and beaten Warrington in the Wardonia Cup. Alan Davies was temporary captain and Wigan had somehow managed to lose £15,000 on the previous season. On returning to Central Park Billy looked and felt extremely fit, according to the *Wigan Observer*, but he told officials that he had played several games in New Zealand when definitely not fit. He was despatched to Leeds, where he underwent an operation to remove a foreign body from his troublesome knee. Eric Ashton was also seeing a Leeds specialist for his ankle injury and all the Wigan tourists were carrying injuries.

They came back into action in dribs and drabs, Brian McTigue being the first on 22 August in a 14–10 home win against Blackpool Borough. Bill Sayer reappeared in the next game against Rochdale, as Wigan won their first five Western Division fixtures. Billy and Frank Carlton played their first games on 8 September, when more than 17,000 assembled at Central Park for a first round Lancashire Cup tie against Warrington. Billy took over the captaincy from Davies and scored a cracking try after 20 minutes following the best move of the match. He ran the last 25 yards before making short work of Tommy Conroy's challenge. He also potted a second half penalty goal, missed two other shots and made a fantastic cover tackle on Warrington's Welsh second-rower Idwal Fisher to save a try. Warrington were beaten 11–3.

And so was Billy, at least temporarily. His knee had flared up again and another operation was necessary. He missed the next 10 games and did not return to the Wigan team until November. In the meantime much water passed down the River Douglas and past Central Park. Wigan gradually got all their tourists back into action, but the team was clearly not firing on all cylinders. Workington Town dispatched them from the Lancashire Cup in the second round and repeated the dose in thrashing Wigan 27–9 in the semi-final of the Western Division Championship. The First Division Championship campaign got off to a stuttering start with defeats at Featherstone and Halifax, home wins against Bramley and Hull and a drawn game against Oldham, in which Brian McTigue got his marching orders.

Although rumours that Eric Ashton was bound for Eastern Suburbs in Australia came to nothing, there were personnel changes for the fans to ponder. Fred Griffiths had agreed to join North Sydney, while two Rhodesians had joined Wigan. John Winton, a goalkicking full-back, was to be Griffiths's replacement, although he arrived before Fred left, while winger Trevor Lake, a junior Springbok, added strength to the flanks. Wigan were also confident that they had finally solved their problem at scrum-half by signing Oldham's test player Frank Pitchford, in whom they had been interested for the last two years. On the debit side Norman Cherrington was sold to Huddersfield and the popular Frank Collier had been listed at £5,500. An even bigger surprise though was the listing of Dave Bolton at £10,500.

Billy was certainly being missed as Wigan adjusted to all the changes and Cyril Briggs lamented his absence in the *Rugby Leaguer:* "The name of Boston can do a lot at Central Park, even if it is only spoken. It has been known to start fights in pubs, between schoolchildren, and autograph hunters, but Billy is best seen when fighting his way to the line... One player does not make a team, or else the Wigan pack would be lost without the services of Brian McTigue. But Boston means a tremendous boost to the Wigan team, and someone to throw the ball to when the defence is in danger. Billy always finds a way out of the tightest of corners."

There was much rejoicing when Billy finally got back on to the field at Bramley on 10 November. Remarkably, it was the only time Billy ever played against Bramley. At half-time Wigan were 7–0 down, but recovered to win 19–9. Billy, Carlton and Lyon all had tries disallowed although Billy showed that he was still a dangerous opponent.

A week later Wigan threw away an 11–3 lead to lose 13–11 at home to Featherstone. Their topsy-turvy form continued at The Boulevard on 24 November with a stunning 34–0 drubbing of Hull. The game was effectively over after quarter of an hour when Wigan had 19 points on the board. Ashton scored a hat-trick before half-time and sent Billy roaring over for his first try in First Division rugby league. It was a happy day for Fred Griffiths to say good-bye to Wigan as he kicked eight goals and scored a try. A young, injured, Clive Sullivan was in the crowd and 'Old Faithful', the Hull correspondent of the *Rugby Leaguer*, mused, "Likened by many to be a younger edition of Billy Boston, I wonder what Clive thought when he saw the incomparable Billy on the warpath in one of his bull-dozing, fear-not-man-nor-beast runs which cut through the Hull back division."

Unsurprisingly, Billy's injury mishaps had cost him his place in the Great Britain team, which went down 17–12 to France at Perpignan on Sunday 2 December. Injuries, staleness and loss of form had caused the selectors to radically alter the side from the one that had swept Australia aside. Only five of the 1962 tourists played at Perpignan, and Eric Ashton was the only Wigan player. Billy's place had gone to the splendid young Bill Burgess from Barrow. Instead Billy moved into the centre and took over the captaincy for Wigan's home game with Halifax, who had walloped them 33–10 at Thrum Hall just five weeks earlier. This time it was different. Wigan won 39–0 with Collier, now off the transfer list, McTigue and Evans completely dominating the forward exchanges, while the *Wigan Observer* noted, "Billy Boston and Alan Davies were giants in the centre." Billy bagged two of Wigan's seven tries and John Winton landed nine goals.

Oldham were next to feel the power of a resurgent Wigan, going under 19–0 at Watersheddings. Alan Davies played a blinder against his old club, opposite Keith Holden, scoring a fantastic try after a curving 65-yard run. Wigan had scored 92 points in their last three games and conceded none. The new First Division was so competitive that Wigan's winning spurt had taken them from mid-table to second, a point behind Widnes, while Hull and Oldham, so recently among the game's elite, were joint bottom.

Another excellent win, 15–3 over Swinton in dismal conditions, set up a mouth-watering top of the table clash at Widnes on 22 December. Billy filled in at full-back, when Dave Bolton withdrew because of a boil on his arm. The *Wigan Observer* said: "Boston did nothing wrong and looked at home in the number one jersey but there were times... when his strong link-up bursts could have been better exploited." Billy saved a certain try when he took South African winger Johnny Gaydon into touch at the corner but Widnes, inspired by Vince Karalius at his best, proved too good and ran out 14–2 winners. Referee Eric Clay missed the first 20 minutes, having been delayed by a nasty West Lancashire mist and a burst water main.

Billy then got another rest for almost three months and so did everyone else in rugby league. The Great Freeze closed the sport down completely, beginning with a wipe-out of the Christmas and Boxing Day fixtures. It did not relax its grip until March, having comprehensively ruined all Challenge Cup arrangements, as well as creating a monstrous backlog of league fixtures. Just a handful of games were staged in the course of the Great Freeze. Wigan's directors refused to sand Central Park or resort to chemicals to defrost the pitch, as Widnes had done successfully with a substance sinisterly known as GL5. They did, however, attempt to keep the players fit by taking them to Blackpool to train on the beach several times. At the end of January the RFL decided to extend the season until 24 May. That must have come as a welcome relief to Wigan's latest signing, Kia Bose, a Fijian rugby union international stand-off, who arrived in February amid the snow and ice. It looked like Billy, at least, would get some match practice, when he was selected at right centre for Wales against France at Toulouse on 17 February. Billy was set to figure in a threequarter line containing three black Cardiffians, Colin Dixon and Johnny Freeman forming the left wing pairing, with Workington's Ray Glastonbury partnering Billy. Unfortunately, Billy contracted influenza and had to withdraw.

He finally saw match action with Wigan on Monday 4 March, when Wigan won a floodlit friendly at Leigh by 46–11. Billy failed to score despite Wigan picking up 10 tries. Three days later, on Thursday, Wigan played at Hull in their much delayed first round Challenge Cup tie, having, most unusually, had an overnight stay at York. Jack Winstanley reported that Wigan "gave a miserable performance", although that was perhaps unsurprising in view of the heavy pitch, unfit players and lack of match practice. Wigan led 2–0 at half-time and 4–0 after 77 minutes, thanks to two penalties by Ashton. At that point Billy sealed the victory at 7–0 with the only try of the tie after a break by Stan McLeod. Billy's try enabled him to equal Johnny Ring's Wigan club record of 368 tries. Ring, a fellow Welshman, had scored his mammoth total between 1922 and 1931.

Two days later, Billy again scored the only try of the match in a workmanlike 9–0 win at Swinton to break Ring's record. The try, which opened the scoring in the 31st minute, came via Pitchford, Barton and McTigue, who got Billy away down the touch-line. A powerful run, knocking off Bonser and Halliwell en route, took him over at the corner. It was the last time Swinton lost in the league that season, as they went on to lift the Championship, having at one point been bottom of the table.

Matches were coming thick and fast for all the clubs now, but Wigan had a full week before they met seemingly perennial opponents Leeds in the second round of the Challenge Cup at Central Park. Leeds, missing four star players, certainly gave the crowd of 27,819 a shock. They took an early 5–0 lead when Robin Dewhurst scored between the sticks and converted his own try. Three minutes later classic Wigan manoeuvring and subterfuge brought an equalising try. Play swung towards Billy's wing, drawing half-a-dozen Leeds coverers, all expecting Ashton to unleash Billy. Instead he threw the ball inside to McTigue, who drew the last elements of the defence before sending Billy flying over, Ashton kicking the goal. Leeds regained the lead on 30 minutes, when Dewhurst hoofed over a 50-yard penalty and at the break Leeds were 7–5 ahead. Ashton hit the post with a penalty before Frank Collier was sent off after 57 minutes for a bad tackle on Louis Neumann and when stand-off Rees dropped a 30-yard goal for Leeds on the hour to make it 9–5, Wigan seemed dead and buried.

Twelve minutes from time Ashton landed a penalty and there were only two points in it. Ashton passed up the chance to kick another penalty and elected to put the ball into touch at the corner in the hope of winning the ensuing five-yard scrum. Sayer obliged and the old firm went into stunning, if familiar, action. Pitchford and McLeod worked a scissors and whipped the ball to Ashton. Billy rocketed inside for Eric's pass and bounced clear to the posts. Ashton's goal put Wigan ahead for the first time and Jack Winstanley noted, probably with considerable understatement, "a thousand smiles returned to the terraces". Eric and Billy had worked the oracle yet again. The boot was now on the other foot. Leeds lost Fred Pickup, sent off after a dust-up with Pitchford, and Wigan scored eight more points against another Rees drop-goal to win 20–11.

It had been a good week for Billy. Before the Cup game he and his team-mates had been presented with tankards for winning the third period of the Mackeson points scoring competition and Jack Winstanley's brochure, celebrating Billy's 10th anniversary at Wigan, *The Billy Boston Story* had hit the bookstalls. To top it all, he had been selected for Great Britain's test against France at Wigan on 3 April.

However, all was not plain sailing. A chest injury kept Billy out of Wigan's 22–20 home defeat against Workington Town on 23 March, although he returned to the side three days later at right centre in another defeat, 20–11, in a brilliantly contested game at St Helens. He suffered a recurrence of his chest injury and moved to full-back for the second half. The *Wigan Observer* was much taken by Alex Murphy's great performance for Saints, but also complained that he "again indulged in the kind of niggling 'monkey tricks', which far too often pay scant respect to sportsmanship and authority". Not that such criticism would have much effect on the Great Britain scrum-half.

Billy's bruised chest kept him out of Wigan's 3–2 win at Huddersfield on 30 March and there was anxiety that he would be ruled out of the Central Park test match and Wigan's third round Challenge Cup tie.

However, Billy was made of pretty stern stuff and duly turned out against France on Wednesday, 3 April. There were 19,487 spectators present that evening for what turned out to be Billy's last test match, his 31st. It was fitting that it should have been played at Central Park and that his long time colleagues Eric Ashton, Dave Bolton and Brian McTigue were also in the team. Unfortunately, the French, after beating Great Britain three times in a row, hardly competed and were thrashed 42–4. Neil Fox set a new British record of 21 points, a try and nine goals. Billy signed off by roaring over for his 24th test try.

Three days later 7,500 Wigan fans travelled to Watersheddings for another all-ticket full house third round Challenge Cup tie against Oldham. Although Oldham were not the force they had been in the 1950s, a hard struggle was anticipated by the 22,301 onlookers. What they got was a master class from Wigan. The Oldham pack was annihilated in the face of a Wigan forward display which was "almost frightening in its ferocity", according to the *Wigan Observer*. Oldham, on a £60 a man bonus, fell behind after 15 minutes when Bolton scored from a scintillating movement and eight minutes later Billy was almost over only to be balked by three tacklers at the corner flag. From the scrum Evans shot down the blind-side, while Pitchford ran on the open-side as a decoy. Billy took Evans's pass at an alarming velocity and bored through, over or past Parker, Simms and Gaskell for a fabulous try at the corner. It was all over when Lyon romped over for a third Wigan try in the 32nd minute. Wigan led 13–0 at half-time and the only other score was a late converted try to Frank Carlton. Oldham scrum-half Gaskell was sent off two minutes from time for striking Pitchford. Despite the victory, there was a price to pay for Billy and Wigan. John Barton and Roy Evans picked up injuries and Billy sustained a shoulder injury and "was like a one-armed man for the whole of the second half, although he shirked nothing."

With fixtures beginning to pile up and the Challenge Cup semi-finals just two weeks ahead, Wigan were compelled to field weakened sides for the three Easter games and lost the lot, pretty comprehensively. Billy's bruised shoulder kept him out of them all. The semi-final pitted Wigan against a rising Hull KR at Headingley on 20 April. Wigan spent a couple of days at Ilkley preparing for the game, which took place in continuous rain. Billy received a pain-killing injection for his shoulder 15 minutes before kick-off and it obviously worked. The *Rugby Leaguer* reported that early in the proceedings: "When Wigan got the ball Bolton linked with Ashton to send Boston bouncing down the wing. And what bounce! He sent one opponent skittling, but paid for it as reinforcement, in the shape of three determined defenders, dropped on him in a cascade of arms and legs. The crowd loved it. I think Boston did, too... Then Boston bounced in again, and Rovers' Blackmore almost bounced out as the Wigan idol smashed him into the mud with a tremendous smother tackle."

Poor old Mike Blackmore had a torrid time against Billy – "The second half almost fell in on Blackmore. Boston caught him with another of those smother tackles", while later "Smash! Boston caught Blackmore with yet another smother tackle. Blackmore got up, absolutely bewildered." Billy's duel with Blackmore apart, Wigan played magical football to win 18–4. Alan Davies scored a hat-trick, Dave Bolton claimed the remaining try and Eric Ashton kicked three goals. When Davies scored the final try, Ashton took the conversion and Billy, "ever the showman, stood joking with the crowd. Rovers stood with heads bowed, thoroughly dejected."

Although Wigan had more or less given up on the chase for the League Championship title, having dropped to around mid-table, they followed their Cup success with super wins at Warrington and at home against Leeds. Billy missed the former and was very quiet in the latter after taking another knock to his shoulder. Apart from Billy, Wigan also had injury worries with Barton, McTigue and Pitchford as Wembley approached. Billy missed a home defeat by Widnes on 1 May, but proved he was fit enough three days later in a 19–15 home win over Hull KR. He scored Wigan's first try in the sixth minute. However, it was a converted try by Trevor Lake 50 seconds from time that clinched the victory.

After playing eight games in 18 days Wigan had a clear week to prepare for the Challenge Cup Final against Wakefield Trinity. They took the 13 men expected to play in the final plus Trevor Lake, Jim Belshaw and Tony Stephens to Blackpool on Sunday for several days' preparation. A Leeds specialist declared Billy's shoulder 100 per cent fit and Billy told the press, "I think we'll win and win easily". The Wigan players trained at Blackpool Borough and enjoyed Turkish baths, golf and a boxing promotion at the Winter Gardens before departing for their London base at the Hendon Hall hotel on the Thursday. They wound down on Friday with a trip to the London Palladium to see Sammy Davis, Junior.

The sun shone benignly at Wembley on 11 May for another dream final. Wakefield Trinity versus Wigan was the match everyone had anticipated the previous season, when the two teams had been outstanding. Strangely, neither side had won anything in 1962–63 so far, but both were full of match-winners and personalities and both had tremendous pedigrees at Wembley in recent years. Trinity were the Cup holders and had also won at Wembley in 1960, while Billy and several of his Wigan colleagues were ready for their fourth final in five years. Despite Wakefield's undoubted class, Wigan were considered firm favourites. Leslie Woodhead, for example, endorsed the bookies' view in the *Liverpool Echo and Evening Express* on 4 May, writing: "My view is that Wigan on their day are unbeatable. No team in the Rugby League can stay the pace with them when they hit top form."

There was quite a stir when Wigan entered the arena in red tracksuits with "a glaring advertisement for a firm of sports outfitters [Litesome]". Overt sponsorship was not strictly allowed in those days and the always strongly opinionated Eric Thompson, of the *Lancashire Evening Post*, grizzled: "I must agree that it looked like commercialism gone too far. This big occasion of the season was one time when Wigan fans wanted to see their team coming out in the famous cherry-and-white jerseys... not wrapped up like teddy bears."

The teams were introduced to Field-Marshall Montgomery before the game and lined up as follows:

*Wakefield Trinity:* Round, Greenwood, Brooke, Fox, Coetzer, Poynton, Holliday, Wilkinson, Kosanovic, Sampson, Vines, Turner (captain), Pearman

*Wigan:* Bolton, Boston, Ashton (captain), Davies, Carlton, McLeod, Pitchford, Barton, Sayer, McTigue, Collier, Lyon, Evans

The introductions to 'Monty' gave rise to one of rugby league's classic tales. It was noticed that there was a good deal of ribaldry between Viscount Montgomery and the sometimes whimsical Wigan second-rower Frank Collier. Eric Thompson explained: "Rugby League chairman Mr Wilfred Spaven said: 'Frank added a few years to his age though he would probably be the first to get annoyed at it if it was to be given as his football age'. Collier saluted smartly when he was presented to Monty. 'Nice to see you again, sir', said Frank. Replied Monty, 'Where have we met before?' 'Don't you remember Alamein?' said Frank. 'How old are you?' asked Monty. Back came the reply: '35'.

A puzzled Monty went back to the Royal Box and half way through the game turned to Mr Spaven and said: 'That Wigan forward couldn't have been at Alamein. If he's 35 he would have been less than 15 then and we didn't have any schoolchildren at Alamein. And if he is 35 he is too old to be running about out there'. Collier, of course, had added five years to his age."

The oldest players on the field were, in fact, rival props Jack Wilkinson, making a record fifth Wembley appearance, and Brian McTigue. Both were three months short of their 33rd birthdays. It was in the area of experience that many pundits believed Wigan had a vital edge. Trinity were fielding some very inexperienced men in Ian Brooke, Malcolm Sampson, Roger Pearman, who was playing only his seventh first class game, and Gert 'Oupa' Coetzer. Coetzer, a South African, in his 15th first team appearance, was facing Billy and, like Billy, was suffering from a severe shoulder injury, for which he needed a painkilling injection prior to playing.

Wigan dominated the first 20 minutes, stretching Trinity to breaking point on several occasions but failed to register any points. Early on Billy was brought to earth just short of the goal-line and McLeod and Carlton almost got over. Eric Ashton did get over near the corner flag, but was adjudged by referee Dennis Davies to have made a double movement and penalised for his trouble. Eric always maintained that the try was legitimate and Billy was on the spot and equally sure that Eric scored. Ashton was doing all he could to inspire Wigan, but his goalkicking was awry and he missed several penalty attempts in the first half hour, while on another occasion he broke through beautifully over the half-way line but found that Billy had failed to support his break. The Wigan forwards began to fade and the two minutes before half-time turned fortunes Wakefield's way. Firstly, Dave Bolton flew up into the line in anticipation of a drop-goal attempt from Neil Fox, but Keith Holliday had only feinted to serve Fox. Instead he popped a beautiful inside ball to Malcolm Sampson who careered past two nonplussed defenders to plant the ball under the posts. Fox's conversion gave Trinity a 5–0 lead. Worse followed as Bolton was knocked unconscious after backing up a break by Geoff Lyon and carried off just as half-time arrived. He did not reappear for the first 18 minutes of the second half.

Straight after the resumption Wigan hopes rose when Frank Pitchford dashed over for a try at the corner to make the score 5–3. Wakefield stretched their lead to 10–3, however, in the 48th minute when Coetzer went over at the opposite corner and Fox landed a brilliant conversion. Fox and Ashton traded penalty goals and Wigan trailed 12–7, when the game's crucial moment occurred. Bolton, still dazed, broke through across his own '25', with Eric and Billy outside him and the possibility of a try unfolding. However, Bolton suddenly found Harold Poynton had intercepted his pass and was scuttling 30 yards to the line for another converted try. With only 12 minutes remaining Wigan were 10 points adrift. Carlton sped over near the flag to make it 17–10, but Trinity finished with a flourish. Coetzer went in for his second try after splendid work from Pearman and in the dying seconds Brooke added a fifth try and Trinity finished 25–10 winners.

For the neutrals and Trinity supporters the game was wonderful. The *Daily Mail's* Derek Marshall wrote: "It was the Cup Final that enraptured TV millions, the match in which Harold Poynton joined an immortal list of Lance Todd trophy winners, and Wakefield threw back the shutters to let a national audience see Rugby League in all its glory." Jack Paul commented in the *Sunday Express:* "Underdogs Trinity kept the Rugby League Challenge Cup yesterday with the finest football-filled display of teamwork I have seen at Wembley."

For Wigan and their fans the 1963 Cup Final was a disaster. Jack Paul said: "Wigan were over-confident in my reckoning. Early on they played without either drive or urgency, always with the air that they felt that the tries would eventually come – and indeed it looked that way. But there was no excuse for scrum-half Pitchford kicking when Trinity's Kosanovic was winning the [first half] scrums 2–1, and for sloppy backing-up before Wakefield's tackling had assumed its rock-like quality of later stages. And Wigan paid the penalty for their shocking finishing." Derek Marshall observed: "It was a day of pride and of sadness too, for it marked the end of a once-great Wigan pack. In my belief it was not David Bolton's misfortunes that cost Wigan the Cup but the forwards' tacit admission that they could no longer stay the pace on the spacious Wembley pitch."

Billy came in for his share of criticism too. The *Wigan Observer* wailed: "Billy Boston had a most ineffective match. Apart from some strong tackles early in the game and that inside dash which led indirectly to Carlton's try, Boston was unable to exert any influence at all on the game." Derek Marshall mused that "Disillusioned Wigan supporters are still wondering what witchcraft induced Billy Boston to labour so listlessly on the wing" and declared that Gert Coetzer "gave Billy Boston one of the blackest afternoons of his career".

The *Rugby Leaguer's* Cyril Briggs's disappointment was so intense that he wrote: "Billy Boston on the right wing, I should say, is ready for hanging up his boots. There is not the same drive behind the burly winger's bursts that there used to be, although it is appreciated that Billy is no chicken when it comes to age." Billy was not yet 29. He also had a go at Brian McTigue: "He is not an 80 minute player any longer. He plays in fits and starts. On this Wigan performance, a few youngsters ought to be given a chance to show their worth." Cyril's ultimate criticism read, "To put it in three words, Wigan were pathetic."

All manner of reasons were trotted out for Wigan's demise. They were over-confident; there were too many veterans in the side; there was even a suggestion that the Blackpool ozone had tired the players out, although Eric Ashton pointed out that they had gone to Blackpool in 1958 and 1959, when it appeared to have done them no harm. The most popular theory was that Fred Griffiths's departure caused a big problem at full-back and in the goalkicking department. It was argued, with considerable justification, that moving Dave Bolton to full-back had back-fired as he was more needed at stand-off. Bolton was a big attacking danger from full-back, but he was taking some fearful hidings from head-hunters and obstructionists. Far from being washed up as a winger, some critics thought that Billy was the answer to the full-back conundrum. A reader of the *Lancashire Evening*

Referee D.T.H. Davies disallows Eric Ashton's try at Wembley for Wigan. Gert Coetzer made the tackle, while Neil Fox looks at the referee hopefully.

*Post* suggested: "Boston is now the natural for the full-back berth. He can kick well, can handle well, tackles terrifically and has a great positional sense... and teams would think twice about trying to knock Boston down. And if anybody could make use of that extra breathing space to get into full sail, it is Boston rather than Bolton."

Four days after the disappointment of Wembley, Wigan journeyed to Hull KR and earned a runaway 34–12 win. The forwards seemed revitalised and six sparkling tries were scored. Billy bounced back to form, blotting out the left wing pairing of Blackmore and Murphy. It always took at least two Rovers to stop him and he grabbed two tries, his first a typical blockbuster to the posts after Ashton had released him. Raymond Fletcher of the *Rugby Leaguer* reported: "Billy Boston finished? I don't know about that. I saw him score a try last week that suggests if he is 'finished' most of the others haven't even 'started'."

Wigan still had six league fixtures to fulfil between 18 and 29 May, but Billy's shoulder was too shot to allow him to continue and he missed the lot. Wigan only won one of the six and conceded a double to Wakefield to rub salt into their recently acquired wounds. Even at that stage in the season Wigan went out and bought yet another scrum-half, taking the former Scottish rugby union international Brian Shillinglaw from Whitehaven for £5,500. Wigan had sold the loyal and dependable Terry Entwistle to Leigh barely a month before.

The season had been a very mixed affair for both Billy and for Wigan. The team had got to Wembley, of course, but had finished only eighth in the First Division with a 50 per cent record. They were still the best supported club in the land, but the combination of bad weather, congested fixtures and new league format had reduced their average league crowd by almost 2,500 to 14,890, the lowest since 1953–54.

On a personal level Billy had endured a season of highs and lows. The highs included a fourth Wembley final, beating Johnny Ring's record aggregate of tries for Wigan and a late recall to the test side. On the downside injuries had ruined his season, he had played in only 18 of Wigan's 46 games and for the first time he had failed to top the Wigan try-scorers. Billy had finished at the top for the past eight seasons – another club record – but had just 12 tries to his credit for 1962–63. Frank Carlton topped the list with 23 tries, followed by Alan Davies on 20 and Stan McLeod on 14.

The season did, however, close with the welcome news that Wigan had granted Billy a testimonial season in 1963–64.

## 1962–63

Wigan finished 8th in the League: P30, W14, L14, D2, For 476, Against 393
Boston scored 12 tries and 1 goal for Wigan, plus 1 try in representative rugby league

| Date | Opponent | Score | Boston | Crowd | |
|------|----------|-------|--------|-------|---|
| 18 August | Liverpool City | 34-7 | dnp | 1,583 | WD |
| 22 August | **Blackpool B** | 14–10 | dnp | 10,661 | WD |
| 25 August | **Rochdale H** | 56-0 | dnp | 9,378 | WD |
| 29 August | Whitehaven | 31-7 | dnp | 4,913 | WD |
| 1 September | **Liverpool City** | 31–15 | dnp | 8,142 | WD |
| 8 September | **Warrington** | 11–3 | 1T, 1G | 17,219 | LC1 |
| 15 September | Blackpool B | 19–10 | dnp | 3,500 | WD |
| 17 September | Workington T | 8–16 | dnp | 9,052 | LC 2 |
| 22 September | **Whitehaven** | 22–13 | dnp | 10,272 | WD |
| 29 September | Rochdale H | 6–10 | dnp | 3,615 | WD |
| 6 October | **Bramley** | 30-7 | dnp | 12,252 | |
| 13 October | Featherstone R | 10–20 | dnp | 7,616 | |
| 15 October | Workington T | 9–27 | dnp | 7,597 | WD SF |
| 20 October | **Hull** | 28–11 | dnp | 13,716 | |
| 27 October | Halifax | 10–33 | dnp | 6,862 | |
| 3 November | **Oldham** | 14–14 | dnp | 13,804 | |
| 10 November | Bramley | 19-9 | | 3,435 | |
| 17 November | **Featherstone R** | 11–13 | | 11,397 | |
| 24 November | Hull | 34-0 | 1T | 8,200 | |
| 1 December | **Halifax** | 39-0 | 2T | 13,096 | |
| 8 December | Oldham | 19-0 | | 8,429 | |
| 15 December | **Swinton** | 15-3 | | 9,691 | |
| 22 December | Widnes | 2–14 | | 10,529 | |
| 7 March | Hull | 7-0 | 1T | 10,299 | Cup 1 |
| 9 March | Swinton | 9-0 | 1T | 10,672 | |
| 16 March | **Leeds** | 20–11 | 2T | 27,819 | Cup 2 |
| 23 March | **Workington T** | 20–22 | dnp | 17,307 | |
| 26 March | St Helens | 11–20 | | 21,653 | |
| 30 March | Huddersfield | 3-2 | dnp | 6,473 | |
| 6 April | Oldham | 18-0 | 1T | 22,301 | Cup 3 |
| 12 April | **St Helens** | 4–24 | dnp | 40,996 | |
| 13 April | Leeds | 3–16 | dnp | 12,941 | |
| 15 April | Castleford | 7–18 | dnp | 5,700 | |
| 20 April | Hull KR (at Leeds) | 18-4 | | 21,479 | Cup SF |
| 24 April | Warrington | 16–15 | dnp | 11,131 | |
| 27 April | **Leeds** | 32-8 | | 14,252 | |
| 1 May | **Widnes** | 8–20 | dnp | 20,577 | |
| 4 May | **Hull KR** | 19–15 | 1T | 12,763 | |
| 11 May | Wakefield T (at Wembley) | 10–25 | | 84,492 | Cup Final |
| 15 May | Hull KR | 34–12 | 2T | 9,481 | |
| 18 May | **Wakefield T** | 13–21 | dnp | 16,194 | |
| 20 May | Workington T | 6-8 | dnp | 2,863 | |
| 22 May | **Huddersfield** | 21-7 | dnp | 8,746 | |
| 25 May | Wakefield T | 8–21 | dnp | 9,028 | |
| 27 May | **Castleford** | 18–18 | dnp | 7,823 | |
| 29 May | **Warrington** | 13–22 | dnp | 10,739 | |

## Boston's representative matches:

| Date | For | Opponent | Score | Boston | Venue |
|------|-----|----------|-------|--------|-------|
| 3 April | Great Britain | France | 42-4 | 1T | Wigan |

159

In action against Featherstone Rovers in January 1964

# 15. 1963–64 Transfer listed & two divisions

The late summer of 1963 saw the usual build-up to Wigan's season. On 5 August the Wigan sevens tournament was won for the sixth year in a row, when Oldham were beaten 16–13 in the final after extra time before a crowd of 9,807. It was the day before Billy's 29th birthday, but he was not celebrating too hard. His shoulder was still not right and it certainly was not worth risking it for a game of sevens. The shoulder had given him sufficient pain and worry to stop him from playing any cricket at all. Billy was selected to play centre for the Blues in the public trial match on 10 August but cried off 20 minutes before kick-off.

The following Tuesday, 13 August, the front page of the *Wigan Observer* blazed with the headline "Billy Boston goes on the transfer list".

The article below the headline ran: "Inimitable Billy Boston, the rugby league star who probably has pulled in more spectators to Central Park than any other player, has been placed on the transfer list by Wigan – on the eve of his benefit season. The fee is £10,000 ... Boston was too stunned to comment about his future. And today the town was buzzing with speculation."

This had come like a bolt out of the blue for Billy. The directors had given no indication of their intention to list him and Billy thought the fee was prohibitive anyway. They may have thought he was swinging the lead about his shoulder because a specialist had declared it sound. Billy told Jack Winstanley with some justification, "If I can't throw a cricket ball, my arm can hardly be fit for playing rugby league." Some people wondered at the size of the fee. If Billy was on the way out, as the doom mongers had predicted after the Cup Final, how come the board thought he was worth so much? His heir apparent in the test team Barrow's Bill Burgess had, coincidentally, just been transfer listed at £18,000, the biggest fee ever announced. Maybe there was a connection, mused some Wigan watchers. Then there was the matter of his testimonial year. Concerts had already taken place for it. A cricket match, rugby match collections and a benefit dance at the Empress Hall in September had already been arranged. Billy did not need this distraction.

He missed the Wardonia Cup match on 17 August, when Warrington whacked Wigan 31–5 at Central Park. Wigan fans were already apprehensive about the 1963–64 season and a dispute over match pay organised by players of the self-styled 'Big Five' clubs (Wigan, St Helens, Leeds, Widnes and Wakefield) just added to the uncertainty. The players were demanding home terms of £16 a win and £8 a defeat for Division One fixtures and away terms of £20 and £10 respectively. The Widnes players were the first to capitulate and the others quickly followed in time for the opening league matches. One good piece of news for the Wigan faithful was the signing of Billy's 1962 tour colleague, Laurie Gilfedder, who cost the club £8,000 from Warrington. Laurie would at a stroke solve Wigan's goalkicking problem and add some zest to the pack's back row.

More good news was Billy's appearance in the opening fixture on 24 August, when Wigan beat Widnes 10–3 at Central Park. Billy claimed Wigan's first try of the season a minute before half-time, when he took a long pass from stand-off Ashton and brushed through tackles by Karalius and Heyes to touch down at the flag. Vince Karalius told the Wigan chairman, Joe Taylor, "I wish you wouldn't play Boston against us." The *Wigan Observer* commented: "Perhaps the biggest single impact was made by the return to the Central Park fold of Billy Boston. To say the least, Boston managed to show that he is still a great character to be reckoned with by any opposition." Billy's enduring popularity was rewarded by a collection, which contributed £114 to his testimonial fund.

Four days later Wigan fell 16–4 at champions Swinton, Billy moving to right centre with Trevor Lake outside him. Lake took over the left wing spot from Frank Carlton for the fixture at Huddersfield on 31 August and stayed there for the rest of the season. At Fartown Billy reverted to the right wing and he and Lake both claimed three tries in a 29–14 win. Wigan won the first half scrums 15–2 but, amazingly, were 10–0 down after 25 minutes. Billy was the match winner scoring his first try in the 37th minute. After collecting a Roy Evans pass he blasted through the tackles of Bowman and Curry to score at the corner, pulling Wigan back to 12–12. For his second try he took a pass from Bolton and "treated the tackles of Bowman, Curry and Haywood with contempt." He bounced over for his third "leaving Curry with more unpleasant memories." However, it was another incident that stuck in the memories of those who witnessed it. The *Wigan Observer* reported: "In the dying seconds Boston turned on a spectacular run which must have made Huddersfield supporters think that the great Lionel Cooper had come out of retirement. Put in possession by Ashton 65 yards from the Huddersfield line, Boston was faced by four defenders spaced at 15-yard intervals. For some time Boston has concentrated on rather shorter runs than this but here he set off like a two-year-old. The first two men waiting for him were handed off like pieces of straw and the second two found themselves holding Boston's thighs one second and thin air the next. Just when it seemed that he might squeeze in, two more Huddersfield men hustled him over the touch-line a few inches short of the corner flag."

Billy was certainly back. Leeds, at Central Park, were next to feel the power he still packed. He and Ashton scored first half tries to give Wigan a 10–4 interval lead, but eight points in the last eight minutes were required to finally see off the Loiners. Billy scored his sixth try in five games in an easy 34–12 win at Barrow in the first round of the Lancashire Cup on 7 September. Eric Ashton continually used Billy as a foil to carve huge openings in the Barrovians' defence.

Two days later, on a Monday evening, Wigan met Swinton before a crowd of 20,190 at Central Park. Swinton had won 21 consecutive league matches, but came unstuck against Wigan, who won 13–0. Gilfedder booted five goals but Trevor Lake's try, a 70-yarder in which he gloriously beat four men, was the highlight.

Wigan fans were gleeful the day after the triumph against Swinton when they heard that the board had taken Billy off the transfer list. It had been an uncomfortable month for all concerned. Another pleasant reminder of times past was the visit of Jim Sullivan to Central Park on 17 September, his first since his stroke.

However, there was consternation when Wigan went down 7–5 at home to Second Division Leigh in the second round of the Lancashire Cup on 18 September. Another 20,000 crowd looked on disconsolately as Leigh smothered Wigan out of the game, successfully shackling mainsprings Ashton and McTigue and restricting Billy to a solitary running chance.

Billy missed Wigan's 20–16 home win against Hull KR, after which it was announced that Eric Ashton was to be given a six weeks trial as player-coach. Griff Jenkins was to stay with the club in a scouting capacity. Ashton's first game in charge was at Keighley on 28 September, when the home team were overwhelmed 48–9. Lake claimed a hat-trick before Billy roared in for two tries after great touch-line bursts, shoving off numerous tacklers. However, the game at Lawkholme Lane was one of those rare occasions when Billy was subjected to abuse. He was reported to have turned angrily on several youths, who shouted abuse and threw sods at him as he signed autographs on the field after the final whistle. Typically, the youths ran off when Billy turned on them. The *Wigan Observer* pointed out that it was also at Keighley in a Challenge Cup-tie that a woman had hit him with her handbag and that cushions had been thrown at him as he left the field. In an amazing coincidence there had been trouble the same afternoon at Wilderspool, where Warrington played Halifax. The *Wigan Observer* ran a headline: "Colour Shame". Billy's former club-mate Keith Holden and Colin Dixon had been involved in a punch-up after the final whistle, allegedly because of some uncomplimentary remarks made by Holden. Johnny Freeman had joined in and all three were reported to the RFL. Holden, to his credit, was man enough to publicly apologise for his behaviour. The fact that the *Observer* chose to run the story showed just how unusual racial discrimination or abuse was within the game. It is often forgotten just how cosmopolitan English rugby league was at that time. Billy played with and against men from all the home nations, France, Italy, Yugoslavia, USA, Australia and New Zealand. He played against black, white and coloured (mixed race) South Africans, Rhodesians, Fijians, Tongans, Maoris and Australian Aborigines. The M62 corridor had not yet been invented.

The Western Division Championship had been changed from an early season competition to a season long event and Wigan fancied their chances of winning it, especially as their four opponents were from the Second Division. Eric Ashton must have wondered whether his decision to take the player-coach responsibility was wise after his side's opening fixture in the competition on 5 October. Rochdale Hornets sprang a real surprise by winning 14–13 at Central Park, despite being overwhelmed in the scrums and losing scrum-half Johnny Fishwick, who was sent off after 65 minutes. At least the coach could not fault Billy, who scored all three of Wigan's tries between the 55th and 60th minutes – an almost unbelievable achievement. For the first he slid past a desperate challenge by Evans; the second followed good approach play from Alan Davies and Frankie Parr; finally, he latched on to a kick through by Jeff Bootle, toed the ball forward and touched down.

Wigan's dismal performance against Rochdale was followed by a scrappy win at Warrington, which was televised, injury preventing Billy from playing. He returned on 19 October for the home game against Wakefield Trinity, with whom Wigan had plenty of scores to settle after the previous season. Ashton decided to pick Billy at full-back and Jack Winstanley reckoned that Wigan's 31–7 win was their most brilliant performance since beating Halifax 26–0 at Thrum Hall in the Cup in 1959. Of Billy he wrote: "Billy Boston? Well, you just can't keep the big fellow down. His full-back display was packed with power and penetration and his timely runs from behind the Wigan team had a tremendous influence on the game. Time after time he disposed of two or three men in clearing his line and twice became an extra centre as he supplied the final passes for two of Lake's three tries... The Great Britain selectors should find a place for him in the second test – wing, full-back or centre!"

Billy's next five games were also as full-back. On 26 September Blackpool Borough were butchered 77–8 in a Western Division fixture. Eleven Wigan players shared 17 tries, Lake grabbing another four, while Gilfedder kicked 13 goals. Billy had little to do on defence and contributed one try. An impressive 14–2 win at Widnes kept Wigan in second place in the league, two points behind Swinton, but with a game in hand. It also persuaded the board to make Eric Ashton player-coach on a five-year contract. Ashton, who had captained Great Britain in the first two Ashes tests, both disastrous defeats, decided to retire from international rugby to concentrate on his responsibilities with Wigan. His honeymoon period was quickly over. Wigan lost 18–12 at home to Castleford, Billy running strongly for one of his side's two tries. Then, minus Billy, they went down 18–10 to the Australians, in a Monday afternoon encounter because the game had been fogged off on the Saturday. Five days later they were fortunate to escape with an 8–8 draw at home to Workington and Billy's run at full-back came to an end after an ignominious 20–7 defeat at Second Division neighbours Leigh in a Western Division match. That defeat effectively killed off any hopes of winning the competition, or even qualifying for its play-offs. The nature of the defeat was shocking, the finishing of Davies and Lake was too bad to be true and Wigan's handling beggared belief. Scrum-halves Parr and Entwistle were sent off for fighting three minutes from time and as far as Wigan were concerned the only positive was a sound debut from Chris Hesketh at stand-off.

The fall-out saw six players dropped, including three former test players – Billy, Bill Sayer and Brian McTigue. The Wigan performances did not markedly improve with a scratchy home win against Keighley and another defeat at Featherstone. While Wigan were losing at Post Office Road on 14 December, Wigan 'A' were seeing off Workington Town 'A' 34–5 at Central Park. Billy rampaged over for a couple of tries in a superb display of power.

Wigan restored Billy to their right wing for their trip to Thrum Hall on 28 December. Halifax were seeking their eighth consecutive victory, but Wigan pulled off a great 16–10 success, despite losing the scrums 20–10. McTigue was in magnificent form and Billy gave his opponents no end of trouble, having tries disallowed at the beginning and end of the 80 minutes. Although Billy failed to score at Halifax he did score in the next six games, none of which were lost. On New Year's Day Wigan travelled to Workington, who had become something of a bogey side to them. Not this time, though, as, taking advantage of a gale force wind, Wigan built up an 18–0 lead in the first half-hour. Billy put them 3–0 ahead after 12 minutes after John Winton linked up well to send him in at the corner. The *Wigan Observer* noted, "Billy Boston displayed some of his old keenness on the right wing" and praised Wigan's apparent good team spirit. In spite of that reported good spirit no fewer than six potential first teamers were on the transfer list at "reduced rates" – Bootle, Carlton, Collier, Pitchford, Sayer and Woosey.

On 4 January Wigan won a Western Division match at Rochdale 35–16 with Trevor Lake getting another hat-trick, while Billy touched down in each half and enjoyed a ding-dong tussle with the giant Fijian Joe Levula. At that point in the season Lake led the try-scorers with 27 followed by Barrow's Bill Burgess on 21, Swinton's Johnny Stopford with 17 and Oldham's Trevor Simms and Billy with 16 each. On 11 January the Wigan fans showed how much they appreciated Billy when a cheque for £1,330 from his testimonial was presented to him before the game against Warrington – a record for the club. Billy repaid them by scoring the last points in the 66th minute in a 13–5 win. Frank Collier created the try after snapping up a loose ball. The ball was shipped to the right and Gilfedder threw an overhead pass to Billy, who slid over at the flag with Brian Glover draped around him. It was the popular Frank Collier's last match as a cherry and white as he was soon to be snapped up by Widnes, with whom he won the Lance Todd trophy at Wembley a few months later.

Two weeks later Wigan scraped home 15–14 against Featherstone at Central Park in a memorable game, having had, according to the *Wigan Observer*, 85 per cent of the play. It noted: "Boston had a splendidly alert game on the right wing. His powerhouse finishing brought him his 398th (sic) try for Wigan and he had another score disallowed after scattering five defenders... His brilliant tackling of the centres stopped several tries and made fans wonder where the Wigan second-rowers were!"

On 1 February, Wigan had a very open, absorbing game at Belle Vue against Wakefield Trinity. Billy had been having a frustrating game. He had had a try disallowed when the touch-judge ruled his foot in touch. The crowd jeered him when he looked askance at the official. Colin Greenwood and Don Metcalfe had stopped him on several occasions much to the delight of the Trinity fans, both Wakefield's tries had come down his wing and he had conceded a penalty goal to Neil Fox when he had body-checked Greenwood in full flight. By the 45th minute Wigan were 8–2 behind. The game was changed dramatically with two tries under the sticks within eight minutes. The first followed a scrum 40 yards out and was a master-stroke by Ashton, who motioned Billy to come inside if Sayer won the ball. Wakefield spotted the ruse so Ashton turned and switched the play and sent McLeod haring to the posts, while three defenders were left wondering why Billy had not got the ball. The winning try was initiated by Brian Shillinglaw, who found a chink in Wakefield's left flank. Billy swiftly came infield, took the scrum-half's pass and swept past and through four would-be heroes to touch down, Gilfedder converting.

Wigan's 12–8 victory put them in good heart for their next opponents – Swinton in the first round of the Challenge Cup on 8 February. That was as hard a tie as could be imagined. Swinton were still top of the league and Wigan were second. Wigan made sure the tie took place by covering the field with 12 tons of straw and were rewarded with an attendance of 31,752, who witnessed one of the most electrifying and ferocious games to have taken place at venerable Central Park. The *Sunday Telegraph's* Gavin Gray wrote: "It was a hard game. At times it was hectic, vigorous and rough. Tempers became frayed; fists flew; cautions were administered and names taken. But the game never lost its thrills; never lost its excitement". Jack Nott, in the *News of the World*, observed: "This was a battle of the dinosaurs. It was action-packed. It pulsated. But there were discords in this melody of movement – the flash of hate, the flying fist, the punch and the counter-punch." Billy was at the eye of the storm.

Wigan looked likely winners when they led 10–0 after 25 minutes, Davies and Shillinglaw ripping through for tries and Gilfedder landing two goals but by half-time Swinton had pulled back to 10–5. On 47 minutes Gilfedder kicked a penalty – his 99th goal of the season – and Wigan led 12–5. By the 57th minute Swinton had turned the game on its head and led 15–12 after pilfering two converted tries. In between them Eric Ashton had been knocked unconscious after falling on a kick-through and was taken from the field for a few minutes. He could not remember anything, but Billy could. Tough Swinton stand-off George Parkinson had done the damage to Ashton and Billy avenged his captain. The *Wigan Observer* wrote that Billy "appeared to be using him as a tent peg before the two were dragged apart." Both players were cautioned and Billy was probably lucky not to have been sent off. It was fortunate for Wigan that Billy did remain on the pitch for he saved the game with 12 minutes remaining with a memorable score. Wigan were awarded a penalty on the Swinton '25' and Gilfedder elected to put in a cross-kick or an up-and-under, depending on which report is to be believed, towards Billy's wing, rather than kicking for goal. Billy and Eric went for the ball, which somehow bounced in no-man's land. Johnny Stopford and John Fleet went after it for Swinton. No one seemed able to lay hands on the ball until Billy swept in and as Jack Nott wrote: "Boston's big hands make no mistake. He is hit three times on his flank run. He staggers. But he makes it." The score was 15–15 and the crowd was beside itself. Gilfedder's touch-line conversion just missed and there was still time for Swinton full-back Ken Gowers to miss a 50-yard penalty goal and then send a drop-goal attempt fizzing wide of the goal.

Wigan should have won. They had a scrum advantage of 24–14 and penalties went their way 10–8, while the *Wigan Observer* maintained, "Wigan played 90 per cent of the football". It had been only the second time Wigan had drawn at Central Park in a Challenge Cup tie. The replay three days later attracted a crowd of 26,891 to Station Road. Wigan dominated territorially and in the scrums but lacked imagination on attack and Swinton put them to the sword. Stopford scored two tries down Billy's flank but Billy was by far the best of Wigan's threequarters. Once he sailed past three defenders to touch down but had stepped into touch. This time there was no escape for Wigan who were 13–0 down with six minutes left and made the score respectable with a forlorn flourish of eight points.

Wigan won their next six games, including three fairly meaningless Western Division fixtures, but there was a certain sense of anticlimax after their expulsion from the Challenge Cup. On 7 March there was a splendid 21–7 win at Leeds, where Billy put in several great barnstorming runs. However, he made an uncharacteristic error when he crossed for a try. Before touching down he decided to 'remove' Leeds' forward Louis Neumann, a task he achieved, but in the process put his foot over the touch-in-goal line. He also picked up a badly bruised eye at Headingley. The following Saturday Billy captained Wigan to a 21–2 win against Hull on a mud-bound Central Park. Laurie Gilfedder kicked a seemingly impossible 55-yard penalty out of the morass, soon after which Billy was forced to retire with "a very severe closed eye injury".

With Swinton progressing through the Cup rounds Wigan were able to take over the league leadership, but were always in danger of being overhauled by the Lions who had matches in hand. Wigan were delighted when the RL Council voted to abandon two divisions for the following season and were one of the prime movers in securing that reversal of policy. They did, however, find the maligned Western Division games useful for blooding youngsters, playing 17 year-old Kevin O'Loughlin at stand-off in a 12–7 win at Liverpool City on 15 February. The even more precocious winger Bill Francis was also given his debut, outside Billy in the return fixture on Easter Saturday, 28 March, when Wigan won 12–0. Billy, captaining the side, played as well as anyone, according to the *Wigan Observer*, but "his urgings were to no avail". Late in the game Francis chased down the right wing, drew the full-back and sent Billy in for Wigan's second try – a good start for a player many thought would eventually assume Billy's mantle.

The day before the Liverpool match, Wigan had gone to St Helens for the Good Friday derby and drawn a crowd exceeding 25,000. Unfortunately, the *Wigan Observer* described the game as "unworthy of such a crowd" and referred to Wigan and Saints as "two teams of fast-fading stars." St Helens won 11–5, thanks largely to four penalty goals from Kel Coslett. Billy, again at centre, was by far the best back in the side and seemed the only man who could cause Saints any anxiety. The *Observer's* headline was "Boston lone star" and its reporter noted that Billy "made a monkey out of Brian Todd every time he had the ball." As well as saving two certain tries, Billy scored the only Wigan try, when he accepted Carlton's pass to score after another up-and-under from Gilfedder.

On Easter Monday Wigan hammered Hunslet 31–4 with young Chris Hesketh nabbing three tries. Billy's mind was probably pre-occupied, as the next day Joan gave birth to Angela, the couple's fourth daughter.

On 4 April Billy captained Wigan to an extraordinarily easy 38–12 win at Hull, where Trevor Lake ran riot with four tries before a strangely silent Boulevard crowd. At that point in the season Wigan had played 25 league games and were seven points clear of Swinton at the top of the table. Although Swinton had four games in hand, Wigan had a very good chance of becoming champions. However, their hopes dimmed considerably at Castleford where the home team ran up a 17–0 half-time lead before Billy scored Wigan's first try following a clever blind-side break by Roy Evans. A 24–14 defeat was made even more unpalatable by a groin injury to Eric Ashton, which finished his season and left Billy to skipper the side in their last four fixtures.

On Monday, 13 April Wigan regained some hope of winning the title with a smashing 33–11 win at Hunslet, when full-back Ray Ashby, Liverpool City's test full-back, made his debut for Wigan. Billy unfortunately spent most of the match as a passenger, having damaged an ankle. The following Friday Wigan hit rock bottom against Halifax, who fielded almost a reserve side. Wigan scraped a 3–3 draw thanks to a 27th minute try from Billy, who charged 15 yards to the line from a McTigue pass. Wigan won the scrums 18–12 as referee Geraghty played a solo on his whistle and the *Wigan Observer* lamented, "Wigan looked as stale as last year's bread". Billy's try was his 400th for Wigan, but the achievement went unnoticed as the record keepers had many wires crossed.

Wigan's season concluded with defeats by St Helens at Central Park and away to Challenge Cup finalists Hull KR. Barring miracles they had entirely blown their chance of taking the Championship. They had taken 44 points from their 30 league fixtures. Swinton still had six games to play and already had 40 points. The Lions won five of those six games and took the title with 50 points. Wigan had not even managed to qualify for the Western Division play-offs, finishing sixth behind Swinton, St Helens, Oldham, Widnes and Workington Town.

The only thing Wigan did win was the Mackeson Trophy, and the 200 guineas which went with it, as the highest scoring team of the season. Most clubs would have been satisfied to finish as runners-up for the Championship, but Wigan were not happy at all with the 1963–64 season. Early exits in both major knock-out competitions and failure in the Western Division had diluted the fans' interest. Disturbingly, average league crowds at Central Park had dropped to 12,287 - 2,600 down on the previous season. The two division experiment had seen a catastrophic fall of more than 5,000 per league game at Central Park since 1961–62.

Something had to be done and the most strident call was for Wigan to bring in new blood to replace their ageing stars. Billy had supposedly fallen into that category at the end of 1962–63, but he had convincingly debunked that theory with 26 tries for Wigan, which gave him ninth place in the leading try-scorers' list. Swinton's Wigan-born Johnny Stopford had finished top with 45, two ahead of Trevor Lake, Wigan's new wing wonder.

## 1963–64

Wigan finished 2nd in the League: P30, W21, L7, D2, For 530, Against 294
Boston scored 26 tries for Wigan

| Date | Opponent | Score | Boston | Crowd | |
|------|----------|-------|--------|-------|---|
| 24 August | **Widnes** | 10–3 | 1T | 13,864 | |
| 28 August | Swinton | 4–16 | | 15,106 | |
| 31 August | Huddersfield | 29–14 | 3T | 8,438 | |
| 4 September | **Leeds** | 22–6 | 1T | 15,289 | |
| 7 September | Barrow | 34–12 | 1T | 5,429 | LC1 |
| 9 September | **Swinton** | 13–0 | | 20,190 | |
| 18 September | **Leigh** | 5–7 | | 20,848 | LC2 |
| 21 September | **Hull KR** | 20–16 | dnp | 10,403 | |
| 28 September | Keighley | 48–9 | 2T | 3,760 | |
| 5 October | **Rochdale H** | 13–14 | 3T | 8,080 | WD |
| 12 October | Warrington | 13–6 | dnp | 10,894 | |
| 19 October | **Wakefield T** | 31–7 | | 15,075 | |
| 26 October | **Blackpool B** | 77–8 | 1T | 9,626 | WD |
| 2 November | Widnes | 14–2 | | 11,037 | |
| 9 November | **Castleford** | 12–18 | 1T | 8,691 | |
| 18 November | **Australians** | 10–18 | dnp | 11,746 | Tour |
| 23 November | **Workington T** | 8–8 | | 10,085 | |
| 30 November | Leigh | 7–20 | | 7,712 | WD |
| 7 December | **Keighley** | 18–4 | dnp | 8,040 | |
| 14 December | Featherstone R | 13–17 | dnp | 3,869 | |
| 28 December | Halifax | 16–10 | | 10,107 | |
| 1 January | Workington T | 18–5 | 1T | 4,190 | |
| 4 January | Rochdale H | 35–16 | 2T | 3,190 | WD |
| 11 January | **Warrington** | 13–5 | 1T | 14,318 | |
| 25 January | **Featherstone R** | 15–14 | 1T | 11,494 | |
| 1 February | Wakefield T | 12–8 | 1T | 9,534 | |
| 8 February | **Swinton** | 15–15 | 1T | 31,752 | Cup 1 |
| 12 February | Swinton | 8–13 | | 26,891 | Replay |
| 15 February | Liverpool City | 12–7 | | 1,794 | WD |
| 22 February | **Huddersfield** | 8–7 | dnp | 9,030 | |
| 29 February | **Leigh** | 20–12 | 1T | 12,002 | WD |
| 7 March | Leeds | 21–7 | | 6,129 | |
| 14 March | **Hull** | 21–2 | | 5,017 | |
| 21 March | Blackpool B | 25–18 | dnp | 2,350 | WD |
| 27 March | St Helens | 5–11 | 1T | 25,640 | |
| 28 March | **Liverpool City** | 12–0 | 1T | 6,499 | WD |
| 30 March | **Hunslet** | 31–4 | | 11,722 | |
| 4 April | Hull | 38–12 | | 5,000 | |
| 10 April | Castleford | 14–24 | 1T | 12,000 | |
| 13 April | Hunslet | 33–11 | | 3,748 | |
| 17 April | **Halifax** | 3–3 | 1T | 10,731 | |
| 22 April | **St Helens** | 13–22 | 1T | 20,358 | |
| 25 April | Hull KR | 14–23 | | 9,106 | |

# 16. 1964–65 Wembley winners again

All manner of changes assailed rugby league supporters at the start of the 1964–65 season. Apart from the return to one division, there was to be a top 16 play-off to decide the champions, which was completely off the wall in terms of logic, but crucially might prove to be a crowd-puller. A revolutionary development was the introduction of substitutes, two per team being allowed, but only for injured players and only up to half-time.

There were also changes to the laws of the game. Henceforth penalty kicks were to be taken from the mark at which offences occurred, whereas previously the kick was taken 10 yards further back and the offending side stood on the mark. It would probably mean that more goals would be kicked. The five-yard scrum was abolished, as was drop-kicking from the kick-off after an unconverted try, while minor adjustments were made to scrimmaging to ensure that the ball emerged between the second-row and loose-forward. For supporters there was a price hike for adult men from half a crown (12½p) to three shillings (15p).

The reason for all this change was the steep decline in attendances experienced in recent years. Only Wigan and St Helens had averaged five figure attendances in 1963–64 and most clubs were reliant on pools to provide the necessary income to survive. Bradford Northern had gone bust in 1963 although a new club had been formed for the start of the new season. Northern's demise had been a massive shock to many in rugby league and solutions to the lack of support throughout the game were desperately being sought.

The game had definitely declined in crowd-pulling appeal. Many thought offside and obstructionist play was responsible, others that there was too much violence, while some believed that the ban on signing Australians and New Zealand players robbed the game of personalities, skills and excitement and that their replacement by South African and Fijian rugby union players was no real compensation. Certainly wingers were no longer scoring tries in the numbers fans had grown accustomed to, a sure sign that the nature of the game had changed and not for the better.

There was change for Billy and Joan too. They entered the licensing trade, taking over at The Bush in Belle Green Lane, Higher Ince. Joan recalls: "The Bush was renowned for its great ale. It was so good that a lot of the miners' wives used to come with jugs and bottles for a few pints for their husbands for when they came off their shifts at the pit. We would have queues of them by 11 o'clock and we didn't even open until 12. It was great for Billy, but not so good for me. He would go out to training and then come back with some of the boys, play cards and have a good time. I would still be up at one in the morning cleaning glasses and whatnot. I had to go and pick the kids up from school by half-past three and then walk up the hill and there'd be another queue waiting. That hill was about a mile and half long. After a few months I'd had enough. I didn't drive in those days and one night we had decided to go to a club after closing. The car wouldn't start so Billy and the people we were going with told me to get in the driver's seat, while they pushed it to get it started. Well, of course, it was on that hill and away it went. I didn't even know where the brakes were. Fortunately, it finally came to a stop at the bottom of the hill – right outside the police station. I can laugh about it now!"

On the playing field Billy was again given the vice-captaincy, with Eric Ashton continuing as skipper, and was a member of the Wigan VII which won the annual sevens tournament at Central Park on 3 August. They beat Huddersfield 5–3 and St Helens 11–8 before defeating Halifax 15–11 in the final, when Billy scored a try and kicked a goal. The Wigan team was Boston, Lake, Parr, Hill, Hesketh, Clarke and Lyon. Of particular interest to the crowd of 9,723 was the appearance of Cliff Hill, a stand-off of immense promise from Newton-le-Willows rugby union club, who had been signed during the close season. His signing proved especially important because Dave Bolton had announced he was emigrating to Australia and had played his last game for Wigan. Dave would be a hard act to follow. Wigan put him on the list at £5,000, probably realising that there would be problems when it came to negotiating a transfer if he were to find a club in Sydney.

Wigan regained the Wardonia Cup on 15 August with a scrappy 9–8 win at Wilderspool, Ashton scoring Wigan's try and Gilfedder kicking three goals. Ten minutes from time in this charitable affair Ray Ashby and Keith Holden were sent off. Billy and Trevor Lake might as well have been on the terraces. That was exactly where Billy was at half-time in the opening league fixture a week later. The match was at Swinton and was televised. It was a terrible game, which Wigan lost 9–3, Billy belting 20 yards for his side's only try. During the interval Billy jumped over the perimeter wall to confront a spectator, who had been yelling insults at him from the kick-off. At first they had been the usual sort but then had degenerated into remarks about race. The *Wigan Observer* noted, "The spectator laughed about the incident but, significantly, only after Boston had gone into the dressing-room". It added that no official action would be taken.

Cyril Briggs, editor of the *Rugby Leaguer*, spoke for real rugby league fans: "I was stunned to read that there had been some objectionable remarks made about Bill Boston by a spectator at the Swinton v Wigan game. This sort of thing causes a nasty taste in the mouths of most of us. I hope that the Swinton officials will put a piece in their programme deprecating such conduct by a spectator... I thought that we had got over all this colour bar business years ago. There were some comments, (at which most of us at times were most annoyed) about Cumberbatch, who played for Broughton... Then Roy Francis had every reason to complain to me about certain attitudes. Bill Boston and all who have darker skins than ours should ignore the comments of a very few. The coloured players, past and present, have brought greater skill and honour to our game. I hope that the Wigan winger and his friends will forget this incident and remember that the stupid few don't talk for all of us. More power to Bill, Roy, Johnny Freeman, Colin Dixon and others. We hope they will be with us in the RL game for a long time."

Four days after the Swinton defeat Wigan made heavy weather of beating Blackpool Borough at Central Park. Eric Ashton was not pleased and uncharacteristically was reduced to issuing "none-too-gentle instructions clearly audible from the press box". Lake and Gilfedder did all Wigan's scoring. However, the *Wigan Observer* reported: "Billy Boston was in rare fettle on the right wing. His play always had a keen edge". Kia Bose scored seven points for Blackpool and "one of his second half tackles on Boston was a gem of courage and timing."

Wigan hit their stride on 29 August with a 34–4 win against Whitehaven, Billy grabbing a couple of tries and Trevor Lake a hat-trick. A handsome 30–9 victory at Leigh followed with Billy picking up two more tries. The *Wigan Observer* wrote: "Boston's second try was a thunderbolt. A slick passing movement drew the Leigh cover defence to the right – but they never saw Boston as he took a long pass at full speed and cut inside in a 30 yards run to the posts."

The Lancashire Cup on 5 September brought Griff Jenkins back to Central Park with Salford. Wigan walloped them 36–6. Tom Groves reported: "Boston was always dangerous in possession. He is still remarkably fast and it was unfortunate that one or two prearranged bursts in-field came unstuck at the vital moment. Late in the game he scored two tries". Seven tries in the first five games indicated that Billy was far from a spent force.

A record 32–0 win at Featherstone brought Wigan's fifth win in a row. Lake ran in four tries, including a 75-yarder, while Billy made some tremendous runs without any tangible results. Wigan's run of success came to a halt on Monday 14 September in the familiar surroundings of Station Road. Swinton turfed them out of the Lancashire Cup with an 11–5 victory on a slippy pitch with John Stopford scoring the crucial try.

Around this time there were several changes in personnel at Central Park. Secretary Jack Wood was appointed secretary of Lancashire County Cricket Club and was succeeded by a fellow Yorkshireman, Ken Senior. An unhappy John Winton was transfer listed at £2,000 and Billy acquired a Welshman as a playing colleague. Peter Davies, a 24 year-old second-rower signed from Neath for £2,500. He was described as "the iron man of Neath" and was the first Welshman to join Wigan since 1961. He made his debut against Castleford on 26 September, but was hugely disappointing in a 33–13 win and never made the first team again. Eric Ashton claimed 18 points and Billy scored a try and lost the ball in trying to touch down for another. Wigan's form was certainly picking up and as October dawned they were third in the league behind St Helens and Hull.

Cliff Hill had established himself as a *wunderkind* in Wigan's number six jersey and scored his first hat-trick in a 45–12 rout of Blackpool Borough on 3 October. Billy went in for two tries in the last 11 minutes and hooker Colin Clarke scored a sizzling 60-yarder. An even bigger victory followed on 10 October, when Barrow were battered 49–0 at Central Park. It was a real red-letter day for Billy, who was chasing his 500th try in first class matches. He achieved the distinction in rare style by scoring four, although there was plenty of confusion in the press and among record keepers as to which of the four actually was his 500th. Research shows that it was his first after only three minutes, when he went over after brilliant play by Ashby and Ashton. The crowd and players were under the impression that it was his third around the hour mark, when, appropriately enough, Ashton's inside pass to Billy did the trick. That was when part of the crowd jumped over the walls and mobbed their hero and players from both sides rushed to congratulate him. First or third, it was a hell of a milestone. Only Brian Bevan had reached it prior to Billy and only Martin Offiah has done so since – if his tries in Australian rugby league are included.

The *Wigan Observer* extolled his achievement: "I for one salute him. The fact that he is still the terror of the best defences in the game, having lost the outstanding pace, which accompanies most class wingers, bears testimony to his great class as a footballer. So does his present position as second leading try-scorer [to Trevor Lake]... While Boston was giving Mike Murray a daylight nightmare, there was a rare old shindig on the opposite side of the field where Lake and Burgess, Barrow's international winger, were locked (and I mean that) in combat as closely as Siamese twins. I'll swear that if Lake had gone for a programme, Burgess would have followed him... Burgess even followed Lake when he switched wings with Billy Boston!" In recognition of Billy's feat, Wigan applied to the Rugby League Council for permission to make a gift to him.

Billy and Trevor Lake continued to cause havoc to opposing defences. Both scored two tries in a home 18–5 success against Featherstone on 30 October. Billy's first followed a classic piece of combination with Ashton: "Boston, taking Ashton's inside pass, beat the Featherstone cover defence with no more than a shrug of his shoulders followed by a change of direction". The second came from a similar Ashton back-flip. Lake's first saw him fly "like a human bullet" after a long pass from Gilfedder, while his second was more prosaic and followed a dash from dummy-half by Parr.

Although Wigan's next match at Halifax was, according to the *Wigan Observer*, "a battle as dour as the Yorkshire moors which surround Thrum Hall", it was nonetheless a

171

memorable affair. Wigan were second in the table and Halifax fourth, and until the 70th minute there was nothing to separate the sides with the score locked at 7–7. At that point a fantastic try by Lake from the centre spot to the corner flag broke the Yorkshire side's resistance and Lake went on to complete his hat-trick, twice finishing off fine work by Parr. Wigan thus swept to a 20–7 victory. Amazingly, Lake had been told in his youth that polio in his shoulder would curtail any sporting aspirations he held. Billy's best work was done in defence, blotting out Freeman and making some devastating tackles on Welsh full-back Ronnie James, as he came through the middle on dangerous runs.

On 14 November Wigan sought their eighth consecutive league victory, when they entertained Widnes. Their run ended with Widnes's 10–3 triumph. Wigan's pack was out-muscled and the side's only plan seemed to be to get the ball to Lake, but the passes he received were of the hospital variety. On the other wing, Billy's power was grossly neglected, although he did register Wigan's only try, going over from a play-the-ball after being stopped inches short. It was Billy's 17th try of the season in his 15th match and he would not score another until February. He failed to score in his next eight matches – one of the most barren periods of his career. He was not too concerned, however, as Wigan kept winning, when he did play.

Good wins at Oldham and at home against Halifax kept Wigan in second place. Billy had a splendid game in the return against Halifax, crushing several raids with hard, timely tackles, one of which caused Freeman to drop the ball as he touched down. However, he received a severely bruised thigh, which kept him out of Wigan's first three games in December. The first, a 17–0 defeat at Castleford, where Wigan were nilled for the first time since Warrington also beat them 17–0 on April Fools' Day in 1961, was especially costly as Lake pulled his hamstring and missed the next six games. A home defeat by Workington was a shock and drew a miserable crowd of only 4,034 – the lowest for a league or cup game at Central Park since the war. There was a much healthier attendance of over 15,000 for the next home game, when Billy resumed activities in a 13–6 win over Leigh on Boxing Day. Billy's explosive runs required up to five men to stop him and he often left the Leigh defence in tatters.

The New Year opened badly for Wigan with a 15–8 home loss to Warrington. Although the Wigan pack won the scrums 15–9, "the forwards played like strangers" and "most of Wigan's play was unskilled labour of the lowest quality", was the *Wigan Observer's* damning indictment. Billy received the first of his two passes after 72 minutes, prompting the *Observer* to comment: "The unfortunate point is that Wigan only have one Billy Boston. They could do with two or three Billy Bostons at this very moment." Fortunately, the forwards shook off their torpor at Workington eight days later and the game was won 8–5 with a try by Shillinglaw with only 30 seconds remaining. That victory began another eight match winning sequence, the remaining seven all being home fixtures – a most unusual state of affairs.

Wigan strengthened their pack by signing prop Danny Gardiner from Workington Town for £4,750, although they failed with a bid for Leeds' South African forward Louis Neumann. Gardiner, a massive man with a combative attitude, made his debut in a 7–3 win against champions Swinton. It was, however, the old maestro, Brian McTigue, who took the eye and produced Wigan's solitary try when he shouldered two men out of the way, fell to weight of numbers, but popped an exquisite try-scoring pass to Colin Clarke. McTigue was described as "a giant among striplings". Billy played centre alongside Ashton against the Lions and it was the last time that he would ever start a match in that position. Wigan, despite their anti-television stance, allowed ITV to televise 30 minutes of the game. Wigan

172

received a fee of £150 and £1,000 went to the RFL's television fund. Wigan relaxed their principles because, like every other club, they stood to make £1,000 from the fund at the season's end and in straitened circumstances they needed the money.

On 23 January Billy almost experienced defeat for the first time against Liverpool City at a mud-bound Central Park. Colin Clarke was sent off for kicking on the hour and Billy and Eric mysteriously seemed to have their wires crossed all afternoon. It took four penalty goals and two try-saving tackles from full-back John Winton to see Wigan through 8–5. Rochdale gave Wigan another hard time before going down 21–11. Before the game Beethoven's *Fifth Symphony* was played over the tannoy and a minute's silence was observed following the death of Sir Winston Churchill. Billy crashed through two tackles to send Ray Ashby over after Hornets had established a 7–0 lead. All afternoon he took an awful lot of stopping although Stan Owen, belligerent as a rhino, did stop him once and Billy came up very angry.

As the Challenge Cup ties approached Wigan sold Jack Gregory to Rochdale for £350 and paid out £3,000 to Warrington for their former Wigan centre Keith Holden, who had announced his retirement in December. They also signed Castleford's goalkicking forward John Clark. The Dave Bolton problem was finally solved when Balmain paid Wigan £3,200 for his services. Holden and Clark made their debuts on 6 February, when Wigan beat Barrow 16–0 in the first round of the Cup. They led 13–0 at the break, but did not score again until the 73rd minute when Billy broke his try drought after clever play by Ashton.

League victories over Salford and Oldham followed, but the only thing on the Wigan fans' minds was the second round of the Challenge Cup on 27 February. The draw had pitted Wigan against St Helens at Central Park. St Helens had already won the Lancashire Cup and had only lost two league matches. Although Wigan had recently toppled Saints from the league leadership, the Knowsley Road men were only two points adrift with four games in hand. St Helens were 3–1 favourites for the Cup, while Wigan were third favourites at 5–1. None of this mattered to the Wigan support, as long as revenge for Wembley 1961 was achieved. Wigan certainly took the tie seriously with special daylight training. Eric Ashton had the players out walking on the Tuesday morning, followed by lunch at Central Park, some short films, tactical talks and training. More of the same followed on Thursday as Ashton prepared the team mentally and physically. The board offered the team £40 a man to win, although pay was probably irrelevant in this case.

The tie was a real thriller, hard and uncompromising, with flashes of individual brilliance. Billy hurt his shoulder in the first tackle of the match after fielding Alex Murphy's kick-off but he hid it well. In the 14th minute he blasted past Len Killeen, Tony Barrow, Ray French and Kel Coslett in a stupendous touch-line burst and touched down in the corner. Unfortunately for Billy, Alex Murphy had raced across the field just in time to jump on his back and unbalance him. The referee, Mr Appleyard, ruled that Billy had not grounded the ball properly and had hit the flag. There was no score until the 38th minute, when Gilfedder kicked a goal after Coslett had blatantly obstructed an Ashton kick-through and chase. Only Eric knew that Billy's shoulder was horribly bruised and Billy bravely battled on until half-time, when he was replaced by Alan Davies. Davies still had time to be cautioned three times in the remaining 40 minutes as the battle got ever more heated. On 50 minutes Saints equalised with a Coslett penalty after Ashby obstructed Doug Laughton. A minute later Brian McTigue took the ball just inside his own half, shouldered his way between two Saints' forwards, coolly drew Coslett and delivered a precision pass to Roy Evans bursting through on his right. Evans sprinted 45 yards to the posts, supported all the way by Colin Clarke and hotly pursued by Billy Benyon. Gilfedder's simple conversion ended the scoring at 7–2 in Wigan's favour. It had been an absolute triumph for Wigan's sometimes maligned forwards, who had played with ruthless efficiency, inspired by their evergreen genius Brian McTigue. The crowd of almost 40,000 had certainly had their money's worth.

Anti-climax followed with a shock 5–0 defeat at Barrow, when Billy captained the side until Ashton replaced Davies at the break. The following week Wigan travelled to the northwest again for their Challenge Cup quarter-final with Workington Town, as hard a challenge in its own way as the St Helens game. Cup fever had infected Cumberland as well as Wigan and Derwent Park housed a record crowd of 17,741, which eclipsed the old record of 17,006 that attended a 1957 Cup clash against Warrington. At least 5,000 of the crowd were Wiganers. It was not a great game, but it was a riveting spectacle, despite the creeping barrage of the Workington forwards. The scrums were shared 10–10, although Town seemed to have far of the more of the ball and Wigan's defence was under considerable strain. Billy did not have much to do on his wing in attack but contributed his usual share in defence. Wigan took the two real chances that fell to them. The only score of the first half came from a beautifully worked passing move between Evans and Clarke, which brought the hooker a try, converted by Gilfedder. Billy's old rival for the Great Britain number two jersey, Ike Southward, potted two penalties early in the second half, reducing Wigan's lead to 5–4. However, he crucially missed four reasonable shots. It was Ike's failure to find touch with a penalty 10 minutes from time, which gave Wigan the opportunity to kill off Town's challenge. Ashby fielded the kick and fed Cliff Hill, who zipped 60 yards for one of the most spectacular tries seen at Derwent Park in years. Gilfedder's conversion sealed a 10–4 win. Another Challenge Cup semi-final beckoned Billy and Wigan.

Big games continued as Wigan travelled to St Helens on 23 March for a Tuesday night match under Saints' new floodlights. While a crowd of more than 16,000 was reasonable it was nowhere near as high as for a traditional holiday afternoon derby. Wigan again accounted for Saints, Frankie Parr scoring the only two tries of the game, which Wigan won 10–6. The victory took Wigan back to the top of the league and was achieved on the back of heroic defence in the face of a 26–9 thrashing in the scrums.

Cliff Hill suffered a broken nose, although it did not keep him out of Wigan's next game, when Wigan returned to Knowsley Road 11 days later for their Challenge Cup semi-final against Swinton. The expected tough test did not arise and Wigan were far too good for the Lions. Eric Thompson wrote in the *Evening Post and Chronicle*, "Truth is that this semi-final – one of the most one-sided I have seen – looked like 'Men against Boys'." Tries from Holden, Clarke and Lake set up a 13–2 interval lead and a couple of stupendous second half tries from Hill and Lake wrapped up a 25–10 victory. Billy failed to get on the scoresheet, but one of his efforts was truly memorable. Thompson described it as "a super-human effort that only he can make. This even exceeded the normal prodigious Boston power, however, carrying three men with him at various stages in a make-or-burst effort, although brought to his knees. Despite this he almost stumbled over the line and I don't think anyone would have begrudged a try for this. But all he got at the finish of it was his hand trodden on. He was almost tempted to hit out for this, but referee Eric Clay restrained him."

Before Billy could relish his fifth Wembley final Wigan had six league fixtures to negotiate. Moreover, they had a pretty good chance to finish as league leaders as St Helens had lost four consecutive matches and the struggle at the top had developed into a veritable scramble between Warrington, Wakefield, Castleford, Wigan and St Helens. Wigan pasted Rochdale 30–6 at the Athletic Grounds on 6 April with Billy putting in a rip-roaring display with three tries. The first of his tries followed protests by several Hornets about a tackle by Gilfedder on Rochdale winger Pratt. Billy just got on with the job, took the ball 50 yards out, outpaced Apisai Toga and simply steamrollered through Johnny Noon's tackle.

Billy dominated the match in the second half and drew great applause from the Rochdale supporters. However, Mr Eric Siddall from Altrincham may not have been so well disposed towards Billy. He had come in as a substitute touch-judge at the last minute and Billy broke his leg during one of his touch-line dashes. Eric Ashton told the press: "Billy just broke the line with his foot and the touch-judge tripped himself up as he moved forward to raise his flag. I felt awfully sorry for him". Mr Siddall was stretchered off and taken to hospital.

Billy scored the 10th of 11 Wigan tries and had several near misses in a 47–12 home demolition of Huddersfield, but then two defeats within six days ruined hopes of a top of the table position. An under-strength Widnes embarrassed an impotent Wigan 18–0 on 12 April. Then St Helens gained some compensation for recent reverses with a 16–8 win at Central Park on Good Friday. John Barton suffered a broken arm in the first half, thereby losing the chance to play at Wembley, while the defeat also eradicated any hope Wigan had of lifting the Lancashire League Championship, which ultimately went to Saints. Billy scored his 24th try of the season in a convincing 28–3 win at Warrington on Easter Saturday and on Easter Monday captained the side at Salford. Arctic conditions prevailed and there was a freak hailstorm. Salford played well, but Wigan's 17–2 win gave them the two points that sealed second place in the table. St Helens finished top with 56 points, followed by Wigan with 52, Castleford 51, Wakefield Trinity 50 and Warrington 49.

Wigan thus qualified for a home tie against 15th placed Featherstone Rovers in the new-fangled Top 16 play-offs on 24 April. Whether Wembleyitis had set in was debatable but Wigan were licked by the Rovers, who won 15–8. Both Wigan's tries were scored in the last four minutes and they had no answer to Don Fox, who scored two tries and three goals. The *Wigan Observer* reported that Fox "dominated play with the aplomb of a man conducting a brass band at a Sunday afternoon recital in the park". Worryingly, Brian McTigue was led off after 10 minutes with a recurrence of a shoulder injury and Billy damaged his leg in the second half. Wigan had a fortnight to recuperate for their date at Wembley on 8 May with Hunslet, shock conquerors of Wakefield Trinity in the semi-finals.

Few people gave Hunslet much of a chance to lift the Challenge Cup. They had finished 14th in the league and had a points ratio of 477–466 in their 34 games. Compared to Wigan's 626–260 points ratio, it hardly seemed a fair contest. The bookmakers had Wigan at 3–1 on and Hunslet at 9–4. Most critics predicted that Hunslet would have to play a tight game to restrict Wigan's superior pace and finesse. The only Hunslet player to have experience of Wembley was hooker Bernard Prior, who had won the Cup with Leeds in 1957. Wigan's three wise old men, Billy, Eric Ashton and Brian McTigue were all playing in their fifth Wembley final, emulating the record set by Jack Wilkinson of Halifax and Wakefield Trinity fame. However, the only other Wigan players in the starting XIII with Wembley experience were Keith Holden and Roy Evans. Wigan sprang a surprise by playing Tony Stephens in the second-row instead of Geoff Lyon.

It was noticeable that Billy's right knee was heavily bandaged as the teams walked out to be presented to Princess Alexandra. The day had begun overcast but the threat of rain did not materialise and playing conditions were almost perfect. The teams were:

*Wigan:* Ashby, Boston, Ashton (capt), Holden, Lake, Hill, Parr, Gardiner, Clarke, McTigue, Stephens, Evans, Gilfedder. Substitutes: O'Loughlin, Lyon (neither played)

*Hunslet:* Langton, Griffiths, Shelton, Preece, Lee, Gabbitas, Marchant, Hartley, Prior, Eyre, Gunney, Ramsey, Ward (capt). Substitutes: Render, Baldwinson (neither played)

Contrary to expectations, the 1965 Challenge Cup Final proved to be an absolute classic. From the first whistle to the last there was barely an opportunity to draw breath for players and onlookers alike. Comparing the game to the previous week's FA Cup Final between Leeds United and Liverpool, the *Sunday Express's* Keith Macklin declared: "It was a splendid game, one of the best ever seen at Wembley. These two sides were a credit to the game, and we got more excitement in yesterday's 80 minutes than we got in the first 90 minutes of football by computer at Wembley last Saturday." The *Sunday Mirror's* Eddie Waring described the match as "the greatest Rugby League Cup Final of them all". Leslie Woodhead wrote in the *Liverpool Echo and Evening Express:* "Spectacular scoring, a thrilling seesaw in the run of play and brilliant goal-kicking made it a final to remember".

The game began dramatically. Alan Marchant hoofed the ball straight into touch from Hunslet's kick-off and Laurie Gilfedder promptly put over the resultant penalty kick from the centre. Hunslet equalised within three minutes when Billy Langton banged over a penalty goal after Alan Preece had been obstructed. Then Preece got past Ashton and broke clear "before the mighty Boston dropped him" 20 yards from Wigan's line. Wigan then survived a close shave after 14 minutes when Hunslet's big Welsh winger John Griffiths drove over at the corner and was buffeted by Trevor Lake over the in-goal touch-line. Most people thought it was a try, but referee Joe Manley ruled no-score after consulting his touch-judge, deciding Griffiths had lost the ball inches from touching down.

Three minutes later Wigan capitalised on their escape by scoring the first try. Lovely passing got the ball to Holden out on the right and with Billy and Ashton available to score, the centre dived headlong to touch down and Wigan led 5–2. Langton kicked a second penalty following a scrum offence after 25 minutes and it was 5–4. Ashton and Ashby released Billy on a devastating 45-yard run and there were gasps as he bumped off Preece and went hard for the corner but Langton brought him down just in time. Langton hurt his shoulder in his heroic effort, but remained on the field. On the half hour Gilfedder potted a fine penalty and five minutes later Wigan led 12–4. A Wigan raid down Billy's wing petered out, but the ball was flashed to the other flank, where Holden expertly put Lake over for a delightful try. Gilfedder superbly kicked the conversion from wide out. Anyone who thought that Hunslet would crumble was mistaken. On the stroke of half-time Billy's former fly-half in the Royal Signals XV, Brian Gabbitas, sent Geoff Shelton away and the powerful centre slid between the posts for a converted try. Wigan went in at half-time with a 12–9 advantage.

The second half was no less thrilling. Early on Geoff Gunney was sent crashing to the ground in a three-man tackle and, when the players had disentangled themselves, Billy and Cliff Hill got a few choice words from the referee. In the 45th minute Evans sent Gilfedder scorching 30 yards to the corner for a superb try, to which Ashton added an almost equally brilliant goal. Just before the hour Ashby broke through and sent Lake on a tremendous run to the corner flag. Griffiths chased him all the way, but was unable to prevent Lake from soaring spectacularly over for a try that brought the house down and gave Wigan a seemingly unassailable 20–9 lead. Hunslet just would not give in though. A quarter of an hour was left when Gabbitas shattered the Wigan defence, slipped an exquisite pass to Griffiths and watched admiringly as the winger held off Ashby and Ashton before plunging over for another glorious try, which Langton goaled. With three minutes left Hunslet had the whole stadium rocking with excitement as they pulled up to 20–16 when Langton kicked his fifth goal after Wigan were penalised in front of their posts. Discretion finally got the better of valour in the last few minutes when Wigan got possession and decided to keep it.

Billy went up to the Royal Box behind his captain to receive his third winners' medal. Eddie Waring commented in the *Sunday Mirror:* "Wigan, as always, were mighty, and although Billy Boston did not score, he wiped out the memory of two years ago when Wigan were hammered by Wakefield and Boston was assumed to be a 'write-off'." When the winning side descended back to the pitch, Leslie Woodhead wrote: "The perfect finishing touch of this memorable final, following the presentation by Princess Alexandra, came from Wigan player-coach Eric Ashton. With a fitting gesture he handed the trophy to Wigan's young half-back pair Frank Parr and Cliff Hill to lead the lap of honour, while Ashton, Boston and McTigue, the three men making their fifth Wembley appearances, dropped back to the rear of the team in the jubilant race round the pitch." Woodhead added, "Billy Boston did not disappoint his fans with some thrilling touch-line power bursts and one vital try-saving tackle on Hunslet winger Brian Lee late in the game." The *Rugby Leaguer* observed: "We are never likely to forget the forceful runs of Griffiths and Boston on the respective right wings. Their dashes thrilled the folk who were on terrace and stand and watching on TV – this time in millions and not mere thousands."

Billy told the press: "When the score was 20–9 in our favour Hunslet should have been a goner. Amazingly, though, we let up. We suddenly lacked the killer punch when we needed it". In later years he said in an interview for the *Wigan Observer:* "While an awful lot of people single out [the Hunslet final] and are still talking about it, for me that was something of a 'tick-and-pass final! Against Hunslet, we always thought Wigan could step it up a gear. We were never in any serious danger of being beaten". Keith Macklin's report indicated that Eric Ashton had a similar view: "[the] Wigan skipper... was one of the few men who did not think Hunslet were in the game with a chance at any stage. He told me, 'We always seemed to have a lot of points to spare, and even when they scored, I felt we were just as likely get another as they were'."

The Wigan party returned home on Sunday night. An ecstatic 40,000 locals waited for their heroes at the North-Western Station, the town hall or lined the streets on a sunny evening. The mayor and mayoress, Councillor and Mrs Gerald Lewthwaite, and the town clerk, Mr Allan Royle and his wife, met the team on the town hall steps. The coach back to Central Park arrived 20 minutes behind schedule, where the forecourt and its environs were jammed with fans, chanting "Wigan, Wigan, Wigan". The *Evening Post and Chronicle* reported, "Ashton held the coveted trophy aloft and as the other players stepped out of the coach, the biggest cheer went up when Billy Boston and Ray Ashby appeared". Ashby was cheered because he had shared the Lance Todd Trophy with Billy's old Army friend Brian Gabbitas, the first time this had happened. Billy was cheered because he was Billy.

Season 1964–65 had gone well for Billy. He had been largely injury free and missed only three of Wigan's 42 matches. He had reached the fabulous landmark of 500 tries in his career and had won at Wembley for the third time. He was seventh in the season's leading try-scorers list with 24 tries – the perfect answer to those who had written him off.

Wigan had won the Cup for the third time in seven years and finished second in the league. The town was still a hotbed of the game, but overall support for rugby league was on the wane. Wigan's average crowd at 10,694 was still the biggest in the league, but had fallen by 1,600 on the previous season. Wigan RLFC reported a loss of £7,264 for 1964–65. Amazingly for a successful side, only one Wigan player won representative honours. Ray Ashby played a test against France and was a non-playing substitute for Lancashire in the Roses Match.

**Wembley 1965**

Eric Ashton introduces HRH Princess Alexandra to Trevor Lake while
Keith Holden, Billy and Ray Ashby await their introductions.

Billy celebrates Keith Holden's try.

Billy leaves the Hunslet defence in his wake with a run down the touchline.

Eric Ashton receives the Cup from Princess Alexandra, with Ray Ashby and Billy
waiting to receive their medals.

## 1964–65

Wigan finished 2nd in the League: P34, W26, L8, For 626, Against 260
Boston scored 24 tries for Wigan

| Date | Opponent | Score | Boston | Crowd | |
|------|----------|-------|--------|-------|--|
| 22 August | Swinton | 3- 9 | 1T | 9,500 | |
| 26 August | **Blackpool B** | 15–10 | | 7,320 | |
| 29 August | **Whitehaven** | 34–4 | 2T | 6,310 | |
| 2 September | Leigh | 30–9 | 2T | 9,000 | |
| 5 September | **Salford** | 36–6 | 2T | 8,135 | LC1 |
| 12 September | Featherstone R | 32–0 | | 4,474 | |
| 14 September | Swinton | 5–11 | | 13,422 | LC2 |
| 19 September | Liverpool City | 34–5 | | 1,100 | |
| 26 September | **Castleford** | 33–13 | 1T | 11,946 | |
| 3 October | Blackpool B | 45–12 | 2T | 5,550 | |
| 10 October | **Barrow** | 49–0 | 4T | 10,687 | |
| 17 October | Huddersfield | 15–5 | | 7,646 | |
| 31 October | **Featherstone R** | 18–5 | 2T | 10,000 | |
| 7 November | Halifax | 20–7 | | 10,107 | |
| 14 November | **Widnes** | 3–10 | 1T | 10,021 | |
| 21 November | Oldham | 18–9 | | 10,365 | |
| 28 November | **Halifax** | 13–0 | | 10,214 | |
| 5 December | Castleford | 0–17 | dnp | 5,765 | |
| 12 December | **Workington T** | 8–13 | dnp | 4,034 | |
| 19 December | Whitehaven | 15–3 | dnp | 2,260 | |
| 26 December | **Leigh** | 13–6 | | 15,056 | |
| 1 January | **Warrington** | 8–15 | | 15,293 | |
| 9 January | Workington T | 8–5 | | 2,900 | |
| 16 January | **Swinton** | 7–3 | | 7,261 | |
| 23 January | **Liverpool City** | 8–5 | | 5,541 | |
| 30 January | **Rochdale H** | 21–11 | | 7,201 | |
| 6 February | **Barrow** | 16–0 | 1T | 13,217 | Cup 1 |
| 13 February | **Salford** | 16–4 | | 8,544 | |
| 20 February | **Oldham** | 20–12 | 1T | 9,825 | |
| 27 February | **St Helens** | 7- 2 | | 39,938 | Cup 2 |
| 6 March | Barrow | 0–5 | | 3,950 | |
| 13 March | Workington T | 10–4 | | 17,741 | Cup 3 |
| 23 March | St Helens | 10–6 | | 16,424 | |
| 3 April | Swinton | 25–10 | | 26,658 | Cup SF (at St Helens) |
| 6 April | Rochdale H | 30–6 | 3T | 2,708 | |
| 10 April | **Huddersfield** | 47–12 | 1T | 7,757 | |
| 12 April | Widnes | 0–18 | | 6,775 | |
| 16 April | **St Helens** | 8–16 | | 34,796 | |
| 17 April | Warrington | 28–3 | 1T | 11,217 | |
| 19 April | Salford | 17–2 | | 6,853 | |
| 24 April | **Featherstone R** | 8–15 | | 11,369 | CH 1 |
| 8 May | Hunslet | 20–16 | | 89,016 | Cup Final (at Wembley) |

# 17. 1965–66 Wembley finale

Billy was not fit for the start of the 1965–66 season because of a recurring knee injury. In his absence Wigan failed to win their own sevens tournament for the first time, Warrington beating Widnes 19–15 in the final after Huddersfield had put the hosts out in the first round. Wigan did, however, win the Crystal Palace sevens on 12 August, when a try by Trevor Lake in the last seconds enabled them to beat Workington Town 14–13 in the final. The tournament was one of rugby league's contributions to an International Sports Festival. Billy also missed Wigan's 38–17 rout of Warrington in the Wardonia Cup and the first three league games of the season, all of which were won.

He picked a bad game for his first appearance on 28 August as Oldham inflicted an embarrassing 23–8 beating on Wigan at Central Park. Oldham's forwards scored four of their five tries and John Winton, who had left Wigan for £2,500 the previous March, kicked four goals against his former colleagues. A reversal of fortune followed two days later with a good win at Leigh. However, Billy sustained a chest injury, which kept him out of a desperately close 13–12 win at Liverpool City. He recovered in time for Wigan's game against the 1965 Kiwis on 4 September. It would be his last game against the New Zealanders and it was not a happy finale as Wigan, minus four regulars, lost 17–12. In heavy conditions, the ball was like the proverbial bar of soap, and Wigan's play was extremely unadventurous. They were lucky to lose by so few points. The *Wigan Observer* dolefully criticised Billy's performance, "I fear the buffetings, which he has taken in his long and illustrious career, are now beginning to have a really marked effect on him".

A week later, Billy made his 400th appearance for Wigan in a wonderful first round Lancashire Cup tie against Whitehaven at Central Park. He celebrated by scoring Wigan's first try, playing the ball to himself after he had been brought down near the 'Haven goal-line to level the score at 5–5. Injury forced him off at half-time and he could only watch as Wigan swept to a 21–9 lead between the 37th and 50th minutes. The Cumbrians had levelled the game at 23–23 by the 71st minute, only to lose it when Ashton landed a sublime penalty goal from the touch-line. Wigan's up-and-down form continued in the second round at Oldham on 16 September. Wigan fielded Harry Major at loose-forward, whom they had signed from Oldham for £4,000 just 24 hours earlier. It was not an auspicious debut as he was sent off just after half-time after an incident with Peter Smethurst and landed a three-match suspension. Wigan were leathered 28–13 although Billy brought the crowd to its feet with a try from half-way, when he chased and gathered a kick-through from Ashton at a rate of knots which seemed to throw off the years.

Two days later Billy was the match-breaker in a 20–11 home win against Hull KR. Immediately after half-time, when Rovers led 7–4, they lost the ball a few yards from their own line. Billy pounced on it and shouldered three unfortunates out of his path. Eleven points in 12 minutes swung the game Wigan's way as Holden and Ashton set up a try for Lake. Billy then received a peach of a pass from Holden, who had drawn three defenders, and thundered over at the corner.

A dose of 'flu kept Billy out of Wigan's 12–9 victory at Castleford on Friday 24 September, a game that marked Castleford's first league fixture under their new floodlights. The following Tuesday Wigan played a friendly at Wilderspool to inaugurate Warrington's newly installed lights, losing 9–5 on a vile night. The trend to install floodlights was certainly catching on and the BBC introduced their BBC2 Floodlit Trophy competition in the autumn of 1965. It was played on Tuesday nights and was a source of additional income for those clubs wise enough to invest in lighting. Wigan had not yet got round to acquiring lights, but had begun to build a new social club at the enormous cost of £45,000. They were intending to install lights, although certainly not with a view to entering the Floodlit Trophy as they were still dead set against live televising of their home games.

On 2 October Castleford, with a weakened side, gained a shock 10–8 win at Central Park after Roger Millward landed a late match-winning penalty. The game proved to be Frank Carlton's final appearance of a distinguished career. A week later Wigan trounced Blackpool Borough 43–19 with Billy bouncing over for two well-taken tries. With a little luck he might have had a couple more. Significantly, however, that game marked the break-up of Billy's wing-centre partnership with Eric Ashton for the next couple of years. Although he would never be too far away from Billy, for the next couple of years Ashton played at left centre. For the rest of the 1965–66 season Billy's centre partner was initially Keith Holden and then David Stephens, a former Yorkshire rugby union player and an even-timer on the track, who had joined Wigan at the start of August. Ashton was just about to embark on his testimonial year. He was following Bill Sayer, who had recently received £1,050 for his testimonial.

Billy received a plaque from director Joe Taylor before the game against Swinton on 16 October marking his achievement of scoring 500 tries. Billy was also captain that afternoon in Ashton's absence. Danny Gardiner was sent off after half an hour and that cost Wigan the game, Swinton running in three tries to none in their 13–8 success. Bill Sayer made his 295th and last appearance for Wigan, being transferred to arch rivals St Helens for £1,750 a few weeks later. Another Friday night floodlit game followed at Oldham, where Wigan sprang back to form with a 16–6 win. The *Wigan Observer* commented: "Boston, who appears to have a special liking for the Oldham ground, had a splendid first half and some of the game's sparkle faded when he retired during the interval with a leg injury". Billy was a try-scorer in a 51–2 beating of Blackpool, their biggest win of the campaign, but there was a dire 14–4 loss at Warrington before Wigan embarked on another winning streak.

On 20 November Billy had the novel experience of being a substitute for the home game against fellow top-four contenders Workington Town. Cliff Hill captained the team for the first time, as Ashton was injured and Billy on the bench. Australian forward Bill Cane made his debut for Wigan, but was replaced at half-time by Geoff Lyon and never played again. Billy also got on in the second half, replacing Chris Hesketh and, according to the *Wigan Observer*, "Showed a glimpse of his old power by trampling on Bell and Charlton to score Wigan's fourth try" in their 29–8 victory. Colin Clarke got a hat-trick – an unusual achievement for a hooker. Billy was again brought on as a second half substitute for Frankie Parr against Widnes at Central Park the following Saturday. A late try from acting half-back by Ashton sneaked a 9–8 win for Wigan. It was the last time Billy was used as a substitute.

The vicissitudes of the December weather allowed Wigan to play only two games, both bringing narrow victories. Fourth from bottom Barrow gave fourth from top Wigan an almighty scare at Central Park. It was another occasion when Bill Burgess's limpet-like attention to Trevor Lake caused friction. At one point Eddie Tees almost caused a riot after taking exception to a tackle by Ashby and Lake on Burgess. Billy rushed in and flattened Tees and a huge fracas erupted, fortunately without serious repercussions. Billy was twice stopped inches short in the first half, which closed with Barrow 7–2 up. With a couple of minutes remaining Wigan were clinging to a 9–7 lead, when Billy did well to hang on to a high pass from Cliff Hill. He bounded down the wing, held off two tacklers and delivered a perfect one-handed pass inside to David Stephens, who plunged through two defenders to score the decisive try. After the game Jack Winstanley interviewed Bill Burgess, whom Lake had hit in frustration at his excessively close attention, and put it to him that such tactics were a provocation. Burgess replied: "No, it's all in the game, and you don't see me hitting and running. There's only Vollenhoven among the South Africans who I rate highly. And none of them has been as good as Billy Boston. He was the greatest of all time".

A week after struggling to beat lowly Barrow, Wigan went to second-placed Wakefield and won 13–10. Trinity had been undefeated in their last 14 games and led 10–5 at the break. Wigan's saviour was the Boston-Stephens axis, which claimed all three of their tries in muddy conditions. Billy bagged the first, going in at the corner after capitalising on the approach play of Tony Stephens and David Stephens. David scored the try that equalled the scores at 10–10 and Billy's second won the match 13–10 with seven minutes remaining. The *Wigan Observer's* headline was "Boston slides in to beat Trinity". The try followed a 20-yard arcing "boomerang" pass by McTigue to Parr. Hill and Stephens shifted the ball quickly to Billy 15 yards out. Three defenders barred his way but he took them all over with him in a slithering heap for a try only he could have manufactured.

Ron Barker wrote in the *Rugby Leaguer:* "Boston's critics have been writing him off for a couple of seasons but he keeps confounding them and I still rate him the most powerful winger in the game within 20–30 yards of the opposing try-line. His match-winning try against Wakefield was evidence that he is far from a spent force. In his 12 years at Central Park the human powerhouse has registered some sensational tries. However, for sheer value and as a team morale-booster I think his match-winner is worthy of [special] mention."

January and early February brought a mixed bag of results for Wigan. They only scored 18 points in their first four games of 1966, but collected notable home wins against Warrington and Wakefield, while losing at Hull KR and Workington and Billy failed to get on the score-sheet in all four. January also saw another member of the great Wigan side of the recent past depart, when Roy Evans announced his retirement because of a persistent groin injury. A 10–2 win at Huddersfield on 12 February launched a run of 10 consecutive victories and ignited Wigan's season. Wigan had actually objected to taking the field at a freezing Fartown, which was covered by an inch of snow. John Benn wrote in the *Wigan Observer:* "Boston, in dire trouble with the popular side spectators right from the first minute, when he pole-axed Curry from the kick-off, virtually clinched the game in the 50th minute – without even touching the ball. A mighty break by Lyon, carried on by Parr, sent David Stephens streaking through. And Boston, dreaded even yet, was blatantly used as a decoy as Stephens turned inside and romped over. Senior was so intent on taking Boston that Stephens could have skidded the team coach broad-side-on through the gap which suddenly opened up."

A week later Wigan butchered Whitehaven 39–0, although Billy did not claim any of their nine tries. He did, however, leave a big impression on the Whitehaven tacklers. Jack Winstanley reported: "Billy Boston's rollicking performance must have left Whitehaven defenders wondering what Wigan fed their players on. With almost every chance he got, Boston left a trail of bruised and battered Cumbrians in his wake and it was a matter of regret for many of the spectators that his efforts were not rewarded by at least one try. Certainly he deserved it."

On 26 February Wigan hosted Halifax before a crowd of more than 18,000 in the first round of the Challenge Cup. They won 8–4, enjoyed massive territorial advantage, despite just shading the scrums 16–15, and there were outstanding performances from Billy, Ashton, McTigue and Major. Jack Winstanley described the game as "Wigan draughtsmen versus Halifax blacksmiths". Billy scored his first try since his match-winner at Wakefield in December. He received a pass in the 17th minute 30 yards out, flabbergasted Johnny

Freeman with a side-step off his right foot and ran wide of Ronnie James to the corner for a super try. Geoff Lyon, drafted in on the left wing, scored the only other try of the match after half an hour, going over after a seven-man move gave him an overlap. Two days later Wigan played Rochdale Hornets under floodlights at Watersheddings and scored seven tries in a 35–5 romp, Billy claiming one, as Wigan began to play their best rugby of the season.

A wonderful performance at Swinton on Wednesday 9 March brought a 25–7 win. Billy was involved in a fearful collision with Alan Buckley, who was concussed, and neither returned for the second half. Three days later Barrow were vanquished 22–8 at Craven Park, where Billy received a solitary pass in the first half and that was four yards forward. He was again criminally underused in a 36–8 annihilation of Salford on 15 March, as most clubs strove to catch up on a massive fixture backlog. Three games in six days was hardly ideal preparation for Wigan's second round Cup-tie against Whitehaven. However, Wigan swept the Cumbrians aside by 40–6, scoring seven tries between the 44th and 71st minutes. Trevor Lake crossed for four of them, but Billy had to be content with one.

A week later Wigan passed a much sterner test in front of 22,803 enraptured fans at Central Park. League leaders St Helens left chastened having suffered a 17–8 defeat, only their second of the season. It was a game of high quality and the *Wigan Observer* was in no doubt that "the better side by a mile" prevailed. Wigan fans were especially pleased as their side's performance flew in the face of the decision of the 1966 tour selectors to take only one Wigan player to Australia and New Zealand – Colin Clarke. Wigan's wingers scored all three tries, all gems. Billy's arrived in the 20th minute, when he "swept contemptuously past Benyon and Barrow after sparkling approach work of Ashby and David Stephenson", while "the ever threatening power of Boston was always evident".

Wigan had drawn a tough third round Challenge Cup tie away to Bradford Northern on Saturday 2 April. However, there was huge controversy as the BBC wanted to televise it on *Grandstand*. Wigan had a couple of months previously instigated a revolt against televised matches. The Wigan board had issued a statement describing the televising of live matches as "a creeping paralysis" and had declared they were not going to allow any of their games at Central Park to be televised in 1966–67, adding that if it were legally possible they would also refuse to play on away grounds before the cameras. Consequently, Wigan refused point blank to have the cup tie at Odsal televised and were fined £500 by the RFL and forfeited another £100 from the television pool. Wigan commented, "We want spectators on our terraces, not watching matches on the screen". The RFL and BBC agreed to televise the Warrington versus Leeds tie instead. Perversely, snow fell throughout the north of England and deposited six foot drifts at Odsal, causing the game to be delayed until the following Wednesday evening.

Bradford Northern got their biggest crowd for years – 27,453 – but progressed no further in the Cup. Wigan well merited their 15–6 victory with tries from Ashby, Lake and Ashton and three goals from Gilfedder. Two days later Wigan journeyed to St Helens for the Good Friday derby, but went down 17–10 in another tremendous match, played before a massive crowd of 28,953, some of whom risked life and limb on the stand roofs. Unfortunately for Billy he sustained a knee injury, necessitating fluid being drawn. It was touch-and-go as to whether he would be ready for the semi-final, but by the time Wigan had arranged their three days special daylight training for it, Billy was in the party. He had missed four games, all of which Wigan won to maintain third position in the league.

The Challenge Cup semi-final took place on 23 April. Wigan's opponents at Fartown were sixth-placed Leeds, who were on the verge of one of their golden eras. What was bound to be a testing encounter was exacerbated by the dreadful conditions which the teams faced.

After monsoon-like amounts of rain, the Fartown field was a poisonous concoction of mud and sand, which deteriorated as the game wore on. Hooker Colin Clarke had twisted his knee against Leigh on the previous Monday and prop Tom Woosey took his place. Leeds hooker Alan Lockwood won the first half scrums 7–5 and the second half scrums 12–1. To add to Wigan's problems they lost Laurie Gilfedder after 29 minutes with a sprained ankle and Frankie Parr with a bruised thigh at half-time. None of which seemed to perturb a defiant and inspired Wigan, while Billy played a blinder, scored one of the most important tries of his career and won the match.

He delivered the killer blow as early as the ninth minute, when scrum-half Parr capitalised on great work from Tony Stephens and Brian McTigue. He outmanoeuvred three Loiners before whizzing out a long pass to Billy. There was not far to go but the surface was treacherous and Billy was met by a ferocious shoulder charge from his opposing wing, the tough-tackling Geoff Wriglesworth, which would have sent any other mortal sprawling over the touch-line. However, this was Billy Boston and it was Wriglesworth who was sent flying. Billy crashed over the line at the corner and referee Harry Hunt waved away Leeds' protests that he had hit the flag before touching down. The *Sunday Express's* reporter Keith Macklin asked Billy about the incident and was told: "I touched down cleanly inside the flag. If somebody knocked over the flag, it wasn't me. It must have been the bloke who tackled me". The Leeds captain Harry Poole told Macklin: "On a dry ground, with only half as much ball, we'd have won it. Twice in the second half we had a three-man overlap on the left wing, and it was only perfectly-timed crash tackles by Boston that stopped us." Billy's was the solitary try of the match, the only other scores being penalty goals from Leeds full-back Bev Risman on 42 minutes and Eric Ashton, after 49 and 70 minutes. Billy's barnstorming try had set up another meeting with St Helens at Wembley, Saints having disposed of Dewsbury 12–5 at Swinton in the other semi-final the previous Saturday.

Having finished third in the league behind St Helens and Swinton, Wigan had realistic hopes of a Championship and Cup double, an achievement that had escaped Billy in his long and illustrious career. The quest began on 30 April with a home tie against Widnes in the top 16 play-offs. It was a highly entertaining affair with Wigan trailing 8–2 before levelling at 8–8 by half-time and eventually winning 27–10. Billy gave an astounding performance, which brought him his only hat-trick of the season. He also provided David Stephens with a last minute try with an amazing inside pass. Jack Winstanley commented, "Boston's display generally confirmed the view held by many people – and shared by me – that his natural skill has never been surpassed on the rugby field."

The play-off quarter-final brought Leeds to Central Park on 7 May and Wigan reproduced their superiority over the Loiners with a comfortable 22–5 triumph. With the game scoreless after 23 minutes both hookers, Colin Clarke and Alan Lockwood, were sent off for persistent infringements, both having been cautioned twice already by referee Laurie Gant. Two tries from Tony Stephens paved the way for victory before Billy snatched the third in the 76th minute. Frank Parr put in a devilish kick through around half-way and Billy showed remarkable speed to get to the ball ahead of three Leeds men before diving in for his 19th try of the season. Geoff Lyon finished Leeds off with Wigan's fourth try in the last minute.

Clarke's dismissal earned him a two-match ban, which was considered excessively harsh by many as it meant he would miss the play-off semi-final and Wembley. Wigan would have to make do with no expert ball-winner in two of the most vital matches imaginable and were left ruing the departure of Bill Sayer to St Helens.

Billy tackling Halifax half-back Barry Robinson in the 1966 Championship semi-final.

On the Saturday evening of 14 May, Halifax, the reigning champions, drew a crowd of more than 23,000 to Central Park for the Championship semi-final. They were rewarded with a truly spell-binding match. Alan Thomas gave the game five-star rating in the *Daily Express* and commented, "Wigan showed their fighting spirit in as great a first half as I have ever seen". Halifax were 10–0 ahead after 10 minutes. Wigan, on £50 a man, were level at 10–10 by the 17th minute and there had only been two scrums. Halifax added a penalty to lead 12–10 at half-time and extended their advantage to 17–10 on 42 minutes. Roland Tinker, in the *Halifax Courier*, wrote: "And then came the bouncing bundle of dynamite in the shape of 15-stone Boston. Cooper went for him but was knocked out. Charlie Renilson was ready, however, and just managed to push him out of play". It was Wigan's last throw as they subsided to a 25–12 defeat, ending their hopes of the double.

So Wigan's clash with St Helens at Wembley on 21 May became their last chance to lift silverware in the 1965–66 season. Billy, Eric Ashton and Brian McTigue were carving their own niches in history by becoming the first players to figure in six Wembley finals. The Stadium was sold out and a record Wembley final crowd expected a match to remember.

Prime Minister Harold Wilson was introduced to the two sides before kick-off. His government had been grateful for a Labour landslide in the Wigan area in the recent elections, having won at Wigan, Ince and Westhoughton. Wigan RLFC were hoping for their own landslide of points against their arch rivals. The teams were:

*Wigan:* Ashby, Boston, D. Stephens, Ashton (capt), Lake, Hill, Parr, Gardiner, Woosey, McTigue, A. Stephens, Gilfedder, Major. Substitutes: Hesketh, Lyon (neither played)
*St Helens:* F. Barrow, van Vollenhoven, Murphy (capt), Benyon, Killeen, Harvey, Bishop, Halsall, Sayer, Watson, French, Warlow, Mantle. Substitutes: A. Barrow, Hitchen (neither played)

Once again Wigan had concealed an injury to skipper Eric Ashton, who had to have pain-killing injections for a torn rib cartilage, while make-shift hooker Tom Woosey needed an injection for an ankle injury.

From the start St Helens imposed an iron grip on proceedings. Billy's opposing winger Len Killeen potted a straight 30-yard penalty after only three minutes. Six minutes later he landed the most astonishing goal ever seen at the famous venue – a 60-yard penalty from wide out in his own half – and Wigan were four points down. Their only real response in the early stages came when Billy fielded a kick and went on a blockbusting run which required three Saints to halt. John Mantle dived across Wigan's goal-line for the game's first try after 17 minutes and Killeen's conversion stretched St Helens' lead to 9–0. A Laurie Gilfedder goal was Wigan's only reply after half an hour and Wigan looked beaten at half-time, despite being only 9–2 in arrears.

St Helens were even more dominant after the break. Within four minutes Danny Gardiner had laid out Billy Benyon, who was chasing a kick inside Wigan's '25'. Killeen's fourth goal made it 11–2. Ten minutes later it really was all over for Wigan. Benyon was in possession but, on seeing Billy rapidly bearing down on him, put in a neat grubber-kick to the corner flag, which sat up perfectly for Killeen to gather and touch down. By that stage the Saints faithful were chanting "Easy, Easy", while the Wigan supporters, and many neutrals, were booing the referee, Harry Hunt, and slow handclapping because of his over-strict interpretation of the rules and failure to play advantage. Matters did not improve and in the 71st minute Tommy Bishop kicked through from a play-the-ball, collected a ricochet off Ray Ashby and dived under the posts for another converted try. Alec Murphy applied the *coup de grâce* three minutes from time with a coolly placed 15-yard drop-goal and Saints ran out winners 21–2.

Of course, Wigan had excuses for their wretched performance in a game that drew pretty universal condemnation for its lack of entertainment and niggliness, except from those with St Helens connections. Tom Woosey lost the scrums to Bill Sayer 17–9, which was better than most people expected and a lot more than the passage of time has distorted Woosey's performance into. Forty-odd years later tales now abound of how Wigan only won one scrum. The truth is that they may as well have won only one scrum because St Helens were happy to concede penalties knowing that Wigan would have to kick to touch and thereby risk losing possession anyway. Wigan were in fact awarded 17 penalties to Saints' 9, an exact reversal of the scrum count.

Again, in truth, Wigan's overall performance was woeful. Harold Mather wrote in the *Manchester Guardian*, "This was a display which, on Wigan's normal high standards, was hard to believe". The *Yorkshire Post's* Alfred Drewry agreed: "Wigan, hesitant and clumsy, never moved well. Ashby, a brave full-back, was the only player who did not find the occasion too much for him". The *Liverpool Echo's* Leslie Woodhead noted: "St Helens had the poise, pace and the class. Wigan were disappointing, disjointed and a team which had promised so much in the preceding rounds found themselves outclassed and outplayed when it came to the most important one of all". Jack Paul neatly summed up Wigan's problem in the *Sunday Express:* "St Helens used the lot, especially offside gamesmanship at play-the-balls and referee Harry Hunt, much to my surprise, regularly whistled up to give Wigan penalties instead of allowing them the advantage and playing on".

Eric Ashton told the press: "We were pathetic. Wigan either wins as a team, or flops as one, and believe me, we certainly belly-flopped today." Billy later said: "The 1966 final was ridiculous. Everybody was looking forward to it and there was a crowd of over 98,500... but it became an absolute farce. And I don't accuse Alex Murphy for what happened. I blame the Rugby League for harshly suspending Colin Clarke. Why couldn't they have imposed a fine? I'll always believe it could still have been a cracking final if we'd had 'Clarkie' hooking against Bill Sayer... We never stood the slightest chance".

So Billy's sixth and last Wembley Challenge Cup brought him a third runners-up medal to add to his three winners' medals. Once again people were wondering whether Wigan's dynasty was disintegrating.

Billy breaks away from a St Helens defender.

## 1965–66

Wigan finished 3rd in the League: P34, W27, L7, For 604, Against 302
Boston scored 19 tries for Wigan

| Date | Opponent | Score | Boston | Crowd | |
|------|----------|-------|--------|-------|---|
| 18 August | Whitehaven | 23–10 | dnp | 2,000 | |
| 21 August | Widnes | 12–2 | dnp | 7,822 | |
| 23 August | **Liverpool City** | 22–10 | dnp | 7,313 | |
| 28 August | **Oldham** | 8–23 | | 12,444 | |
| 30 August | Leigh | 25–18 | | 9,500 | |
| 1 September | Liverpool City | 13–12 | dnp | 1,500 | |
| 4 September | **New Zealanders** | 12–17 | | 12,853 | |
| 11 September | **Whitehaven** | 25–23 | 1T | 8,576 | LC1 |
| 16 September | Oldham | 13–28 | 1T | 9,500 | LC2 |
| 18 September | **Hull KR** | 20–11 | 2T | 8,096 | |
| 24 September | Castleford | 12–9 | dnp | 9,203 | |
| 2 October | **Castleford** | 8–10 | | 7,890 | |
| 9 October | Blackpool B | 43–19 | 2T | 4,000 | |
| 16 October | **Swinton** | 8–13 | | 13,162 | |
| 22 October | Oldham | 16–6 | | 8,098 | |
| 30 October | **Blackpool B** | 51–2 | 1T | 6,010 | |
| 13 November | Warrington | 4–14 | | 8,325 | |
| 20 November | **Workington T**\* | 29–8 | 1T | 6,753 | |
| 27 November | **Widnes**\* | 9–8 | | 7,020 | |
| 11 December | **Barrow** | 12–7 | | 5,603 | |
| 18 December | Wakefield T | 13–10 | 2T | 9,736 | |
| 1 January | **Warrington** | 6–0 | | 13,543 | |
| 8 January | Hull KR | 2–15 | | 8,000 | |
| 29 January | **Wakefield T** | 7–5 | | 13,771 | |
| 5 February | Workington T | 3–7 | | 2,829 | |
| 12 February | Huddersfield | 10–2 | | 3,867 | |
| 19 February | **Whitehaven** | 39–0 | | 6,755 | |
| 26 February | **Halifax** | 8–4 | 1T | 18,064 | Cup 1 |
| 28 February | Rochdale H+ | 35–5 | 1T | 2,005 | |
| 9 March | Swinton | 25–7 | | 11,700 | |
| 12 March | Barrow | 22–8 | | 4,500 | |
| 15 March | Salford | 36–8 | | 8,000 | |
| 19 March | **Whitehaven** | 40–6 | 1T | 14,491 | Cup 2 |
| 26 March | **St Helens** | 17–8 | 1T | 22,803 | |
| 6 April | Bradford N | 15–6 | | 27,453 | Cup 3 |
| 8 April | St Helens | 10–17 | | 28,953 | |
| 9 April | **Huddersfield** | 7–2 | dnp | 6,641 | |
| 11 April | **Salford** | 15–7 | dnp | 10,024 | |
| 15 April | **Rochdale H** | 25–12 | dnp | 4,082 | |
| 18 April | **Leigh** | 17–7 | dnp | 9,501 | |
| 23 April | Leeds | 7–2 | 1T | 22,758 | Cup SF (at Fartown) |
| 30 April | **Widnes** | 27–10 | 3T | 13,381 | CH PO1 |
| 7 May | **Leeds** | 22–5 | 1T | 16,064 | CH PO2 |
| 14 May | **Halifax** | 12–25 | | 23,292 | CH SF |
| 21 May | St Helens | 2–21 | | 98,536 | Cup Final (at Wembley) |

\* Appeared as a substitute
+ Played at Oldham

# 18. 1966–67 Lancashire Cup win at last

"Lights, even if not TV cameras... but scant sign of action. This is the picture at Central Park where the directors, under bitter criticism from many quarters, shape up to fight a foreign battle of striving to check an alarming slump in interest. Wigan who have had it so good for so long are in trouble. The nucleus of a great side has grown old together and not all that gracefully. And Wigan's acute lack of automatic potential replacements has been ruthlessly exposed by an exceptional crop of early season injuries. Prospects are as black as thunder."

That is what appeared on the front page of the *Rugby Leaguer* on 26 August 1966 and it was an accurate description of Wigan's woes. Although Wigan had finished third and been Challenge Cup runners-up the previous season, there was a whiff of desperation at Central Park. For the first time that anyone could remember, average league match attendances at Wigan had dipped below 10,000 in 1965–66 and St Helens had taken over as the best-supported club in the league. Wigan's average of 9,495 was 2,000 fewer than Saints' – a sad indictment of the decline in rugby league's fortunes. Wigan's humiliation at Wembley had at least pushed the clubs to agree to a new rule – that a tap kick would go to a team kicking to touch from a penalty. It was hoped that it would open up play and stifle offside play, as well as reduce even further the number of scrums in a match. Billy had scored 19 tries in the previous season, not many by his astronomical standards but still good enough to place him 10th in the try-scoring lists. The constriction on wing play by the mid-1960s was very clear from the fact that the leading try-scorers, Len Killeen and Trevor Lake, had each only scored 32 tries, followed by Bill Burgess and Geoff Wriglesworth with 25 each.

The only good news to come out of the 1966 close season for Wigan was the award of an MBE to Eric Ashton. Unfortunately for Eric, he was about to experience a tough season. Wigan began by failing to regain the sevens title, Oldham taking the Silcock Cup by beating Halifax 16–15 in the final. They also failed to regain the Wardonia Cup on Friday 12 August, going down 10–8 at Warrington.

Billy, now just turned 32 years of age, decided to have a crack at playing in the forwards. With his mighty physique and awesome power he was one winger who would not be regarded as a fish out of water and there were high hopes that he would make a success out of the change from three-quarter to packman. He was consequently selected to play in the second row alongside Geoff Lyon for the opening league fixture at Whitehaven on 17 August. Eric Ashton told the press: "This is a serious experiment. Billy is keen on the move and we think it will give his career a new lease. He may not be as fast as he was but he still has a fair turn of pace. There may be one snag – whether Billy has the stamina to stay the 80 minutes as a forward." Billy told reporters, "Eric and I have already talked about the possibility of me joining the forwards..." But the caution typical of Central Park prompted him to add, "Of course, what finally happens is entirely in the hands of the team selectors... I will play anywhere so long as I get a game."

Whitehaven had finished bottom of the league, but in wet conditions shocked Wigan and the wider rugby league fraternity by winning 16–0. Wigan were losing 2–0 at half-time and four minutes into the second half Ray Ashby was carried off with torn knee ligaments. Billy, "a busy forward in the first half", according to Brian Batty in the *Daily Mail*, was moved to full-back in Ashby's place. John Benn wrote in the *Wigan Observer:* "The much publicised first appearance of Billy Boston – one of the greatest 'turnstile-clickers' of all time – as a forward, rapidly became one of secondary importance as enthusiastic Whitehaven rocked

Wigan... In any event, on this dismal show, there is room for him yet on the right wing – once he is fully fit."

The experiment continued for Wigan's first home game against Halifax, when Brian McTigue filled the hooking role. Matters did not improve, though. By half-time Wigan were sinking fast at 19–4 down. Billy had been taken out of the pack after 20 minutes and returned to the right wing. Jack Winstanley wrote in the *Observer*, "Boston's experimental role as a second-row forward was called off almost before it began and I see no future in it". The Wigan fans were certainly happy to see him in his normal role. Five minutes after the break he scored Wigan's first try of the season. Receiving the ball from Gardiner after a quick tap-penalty 20 yards out, Billy battered through three attempted tackles and took over a final defender with him for a typically belligerent score. Wigan rallied briefly, but finished shell-shocked by a 34–22 defeat, which actually flattered them.

The directors took desperate measures and signed veteran hooker Len McIntyre for £750 from Liverpool City in the hope of rectifying their possession problems. They also gave 'A' team trials to a French threequarter, Henri Cribaillet, who had played for Perpignan, Toulouse and Rouen.

Leigh and Wakefield Trinity both beat Wigan, whose first four league fixtures all ended in defeat. The 18–9 loss at Leigh was illuminated by a wonderful display by Colin Tyrer, who scored all his side's points and left a deep impression on the Wigan board. The 19–7 defeat at Wakefield marked Brian McTigue's last appearance for Wigan – his 422nd. Brian's finale was sadly not acclaimed after 16 years of magnificent service, as he was involved in protracted negotiations to take a player-coach position in Bathurst, New South Wales. Billy regarded Brian as the greatest forward he had ever seen.

Wigan finally broke their duck on 29 August, when they overcame Leigh 18–13 at Central Park. However, another link with the good old days was broken as it proved to be John Barton's last game for Wigan. The old order was certainly changing. Four days later Leigh were beaten again, 18–4 in the first round of the Lancashire Cup at Hilton Park. Eric Ashton turned the game round when he came on from the bench, took over the acting half-back role and destroyed Leigh. Billy converted a try by Geoff Lyon in the 32nd minute but there was a sour note just after half-time when McIntyre was sent off for striking Tyrer, who allegedly bit him.

If Wigan fans thought their team had turned the corner, they were wrong. Billy missed the next game, a 20–10 loss at Blackpool, Wigan's first ever to Borough. Third from bottom of the league was not where Wigan followers expected their team to be. A better show followed with a 24–14 home win over Barrow, when Wigan were reduced to fielding two trialists. John Southey, a Rhodesian, partnered Billy, while John Thompson, a Liverpool forward, played in the front row. John Benn wrote in the *Wigan Observer*, "A Boston speciality try sent fans home happier – if not complacent".

On 14 September Wigan faced their sternest test of the season so far, when St Helens came to Central Park for the second round of the Lancashire Cup. In monsoon conditions the two sides produced a cliff-hanger. Significantly, the right wing pairing of Boston and Ashton was temporarily re-established and it was Billy who provoked the *Wigan Observer's* headline 'Boston blockbuster shatters Saints'. Wigan were trailing 7–6, when a scrum was formed in the 44th minute. Ashton shot out a 20-yard pass to Billy, who had come in from the wing, leaving Benyon helpless. Killeen was left in two minds as Billy rampaged to the corner, striding through full-back Frank Barrow's tackle en route. Gilfedder converted and Saints could conjure up no more than a penalty goal, leaving Wigan with an 11–9 victory and a place in the semi-final. Eric Ashton celebrated a good week by receiving a testimonial cheque for £1,677, breaking Billy's club record.

Within three days Wigan were brought back to earth with a good hiding at Headingley. Leeds won 38–25, but Wigan scored 15 late points. Billy got a breakaway try, but Wigan's shortcomings remained all too apparent, particularly in defence. It had been Leeds's highest score at Headingley against Wigan for 43 years and the defeat left Wigan sixth from the foot of the league. Ironically they were one point better off than Hunslet, with whom they had so recently shared the Wembley limelight. Workington pushed Wigan hard at Central Park on 24 September before going under 28–16 and, according to Neville Haddock in the *Daily Sketch:* "Billy Boston lifted some of the gloom which is hanging over Central Park. The heavyweight winger rumbled in for two tries and revived the memories of happier days... There was nothing fancy by blockbuster Billy after slick passing twice left only Workington winger Keith Davies between him and the line. That situation is too much for one man to face. The first time Davies was simply trampled underfoot. Next thing Billy seemed to take pity and just shunted his opposite number aside with a body-shattering shoulder charge. But as Billy dived through two desperate tackles in a bid to touch down for his hat-trick, the ball was snatched in mid-air – by Davies."

Close on 14,000 fans descended on Central Park on 28 September for the Lancashire Cup semi-final between Wigan and Warrington, wondering which Wigan would turn up this time. They were lucky because Wigan had apparently learned again how to tackle. John Benn described the game in the *Wigan Observer* as "a rousing, robust and often ragged tie". Warrington defended sublimely in the first half and led 7–4 until 14 minutes from the final whistle. At that point Cliff Hill failed to get to a Colin Clarke pass along the Wire '25', but Billy swooped swiftly for the ball, expertly drew the cover and gave an inside pass to David Stephens, who side-stepped his way over for the decisive try, which Gilfedder improved. Two minutes later Ashton sent a soaring drop-goal over the bar and five minutes from time sent Keith Holden over for a final converted try. Wigan had triumphed 16–7 and it was appropriate that the old firm had been instrumental in getting Wigan to their first county cup final for nine years.

Two days later Wigan went to Oldham, who were to be their opponents in the Lancashire Cup Final, and snatched a 16–15 win after trailing 15–8 at half-time. Wigan put in a titanic display of tackling and it was Billy's 68th minute try that sealed their success. Holden placed a kick over the Oldham cover. Billy raced after the ball, adroitly collected an awkward bounce and swept outside Brian Curry and Trevor Simms for a cracking try. He was a try-scorer again on 8 October in a ghastly game at Central Park which Swinton won 16–6, but that reverse was countered six days later at Barrow. The crowd of more than 7,000 was Barrow's best of the 1960s so far, largely because it was the debut of Tom Brophy, the former England rugby union stand-off. Brophy's much-anticipated duel with Cliff Hill was over almost before it began when Wigan's stand-off hurt his wrist and was taken off. Barrow took an eight-point lead before Billy struggled over for a characteristic try in the corner in the 25th minute. Eleven minutes later Ashton scored his first try of the season, using Billy as a decoy, to level the scores at 8–8 and Wigan spoiled Barrow's party by running out 15–13 winners.

Wigan had been interested in a rugby union stand-off of their own – Llanelli's rising star Barry John. They had to settle for signing another outstanding Welsh player, 19-year-old Peter Rowe of Swansea for £2,000. On the debit side Wigan were resigned to losing Trevor Lake, who had agreed to join St George in Sydney at the end of the season.

Momentous decisions were being taken off the field at this period. Wigan, Bradford Northern and Hunslet had told the RFL that they would not take part in any televised games at all, home or away. This came at a time when the BBC2 Floodlit Trophy tournament was expanded to 11 clubs and indicated a lack of forward thinking on the Wigan board's part. Moreover, the Floodlit Trophy became the vehicle for a revolutionary experiment – the four tackle rule. Even before the competition reached its final stages the RFL decided to adopt four tackles and informed clubs that from November games would be played under the limited tackles format.

Oldham and Wigan decided that they would play the Lancashire Cup Final under the old unlimited tackles laws, although Eric Ashton told the press that he believed four tackles would eventually benefit Wigan. The game was played at Station Road, Swinton on Saturday 29 October and drew a crowd of 14,193, a fraction of what would have accrued just a few years earlier. Only two of the Wigan side had been on the winning side in a Lancashire Cup Final – Harry Major and Laurie Gilfedder with Warrington in 1959. Almost incredibly, Billy Boston and Eric Ashton had never collected a winners' medal for the competition, which Wigan had failed to win since 1951. For this distinguished pair, the Lancashire Cup had become the Holy Grail. A winners' medal would complete their collections. Only Oldham stood between them and that achievement. They also stood 10 places higher in the league than Wigan, who were now 19th. However, there was no clear favourite to take the trophy and the teams were:

*Wigan:* Ashby, Boston, Ashton (capt), Holden, Lake, Hill, Parr, Gardiner, Clarke, J. Stephens, Lyon, Gilfedder, Major. Substitutes: D. Stephens, A. Stephens (neither played)

*Oldham:* McLeod, Dolly, McCormack, Donovan, Simms, Warburton, Canning, Wilson, Taylor, Fletcher, Smethurst (capt), Irving, Mooney. Substitutes: Holroyd, Ogden (neither played)

There was not much doubt that for the sentimentalists and neutrals a Wigan win would be welcomed, if only to fittingly round off the careers of two all-time greats. Wigan could not rely on sentiment but they could rely on Eric and Billy. However, Oldham were on £40 a man to win and they fought like demons. John Benn reported in the *Wigan Observer:* "Superb play by Ashton and Holden gave Boston the chance to show them that he still has a nifty side-step when Wigan went ahead in the 10th minute. Boston made his try look so easy after Ashton had beaten two men, thrown off Mooney, and sent Holden veering across to the right-hand touch-line. Holden completely deceived Oldham with a gem of a reverse pass, and Boston did the rest." Gilfedder converted and three minutes later scored another try after good work from Gardiner and Lyon. Tommy Warburton kicked penalties for Oldham in the 26th and 30th minutes, but Parr and Holden worked beautifully to provide Ashton with a brilliant try in the 34th minute. Gilfedder missed the simple conversion and then Ashton sent a drop-goal attempt wide, but Wigan ended the half 11–4 ahead. John Benn noted: "How fitting that the thoroughbred Ashton and the businesslike Boston – searching for work and revelling in challenging four and five men to force him down – should play such a vital part in Wigan's first half booster."

Within eight minutes of the restart Oldham drew level. Warburton kicked his third penalty and then John Donovan swept past Ashby, Ashton and Billy to score wide out. Warburton struck a mighty conversion and the tide seemed to have turned against Wigan. However, Ashton steadied the boat and after 56 minutes the crucial score fell to Wigan. Seven minutes of continuous pressure and more than 30 play-the-balls softened up the Roughyeds' defence before Major found a gap and swivelled to send Clarke surging over despite the attentions of two tacklers for a match-winning try, converted by Gilfedder. Warburton landed his fifth goal on the hour and there was no more scoring, although Wigan had an almighty scare when their former player Stan McLeod lost the ball in a jarring tackle in the last seconds as he attempted to cross at the posts. So Wigan beat Oldham 16–13 and Billy and Eric finally obtained those cherished medals. Ashton received the trophy from the Lancashire president, Billy Williams, an old Salford and test prop. The Oldham players applauded as he accepted the Cup and Billy could not hide his delight. Ashton, however, displayed some displeasure at his side's performance and said: "I wanted this medal. Now I've won it. Naturally, I'm pleased. So is Billy. But I was disappointed at times... We let Oldham off the hook with a stream of daft penalties... I was shouting myself hoarse." In fact Wigan had lost the penalty count 15–5, all 15 of Oldham's coming in a row but astoundingly there had been only three scrums, two of which Wigan won.

It was strangely ironic that in this, the worst season Billy had experienced with Wigan, he should gain the medal that had proved so elusive. He was not to know that he would not play in another major final of any description. The seasons of plenty had been replaced by seasons of barrenness.

On 5 November Wigan staged their first game under the limited tackles law against Wakefield Trinity and there was some good rugby but opinions were divided as to whether the change was for the better. Wigan lost the scrums 17–7, and four minutes from time they lost the match 15–13, when Don Fox stopped dead 40 yards out and dropped a towering goal on the fourth tackle. Peter Rowe made an impressive debut for Wigan, partnering Billy. Unfortunately, Billy sustained a nose injury, which kept him out of Wigan's 40–0 home win over Whitehaven, a result which made up somewhat for that catastrophic defeat in Cumberland on the first day of the season.

A pulsating encounter followed at Thrum Hall that vindicated the new rules for many of those who witnessed it. Cliff Webb reported in the *Wigan Observer:* "Boston seemed to have found an apparently inexhaustible supply of wind throughout this game and was in top form. He contributed many thrilling runs which had the crowd roaring and opened Wigan's account in the first quarter with an unconverted try after Ashby had made the extra man." Five minutes later Colin Dixon scored for Halifax and Ronnie James's conversion left Wigan 5–3 behind at the break. On 50 minutes Ashton, playing stand-off, dropped a peach of a goal from 40 yards. Gilfedder followed with a difficult penalty goal and then hammered another 40-yard drop shot between the sticks to give Wigan a 9–5 lead in the 69th minute. A minute later John Burnett raced in at the corner, but James missed the conversion and Wigan held out for a breathtaking 9–8 win. They had quickly learnt that the drop-goal was going to be a major weapon under limited tackles rugby. Indeed it would become an obsession – an unintended consequence of the law-makers.

There was a joyous occasion for Billy and Joan on 22 November, when their fifth child Stephen was born. The four sisters finally had a brother. Joan recalls: "Billy took me into the hospital when I went into labour. He had not been at any of the births and this time he popped down the corridor, while I got on with the hard work. Then he popped over to a little pub just opposite the hospital. I gave birth really quickly and got a telephone message to Billy to come back. When he arrived he couldn't believe how fast the baby had arrived and he asked 'Have you had it?' When I told him I had and it wasn't a girl, he must have been really shocked because he replied, 'What the bloody hell is it then?' Of course, we were really happy. Nearly all the other Wigan players had sons, so it really pleased Billy. The following week there was a big picture of me and Stephen on the front page of the *Wigan Observer*."

Back on the playing field the drop-goal mania worked against Wigan in their next fixture, which brought a shock 13–10 win for Rochdale Hornets at Central Park. Hornets' centre

Graham Starkey was the game star, kicking five goals, including two crucial drop-goals. Billy edged Wigan 10–9 ahead in the 42nd minute with a fabulous try in which he beat two men and carried four over with him. John Benn commented, "Boston was only just held four times, the desperate Rochdale cover scurrying across like Lilliputians striving to chain down Gulliver!"

Billy's good form continued when Blackpool Borough visited Central Park on 3 December. Billy had knocked up his left hand in training so it was decided to play him on the left wing to protect it and move David Stephens over to right wing. Billy had not played on the left wing for Wigan for 10 years – the day he marked Brian Bevan. The move certainly worked as he scored a hat-trick between the ninth and 21st minutes causing the *Wigan Observer* to run the headline "Boston 3-step tramples Boro". Rowe and Lyon put him in for the first try and Ashton worked the old moves for his second and third. Billy also started a move that brought a try to Stephens after a spectacular 60-yard movement. Billy's performance in a 19–6 win prompted John Benn to describe Billy as "the star who violently refuses to be written off". The *Rugby Leaguer's* Raymond Fletcher, more poetically, wrote, "Like old man river, Boston, now 32, just keeps rolling along".

Billy's hat-trick brought his tally to 15 tries in 19 games, placing him well up the try-scoring lists, even though Wigan were having such a dismal league campaign. That other old stager Tom van Vollenhoven was leading the way with 19. While Billy still rolled on, his erstwhile wing colleague Trevor Lake had been released early from his contract and allowed to go to Australia. He had not played since breaking his nose in the Lancashire Cup Final. Lake had been a gem for Wigan, amassing 132 tries in 140 games. The timing of his leaving suddenly became catastrophic, however. In Wigan's 10–8 win at Liverpool City on 10 December David Stephens suffered horrendous injuries. A broken left leg and dislocated ankle put him out for the rest of the season and probably cost him a Great Britain cap. The extraordinarily versatile Chris Hesketh took over on the left wing for the rest of the season.

The Liverpool City game saw the debut of second-rower Terry Fogerty, a 1966 Lion. Wigan had been after Fogerty for two years and paid Halifax £7,500 for his services. Wigan regarded him as a natural successor to Brian McTigue. Terry certainly had the skills and creativity, if not the drive and temperament. Fogerty and Ashton produced masterly displays in a 20–7 win at Widnes. Cliff Hill scored a hat-trick and Hesketh claimed a great 50-yard try in what was seen as Wigan's best away performance of the season. Billy was taken off at half-time with a slight recurrence of his old knee injury. However, he was fit for the Boxing Day derby at Knowsley Road. Unfortunately, it brought disappointment with an 8–3 defeat, after a scoreless first half. Billy scored the only Wigan try, cruising through three tackles in the 67th minute after superb lead-up play from Fogerty, Parr and Rowe.

Victories over Salford and Warrington took Wigan up to ninth place in the league table and gave cause for optimism. Even a 9–8 setback at Workington on 14 January did not dampen spirits, as Wigan fans felt the adrenalin rush of another potential trip to Wembley, if only Wigan could gain some consistency and avoid more injuries. A brilliant 46–2 home win against Widnes on 28 January was a tremendous fillip. Eric Ashton collected 17 points and Billy zipped in for two tries.

The Challenge Cup first round draw threw up a real toughie for Wigan – Warrington at Wilderspool on 4 February. Close on 14,000 saw a thrill-a-minute cup tie. Wigan won the scrums 17–14 and the penalties 10–7, but never got ahead. At half-time they were 14–5 down and looking as if the first round would be their last. They rescued the game in the last quarter of an hour with a fantastic display of rugby. Ashton, nominally playing at full-back, was everywhere - a truly inspirational figure. It took a monumentally good try from Cliff Hill, in which he baffled five defenders 90 seconds from time, to earn Wigan a replay. Ashton's conversion from under the posts drew the match 19–19. The replay on the following Wednesday attracted a bumper crowd of 25,133 to Central Park. This time Wigan had an overwhelming 20–3 victory, but paid a heavy price. A rib injury caused Ashton to miss the last 30 minutes, while Hill was hurt and hobbled about on the wing for the last 20 minutes and Billy finished the game at full-back.

Following the snatching of a 10–8 win at Huddersfield after trailing 8–0, Wigan met league leaders Leeds at Central Park on 18 February. Billy was acting captain of a fairly depleted team and caused havoc early on when he went over, having cast off four tacklers, only to be recalled for stepping on the touch-line. In the seventh minute disaster struck Billy, who damaged his right arm when he made a try-saving crash tackle on the Leeds captain Harry Poole. He battled on until half-time, when the score was 5–5, but could not continue and Leeds ran out 17–7 winners, completing their first league double over Wigan for 39 years. Billy's injury was so severe that he had an operation the following day, followed by 10 days in hospital. On 5 March the *Daily Mail* reported: "Billy Boston is out of hospital and saying, 'I'll play until I'm 40'. Everyone in rugby league hopes he will too – but there are doubts whether he can play again this season after his recent operation."

Those doubts were well founded. The injury, which turned out to be a badly ruptured bicep, did end Billy's season. Moreover, Wigan's season went into almost terminal decline. While Billy was in hospital Wigan lost 18–6 to Salford in the Challenge Cup second round before the biggest crowd of the season at Central Park – 25,342. It was Wigan's first defeat at home in the Cup since 1954, and Salford's first win at Central Park for a decade. Even more alarmingly, Wigan lost four of their remaining seven league games and failed to qualify for the top 16 play-offs. Their finishing position of 17th was the worst since the club moved to Central Park in 1902. Despite all that, Wigan actually finished top of the league as far as attendances were concerned. At an average of 9,791, they had risen by about 300 on the previous season when they had finished third – and they say there are no such things as miracles.

Billy had finished top of Wigan's try-scorers with 18 – four ahead of the unfortunate David Stephens. Until his injury his form had been good, better perhaps than he or anyone else had a right to expect, in view of Wigan's falling standards. Perhaps it was time to consider his options for the future.

## 1966–67

Wigan finished 17th in the League: P34, W17, L17, For 513, Against 456
Boston scored 18 tries and 1 goal for Wigan

| Date | Opponent | Score | Boston | Crowd | |
|---|---|---|---|---|---|
| 17 August | Whitehaven | 0–16 | | 1,750 | |
| 20 August | **Halifax** | 22–34 | 1T | 8,471 | |
| 24 August | Leigh | 9–18 | | 7,000 | |
| 27 August | Wakefield T | 7–19 | | 6,957 | |
| 29 August | **Leigh** | 18–13 | | 9,537 | |
| 3 September | Leigh | 18–4 | 1G | 9,000 | LC1 |
| 6 September | Blackpool B | 10–20 | dnp | 3,000 | |
| 10 September | **Barrow** | 24–14 | 1T | 7,626 | |
| 14 September | **St Helens** | 11–9 | 1T | 13,141 | LC2 |
| 17 September | Leeds | 25–38 | 1T | 10,117 | |
| 24 September | **Workington T** | 28–16 | 2T | 9,246 | |
| 28 September | **Warrington** | 16–7 | | 13,759 | LCSF |
| 30 September | Oldham | 16–15 | 1T | 8,877 | |
| 8 October | **Swinton** | 6–16 | 1T | 12,576 | |
| 14 October | Barrow | 15–13 | 1T | 7,060 | |
| 22 October | **Huddersfield** | 15–4 | dnp | 7,753 | |
| 29 October | Oldham | 16–13 | 1T | 14,193 | LC Final (at Swinton) |
| 5 November | **Wakefield T** | 13–15 | | 10,473 | |
| 12 November | **Whitehaven** | 40–0 | dnp | 5,431 | |
| 19 November | Halifax | 9–8 | 1T | 6,490 | |
| 26 November | **Rochdale H** | 10–13 | 1T | 6,738 | |
| 3 December | **Blackpool B** | 19–6 | 3T | 4,532 | |
| 10 December | Liverpool City | 10–8 | | 1,100 | |
| 16 December | Widnes | 20–7 | | 5,100 | |
| 26 December | St Helens | 3–8 | 1T | 18,734 | |
| 27 December | **Salford** | 28–11 | | 8,543 | |
| 2 January | **Warrington** | 17–5 | dnp | 15,950 | |
| 14 January | Workington T | 8–9 | | 2,661 | |
| 28 January | **Widnes** | 46–2 | 2T | 10,050 | |
| 4 February | Warrington | 19–19 | | 13,843 | Cup 1 |
| 8 February | **Warrington** | 20–3 | | 25,133 | Replay |
| 11 February | Huddersfield | 10–8 | | 4,266 | |
| 18 February | **Leeds** | 7–17 | | 15,274 | |
| 25 February | **Salford** | 6–18 | dnp | 25,342 | Cup 2 |
| 3 March | Rochdale H | 15–12 | dnp | 5,541 | |
| 8 March | Swinton | 11–4 | dnp | 10,000 | |
| 18 March | **Oldham** | 8–20 | dnp | 7,967 | |
| 24 March | **St Helens** | 7–21 | dnp | 19,996 | |
| 25 March | Warrington | 9–12 | dnp | 6,915 | |
| 27 March | Salford | 4–17 | dnp | 10,000 | |
| 5 April | **Liverpool City** | 24–7 | dnp | 4,681 | |

# 19. 1967–68 Farewell to Central Park

The close season of 1967 was an anxious one for Wigan and their fans. There had to be changes, as no one wanted a repetition of the season just gone. The club had lost a colossal £24,792 on the year and it was obvious that the current team had fallen from the high standards of former times. Letting Chris Hesketh, a future Great Britain captain, go to Salford for £5,000 and Tony Stephens to Swinton for £3,000, did not appear to be too prudent, but signings were made to offset those departures. Colin Tyrer had been signed from Leigh towards the end of the season, after Billy was crocked, and by the start of the new season loose-forward Doug Laughton had been signed from St Helens for £4,500. Cliff Hill was appointed captain and his younger brother David, another stand-off-cum-centre, had been recruited from the Liverpool rugby union club. More young blood was pumped into the team in the shape of two reserve team players, winger Bill Francis and scrum-half Johnny Jackson.

Billy was still suffering from the aftermath of his operation; his upper arm and shoulder just would not come right. He declared himself unfit, even though he had managed to lose almost two stones and was down to 14½ stones. He was an interested – but fretful – spectator as Wigan's campaign began. They lost the Wardonia Cup match again, went out of the Lancashire Cup at home to Salford in the first round and lost four of their first seven league fixtures. Harry Major and Laurie Gilfedder were sold to Leigh for a joint fee of a mere £2,750 and by the middle of September 16 players were on the injured list.

At that point Billy dropped a bombshell. On 15 September the press announced that he had asked for a transfer. The only reason proffered was that "he felt he could not produce the standard required by Wigan". That may or may not have subconsciously meant that he could not produce the standard required by himself. Wisely, the Wigan directors discussed the matter at a lengthy board meeting and the following day the chairman, Ken Broome, told the press: "The board have refused to consider Boston's request for a move. As soon as he is 100 per cent fit he will be back with us. He has had a chat with the board and one or two small matters have been ironed out. Boston has happily accepted the position." The Wigan players certainly wanted Billy back.

Billy prepared for his comeback and in the meantime Wigan got back on track with league wins over Barrow and Oldham and a victory over Widnes in the first round of the BBC2 Floodlit Trophy on 2 October. That game drew a good crowd of almost 10,000 and followed a drawn game against Bradford Northern on 26 September, when Wigan had inaugurated their new £17,500 floodlights, Lord Derby doing the honours. Wigan's board had bowed to the inevitable. Even Wigan could not afford to ignore television and had gone so far as to allow their pre-season sevens tournament to be screened by the BBC. At the same time they had also conceded further ground to the relentless march of commercialism by changing the tournament's name from the Silcock Cup to the Cossack Vodka Trophy. Perhaps the gods were making a point when the floodlights failed twice on the opening night, causing the game to last for 98 minutes.

Eight months after playing his last game Billy finally returned to the cherry and white ranks on Monday 9 October 1967. Batley were the visitors and it was a wretched windswept evening. That did not matter to the fans, who chanted "Boston! Boston!" incessantly before the game commenced and carried on cheering him throughout the game. He gave them plenty of reasons for their adulation by scoring a hat-trick, touching down in the 30th, 48th and 62nd minutes in "the usual style". Remarkably, it was Billy's 50th hat-trick for the club.

Wigan seemed happy to shift the ball to the right wing at every opportunity and John Benn wrote in the *Wigan Observer*, "With star crowd-rousing personalities scattered thin around the pretty artisan world of Rugby League, the 33 year-old Billy Boston is still the greatest in the hearts of hundreds of Wigan fans." He also remarked that the crowd was seeing "a fitter, faster, slimmer Boston". Apart from Billy's triumphant return the game was notable for David Hill's first team debut, a 17 point haul from Colin Tyrer and Peter Rowe's winning of the official man-of-the-match award worth £6. It was only the second time Billy had played against Batley, who must have been pretty fed up, as he had scored four tries on the first occasion.

The following Friday night Wigan met the Australians and attracted the biggest crowd of their tour – 22,779. It was Billy's last appearance against a touring team and, fittingly enough, he finished on the winning side after a thrilling, but unspectacular, encounter. The Kangaroos led 6–5 at half-time with a couple of dubious tries from Billy Smith and Johnny King against a converted try by Ashton. Wigan won the game with a storming finish in the last eight minutes with a try from Francis and a couple of goals from Ashton. Billy was happy to be a winner, but the *Wigan Observer* reported: "Billy Boston, to the utter disbelief of the crowd, fumbled try-making inside passes from Parr and Ashton".

Workington were the next visitors to Central Park, when the Wigan board experimented with a Saturday 5.30 kick-off on 21 October, which surprisingly attracted an attendance of 11,705. It was described by the *Observer* as "a half twilight-and-floodlight match". Wigan won 18–13 on the back of a 29–11 scrum supremacy and Billy was among the try-scorers. Neville Haddock wrote in the *Daily Sketch:* "It all assisted Wigan to look like a mighty power once again. And there is no doubt that, on occasions, they looked genuinely impressive. Unfortunately, it was usually when the old firm of Billy Boston, Eric Ashton and Ray Ashby took a hand. Boston showed he is still a terror 20 yards from the try-line, when Ashby gave him a chance. The winger trampled through one poor defender and galloped over with two more hanging on."

A good win at Swinton, which Billy missed, was followed by a disaster at Huddersfield when Terry Fogerty pole-axed Huddersfield skipper Rob Valentine in the 25th minute. His dismissal cost Wigan the game and underlined Wigan's poor disciplinary record for the season so far, as Fogerty was the fifth of their players to be dismissed. The defeat ended a seven-match winning run and dropped Wigan to ninth place in the league. Billy got back on the try trail on 11 November with a couple in a 30–0 home thrashing of Rochdale Hornets, when a fellow Welshman Colin Standing made his debut in the Wigan pack. Billy was denied a hat-trick within 12 minutes when Fred Lindop ruled out a try from a scrum from a classic Ashton-Boston manoeuvre. He was still the target for rough treatment and Hornets forward Brian Kettleton was sent off in the 67th minute for a distasteful incident after Billy had already been held in a four-man tackle.

Wigan went to St Helens for a BBC2 Floodlit Trophy tie on Wednesday 22 November, after fog had caused it to be called off the previous evening, and won a famous victory. Billy played a blinder and scored a tremendous try – "as only he can", according to John Benn – beating four men in the corner after Tyrer had linked from a scrum. Unfortunately, he had to leave the action in the 80th minute to have a dislocated shoulder put back into place. Saints made the score respectable at 22–11 with their third try in the third minute of injury time. The shoulder problem kept Billy out of action until Wigan returned to Knowsley Road for their Floodlit Trophy semi-final against Leigh on 5 December. The tie was played in diabolical conditions, with swirling rain and on a mud heap of a pitch. Billy lost his chance to play in a Floodlit Trophy final, as the conditions and Leigh's dreadnought defence obliterated any possibility of tries being scored and Wigan went out 10–2. Former Wigan kicker Laurie Gilfedder landed three penalties, one from 52 yards, and a drop-goal. Alex Murphy dropped another goal and was cautioned twice by Eric Clay, who presided over 36 scrums and awarded 25 penalties. History was made as the game was the first event from the north of England to be televised live in colour.

Three days before Christmas Wigan suffered a shock 9–2 defeat at Rochdale, which the *Wigan Observer* described as "an appalling failure". However, it exonerated Billy who "stopped Cook with a murderous tackle under the posts" and almost scored in the dying minutes. Boxing Day brought another defeat, 16–10 at home to St Helens. Billy played a big part in creating a try for Colin Tyrer, which allowed Wigan to lead 5–3 for 28 minutes before Saints piled up 13 points in seven minutes.

The New Year dawned with Wigan standing sixth in the league, behind Bradford Northern, Leeds, Hull KR, Halifax and St Helens. They had pulled off excellent home wins against local rivals Leigh and Warrington. For their 8–4 success against Leigh they were indebted to the old firm of Ashton and Boston. Referee Fred Lindop issued 28 penalties and oversaw 36 scrums in another game beset by dreadful conditions, including a hail storm. Both tries came in the first half. In the 18th minute Billy wandered unnoticed to the left touch-line, took a pass and powered over past a bemused defence. Four minutes before half-time Cliff and David Hill combined to get Ashton moving and Eric bluffed three men into believing he was going to pass to Billy on his outside before streaking through for a classic touchdown. The 11–2 New Year's Day victory over Warrington was highlighted by the debut of another Welshman, Pontypool paratrooper, Steve Price, who played on the left wing and claimed a try.

Wigan did not play for three weeks because of the winter weather, but Billy still found himself on the front page of the *Wigan Observer* on 5 January. He and 52 year-old football star Sir Stanley Matthews were pictured together under the headline "Kings of the Wings". The *Observer* had arranged the meeting in the Springfield Park boardroom on New Year's Day just before Stan's team Port Vale were due to play Wigan Athletic and Billy had to dash off to play against Warrington. Compared to Stan, 33 year-old Billy must have felt like a spring chicken. The *Observer* commented: "No introductions were necessary. Sir Stanley apologised profusely for keeping Billy waiting, shared a few quiet words and then posed for Ian Lambert's exclusive picture. 'All the best, Stan', said Billy as he left. 'Good luck, Billy', said Sir Stanley. An historic meeting was over." The article concluded: "A handshake that spans two worlds, two eras, two of the most glorious careers in the histories of their respective sports... Sir Stanley Matthews, the soccer wingman supreme, meets Billy Boston, one of the all-time greats of Rugby League." Athletic and Port Vale drew 3–3 before a crowd of 1,700, by the way, while 13,493 watched Billy at Central Park. Brian McTigue said a few months later: "I shall always treasure as a keepsake the *Wigan Observer* photograph of Billy shaking hands with Sir Stanley Matthews. Here were two really great sportsmen side by side."

Two days after losing 6–2 at Whitehaven on 20 January, when Eric Clay disallowed a try from Billy after he played the ball to himself, Wigan crushed Oldham 39–3 at Central Park. Billy won the man-of-the-match award and generally caused havoc among the ranks of the Roughyeds. He scored an epic try after Ashton intercepted deep in Wigan's half. Receiving the centre's pass about 45 yards out, Billy pulled clear of McCourt, Buckley and Warburton to gain a try which registered high on the tingle factor scale. Five days later Wigan accounted for Widnes 19–7 at Central Park, owing much to Fogerty's finesse and Laughton's fire, but just as much to "the ageless Boston at his most uncompromising best", according to John Benn. In the 71st minute, after having two tries disallowed, "From Laughton's break and Ashton's pass he thundered 35 yards, ignoring three attempted tackles, pulled his 'back leg' out of the last forlorn challenge and reached over for his try".

The 1968 Challenge Cup trail opened on 3 February, when Wigan made the arduous trip to play Hull at The Boulevard. Five of the Wigan players were probably not really fit to play and Billy was still recovering from the 'flu and recurrent chest trouble in the week leading up to the Cup-tie. Still he took the field and as John Benn reported, "Boston, bless his massive heart, was in magnificent fettle". Led superbly by Ashton, Wigan played a wonderfully disciplined game to win 10–3. Francis and Parr scored tries and Tyrer and Ashton notched a goal each. Billy damaged his right index finger, but lasted the 80 minutes.

On Wednesday 14 February Billy scored the last hat-trick of his career in a 35–7 success against Blackpool Borough. Eric Ashton, playing at full-back, also scored a hat-trick and booted four goals. In a strange but wonderful piece of symmetry, it was also Eric's last hat-trick for Wigan – his 10th. Eric created two of Billy's tries and with a bit more luck Billy might have had five. It was a different story three days later at Workington when Wigan went down 13–2, their fifth consecutive defeat in Cumberland. Neither Billy nor Bill Francis saw the ball for practically the whole game.

There certainly needed to be a big improvement for the following Saturday, when Wigan trekked to Leigh for the second round of the Challenge Cup. The game was an all-ticket affair which rapidly sold out, Wigan returning just two of their allotted 7,000 tickets. The tie proved a true anticlimax. Alex Murphy did not turn out for Leigh, because of a suspected heart problem, and Wigan chalked up an easy 20–2 victory. The *Wigan Observer* complained, "In the event this Cup-tie was a beef-burger without mustard". It was a good day for Danny Gardiner, who claimed his first try since August 1965, but Billy had to be helped from the field in the last minute with a painful rib injury.

The injury kept Billy out of two games, but he was declared fit for Wigan's third round cup tie at Keighley on 16 March. Lawkholme Lane was bursting at the seams with a crowd of 13,320, which more than doubled the ground's record for receipts, paying £3,385. The crowd got "a moderate match" for their money and some "provocative refereeing" from Joe Manley, according to the *Wigan Observer*, which also complained that the scrums were a farce, Keighley were constantly offside and there was plenty of "Keighley fist". By half-time Wigan led 8–2, two wonderful tries having fallen to Francis and David Hill. Billy settled the tie in the 69th minute. A 10-yard scrum was formed and Frank Parr wafted down the blind-side with Billy in tow. The try was inevitable as Billy took Moulding, Aspinall and Jefferson over with him to finish the scoring at 11–2. Parr and Billy repeated the move with equal success in Wigan's following game, a 23–14 home win against Liverpool City, when Bill Francis bagged four tries. It was, however, a miraculous 67th minute tackle by Billy on City's winger Arthur Johnson, which won the match for Wigan as Liverpool came within a whisker of winning. With the semi-finals of the Challenge Cup looming Wigan went to Salford and lost a thrilling seesaw of a match 15–13, losing for the first time in six games.

They were still confident of victory over table-topping Leeds, however, in the semi-final at Swinton on 6 April. A victory would take Billy and Eric to their seventh Wembley final and history indicated that Wigan had won all the semi-finals they had played at Swinton since the war. On the other hand, Wigan were facing a genuinely outstanding team, which had won its last 16 games. The weather was perfect and 30,000 fans anticipated a rare struggle. A Colin Tyrer penalty goal after 12 minutes was cancelled out by one from Bev Risman on the quarter hour to lock the score at 2–2. Billy was much in evidence in the opening half. Early on he clattered into Leeds centre Syd Hynes, giving him a real shaking, and was striding clear 30 yards out after great play from Fogerty and Lyon, only to be recalled for a forward pass. After 30 minutes Billy went for an interception near half-way but missed it by a whisker. John Atkinson took full advantage and scored a super try, which Risman converted to give Leeds a 7–2 lead.

Two minutes before half-time Ashton sent Billy hurtling through 30 yards out. He charged into a barrier of Loiners and took three defenders over the line for what he thought to be a perfectly valid try. Referee Fred Lindop disagreed. Jack Bentley wrote in the *Daily Express:* "That was the closest Wigan got to Wembley this year. Afterwards winger Billy swore solemnly that he had scored. 'It doesn't matter to me. I've been to Wembley. But I know I've scored. I put that ball down, they pulled me to one side, and I looked up to see the referee waving his hands to disallow it. The better team won and good luck to them. But things like that upset a team. They knock you down and give the opposition a boost'. Referee Lindop was bang on the spot having circled into it as Boston bullocked his way through a wall of Leeds flesh. 'Billy dropped the ball the last nine inches before he touched it down. Wigan can blame me, but that's my job', said Fred".

That was basically the end of Wigan's challenge. Leeds played exceptional rugby league in the second half and Wigan had no answers to the questions they posed. The final score of 25–4 may have flattered Leeds a little, but Wigan had been comprehensively whacked. There was to be no seventh Wembley for Billy.

The Easter programme brought more disappointment for Wigan supporters. A 24–13 reverse at St Helens on Good Friday could have been heavier. Tom van Vollenhoven had a lovely afternoon, racing over for three tries and picking up £308 from a half-time collection for his testimonial. The following afternoon brought a 13–6 defeat at Warrington as Wigan gradually fell down the top 16 pecking order.

Even after four consecutive defeats there were still almost 12,000 spectators at Wigan for the Easter Monday clash with Salford. Billy had missed the game at Warrington two days earlier, but if that absence had disappointed his fans, they were in even greater distress and shock shortly before the Salford game kicked off. Ken Senior, Wigan's secretary, addressed the crowd over the tannoy system with the following statement: "It was only this morning that we learned officially that Billy Boston has decided to retire. Today sees him play his last game for Wigan at Central Park". Billy was given the captaincy and led the team out for his last first class game at Central Park in Wigan's recently adopted change colours of all white. It was a glorious afternoon as far as the weather was concerned and Wigan got the result they wanted. "But", said John Benn in the *Wigan Observer*, "the farewell 'blockbuster'... never came. The fans had to be satisfied with one link-up with Ashton, one storming run, and a handful of murderous smother tackles". Salford gave Wigan plenty of trouble, were level at 10–10 at half-time and were only finally subdued by a 10-point burst in the last seven minutes which gave Billy's side a 25–14 victory. At the close of the game both teams queued to shake Billy's hand and hundreds of youngsters flocked on to the field to slap his back or cadge his autograph.

Four days later Jack Winstanley wrote a special article for the *Wigan Observer* saying: "So Billy Boston has decided to call it a day, victim of the inevitable, creeping paralysis called age. Now the Kop choir at Central Park will really have to raise its voice – to fill the sound gap, which his departure will leave on the stands and the terraces of rugby league's most famous ground. It may well need the impact of Boston's retirement to make those who run Wigan Rugby Football Club Limited realise to the full what a golden asset he has been during the last 15 years. I am only sorry Billy Boston didn't choose to bow out in a rather grander manner. I dropped out of the Rugby League scene two seasons ago and I dearly would have liked to have gone back to Central Park to bid farewell to the greatest winger I ever saw. So too, I fancy, would thousands of other people."

Billy was not quite finished yet. Wigan had finished 11th in the league and qualified for the top 16 play-offs. By the quirkiness of the system they could still become champions, but they would have to do it the hard way, with three away ties before the Championship Final. It was certainly a long shot, but Halifax had done it from seventh in 1964–65 and Dewsbury would from eighth in 1972–73. In the event Billy's finale with Wigan became a kind of triumphal procession through the West Riding of Yorkshire.

First up on Saturday 20 April was a last trip to Odsal Stadium, scene of his 1956 nightmare. Sixth placed Bradford Northern played like chumps and Wigan won as they pleased 28–8. The nearest Billy came to a try was soon after half-time, when he was energetically bundled into touch a foot or so from the Bradford goal-line. He had been given a standing ovation at half-time and he was called up "amid thunderous applause" to convert the last two Wigan tries, which he duly did. A police escort was required to clear his way back up the slope at the final whistle, as both sets of fans acclaimed him all the way back to Odsal Top, while some disenchanted Bradford supporters also shouted in a sort of backhanded compliment, "Rubbish, Northern. It's you shower who ought to retire!"

Four days later the quarter-finals presented a trip to Leeds, who had finished seven points clear of Wakefield Trinity, Hull KR and St Helens at the top of the table. Leeds were hoping to do the League and Cup double, while Wigan were keen to exact revenge for their dismissal from the Cup by Leeds just 18 days earlier. It proved a tight struggle. Wigan held the whip hand in the first half and took a 9–2 lead when Billy went in at the corner after a decidedly forward-looking pass from Ashton. Referee Sam Shepherd might have been unpopular with the Headingley crowd for that decision, but he was equally annoying to the Wigan fans in disallowing three Wigan tries, including two by Billy, both for forward passes. Billy was so angry at the second incident that he hurled the ball into the perimeter wall. Leeds made a great rally in the second half and pulled back to 9–7, but with only four minutes remaining Colin Tyrer kicked his fourth penalty goal. Wigan won 11–7 and Billy's progress through Yorkshire continued.

The semi-final, Wigan's third game in a week, took them to Belle Vue on 27 April. Second-placed Wakefield Trinity were also in with a chance of achieving the double and Wigan must have been hoping that Wembleyitis had set in. Unfortunately for Wigan it had not. They got all the bad breaks, lost hooker Colin Clarke with a suspected broken leg just before half-time and referee Dickie Thomas seemed ill-disposed to them, whenever there was a 50–50 decision. It did not help that Trinity were in such good form either. A crowd of 13,318 and countless television viewers saw Trinity win 26–9 to end Billy's final fling with Wigan. Jack Nott wrote in the *News of the World:* "The final verse is written of the Ballad of Bill Boston. Here at Wakefield the curtain was rung down not only on the mighty Wigan revival but on 'Bomber' Bill too... Alas for Boston, the film star flourish was denied him in this his last game. For Ken Batty and Gert Coetzer stayed closer to him than a Siamese twin." At the final whistle thousands poured on to the pitch as a subdued and emotional Billy tried to leave the field. The *Wigan Observer* noted: "Billy was in tears when Trinity skipper Harold Poynton led the farewell cheers and presented him with the match ball, a last memento for his souvenir collection."

So that was that. Fifteen years for Wigan, 487 games, 478 tries, 1,448 points, exciting times, depressing times, elation, adulation, friendship, celebrations, disappointments, memories.

It was not quite over, however. Great Britain were due to visit Australia for the World Cup in the summer and were playing a series of warm-up games, the last of which was at Halifax on 3 May. RFL Secretary Bill Fallowfield invited Billy to play on the right wing for Great Britain. Billy said: "I certainly never thought I would be asked to play for a Great Britain side again. It is a very nice gesture and a great compliment, which I really appreciate." However, Billy had broken his left thumb against Wakefield and was unable to play. The invitation was redirected to his great rival Tom van Vollenhoven, who played and scored a hat-trick in Great Britain's 25–2 success. Voll had also played his last game for St Helens at the same time as Billy in the other Championship semi-final at Hull KR.

Wigan fans had not had the chance to say good-bye properly to their favourite son. So the club applied to the RFL to stage a testimonial match for him at Central Park and permission was granted, provided that Billy gave a written undertaking that it would be his last appearance. As he was to receive the gate takings, as part of what amounted to a second testimonial, a RFL bye-law would have prevented him playing professionally again. The game was fixed for the evening of Friday 26 July and Eric Ashton was the match organiser. Originally a Welsh XIII was to be fielded against Wigan, but the St Helens board kyboshed that idea the week before the game by refusing permission for eight of their players to participate because of the risk of injury so close to the start of the new season. Instead the game was played between Billy Boston's XIII and a Select XIII. Naturally, Billy's team sported cherry and white hoops, while the Select XIII played in blue jerseys. The players were insured for £4,000 each and their total value on the transfer market was computed to be £150,000. A crowd of 9,326 turned up to witness a game played, according to John Benn, "in a wave of unashamed nostalgia and sentiment". The teams were:

*Boston's XIII:* Ashton, Boston, D Stephens (Castleford), Glover (Warrington), Francis, C. Hill, Jackson, J. Stephens, Kemel (Widnes), Fletcher (Oldham), Fogerty, Brady (Warrington), Brennan (Salford)
Substitutes: Ashurst, Williams (Swinton), Mills
*Select XIII:* Dutton (Widnes), Sullivan (Hull), Lewis (Leigh), Rowe, Freeman (Halifax), Watkins (Salford), Prosser (Salford), Halliwell (Salford), Dickens (Blackpool), Webb, Standing, Lyon, Dixon (Halifax).
Substitutes: Boyd, O'Loughlin

Denis (D.T.H.) Davies had the honour of refereeing Billy's Central Park finale and the Select XIII won 58–47 in game that resembled tick and pass rather than rugby league, but no one complained. Billy scored three tries and kicked a goal, much to the delight of his admirers. Fellow Cardiffian Clive Sullivan, recently returned from the World Cup, was the star of the show with five tries and Ray Dutton kicked 11 goals. Appropriately, Billy's first try was provided for him by Eric Ashton, following a break by Geoff Fletcher, and John Benn noted: "There were no 'baddies' to mar the big feature and not a single blue-jerseyed Select player was mean enough to attempt to impede his progress as he rounded unopposed for a try behind the posts. His second was much more like the real thing as he ripped infield and surged through four ineffective tackles for the touchdown. But the wing dreadnought who has scored more 'impossible' tries than anyone I have been privileged to see, bowed out with a planned 'thanks-for-the-memory' try conveniently scored right on time. Seventeen minutes from the end, Billy had come off to give Bill Ashurst a run out. But at the last scrum, Ashton strolled off, signalled to Billy that his final cue-call was due. And straight from the scrum, he started and finished the move, taking the final pass from Swinton's Graham Williams, for his last try at Central Park. It surely was not an accident that the touchdown was only a few feet from the tunnel!"

Nearing the end – playing for Wigan in 1968.

Predictably, Billy had spent those 17 minutes off the field in the Wigan dug-out signing autographs for scores of boys and girls, who probably already had them several times over. When Mr Davies blew the final whistle an epoch had ended. John Benn commented: "As a horde of kids hared across the unblemished 'bowling green' turf to mob him and beg just one more autograph, Billy disappeared up the tunnel for the last time... 'King' Billy, undisputed all-time great, had abdicated."

On the following Monday there was a testimonial concert at the plush new Central Park Social Club. The admission was 10 shillings (50p), more than twice as much as admission to a match, but the place was packed to the rafters. Billy's long-time friend and admirer Georgie Fame, one of Britain's top recording stars of the swinging sixties, topped the bill. His fee was Billy's number two jersey from the testimonial match.

Six months later, on 29 January, 1969, Billy's second testimonial climaxed in a farewell night at Wigan's *King of Clubs*.

Among the guests were the captains of the Leigh, St Helens, Warrington and Widnes clubs and the Liverpool and England soccer star Roger Hunt. However, the most important and, to Billy, the most unexpected guest was his mother Nellie. The *Lancashire Evening News & Chronicle* had arranged for her to travel from Wales and her overnight stay at a local hotel had been kept secret – she had even been registered under a false name, so that no Wigan fan could put two and two together and leak the news to Billy. Nellie received a tremendous ovation and told the press later: "I never anticipated anything like this. I haven't been to Wigan for six years through ill-health, but I think it's marvellous the way Lancashire people have responded to Billy."

Councillor John Hitchmough, the Mayor of Wigan, presented a cheque to Billy as the proceeds of his second testimonial. The figure was almost double that for his first testimonial and easily broke the Wigan record, previously established for Eric Ashton's testimonial. Billy had his own presentations to make, a sign of his well-known generosity. Among them he gave a beautifully inscribed cup to his partner in crime Eric Ashton, which read, "To Eric, from Billy-B with happy memories". Leigh-born Georgie Fame, an avid bowls player, received an inscribed set of specially commissioned Crown Green bowls. Together Billy and Georgie presented a new trophy to be competed for annually by schools in Wigan and Leigh – the Boston-Fame Cup.

## 1967–68

Wigan finished 11th in the League: P34, W21, L13, For 602, Against 350
Boston scored 16 tries and 2 goals for Wigan

| Date | Opponent | Score | Boston | Crowd | |
|---|---|---|---|---|---|
| 19 August | **Salford** | 14–18 | dnp | 10,592 | LC1 |
| 23 August | Liverpool City | 16–7 | dnp | 1,500 | |
| 26 August | **Bramley** | 53–8 | dnp | 5,914 | |
| 28 August | Leigh | 9–12 | dnp | 10,300 | |
| 2 September | **Swinton** | 12–15 | dnp | 9,215 | |
| 9 September | Dewsbury | 10–11 | dnp | 4,300 | |
| 16 September | Blackpool B | 29–2 | dnp | 3,000 | |
| 19 September | Widnes | 5–24 | dnp | 6,000 | |
| 23 September | **Barrow** | 22–12 | dnp | 6,613 | |
| 30 September | Oldham | 17–13 | dnp | 5,053 | |
| 2 October | **Widnes** | 32–6 | dnp | 9,585 | FT1 |
| 9 October | **Batley** | 35–5 | 3T | 9,164 | |
| 13 October | **Australians** | 12–6 | | 22,779 | Tour |
| 21 October | **Workington T** | 18–13 | 1T | 11,705 | |
| 28 October | Swinton | 13–11 | dnp | 6,300 | |
| 4 November | Huddersfield | 7–14 | | 4,585 | |
| 11 November | **Rochdale H** | 30–0 | 2T | 5,932 | |
| 18 November | Bramley | 10–5 | dnp | 2,200 | |
| 22 November | St Helens | 22–11 | 1T | 15,004 | FT2 |
| 24 November | **Dewsbury** | 16–20 | dnp | 7,410 | |
| 1 December | **Whitehaven** | 31–7 | dnp | 6,239 | |
| 5 December | Leigh | 2–10 | | 11,000 | FT SF (at St Helens) |
| 13 December | **Batley+** | 11–4 | dnp | 4,934 | |
| 22 December | Rochdale H | 2–9 | | 2,425 | |
| 26 December | **St Helens** | 10–16 | | 22,069 | |
| 30 December | **Leigh** | 8–4 | 1T | 15,202 | |
| 1 January | **Warrington** | 11–2 | | 13,493 | |
| 20 January | Whitehaven | 2–6 | | 1,200 | |
| 22 January | **Oldham** | 39–3 | 1T | 8,782 | |
| 27 January | **Widnes** | 19–7 | 1T | 9,049 | |
| 3 February | Hull | 10–3 | | 9,600 | Cup 1 |
| 14 February | **Blackpool B** | 35–7 | 3T | 6,728 | |
| 17 February | Workington T | 2–13 | | 2,741 | |
| 24 February | Leigh | 20–2 | | 22,660 | Cup 2 |
| 1 March | Barrow | 19–12 | dnp | 4,560 | |
| 9 March | **Huddersfield** | 31–8 | dnp | 8,330 | |
| 16 March | Keighley | 11–2 | 1T | 13,320 | Cup 3 |
| 25 March | **Liverpool City** | 23–14 | 1T | 6,000 | |
| 29 March | Salford | 13–15 | | 10,000 | |
| 6 April | Leeds | 4–25 | | 30,058 | Cup SF (at Swinton) |
| 12 April | St Helens | 13–24 | | 17,513 | |
| 13 April | Warrington | 6–13 | dnp | 6,588 | |
| 15 April | **Salford** | 25–14 | | 11,854 | |
| 20 April | Bradford N | 28–8 | 2G | 12,783 | CH 1 |
| 24 April | Leeds | 11–7 | 1T | 15,861 | CH 2 |
| 27 April | Wakefield T | 9–26 | | 13,318 | CH SF |

+ Away fixture switched to Wigan

# 20.  1969–70 Blackpool Borough

After 18 months in retirement, Billy decided to play rugby league again. Joan says it was because he was bored! The announcement of his return to action came on 29 November, 1969, when the press reported that he was to join Blackpool Borough after considering offers from Oldham and Warrington. Billy said he would need another month to get fit. In the meantime Billy had sought and received permission from the Rugby League Management Committee to resume playing despite the complication presented by his receipt of a second testimonial.

George Lunn, the Blackpool secretary, observed in the *Rugby Leaguer:* "There are two schools of thought about Boston. Some supporters feel the Boro have too many 'veterans' in the team and it is a short-sighted policy bringing in yet another. On the other hand there are those who point out that Boston's power and experience could possibly win the Boro more matches because there is a lack of power near the line. Just now Boro need wins to revive their spirits."

Blackpool certainly did need wins. When Billy made his debut they had only three league victories to their credit in 18 matches and only Huyton were below them in the table. The club had just experienced its worst year since its foundation in 1954. Matters were so dire that the club was not even running an 'A' team. Billy might have looked with envious interest at how Wigan were doing. His old side were fifth in the league, had just lost to Leigh in the final of the BBC2 Floodlit Trophy and were threatening to bring back a taste of the good old days to Central Park. There was, however, no shortage of familiar faces at Borough Park, which down the years had become a home from home for past Wigan players. Keith Holden was the player-coach and among Billy's new team-mates were Terry Entwistle and Ray Ashby, while Joe Egan's son, Joe junior, was the hooker. In the recent past Brian McTigue, Dave Bolton and Kia Bose had also turned out for Blackpool.

Blackpool Borough was a culture shock for Billy. He recalls: "At Wigan I was used to going down to Central Park and all my kit would be laid out and in order. My boots were cleaned and all the playing gear had been washed and ironed. Everything was done for the players in that respect. When I went to Blackpool Joan was ready to throw me out of the house. All the muddy and torn kit had to be brought home. The players were expected to sort it out themselves. I suppose we didn't know we had been born at Wigan!

I did not drive in those days, but travelled to and from Blackpool by car with some of the other lads from Wigan. Soon after I joined Borough we stopped for a drink on the way back from training and one player said, 'I got paid for the Whitehaven match'. Another said, 'Yes, and I got paid for the Huyton game' and someone else chirped, 'I finally got paid for the Huddersfield game'. I thought that was funny because some of those games must have been played six weeks ago and they were only getting paid now. I decided I wasn't having any of that and went to see the secretary and told him I wanted to be paid on time, every week. Still, I enjoyed my time with Blackpool. It was different from Wigan – not as serious."

Billy made his debut for Blackpool on the afternoon of Friday 26 December 1969 in a home fixture against Rochdale Hornets. The programme notes for the game said: "Billy is now 35 years of age – the same age as Henry Cooper (and nobody can lick **him** says Billy). Having retired officially from the game at the end of season 1967–68, Billy once again feels the urge to return, and hopes that for a couple of seasons he can do the Boro a power of good. Assuming all goes well, Billy should be fully match fit by the time the cup ties come around, and if he can only help the lads to have a bit of a run in the Cup and to be pressing for promotion next season his signing will have been well worthwhile".

Making his Blackpool debut on the left wing was another former Great Britain star John Stopford, of Swinton fame, who had also come out of retirement. Their signings certainly provoked interest among the latent support for rugby league in Blackpool. Borough's previous home game against Workington Town had drawn an attendance of just 250. Billy's debut attracted the club's best crowd of the season – 3,447. The teams were:

*Blackpool Borough:* Curry, Boston, Colloby, Ashby, Stopford, Entwistle, Darbyshire, Goddard, Egan, Watson, Holden, D. Walker, Farrell.
Substitutes: Hall, Fairhurst
*Rochdale Hornets:* Chamberlain, Dolly, Corcoran, Taylor, Pimblett, Tees, Rabbitt, Brown, Clarke, Snape, Murray, Hodkinson, Delooze
Substitutes: Crowther, Mooney

Billy was used to scoring tries against the Hornets, having piled up 35 in 23 appearances against them for Wigan. He added another from a short, characteristically block-busting run but had to go looking for action, as Borough found it almost impossible to get the ball to their wings. John Stopford had an unfortunate beginning with Blackpool as he collided with a team-mate and had to have nine stitches in a cut caused by their clash. By half-time Hornets had established a 13–0 lead and ran out winners by 20–6, second-rower Don Walker scoring Borough's other try. It had been one of Borough's worst displays of the season. Nor would Billy's Boxing Day have been brightened up when he heard of Wigan's unbelievable 53–11 humiliation at the hands of St Helens at Central Park.

Just how precarious things were at Blackpool was shown when there were just a handful of players at the training session prior to their New Year's Day fixture at Salford. On match day only 12 players were available and three amateurs were drafted in to make up the numbers, Billy being one of the absentees with a dose of 'flu. A 36–14 defeat was probably a better than expected outcome. Billy was back for the next game, a home encounter with Hunslet on Sunday 11 January. After turning round 5–4 down, Blackpool performed heroically in dreadful conditions to win 9–5. Billy was the match-winner with a storming try in which he beat four men. Unfortunately there were only 450 spectators to witness it. Billy was a try-scorer for his third consecutive match in a close run affair at Rochdale on 24 January, when Borough led for an hour before succumbing 14–8.

Borough had entered on a nine-match losing run, an experience Billy had never suffered at Wigan. He missed several of those defeats, but became accustomed to losing pay and not seeing the ball. The biggest game Billy played for Blackpool was their first round Challenge Cup tie at Oldham on 7 February. Oldham were a couple of places above Borough in the league so it was not a lost cause. Watersheddings was at its worst and the playing conditions were terrible. However, Blackpool put up a great show only to lose 5–0. Welsh winger Mike Elliott claimed the game's only try in the first half, while Oldham's other winger Phil Larder booted the only goal of the game in the second half. It was Billy's last appearance in the Challenge Cup and a far cry from the glamour of Wembley.

Billy's next game a month later saw Blackpool defeated 15–4 by Bramley at Borough Park before a crowd of only 200, the lowest before which he had ever played in senior rugby league. Four days later he had another unwelcome experience when Borough went down 50–0 at Warrington, the first and only time he had been in a side that conceded a half-century. To their credit, Borough bounced back and with a patched-up team pushed Swinton to the limit before going down 20–16 on 14 March. Billy was among the try-scorers but suffered bruised ribs, which caused him to miss five matches. He returned to the fray for the last game of the season on 4 April, scoring his fifth try for the club, when Borough defeated Batley 19–9. The victory was not enough to raise Blackpool from the bottom of the league. They took the wooden spoon with a record of six wins and 28 defeats, exactly the same as Oldham, but with a much worse points average. If he wanted a reminder of the good old days, Wigan provided it by winning the Lancashire League Championship and reaching Wembley, where they lost a controversial final to Castleford.

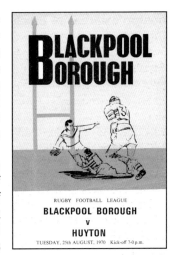

RUGBY FOOTBALL LEAGUE

**BLACKPOOL BOROUGH**

v

**HUYTON**

TUESDAY, 25th AUGUST, 1970   Kick-off 7-0 p.m.

There was surprise that Billy carried on at Blackpool for the 1970–71 season. George Lunn wrote in the *Rugby Leaguer* of 19 August 1970: "Great news for all rugby league fans, one of the game's outstanding personalities, Billy Boston, will be back with the Boro to delight spectators again. He has trained nearly all summer and is fitter than for a long time. He has tackled all the training sessions under Johnny Stopford like a youngster starting out on his career. Yes, Billy B will be back with a bounce."

John Stopford had taken over as player-coach from Keith Holden, who remained as a player. Hopes were high that Borough would rise up the table but they made a bad start to the season, losing 30–0 at Workington Town on 22 August. Three days later they lost 10–5 at home to Huyton, when Billy played in the second-row. It proved to be Billy's last game as a professional rugby league player. The teams for his finale were:

*Blackpool Borough:* Entwistle, Johnson, Holden, Stopford, Colloby, Cassidy, Bishop, Wilkinson, Martland, Shaw, Hall, Boston, Farrell
Substitutes: Fairhurst, P Walker
*Huyton:* Westhead, Leatherbarrow, Bright, Catterall, McDonnell, McGillicuddy, Smith, Payne, Stevens, Wright, Bonser, Wills, Davies
Substitutes: Harrison, Bevan

It was the end of a monumental career.

## Boston's career at Blackpool Borough

### Season 1969-70

| Date | Opponent | Score | Boston | Crowd | |
|------|----------|-------|--------|-------|---|
| 26 December | **Rochdale H** | 6–20 | 1T | 3,447 | |
| 11 January | **Hunslet** | 9– 5 | 1T | 425 | |
| 24 January | Rochdale H | 8–14 | 1T | 1,531 | |
| 1 February | Huddersfield | 10–18 | | 2,242 | |
| 7 February | Oldham | 0–5 | | 2,800 | Cup 1 |
| 7 March | **Bramley** | 4–15 | | 200 | |
| 11 March | Warrington+ | 0–50 | | 2,042 | |
| 14 March | **Swinton** | 16–20 | 1T | 950 | |
| 4 April | **Batley** | 19– 9 | 1T | 500 | |

+ Home fixture switched to Warrington

### Season 1970-71

| Date | Opponent | Score | Boston | Crowd |
|------|----------|-------|--------|-------|
| 22 August | Workington T | 0–30 | | 1,617 |
| 25 August | **Huyton** | 5–10 | | 500 |

All Billy's appearances for Blackpool Borough were as a right-winger, except for his last game against Huyton, when he played in the second-row.

# 21. Retirement

Billy's playing days ended a few weeks after his 36th birthday and, barring the odd testimonial or charity game, he never troubled the scorers again. Nor did he take to coaching. Many former great players at least have a dabble at coaching before they decide that it is not for them, but Billy appears never to have been tempted.

Billy and Joan took over the licence of The Griffin in Standishgate, a pub within a few drop kicks of Central Park. They reigned there from 1982 to 1995 before retiring. The Griffin became a popular meeting place for rugby league fans and helped to keep Billy well and truly in the public eye and in the heart of the community. Joan says: "There was never any trouble at The Griffin and it was a real home for us. They built it around the same time as Central Park and originally it had a thatched roof." It was at The Griffin that Billy had his nearest brush with active involvement with the game. In 1988 a group of his customers decided to form a team and were admitted to the Wigan Amateur Rugby League under the title of Griffin Dragons, playing successfully for several years.

Although Billy was not directly involved in playing or administering the game, rugby league never forgot him and the past quarter of a century has seen him honoured time and again both in League land and Wales. For example, in August 1984 he was invited to the Exchange Buildings in Butetown to receive one of 100 scrolls presented to 100 of the district's successful sportsmen and women, an event which was part of the Butetown Carnival. Fellow rugby league wingers Clive Sullivan and Frank Wilson also received scrolls, while a special tribute was paid to the founders of Billy's old club, Cardiff IAC. Many such similar functions meant that Billy was unlikely to lose touch with his family roots, as trips to Wales were frequent.

In October 1988 Billy received rugby league's ultimate accolade when he was one of nine inaugural inductees to the Rugby League Hall of Fame. Remarkably, two other Cardiffians, Jim Sullivan and Gus Risman, were among the nine, along with Billy Batten, Brian Bevan, Alex Murphy, Jonty Parkin, Albert Rosenfeld and Harold Wagstaff. In the intervening years the Hall of Fame has admitted another eight players – Neil Fox in 1989, Vince Karalius, Tom van Vollenhoven and Roger Millward in 2000, and Eric Ashton, Douglas Clark, Ellery Hanley and Martin Hodgson in 2005.

Barely four months after his elevation to the Rugby League Hall of Fame Billy received another tremendous honour. On 3 February 1989 he opened the Welsh Sports Hall of Fame at the new South Glamorgan County Council headquarters at Cardiff Bay's Atlantic Wharf. The Council leader Lord Brooks of Tremorfa unveiled a Roll of Honour containing the names of 10 of Wales's greatest sportsmen and women. Billy's was first on the list. His nine peers were Lynn Davies (Athletics), Jim Driscoll (Boxing), Ken Jones (Rugby Union), Sir Harry Llewellyn (Equestrian), Billy Meredith (Association Football), Sheila Morrow (Hockey), Jack Peterson (Boxing), Dai Rees (Golf) and Kirsty Wade (Athletics). The citation for the Roll of Honour reads, "Inclusion in the Roll of Honour is for those people who, by their achievement and by their example and conduct, in and beyond the sporting arena, have brought distinction to themselves and credit to Wales". Billy certainly fulfilled the criteria.

He told the *South Wales Echo* he had one regret: "All I have achieved in rugby league I would have given over for just one Welsh cap. That was my biggest ambition. I always wanted to play for Wales and I went to Neath because Cardiff didn't want to know me but it's worked out for the best. There was a lot of colour prejudice at the time and I don't think

Angela, Joan, Billy, Stephen, Karen and Christine outside Buckingham Palace
after Billy received the MBE. Lisa was missing as she was ill.

Mine host at The Griffin

Stephen, Karen, Christine, Lisa and Angela in the 1960s.

A more recent picture: Karen, Lisa, Stephen, Christine, Angela.

The Welsh Sports Hall of Fame reunited Billy with his 1965 Wembley jersey. They promptly took it back in order to display it in their historic collection. Billy had given it away years before.

Cardiff International Athletic Club reunion 23 June 1989. Gerald Ernest, Sammy John, Alec Neil, Arthur Duarte, Billy, Wilf Rogers, George Ernest.

I would ever have played for Wales in those days. I never wanted to sign for rugby league, but I saw the doors weren't open here and there were no signs I would ever get anything". Without a trace of bitterness, according to the *Echo*, Billy added: "I might have been born in Cardiff but I have never been offered a ticket to watch Wales. It's like trying to get into the Kremlin. But things are changing to the good. It should be better for other people who make the grade. I hope there's a lot of people from the Docks that make it and don't have the obstacles I had to face."

Billy was the first of nine rugby league players to be elevated to the Welsh Sports Hall of Fame, an indication that barriers were indeed being broken in the Welsh sporting establishment's attitude to that other game. Billy has been followed into the Welsh Sports Hall of Fame by Jim Sullivan in 1992, Lewis Jones in 1998, Gus Risman in 2000, Jonathan Davies and Willie Davies in 2003, Trevor Foster in 2004 and Clive Sullivan in 2009.

In 1995, to celebrate the centenary of rugby league, *Open Rugby* magazine selected a Great Britain Immortals XIII covering the whole history of the game. Billy won the right wing spot in the following side: Jim Sullivan, Billy Boston, Harold Wagstaff, Neil Fox, Mick Sullivan, Roger Millward, Alex Murphy, Alan Prescott, Joe Egan, Brian McTigue, Martin Hodgson, Dick Huddart and Ellery Hanley.

In February 1996, soon after Billy retired from The Griffin, he was hit by a car, which had been stolen. He was thrown in the air and received multiple injuries, including a broken right femur. Doctors told him that only his remarkable strength had seen him through.

On Wednesday 24 July, 1996, a few months after the car incident, Billy and Joan attended an Investiture at Buckingham Palace, where Billy received the MBE from the Queen. The Investiture began at 11 in the morning and the programme explained that awards for "admission to the Order of the British Empire [are] for either meritorious military service or civilian service to the Crown". Billy's citation was "for services to the Community in Wigan". Although the award was one of the highlights of his life it still rankles a little with Billy that no mention of his involvement with rugby league was included. All the other rugby league players, who have been similarly honoured, received their award "for services to rugby league". There was, however, another who did not - Billy's compatriot, that splendid man of the people, Trevor Foster, who earned his MBE "for services to the Community in Bradford". In that respect it is hard to imagine Billy in better company.

Apart from Joan, only two guests were allowed to accompany Billy into Buckingham Palace for the ceremony. Having five children was therefore a problem. Lisa was poorly in hospital but the remaining four drew lots for the privilege and Karen and Stephen won. Angela and Christine went to London with the family but had to remain outside the Palace. Joan recalls: "Bill was so nervous he ended up soaking wet with sweat. Karen and I left him briefly to have a nosey in the Palace toilets, as anyone would! When we had finished we could not find Bill anywhere. A photographer approached us and said, 'I am supposed to take a photograph of Mr Boston and his family. Where is he?' We couldn't tell him, of course. We searched and searched and eventually found him outside Buckingham Palace having a smoke. Once anyone leaves the Palace gates, they are not allowed back in. So we never did get an official photograph of the event, thanks to Bill. The one that was used in the papers was taken in our own garden, although we did take some of our own photos outside Buckingham Palace."

Honours continued to rain on Billy. In 1999 he was awarded the Tom Mitchell Lion of the Year Trophy by the British Rugby League Lions Association, while in 2000 he was made a Freeman of the Borough of Wigan, a rare accolade indeed for a sportsman. Additionally in October 2000, Billy, Trevor Foster and Neil Fox were invited to Rugby by Rugby School and

Rugby Borough Council to witness the unveiling of brass plaques in honour of their achievements in rugby league. The plaques commemorated 58 illustrious rugby men, mostly, of course, union figures, and formed part of a mile-long Pathway of Fame around the town. Brian Bevan is also honoured with a plaque.

On 1 March 2001 – St David's Day – "at a special evening to celebrate the entire Butetown community", according to the *South Wales Echo*, "Boston the Brilliant was presented with a framed painting to commemorate his contribution to rugby ... He was thrilled to bits. 'It is a tremendous honour', Billy said. 'I am Butetown born and bred and these are my people. They all did so much for me when I was starting out in my career. It is very touching that they want to honour my achievements. I still live in Wigan, but this will always be my home. I've still got lots of family here and visit as often as I can. I wouldn't have missed this for the world'."

In January 2003, in an unlikely but well deserved innovation, Billy was awarded a third testimonial year in recognition of the 50 years he had given to Wigan since going north in 1953. Four months later on 29 April, Billy was named as the Welsh Sports Hall of Fame's greatest rugby league player at Cardiff City Hall. The Hall of Fame also nominated him as right winger in its Greatest Welsh Rugby League XIII. The team was Jim Sullivan (captain), Billy Boston, Gus Risman, Jonathan Davies, Johnny Ring, Lewis Jones, Johnny Rogers, Jim Mills, Keiron Cunningham, John Mantle, Trevor Foster, Joe Thompson and Kel Coslett. There were a few pretty contentious selections in that XIII but Billy's was indisputable.

New ground was broken on 15 April 2004 when Billy led out Wigan against the old enemy St Helens in the final of the Challenge Cup. Club chairmen usually lead out their teams on such occasions. The occasion was made even more special for Billy because the final was staged at Cardiff's Millennium Stadium. The local boy really "had done good". Billy told the *Western Mail*, "I just hope my gammy knees will hold me up". They did, Billy got a rapturous welcome from the crowd but Wigan lost 32–16. In his 2007 book *St Helen's Stories* Alun Wyn Bevan wrote, "A player who combined the speed of Martin Offiah, the guile and magic of Gerald Davies and the power of John Bevan is a mouth-watering prospect. One such was Billy Boston. And in Cardiff on that April afternoon, he was the object of the dignified respect of the common man and woman; the common men and women of Wigan and the North of England! ... There were similarities in background and geography [between Wales and Wigan] maybe, but Saturday April 15, 2004 proved that the citizens of Wigan were warmer, fairer, cleverer and wiser than us Welshmen. Undoubtedly, if a role model for a better future is required, Billy Boston's your man."

On 12 April 2005 the *Wigan Observer* reporter Andy Williams wrote, "A new Wigan health centre is to be named after one of the town's most famous sporting sons. Wigan rugby legend Billy Boston has been chosen as the preferred title of the Frog Lane health centre. Chairman of Ashton, Leigh and Wigan Primary Care Trust, Lynne Liptrot, said: 'Billy is one of the most, if not the most, famous Wigan sportsman and works tirelessly for charity within the borough. He is recognised and treasured throughout the borough. When we were having discussions about what to call the new centre, we asked the question, if you think of Wigan, who do you think of and Billy Boston was the first name on everyone's lips. For all the things he's done for the town, it's so nice to be able to give him something in return finally'... Billy said: 'I am very proud that they have decided to name this after me. It's humbling. I can't believe they chose someone like me for so great an honour. I have been to look at the site and it is absolutely massive. It will be a fantastic place'."

The centre was opened the following year by Billy and is known as Billy Boston House, a truly appropriate tribute to this great man from his adopted community. Perhaps it is now time for the Rugby Football League to honour Billy with its own major accolade – Life Membership. Very few former players have been awarded Life Membership of the RFL, Billy's illustrious centre partner Eric Ashton being one of them. If a man is revered enough to be admitted to the Rugby League Hall of Fame, he is surely worthy of Life Membership of the RFL and that applies to the other living members of the Hall of Fame.

Even today in 2009 Billy steals headlines, as the naming of the Boston Stand at the DW Stadium reinforces his celebrity, as will the exhibition at the Wigan History Shop celebrating him as "Wigan Borough's Greatest Ever Rugby Legend".

As this book goes to press Billy and Joan have shared 53 years of marriage and can enjoy watching the development and progress of their five children, 14 grandchildren and 11 great-grandchildren. Billy's passion for sport remains undimmed and he is a regular follower of Wigan and the game in general. He loves watching televised sport too, particularly football and enjoys a flutter on the horses, but is no longer able to indulge his former passion for playing darts. As far as rugby league is concerned, he envies the full-time nature of the modern game and wonders how much fitter he might have been if he could have enjoyed the benefits of structured training, rest and diet. However, he says he would not like to be a winger under modern conditions. Despite his admiration for some aspects of the modern game, he regrets the passing of old style wing play. It is certainly true that his era probably saw wing play at its most vibrant. There are certainly no van Vollenhovens, Sullivans, Bevans, Coopers or Bostons around today.

So, what should be Billy's epitaph? Perhaps Arthur Duarte hit the right note when he wrote in *The Boys from the Bay*: "A Wigan supporter was once asked what he admired about Billy Boston. He replied, 'When Billy scores his tries there is no bloody fuss. He is a showman but doesn't show off'."

# Appendix: Statistics and Records

**Playing Record**

**Wigan** – Debut 21 November 1953 versus Barrow (home)

|  | A | T | G | P |
|---|---|---|---|---|
| 1953–54 | 10 | 14 | 0 | 42 |
| 1954–55 | 31 | 31 | 3 | 99 |
| 1955–56 | 29 | 43 | 0 | 129 |
| 1956–57 | 35 | 50 | 0 | 150 |
| 1957–58 | 37 | 41 | 0 | 123 |
| 1958–59 | 45 | 54 | 0 | 162 |
| 1959–60 | 38 | 46 | 0 | 138 |
| 1960–61 | 38 | 35 | 0 | 105 |
| 1961–62 | 40 | 49 | 0 | 147 |
| 1962–63 | 18 | 12 | 1 | 38 |
| 1963–64 | 36 | 26 | 0 | 78 |
| 1964–65 | 39 | 24 | 0 | 72 |
| 1965–66 | 34+2 | 19 | 0 | 57 |
| 1966–67 | 29 | 18 | 1 | 56 |
| 1967–68 | 27 | 16 | 2 | 52 |
| **Totals** | **486+2** | **478** | **7** | **1448** |

Last game – 27 April 1968 versus Wakefield Trinity (away), Championship semi-final

**Blackpool Borough** – Debut 26 December 1969 versus Rochdale Hornets (home)

|  | A | T | G | P |
|---|---|---|---|---|
| 1969–70 | 9 | 5 | 0 | 15 |
| 1970–71 | 2 | 0 | 0 | 0 |
| **Totals** | **11** | **5** | **0** | **15** |

Last game – 25 August 1970 versus Huyton (home)

| Career Record | A | T | G | P |
|---|---|---|---|---|
| Wigan | 486+2 | 478 | 7 | 1448 |
| Blackpool Borough | 11 | 5 | 0 | 15 |
| Tests | 31 | 24 | 0 | 72 |
| Internationals | 3 | 6 | 0 | 18 |
| Representative games | 4 | 5 | 0 | 15 |
| 1954 Tour* | 13 | 30 | 0 | 90 |
| 1957 World Cup Tour* | 1 | 4 | 0 | 12 |
| 1962 Tour* | 13 | 19 | 0 | 57 |
| **Totals** | **562+2** | **571** | **7** | **1727** |

*Excluding tests

**Representative Career**

## Tests (31)

| | | | |
|---|---|---|---|
| Great Britain 38 Australia 21 | 3 July 1954 | Brisbane | 2 tries |
| Great Britain 16 Australia 20 | 17 July 1954 | Sydney | |
| Great Britain 27 New Zealand 7 | 24 July 1954 | Auckland | 4 tries |
| Great Britain 14 New Zealand 20 | 31 July 1954 | Greymouth | |
| Great Britain 12 New Zealand 6 | 14 August 1954 | Auckland | |
| Great Britain 25 New Zealand 6 | 8 October 1955 | Swinton | 1 try |
| Great Britain 21 Australia 10 | 17 November 1956 | Wigan | 2 tries |
| Great Britain 9 Australia 22 | 1 December 1956 | Bradford | |
| Great Britain 19 Australia 0 | 15 December 1956 | Swinton | 1 try |
| Great Britain 45 France 12 | 26 January 1957 | Leeds | 1 try |
| Great Britain 19 France 19 | 3 March 1957 | Toulouse | 1 try |
| Great Britain 29 France 14 | 10 April 1957 | St. Helens | |
| Great Britain 23 France 5 + | 15 June 1957 | Sydney | 1 try |
| Great Britain 6 Australia 31 + | 17 June 1957 | Sydney | |
| Great Britain 25 France 14 | 3 November 1957 | Toulouse | |
| Great Britain 44 France 15 | 23 November 1957 | Wigan | 1 try |
| Great Britain 23 France 9 | 2 March 1958 | Grenoble | 1 try |
| Great Britain 14 Australia 22 | 17 October 1959 | Swinton | 1 try |
| Great Britain 10 Australia 3 + | 8 October 1960 | Bradford | 1 try |
| Great Britain 21 France 10 | 11 December 1960 | Bordeaux | |
| Great Britain 27 France 8 | 28 January 1961 | St Helens | 1 try |
| Great Britain 11 New Zealand 29 | 30 September 1961 | Leeds | 2 tries |
| Great Britain 23 New Zealand 10 | 21 October 1961 | Bradford | |
| Great Britain 35 New Zealand 19 | 4 November 1961 | Swinton | |
| Great Britain 15 France 20 | 17 February 1962 | Wigan | |
| Great Britain 13 France 23 | 11 March 1962 | Perpignan | |
| Great Britain 31 Australia 12 | 9 June 1962 | Sydney | 1 try |
| Great Britain 17 Australia 10 | 30 June 1962 | Brisbane | 2 tries |
| Great Britain 17 Australia 18 | 14 July 1962 | Sydney | |
| Great Britain 8 New Zealand 27 | 11 August 1962 | Auckland | |
| Great Britain 42 France 4 | 3 April 1963 | Wigan | 1 try |

+ World Cup

## Internationals (3)

| | | | |
|---|---|---|---|
| Great Britain 17 France 8 | 27 April 1954 | Bradford | 1 try |
| Other Nationalities 33 England 16 | 12 September 1955 | Wigan | 3 tries |
| Other Nationalities 32 France 19 | 19 October 1955 | Leigh | 2 tries |

## Playing record for Wigan against other teams

| | A | T | G | FTS |
|---|---|---|---|---|
| Barrow | 24 | 31 | 0 | 5 |
| Batley | 2 | 7 | 0 | 0 |
| Belle Vue Rangers | 2 | 3 | 1 | 1 |
| Blackpool B | 20 | 39 | 0 | 3 |
| Bradford N | 5 | 4 | 2 | 2 |
| Bramley | 1 | 0 | 0 | 1 |
| Castleford | 4 | 3 | 0 | 1 |
| Dewsbury | 4 | 18 | 0 | 0 |
| Featherstone R | 8 | 8 | 0 | 4 |
| Halifax | 27 | 20 | 0 | 12 |
| Huddersfield | 15 | 10 | 0 | 8 |
| Hull | 15 | 18 | 0 | 6 |
| Hull KR | 10 | 12 | 0 | 3 |
| Hunslet | 14 | 13 | 0 | 7 |
| Keighley | 5 | 4 | 0 | 2 |
| Leeds | 23 | 19 | 0 | 10 |
| Leigh | 31 | 13 | 1 | 20 |
| Liverpool City | 20 | 29 | 0 | 6 |
| Oldham | 29 | 14 | 0 | 17 |
| Rochdale H | 23 | 35 | 0 | 6 |
| St Helens | 31 | 12 | 0 | 20 |
| Salford | 23 | 30 | 2 | 8 |
| Swinton | 30 | 25 | 0 | 17 |
| Wakefield T | 23 | 16 | 0 | 12 |
| Warrington | 24 | 16 | 1 | 12 |
| Whitehaven | 21 | 30 | 0 | 8 |
| Widnes | 24 | 28 | 0 | 10 |
| Workington T | 24 | 17 | 0 | 13 |
| Latchford Albion | 1 | 2 | 0 | 0 |
| Australians | 3 | 1 | 0 | 2 |
| New Zealanders | 2 | 1 | 0 | 1 |
| **Totals** | **488** | **478** | **7** | **217** |

FTS – Failed to score. Note – Billy never played against Doncaster or York

### Blackpool Borough
11 games played against:
2: Rochdale Hornets (2 t)
1: Batley (1 t), Bramley, Huddersfield, Hunslet (1 try), Huyton, Oldham, Swinton (1 t), Warrington, Workington T

### Appearances in the Wardonia Cup
Wigan played Warrington annually in August for the Wardonia Cup, a charity match staged a week prior to the start of the official season. Billy appeared in seven Wardonia Cup games, scoring three tries. These games, although fiercely contested and well attended, are not included in official records.

| Date & Venue | Score | Crowd | Billy |
|---|---|---|---|
| 7 August 1954 (A) | 17–27 | 12,306 | dnp |
| 13 August 1955 (H) | 10–19 | 14,593 | |
| 11 August 1956 (A) | 16–15 | 8,956 | |
| 10 August 1957 (H) | 15–14 | 15,209 | 1 try |
| 9 August 1958 (A) | 29–21 | 10,096 | 1 try |
| 8 August 1959 (H) | 31–22 | 18,701 | 1 try |
| 6 August 1960 (A) | 31–8 | 10,776 | dnp |
| 12 August 1961 (H) | 26–10 | 17,451 | |
| 11 August 1962 (A) | 12–5 | 7,500 | dnp |
| 17 August 1963 (H) | 5–31 | 9,305 | dnp |
| 15 August 1964 (A) | 9–8 | 7,605 | |
| 14 August 1965 (H) | 38–17 | 10,005 | dnp |
| 12 August 1966 (A) | 8–10 | 5,552 | dnp |
| 12 August 1967 (H) | 8–11 | 5,684 | dnp |

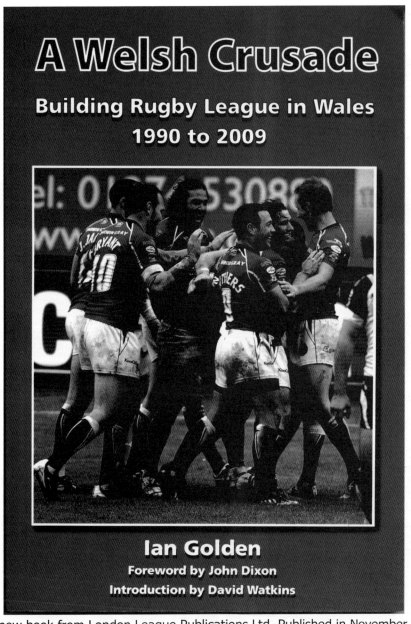

A great new book from London League Publications Ltd. Published in November 2009 at £13.95. Special offer – just £13.00 post free from London League Publications Ltd. Credit card orders via www.llpshop.co.uk , cheques (payable to London League Publications Ltd) to LLP, PO Box 10441, London E14 8WR.

# The British Rugby League Records Book

Graham Williams, Peter Lush & Dave Farrar

A fascinating new book from London League Publications Ltd. Published in November 2009 at £13.95, order for just £13.00 direct from London League Publications Ltd. Credit card orders via www.llpshop.co.uk , cheques (payable to London League Publications Ltd) to LLP, PO Box 10441, London E14 8WR.

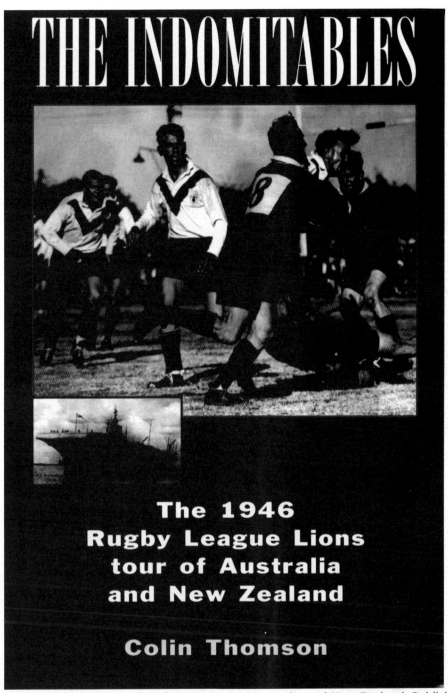

# THE INDOMITABLES

## The 1946 Rugby League Lions tour of Australia and New Zealand

### Colin Thomson

The full story of the greatest British Lions tour to Australia and New Zealand. Published in May at £12.95, order for just £12.00 post-free direct from London League Publications Ltd. Credit card orders via www.llpshop.co.uk , cheques (payable to London League Publications Ltd) to LLP, PO Box 10441, London E14 8WR.

# PETER FOX
## *The Players' Coach*

**Graham Williams & Peter Lush**

Authorised biography of one of the most successful coaches in post-war British Rugby League. Published in June 2008 at £14.95, order for just £10.00 post free direct from London League Publications Ltd. Credit card orders via www.llpshop.co.uk , cheques (payable to London League Publications Ltd) to LLP, PO Box 10441, London E14 8WR.

# Liverpool City RLFC

## Rugby league in a football city

### Mike Brocken

The full story of rugby league's attempts to establish the game on Merseyside. Published in November 2008 at £14.95, order for just £14.00 post free direct from London League Publications Ltd. Credit card orders via www.llpshop.co.uk , cheques (payable to London League Publications Ltd) to LLP, PO Box 10441, London E14 8WR.

## So close to glory

### Warrington Rugby League Football Club 1919 to 1939

**Eddie Fuller & Gary Slater**

Fascinating story of Warrington RLFC between the wars. Published in March 2008 at £12.95, order for just £10.00 post free direct from London League Publications Ltd. Credit card orders via www.llpshop.co.uk , cheques (payable to London League Publications Ltd) to LLP, PO Box 10441, London E14 8WR.